Smart Marketing With the Internet of Things

Dora Simões
University of Aveiro, Portugal

Belem Barbosa
University of Aveiro, Portugal

Sandra Filipe
University of Aveiro, Portugal

I0860997

A volume in the Advances in Marketing, Customer Relationship Management, and E-Services (AMCRMES) Book Series

IGI Global
DISSEMINATOR OF KNOWLEDGE

Published in the United States of America by
IGI Global
Business Science Reference (an imprint of IGI Global)
701 E. Chocolate Avenue
Hershey PA, USA 17033
Tel: 717-533-8845
Fax: 717-533-8661
E-mail: cust@igi-global.com
Web site: http://www.igi-global.com

Copyright © 2019 by IGI Global. All rights reserved. No part of this publication may be reproduced, stored or distributed in any form or by any means, electronic or mechanical, including photocopying, without written permission from the publisher. Product or company names used in this set are for identification purposes only. Inclusion of the names of the products or companies does not indicate a claim of ownership by IGI Global of the trademark or registered trademark.

Library of Congress Cataloging-in-Publication Data

Names: Simoes, Dora, 1970- editor. | Barbosa, Belem, 1971- editor. | Filipe, Sandra, 1973- editor.
Title: Smart marketing with the internet of things / Dora Simoes, Belem Barbosa, and Sandra Filipe, editors.
Description: Hershey : Business Science Reference, [2018]
Identifiers: LCCN 2017054595| ISBN 9781522557630 (hardcover) | ISBN 9781522557647 (ebook)
Subjects: LCSH: Internet marketing.
Classification: LCC HF5415.1265 .S583 2018 | DDC 658.8/72--dc23 LC record available at https://lccn.loc.gov/2017054595

This book is published in the IGI Global book series Advances in Marketing, Customer Relationship Management, and E-Services (AMCRMES) (ISSN: 2327-5502; eISSN: 2327-5529)

British Cataloguing in Publication Data
A Cataloguing in Publication record for this book is available from the British Library.

All work contributed to this book is new, previously-unpublished material. The views expressed in this book are those of the authors, but not necessarily of the publisher.

For electronic access to this publication, please contact: eresources@igi-global.com.

Advances in Marketing, Customer Relationship Management, and E-Services (AMCRMES) Book Series

Eldon Y. Li
National Chengchi University, Taiwan & California Polytechnic State University, USA

ISSN:2327-5502
EISSN:2327-5529

Mission

Business processes, services, and communications are important factors in the management of good customer relationship, which is the foundation of any well organized business. Technology continues to play a vital role in the organization and automation of business processes for marketing, sales, and customer service. These features aid in the attraction of new clients and maintaining existing relationships.

The Advances in Marketing, Customer Relationship Management, and E-Services (AMCRMES) Book Series addresses success factors for customer relationship management, marketing, and electronic services and its performance outcomes. This collection of reference source covers aspects of consumer behavior and marketing business strategies aiming towards researchers, scholars, and practitioners in the fields of marketing management.

Coverage

- Web Mining and Marketing
- Customer Relationship Management
- Mobile services
- Electronic Services
- Text Mining and Marketing
- B2B marketing
- Cases on CRM Implementation
- Social Networking and Marketing
- Ethical Considerations in E-Marketing
- Customer Retention

IGI Global is currently accepting manuscripts for publication within this series. To submit a proposal for a volume in this series, please contact our Acquisition Editors at Acquisitions@igi-global.com or visit: http://www.igi-global.com/publish/.

The Advances in Marketing, Customer Relationship Management, and E-Services (AMCRMES) Book Series (ISSN 2327-5502) is published by IGI Global, 701 E. Chocolate Avenue, Hershey, PA 17033-1240, USA, www.igi-global.com. This series is composed of titles available for purchase individually; each title is edited to be contextually exclusive from any other title within the series. For pricing and ordering information please visit http://www.igi-global.com/book-series/advances-marketing-customer-relationship-management/37150. Postmaster: Send all address changes to above address. Copyright © 2019 IGI Global. All rights, including translation in other languages reserved by the publisher. No part of this series may be reproduced or used in any form or by any means – graphics, electronic, or mechanical, including photocopying, recording, taping, or information and retrieval systems – without written permission from the publisher, except for non commercial, educational use, including classroom teaching purposes. The views expressed in this series are those of the authors, but not necessarily of IGI Global.

Titles in this Series

For a list of additional titles in this series, please visit: www.igi-global.com/book-series

Handbook of Research on Social Marketing and Its Influence on Animal Origin Food Product Consumption
Diana Bogueva (Curtin University, Australia) Dora Marinova (Curtin University, Australia) and Talia Raphaely (Curtin University, Australia)
Business Science Reference • copyright 2018 • 453pp • H/C (ISBN: 9781522547570) • US $325.00 (our price)

Analyzing Attachment and Consumers' Emotions Emerging Research and Opportunities
Giuseppe Pedeliento (University of Bergamo, Italy)
Business Science Reference • copyright 2018 • 308pp • H/C (ISBN: 9781522549840) • US $185.00 (our price)

Building Brand Identity in the Age of Social Media Emerging Research and Opportunities
Amir Ekhlassi (University of Tehran, Iran) Mahdi Niknejhad Moghadam (Sharif University of Technology, Iran) and Amir Mohammad Adibi (University of Tehran, Iran)
Business Science Reference • copyright 2018 • 189pp • H/C (ISBN: 9781522551430) • US $145.00 (our price)

Neuromarketing and Big Data Analytics for Strategic Consumer Engagement Emerging Research and Opportunities
Joana Coutinho de Sousa (Unlimited-Hashtag, Portugal)
Business Science Reference • copyright 2018 • 200pp • H/C (ISBN: 9781522548348) • US $165.00 (our price)

Holistic Approaches to Brand Culture and Communication Across Industries
Sabyasachi Dasgupta (O.P. Jindal Global University, India) Santosh Kumar Biswal (Symbiosis International University, India) and M. Anil Ramesh (Siva Sivani Institute of Management, India)
Business Science Reference • copyright 2018 • 281pp • H/C (ISBN: 9781522531500) • US $225.00 (our price)

Multi-Platform Advertising Strategies in the Global Marketplace
Kenneth C. C. Yang (The University of Texas at El Paso, USA)
Business Science Reference • copyright 2018 • 377pp • H/C (ISBN: 9781522531142) • US $205.00 (our price)

Digital Marketing Strategies for Fashion and Luxury Brands
Wilson Ozuem (University of Gloucestershire, UK) and Yllka Azemi (Indiana University Northwest, USA)
Business Science Reference • copyright 2018 • 460pp • H/C (ISBN: 9781522526971) • US $210.00 (our price)

Exploring the Rise of Fandom in Contemporary Consumer Culture
Cheng Lu Wang (University of New Haven, USA)
Business Science Reference • copyright 2018 • 300pp • H/C (ISBN: 9781522532200) • US $225.00 (our price)

IGI Global
DISSEMINATOR OF KNOWLEDGE

701 East Chocolate Avenue, Hershey, PA 17033, USA
Tel: 717-533-8845 x100 • Fax: 717-533-8661
E-Mail: cust@igi-global.com • www.igi-global.com

Editorial Advisory Board

Pedro Almeida, *University of Aveiro, Portugal*
Ana Carla Amaro, *University of Aveiro, Portugal*
Maria João Antunes, *University of Aveiro, Portugal*
Elodie Attié, *Toulouse School of Management Research, France*
Pedro Beça, *University of Aveiro, Portugal*
Valentina Chkoniya, *University of Aveiro, Portugal*
Tapan Das, *VIT University, India*
Gyu Myoung Lee, *Liverpool John Moores University, UK*
Rui Marques, *University of Aveiro, Portugal*
Óscar Mealha, *University of Aveiro, Portugal*
Ana Melro, *University of Aveiro, Portugal*
Lídia Oliveira, *University of Aveiro, Portugal*
Patrícia Oliveira, *University of Aveiro, Portugal*
Rita Oliveira, *University of Aveiro, Portugal*
Luís Pedro, *University of Aveiro, Portugal*
Filipe Pinto, *Altices Labs, Portugal*
Jorge Remondes, *Instituto Superior de Entre Douro e Vouga, Portugal*
Rui Rodrigues, *Instituto Superior Miguel Torga, Portugal*
Claudia Amaral Santos, *University of Aveiro, Portugal*
Jorge Sa Silva, *University of Coimbra, Portugal*
Telmo Silva, *University of Aveiro, Portugal*
Ana Isabel Veloso, *University of Aveiro, Portugal*

Table of Contents

Detailed Table of Contents

wellbeing, social, and utility values. The importance of each benefit is demonstrated, according to specific targets and to examples of applications. A system of values that represents the promises of the IoT and the central needs of users is also described. Besides, a typology of users should help companies creating or refining targeting strategies and should guide consumers into their acceptance process. Finally, further research directions are discussed.

Section 2
Scopes of Application

Data becomes big data when then the size of data exceeds the ability of our IT systems in terms of 3Vs (volume, velocity, and variety). When the data sets are large and complex, it becomes a great difficult task for handling such voluminous data. This chapter will provide a detailed knowledge of the major concepts and components of big data and also the transformation of big data in to business operations. Collection and storage of big data will not help out in creation of business values. Values and importance are created once when the action starts on data by performing an analysis. Hence, this chapter provides a view on various kinds of analysis that can be done with big data and also the differences between traditional analytics and big data analytics. The transformation of digital data into business values could be in terms of reports, research analyses, recommendations, predictions, and optimizations. In addition to the concept of big data, this chapter discuss about the basic concepts of digital analytics, methods, and techniques for digital analysis.

Today technology evolves in two different directions. The first one is to create a new technology for our requirement and solve the problem, and the second one is to do it with the existing technology. This chapter will discuss in detail augmented reality and its use in the real world and also its application domains like medicine, education, health, gaming, tourism, film and entertainment, architecture, and development. Many think that AR is only for smartphones, but there are different ways to enhance the insight of the world. Augmented realities can be presented on an extensive range of displays, monitors, screens, handheld devices, or glasses. This chapter will provide the information about the key components of AR devices. This chapter gives a view on different types of AR and also projects how the technology can be adapted for multiple purposes based on the required type of view.

The developing number of applications available through smart devices provides an increasing diversity of tourism marketing, destination and city marketing, tourism business marketing, and advertising. In the last decade, marketers have developed more creative practices to attract consumers. These new marketing tools are augmented reality, virtual reality, QR code, near field communication (NFC), geo-tagging, geo-fencing, and geo-targeting applications with the smart technologies, which are considered as a new marketing communication instruments these increase awareness and help get information about tourist and give information to the tourist. This chapter presents the profile of smart marketing applications and their marketing benefits in tourism industry. More specifically, this chapter aimed to achieve the following research objectives: to determine the potentials of the augmented reality, virtual reality, QR code, near field communication (NFC), geo-tagging, geo-fencing, and geo-targeting applications in the tourism industry.

Consumers have become better informed, forcing companies to offer products and services that fit their tastes and preferences. The technologies in the context of internet of things (IoT) have been in increasing demand, by allowing the adaptation and customization of products and services contextualized with the location of consumers functioning and operating in real-time context and location of consumers. In this chapter, two relevant real-time content notification systems based on IoT systems are analyzed. It was concluded that, despite all the advantages associated with the use of these notification services, there are some security limitations: large amount of information collected, it is necessary to manage quickly and effectively to deliver relevant content in a timely manner; need for high bandwidth; considerable reduction of the autonomy of the batteries of the smartphones, of the users due to the necessity of activation of the GPS and the Bluetooth.

Mall advertising is a critical factor for retailers to gain revenue. Traditional mall advertising strategies mainly rely on impression and empiricism which might be inefficient and result in a waste of resources. Recent research demonstrates that the effectiveness of advertisements can be affected by exposure time and relevance to customers. Authors in this chapter propose a data-driven approach to achieve these goals using fine-grained trajectories of customers. They first preprocess the trajectories and model the floorplan. Then detect stopping locations where customers stay for relatively long time and analyze the

Preface

The Internet of Things (IoT), also known as the Internet of Everything, refers to an interconnected network of things, comprising a system where objects and devices from the physical world are connected via wireless and wired Internet connections. These connections through the Internet infrastructures enable cooperation of smart things, and are expected to transform the lives of consumers, managers, and workers alike. It is widely accepted that we are living at a new era of IoT, which demands an update on management and marketing, an in return offers significant opportunities for being more relevant, more effective, and more efficient, independently of the sector or market we are dealing with. In fact, in recent years, the Internet of Things has gained increased popularity in several fields of society and opened several business opportunities. Meanwhile, consumers are showing growing interest in knowing, using, and acquiring smart things, being smartphones and wearables such as smart watches and glasses the most popular.

From the marketing point of view, it is of utmost importance to understand the needs, preferences, and possible applications on daily routines by users and potential users, both in business to consumer and in business to business contexts. IoT is getting increased attention from researchers, practitioners, consumers, and the media. It is expected that IoT will change the way we produce, transform, and consume goods and services, as well as the interaction between organizations and their customers.

In such a context, this book aims to contribute to the knowledge and efficacy of scholars, students, and professionals, by publishing theoretical, empirical, and applied contributions on marketing of the Internet of Things that are particularly relevant for businesses and the society in general. It identifies key technologic facets that support the increasing importance of IoT, and discusses benefits and challenges for business, shedding the light on the changes expected to dominate the next decades. The target audience of this book is composed of researchers, academics, undergraduate and postgraduate students, corporate managers, marketing managers, engineers, and other people working in different sectors that are expected to be influenced by the technological and social changes associated to the Internet of Things.

Smart Marketing with the Internet of Things offers a compilation of 13 contributions about central concepts and business trends and strategies in the current and future IoT Era. The book is organized in three sections: "The Essence," "Scopes of Application," and "Future Trends."

The two chapters that compose the first section of the book introduce the conceptualization of the Internet of Things and present the challenges posed to marketing management.

In the first chapter, "An Overview on IoT and Its Impact on Marketing," Simões, Filipe, and Barbosa explore the challenges IoT for marketing management. They present the main concepts associated to the theme based on the extant literature, considering information management, technological and ethical aspects of its adoption by corporations and consumers, and discuss the expected impacts on different marketing application domains.

The second chapter, "The Acceptance Process of the Internet of Things: How to Improve the Acceptance of the IoT Technology?" by Attié and Meyer-Waarden, discusses the main factors that influence consumer decisions to accept and use the IoT and smart objects, such as ethical, wellbeing, social and utility values. The importance of each benefit is demonstrated, according to specific targets and to examples of applications. Moreover, a system of values that represents the promises of IoT and the central needs of users are also described.

Following is the second section of the book, comprising eight chapters that propose different scopes of application of Internet of Things in business and marketing. They explore alternative technologies and their impact on marketing and management, namely gains in efficiency and customer experience and satisfaction.

In the third chapter, "Big Data and Digital Analytics," Doraikannan and Selvaraj provide detailed information on the major concepts and components of big data and also on the transformation of big data in business operations. The chapter provides a view on various types of analyses that can be done with big data, explaining the differences between traditional analytics and big data analytics. In addition, the authors discuss the basic concepts, methods and techniques of digital analytics.

The fourth chapter is devoted to "Augmented Reality Experiences" and was written by Selvaraj, Doraikannan, and Anantharaman. It explores augmented reality and its use in the real world, including its application in different domains like medicine, education, health, gaming, tourism, film and entertainment, architecture and development. The chapter discusses the key components of augmented reality devices, different types of augmented reality, and also suggests how technology can be adapted for multiple purposes based on the required type of view.

In the fifth chapter, "Advantages of Augmented Reality, Virtual Reality, QR Code, Near Field Communication, Geo-Tagging, Geo-Fencing, and Geo-Targeting for Marketing Tourism Businesses," Çeltek suggests that smart technologies are new marketing communication instruments that increase awareness and help get information about tourist and give information to the tourist. The chapter presents the profile of these smart marketing applications and their marketing benefits in tourism industry.

In the sixth chapter, "Real-Time Notifications: Marketing Applied to the Internet of Things," Soares, Vairinhos, Beça, and Ribeiro present two relevant real-time content notification systems based on IoT systems. The chapter explains the contribution of these systems to a superior user experience that meets users' preferences.

In the seventh chapter, "Data-Driven Mall Advertising," Shen, Lau, and Cao propose a data-driven approach to improve average advertisement exposure time and advertisement relevance using customers' fine-grained trajectories. They first preprocess the trajectories and model the floorplan, then detect stopping locations where customers stay for relatively longer time and analyze the correlation between different locations. They also detect customers' facing directions at each stopping location. The authors propose that appropriate advertising locations and content can be determined according to the correlation of stopping locations and customers' facing direction.

The eighth chapter, "Digital Category Management: How Technology Can Enable the Supplier-Retailer Relationship," by Chkoniya and Mateus, discusses the implications of the new digital empowered shopper for the traditional Category Management. The authors underline the need to enhance business results by focusing on higher collaboration and automation.

In the ninth chapter, "Instant Messaging Chat Bot: Your New Best Friend?" Han focuses on mobile users' current understanding and perceptions of chat bots, in order to provide better insight into instant messaging chat bots as a marketing tool.

In the tenth chapter IoT Sustainability in Higher Education, Rocha, Almeida, and Abreu explore the use of new information technologies in educational practices. The experience and creativity of a panel of experts from the Delphi technique lead to a categorical scale and to the elaboration of an instrument with a preliminary list of indicators to be applied to students and professors and to evaluate the sustainability of IoT in higher education.

Finally, the last three chapters address some business trends, strategies, and opportunities in IoT era.

In the eleventh chapter, "Are Millennials Ready for the Internet of Things?" Barbosa, Filipe, Santos, and Simões focus on Millennials, analyzing their ability and propensity to adopt and adapt new media to their daily routines, discussing the potential of the millennial segment to IoT products and services.

The twelfth chapter, "IoT Digital Service Provider: Towards Smart Living," by Pinto, Borges, and Santiago, presents the integration of IoT on the service provider actuation sphere, answering to customers' new way of living in the digital era. As the authors explain, the advent of IoT enables getting useful insights into customers' characteristics, facilitating the delivery of personalized offers and first-class experiences during the whole consumer journey.

Finally, in the thirteenth chapter, "An Overview of Main IoT Trends Applied to Business and Marketing," Remondes and Afonso explore the main trends of IoT for business and management (Personalization, Interaction, Integration, Analytics, Monitoring and Protection), as well as potential organizational marketing strategies.

As the book demonstrates, the Internet of Things provides a very rich domain and offers numerous opportunities and challenges for marketing. Sooner or later it is expected to be on the top of the agendas of executives all over the world. Hopefully this book will help you find interesting paths and put you ahead of your competition by better approaching IoT in your professional context.

We wish you a pleasant and useful reading!

Dora Simões
University of Aveiro, Portugal

Belem Barbosa
University of Aveiro, Portugal

Sandra Filipe
University of Aveiro, Portugal

Acknowledgment

Editing this book was only possible with the collaboration of many individuals that backed us through the way, some of them part of the IGI-Global Group. We are very grateful for the opportunity to publish with IGI-Global and particularly for the professionalism, rigor, and support that we have witnessed in the past months from all the Publisher's representatives we had contact with.

We would like to thank all the authors that contributed to this book. The authors' knowledge and expertise shared through these pages are particularly valuable, and so was their effort to deal with deadlines, recommendations, and all the guidelines to write each chapter. We hope you are as proud as us of the final result, and wish you the best for your future projects.

Let us also express our gratitude to the reviewers and the advisory board, whose recommendations and guidance were very important to improving each chapter in order to make more relevant contributions to the different target audiences.

Last but not least, we would like to thank the support of our husbands and kids, that stood by us unconditionally. Thanks for letting us work several weekends in the past months – and for being happy for us, no matter what.

Dora Simões
University of Aveiro, Portugal

Belem Barbosa
University of Aveiro, Portugal

Sandra Filipe
University of Aveiro, Portugal

Section 1
The Essence

Chapter 1
An Overview on IoT and Its Impact on Marketing

Dora Simões
University of Aveiro, Portugal

Sandra Filipe
University of Aveiro, Portugal

Belem Barbosa
University of Aveiro, Portugal

ABSTRACT

The internet of things (IoT) is attracting increased attention from researchers, practitioners, consumers, and the media, and it is expected to change dramatically the production and consumption of goods and services, as well as the interaction between organizations and their customers. This chapter explores the challenges of IoT for marketing management. The authors present the main concepts associated to the theme based on the extant literature, considering information management, technological and ethical aspects of its adoption by corporations and consumers, and they discuss the expected impacts on different marketing application domains such as product placement, purchasing behavior, storytelling and communication, customer experience and consumer' brand perception, real-time persona development, and product and content development, among others.

INTRODUCTION

When the web emerged, organizations and people purchased Internet real estate in the form of domain names and built it out with websites. Consumers shopped, and people read the news online, but information applications were typically static and one-way in communication orientation (i.e., provider to consumer). Then web 2.0 gathered steam. Services allowed for dynamic information in a variety of forms and enabled n-way conversations and collaboration. Blogging, liking, tweeting, writing online reviews, sharing videos and photos, and such became commonplace (Kaplan & Haenlein, 2010). With social media, people keep private relatively fewer bits of information and reveal secrets more often. The web

DOI: 10.4018/978-1-5225-5763-0.ch001

Copyright © 2019, IGI Global. Copying or distributing in print or electronic forms without written permission of IGI Global is prohibited.

3.0 comes with the "focus on ways to make the Web "smarter", with machine-facilitated understanding of information promoting a more intuitive and effective user experience" (Laudon & Laudon, 2016). Nowadays a new wave of Internet-connected technologies is gaining steam: the Internet of Things (IoT). IoT gives rise to several applications at level of augmented reality, wearable technology, chatbots, gamification, transmedia, and so on that impact on smart marketing.

Within the Internet of Things paradigm, many of the objects that surround us will become part of a network in one way or another. Radio Frequency IDentification (RFID) and sensor network technologies will rise to meet this new challenge, in which information and communication systems are invisibly embedded in the environment around us (Gubbi, Buyya, Marusic, & Palaniswami, 2013; Miorandi, Sicari, Pellegrini, & Chlamtac, 2012). Consequently, IoT is attracting increased attention from researchers, practitioners, consumers, and the media, and it is expected to change dramatically the production and consumption of goods and services, as well as the interaction between enterprises and customers. On the one hand, it offers new and innovative ways of seeing products and appliances, imagining them communicating together to improve people's everyday lives. On the other hand, it creates new opportunities for marketing activities and strategies. IoT has just started to invade the technology market but little is known about the adoption of smart connected objects by users (Attié & Meyer-Waarden, 2016). Wireless sensor technologies now allow objects to provide information about their environment, context, and location; 'smart' technologies are touted as being able to allow everyday things to 'think and interact' (Ng & Wakenshaw, 2017). The marketing as a set of processes for creating, communicating, delivering, and exchanging offerings that have value for customers, clients, partners, and society at large (Keefe, 2008) should leverage on these advances to generate more value for the businesses.

Under marketing umbrella, Ng and Wakenshaw (2017) present four conceptualizations of IoT. These conceptualizations are developed from the following theoretical constructs: liquification and density of information resources; digital materiality; assemblage and service systems; and modularity and transaction network. In the IoT, liquification further enhances the capacities of digitized objects. Intelligent sensors could provide precise real-time information about the involved devices and integrate with wireless sensors networks to better track and trace things in real time (Da Xu, He, & Li, 2014). Digital materiality refers to what the software embedded in the physical object can do by manipulating the digital representation of the physical object (Yoo et al., 2012). Assemblage refers to objects/devices working together and in this process, the ability to do things that none of these objects could perform on their own (Hoffman & Novak, 2015). Hoffman and Novak (2015) describe assemblage in consumer IoT as a collection of heterogeneous components that interact with each other. Constituents of IoT can be viewed as modules with capabilities that could converge and diverge to create 'thin crossing points' i.e. a boundary and a transaction between the modules' tasks for both the consumer and the producer, by dividing skills and competencies. Individuals could modularize their practices as tasks for the design of thin crossing points that allow for new resources (e.g. Internet-connected constituents) to be brought in and for new transactions to occur (Ng & Wakenshaw, 2014). Modularization in consumer experiential spaces can therefore lead to ways where latent needs could be discovered and fulfilled through new offerings.

For the IoT vision to successfully emerge, the computing paradigm will need to go beyond traditional mobile computing scenarios that use smart phones and portables and evolve into connecting everyday existing objects and embedding intelligence into our environment. This is what characterize the web 4.0 era, but also the promised web 5.0 - a linked web which communicates with us like we communicate with each other. However, despite the overall positive feeling about the IoT's development, and while the IoT brings considerable benefits when it works, this brings several challenges (De Cremer, Nguyen,

& Simkin, 2017). Nevertheless, the application of IoT paradigm on marketing management is yet on its beginning. So, there are many aspects its use and contributions that emerge to explore.

Considering the novelty and potential of IoT, this chapter explores the opportunities and challenges it poses for marketing management. It presents the main concepts associated to the theme based on the extant literature, considering managerial, technological and ethical aspects of its adoption by enterprises and consumers. Also, it is discussed the expected impact on different areas of marketing, such as digital marketing, brand management, marketing research, communication marketing, among others.

BACKGROUND

The term 'Internet-of-Things' (IoT) was first coined by Kevin Ashton in 1999, a technologist and pioneer in the Auto-ID world, in the context of supply chain management (Ashton, 2009, 2013). However, in the past decade, the definition has been more inclusive covering wide range of applications like healthcare, utilities, transport, and so on (Sundmaeker, Guillemin, Friess, & Woelfflé, 2010). More recently has started to gain attraction, and the industry is beginning to wake up to the possibility of every object being part of the Internet, whatever the business proposition might be. Firstly, the term IoT was introduced to describe how IoT can be created by adding Radio-Frequency IDentification (RFID) and other sensors to everyday objects. Over time, the term has evolved into one that describes the IoT as a network of entities that are connected through any form of sensor, enabling these entities, which it is termed as Internet-connected constituents, to be located, identified, and even operated upon. Concerning this evolution, Ng and Wakenshaw (2017) propose the following definition of IoT:

a system of uniquely identifiable and connected constituents (termed as Internet-connected constituents) capable of virtual representation and virtual accessibility leading to an Internet-like structure for remote locating, sensing, and/or operating the constituents with real-time data/information flows between them, thus resulting in the system as a whole being able to be augmented to achieve a greater variety of outcomes in a dynamic and agile manner. (p. 6)

In its essence, IoT is a network of interconnected devices, systems and services within the existing Internet infrastructure. The core of the IoT is that it allows for 'all things connected' in the communication between devices and objects, creating a more direct integration between the physical world and computer-based systems (De Cremer et al., 2017). By capturing and analyzing the data that come from the sensors at the endpoints of the connected objects, the IoT's value lies in its ability to track, measure and create 'smart' devices that bring considerable benefits to individuals, businesses and society. Technology devices are connected to and can receive or transmit data via the Internet; these include computers, laptops, servers, smartphones, tablets, and a variety of other devices that consumers now employ for utilizing the web through a browser or an app (Weinberg, Milne, Andonova, & Hajjat, 2015).

In order to better recognize potential opportunities in IoT, it is important to understand key distinctions between a web-based environment and an IoT-based environment. Weinberg and colleagues (Weinberg et al., 2015) make a good distinction of these concepts concerning 5 dimensions: data, data entry, data sharing, learning and decision making. Consumers in a web-based environment actively manipulate devices to interact directly with the web. For example, a consumer may use a laptop to shop online, direct a browser to a particular webpage for a product at an online store, put a product in a digital shopping cart, and then purchase the product after clicking on checkout and entering relevant transaction information. Consumers can interact with IoT devices, but in many cases, they don't directly enter the data. Rather, IoT devices by themselves monitor and retrieve relevant data from the environment and a person. Providers, marketers, and websites learn about consumers based on their activities inside the digital world, such as shopping online and using social media. Again, these activities may be recorded in the form of cookies or transactional purchase information. These web-related behavioral data can be used for learning consumer behaviors. IoT devices learn about consumers by observing their habits, tendencies, and preferences as well as their environments. Learning is based on behaviors and phenomena in the natural, physical world as opposed to the strictly online world. Marketers use web-related data in making decisions about engaging and serving consumers with respect to their online behaviors. Decisions are not necessarily made in real time from a consumer perspective, as some 'more than immediate' amount of time may pass between the recognition of a consumer problem and the provision of a provider solution. On the other hand, IoT machines are constantly monitoring the environment through sensors and dynamically making decisions and associated changes in real time given these environmental conditions and consumer or other stakeholder preferences.

Nevertheless, with such rapid expansion and spread of its impact, it is surprising that few marketing studies exploring the IoT have yet been conducted. There are still many untapped application areas, numerous challenges and issues that need to be improved, and the full impact for stakeholder groups is far from clearly charted. There are implications for how marketing may effectively embrace the IoT and how the IoT might itself shape marketing (Nguyen & Simkin, 2017). More research is needed to explore the capabilities needed to adopt the IoT in the organization and how these relate to different aspects of marketing, particularly for the relationship-oriented organization that engages in customer relationship marketing, alliances, joint ventures and partnerships. The objective is enhancing the customer relationships with the enterprises, providing strategic capabilities or improving integrated marketing systems. The applications are varied and include value co-creation, adoption and use of wearables, interaction style and consumer resistance to smart products, etc.

However, despite the advantages that come from of IoT to marketing, as Nguyen and Simkin (2017) argues, companies are facing many challenges in managerial, technological and ethical domains. Just consider some of the unanswered questions that need urgent approach:

- How should enterprises develop fully integrated IoT channel and communication strategies to best reflect the wide variety of the IoT options?
- How should IoT enterprises evaluate the consistency of messages across multiple touch points?
- How can marketing effectiveness be measured in an integrated IoT communications system?
- How much control do enterprises have over their customers in this environment?
- How much control should they exert over their customers with so much available data?
- What is the relationship between CRM (Customer Relationship Management) and the IoT in such a data-driven environment?
- How should enterprises develop relationships, alliances and partnerships in an IoT environment?
- What factors affect consumer's engagement with enterprises?
- How can enterprises use the IoT to design and develop a better customer experience?
- What are the optimal metrics and marketing strategies that enterprises should employ with the IoT?

- How are customized ads, promotions and other communications processed by consumers via the IoT as compared to traditional counterparts?
- What are the costs and benefits of organizations adopting the IoT to optimize marketing?

Some directions to answer these questions are explored next.

CONCEPTUALIZATION OF IOT (ON MARKETING)

Although the definition of 'Things' has changed as technology evolved, the main goal of making a computer sense information without the aid of human intervention remains the same. A radical evolution of the current Internet into a network of interconnected objects that not only harvests information from the environment (sensing) and interacts with the physical world (actuation/command/control), but also uses existing Internet standards to provide services for information transfer, analytics, applications, and communications (Gcaba & Dlodlo, 2016). The IoT is what happens when everyday objects have inter-connected microchips in them which enable them to sense their surroundings and report it to other machines or people for actuation of functionalities in these machines or people.

Fueled by the prevalence of devices enabled by open wireless technology such as Bluetooth, RFID, Wi-Fi, and telephonic data services as well as embedded sensor and actuator nodes, IoT has stepped out of its infancy. The evolution is emerging in the interconnection between objects to create a smart environment. Mark Weiser, the forefather of ubiquitous computing, defined a smart environment as ''the physical world that is richly and invisibly interwoven with sensors, actuators, displays, and computational elements, embedded seamlessly in the everyday objects of our lives, and connected through a continuous network'' (Weiser, Gold, & Brown, 1999, p. 694). The advancements and convergence of micro-electro-mechanical systems technology, wireless communications, and digital electronics has resulted in the development of miniature devices having the ability to sense, compute, and communicate wirelessly in short distances. These miniature devices called nodes interconnect to form a wireless sensor networks (WSN) and find wide ranging applications in environmental monitoring, infrastructure monitoring, traffic monitoring, retail, etc. For the realization of a complete IoT vision, efficient, secure, scalable and market oriented computing and storage resourcing is essential. Cloud computing is the most recent paradigm to emerge which promises reliable services delivered through next generation data centers that are based on virtualized storage technologies. This platform acts as a receiver of data from the ubiquitous sensors; as a computer to analyze and interpret the data; as well as providing the user with easy to understand web based visualization. The ubiquitous sensing and processing works in the background, hidden from the user (Gubbi et al., 2013). As we move from static pages web (web 1.0) to ubiquitous computing web (web 4.0 and web 5.0), the need for data-on-demand using sophisticated intuitive queries increase. To take full advantage of the available Internet technology, there is a need to deploy large-scale, platform-independent, wireless sensor network infrastructure that includes data management and processing, actuation and analytics. Cloud computing promises high reliability, scalability and autonomy to provide ubiquitous access, dynamic resource discovery and composability required for the next generation Internet of Things applications.

Based on the early concepts, Gubbi et al. (2013) presented a taxonomy that will aid defining the components required for the Internet of Things from a high level perspective. There are:

- **Hardware:** Made up of sensors, actuators and embedded communication hardware;
- **Middleware:** On demand storage and computing tools for data analytics; and
- **Presentation:** Novel easy to understand visualization and interpretation tools which can be widely accessed on different platforms and which can be designed for different applications.

A marketing focus in an era of IoT is needed because not all IoT technology is adopted by users, regardless of how amazing they may seem. Those that do become accepted would have undergone a process that has traversed fundamental marketing principles – the technology met a consumer need,

and the organization was able to create an offering from that technology, resulting in a purchase decision (Ng & Wakenshaw, 2017). An era of IoT could potentially provide visibility of experiential and consumption contexts that hitherto have not been possible. Ng and Wakenshaw (2017) propose that this visibility into day-to-day contexts would impact on three broad areas of marketing research:

1. The consumer experience;
2. Dispositions and situations;
3. Behaviors and decisions.

Marketing has endeavored to gain insight into how consumers experience the products they purchase. This service experience offers new insights into the emerging value creation and value-in-use (Ng & Smith, 2012). More importantly, the relationship between the consumer and the organization also evolves into a service relationship with experiences that are co-created, inseparable, perishable, heterogeneous, and intangible.

Based on the considerations explained above, next it is presented some important aspects on considering the IoT paradigm on marketing. This analyze is made in three levels: information management, technology, and ethics and safety.

Information Management Aspects

Concerning managerial dimension, Ehret and Wirtz (2017) identify the following three main types of Internet of Things enabled business models:

1. Provision of manufacturing assets, maintenance and repair, and their operation,
2. Innovative information and analytical services that help manufacturing (e.g., based on artificial intelligence, big data and analytics), and
3. New services targeted at end-users (e.g., offering efficient customization by integrating end-users into the manufacturing and supply chain ecosystem).

Nowadays, organizations and individuals generate substantial amounts of data at a very high rate. With an impressing amount of data arriving at a bigger scale, new insights can be obtained from their contents. The latter will help organizations to gain richer insights and improve their competitive position. Moreover, it is generally accepted that relevant information obtained using Big Data technologies will enhance enterprises efficiency and competitiveness (Akoka, Comyn-Wattiau, & Laoufi, 2017). For businesses, the industrial IoT can be useful in many different categories, most notably, those related to asset tracking and inventory control, security, tracking of shipping, location and energy conservation, as well as building profiles of customers and suppliers (De Cremer et al., 2017).

Aside from privacy, which is discussed in its own section, there are many concerns and problems which may prove challenging to manage. More data will be generated, will need to be stored, and will need to be processed. It includes data originated from surveillance footage, embedded and medical devices, entertainment, social media, as well as consumer images (Akoka et al., 2017). Emerging big data opportunities can be classified into several topic areas. Jeanne Ross (MIT) proposed the five key areas of social media, mobile systems, analytics, cloud, and IoT (SMACIT) as significant drivers for enterprise digital transformation (Akoka et al., 2017). Such a classification aims to emphasize the relations of these technologies with big data characteristics. IoT, mobile and social network are major sources of big data, but there are others. Analytics related to unstructured data, which constitute the main source of big data, such as text, audio, video, and social media data (Marques & Batista, 2017). Enterprises are learning to take advantage of it. They use real-time information from sensors, RFID to understand their business environments and to create new products and services. So, new technologies and algorithms for processing and storing data will be needed (Weinberg et al., 2015).

Ownership is also a concern. Who owns the data in a system where a variety of parties co-creates and adds value? This has been an issue in social media and in other cases where data are generated or shared through third-party agents. In addition to concerns related to data processing, storage, and ownership, unanswered questions regarding interoperability, communication, and standards will need to be addressed (Marques & Batista, 2017). Providers and manufacturers will employ a variety of different approaches with respect to IoT, such as data structures and communications, but for devices to ultimately work together, some sort of coordination or set of standards will need to be defined (Akoka et al., 2017).

Technological Aspects

At the core of IoT devices is computer technology with associated programs and hardware for sensing, communicating, and delivering benefits. A telephone becomes a computer with phone-calling capabilities (e.g., smartphone); a watch becomes a computer and communication device that can keep time (e.g. smartwatch); an automobile becomes a computer on wheels (e.g., self-driving cars). And a central part of computer-based technology is data and data processing (Weinberg et al., 2015). Thinking more like a technologist does not suggest thinking less like or about people. As the web and social media utilization have become more commonplace, the users of these technologies expect greater speed in response, information flow, and problem solving. Indeed, more people expect their problems to be handled in real time, and for corresponding solutions to be quickly developed and delivered. Although the web applications and tools of today allow for faster input and response than did the first generation of web solutions, the need for speed will increase with IoT. IoT will further increase the speed of and possibility for real-time, solution-related actions to problems. It will be critical not only for people to design machines that can deliver real-time solutions but also for employees of organizations to think, respond, and act faster in IoT contexts.

For technology to disappear from the consciousness of the user, the IoT demands (Gubbi et al., 2013):

1. A shared understanding of the situation of its users and their appliances,
2. Software architectures and pervasive communication networks to process and convey the contextual information to where it is relevant, and
3. The analytics tools that aim for autonomous and smart behaviour.

Ethical and Security Aspects

Information and market intelligence create a smart and intelligent environment, which is an essential component to a functional IoT system and network (Quirk, 2017). However, when organizations distort, hinder or otherwise manipulate information flows, several ethical or security aspects are compromised. The pervasive belief is that the IoT will enhance customers' lives and make them 'smarter' (intelligent), while at the same time feed data to develop the enterprise' competitive behaviour, making it possible to more directly, for example, target, monitor and deliver more specific and customized experiences. From cameras to industrial controls to GPS (Global Positioning System), the increased connectivity of devices leads to increased data and accordingly to security threats. These risks include cybercrime and fraud and encompass examples such as privacy infringement, hacking, espionage and market manipulation through Internet forums and various connected social networks (De Cremer et al., 2017). As the push towards IoT, smart devices and big data makes clear, these risks become more and more pronounced over time, when an increasing amount of information is gathered about organizations and their stakeholders.

De Cremer and colleagues (2017) classify the ethical behaviours in four levels. The issues enhanced are also corroborate in works of Peppers and Rogers (2016) and of Weinberg et al. (2015). They are:

- **Information and Intelligence:** As the IoT involves tracking, monitoring and assembling detailed information about customers to serve them better, there is a potential for the misuse of information, where vital information is used in ways that customers disapprove. IoT organizations that are able to collect and integrate information from a variety of sources may sell these to third-party enterprises and other organizations to use without the customer 's knowledge or permission. Supplemented with additional information purchased from data brokers, organizations possess unique knowledge about their customers' behaviours, which provides the basis for carefully targeted and customised promotional campaigns based on detailed knowledge. For example, spamming is an unwanted intrusion, and the Internet has led to many different forms of communication and intrusion, including pop-up ads and unsolicited e-mails offering various unwanted services.
- **Transaction:** Involves offering the customer products and services with 'hidden' and unexpected costs and conditions, restricting the alternatives available, or ignoring the needs of some customers, so that these IoT organizations can maximise their profits from each transaction. Examples include complex pricing alternatives of IoT subscriptions, or complicated usage rates that make comparisons of price and fees among IoT service providers very difficult. Other example is that penalties may be imposed for disconnecting certain IoT units or perhaps, when customers with an 'adaptable pricing plan' miss a payment, this may result in financial consequences.
- **Relationship:** With the IoT in place, impeccable knowledge on customers exists, resulting in micro segmentation and customization schemes based on their buying behavior characteristics and their economic attractiveness. IoT providers can make it difficult and costly for customers to

change service providers to retain customers. An example is when a breakdown of the IoT may occur in situations where the organization discriminates the needs of some customers and ignoring others, because they consider their profit margins to be more important than their relationships.

- **Integrity Challenge:** Consider service providers' deliberate attempts at manipulating market conditions to take advantage of the situation, while disadvantaging the other party. An IoT organization may put pressure on their staff to up-sell and cross-sell, resulting in customers being sold products they do not need, leading to the connection of more units than warranted. For example, a beverage brand developing a smart vending machine that would raise the price when the weather was hot, or when a customer found that a product which he bought dropped in price when he deleted the cookies on his computer, suggesting that the enterprise had tracked his behavior and raised the price due to his interest in that product.

Weinberg and colleagues (2015) highlight also that the security breach associated with IoT could be costlier. They recall that IoT devices connect physical objects to the Internet. Hacking into a database of information is one thing; hacking into a physical device in the proximity of a person and gaining control of it could be disastrous. The authors cite the case of the automobiles to imagine the outcome of someone wrestling away control of a motor vehicle. Imagine the risk with respect to health care. The effectiveness and degree of care associated with connectivity to a consumer's vital signs and systems can be comforting on the benefit side (Shepardson, 2015). There is greater need for privacy and security lock-down when it comes to IoT.

Given the increased importance of privacy in a more advanced technological and connected world, it is critical for privacy to be a more common consideration throughout an organization and the various processes employed in serving customers and solving their problems (Attié & Meyer-Waarden, 2016). The consumers also perceive risks that can be financial, functional, physical, social, psychological, temporal, and so on. Again, in a world with significant increases in connectivity, data, personal sensitivity of data, data transmission, and potential impact of data on a consumer's being, a consumer's trust and relationships will be based more on how well privacy is respected and maintained. Indeed, an organization's management of privacy is becoming increasingly representative of its respect for consumers and, in turn, consumers' trust in the organization and brand. Organizations that plan to employ or develop IoT, entwined solutions to problems should devote careful attention to a variety of areas, but mainly including information management, technology development, and ethical and privacy concerns.

IMPACTS OF IOT ON MARKETING AND APPLICATION DOMAIN PROPOSALS

The growing use of the IoT to facilitate marketing activities reveals the importance of understanding the growing challenges for organizations and their stakeholders, and the managerial and policy implications.

Consumers will have a heightened awareness that data associated with their being, actions, thoughts, and emotions are indeed a currency and are associated with their humanness. In a similar vein, targeted influence maximization of online advertisements is subject to the latency tolerance of a potential customer online (Kejariwal & Orsini, 2016). Thus, as society - including its business landscape - moves into a more ubiquitous technology and information era, consumers will place greater emphasis and importance on data ownership and data flow-related issues such as privacy, and relatively lesser weight on traditional marketing factors such as the marketing mix. Note that marketing mix elements are of the hand of the marketer, but consumer data are generated by and of the consumer. These data are reflections of consumers and can be used to characterize and control them. Thus, organizational and marketer performance constructs, such as reputation and brand perceptions, will be based increasingly on privacy and respect for consumer data, which in turn can signal respect for consumers (Weinberg et al., 2015).

The Internet of Things (IoT) is progressing from a hi-tech vision to everyday reality, powered up by mobile devices bringing interconnectivity into the lives and homes of consumers. The convenience of connected devices is driving a sharp increase in technology of wearable devices and it is predicted that the utilization of wearable devices will double in the very near future. A new era for advertisers has silently come to its stage. With connections established between everything from wearables to cars and even to the bulletin over the buildings, smart devices and products have created an array of new channels and screens for advertisers (Lee, Chen, Chiang, Chen, & Liu, 2016). Consumer's consumption behavior and common contact points could be recorded by these smart devices, which enable marketers to effectively communicate with target customers by customized advertisements. The real time and customized advertisement would attract people and enhance the conversions rate.

There are several application domains which will be impacted by the Internet of Things. In marketing context, some cases are emerging. Look for some ones in the following paragraphs. The Table 1 resume the application domains, the scope and the main technologies.

In the work of Lee and colleagues (2016), the authors apply 2D animation to media of mobile devices over IoT infrastructure along with the real-time plot and product placement to serve the purpose of in-

Table 1. Examples of several marketing application domains of IoT.

Application domain	Scope	Authors	Technologies
Product placement	mobile advertising	Lee and colleagues (2016)	CPS (Cyber-Physical System), Location-based Animation Plot-Placement System (LAPS), GPS, Wi-Fi
Purchasing behaviour, storytelling and communication	tourism	Gcaba and Dlodlo (2016)	TOTEM (Tale of Things and Electronic Memory), Near-field communications (NFC), RFID and QR codes, cloud database.
Customer experience and consumer' brand perception	health and fitness, smart products	Balaji and Roy (2017), Canhoto and Arp (2017), Wu, Chen and Dou (2017), Mani and Chouk (2017)	Wearable technology
Real time buyer personas' development	buyer personas based on public social media data	An, Cho, Kwak, Jansen and Hassen (2016)	Automatic persona generation system
Product and content development	• bathroom that collect data (use of shampoo, toothpaste, shower gel, etc.) • toilet that liberate information about the state of the urine • doorbell/lock and camera assemblage that enables the homeowner to see who is at their front door and to speak and interact with the visitor • clothes with sensors have digital materiality in that they can record representations of their use in a digital format	Parry, Brax, Maull and Ng (2016); Ng and Wakenshaw (2017); Hoffman and Novak (2015), Guinard, Trifa, Mattern and Wilde (2011)	Sensor, RFID, software offerings in the health and wellbeing

ternet advertising. A prototype of a CPS (Cyber-Physical System) was designed where the consumers could derive it and be encouraged to location-based shopping; or, they could get the tour information immediately while they are moving. To facilitate mobile advertising over the IoT infrastructure and cloud computing, a Location-based Animation Plot-Placement System (LAPS) was developed. The software client of LAPS resident in user's mobile device and would be notifying the server side of LAPS the location info (which metro station/entrance/floor), the route and the moving direction to discover and predict the user's destination and some potential stop-by stations. The operation of LAPS is to obtain the user information of location via the GPS, WiFi or any other wireless schemes within the mobile device then the moving routes could be analyzed, calculated and speculated while the information is updated periodically. With the flow of plot-placement strategy designed for LAPS, the location plotted segment of animation would be transmitted as a streaming multimedia service.

The work of Gcaba and Dlodlo (2016) focused on identifying potential applications of the IoT in tourism. In their study, they determine that in marketing tourism, it involves the collection and processing of sales data to understand the purchasing behavior, storytelling for memories of objects, and enabling communication between tourist and seller:

- **Purchasing Behavior:** The integration of telecommunication technologies with social media enables interaction between people and things. Near-field communications (NFC), radio-frequency identifiers (RFID) and QR codes link the identifier to an IoT platform for processing the data. For example, the store that has sold hand-crafted souvenirs now has more information about the destination of the goods, the retailer gets a report of the purchasing behaviour of tourists across the globe.
- **Storytelling:** As more of our objects and environments become actuated, connected and data-enabled, these enchanted objects are developing the capacity to contain their own stories. An object can remember its history and can understand how it is used, can talk to other objects around it to understand its environment. For example, the wine bottle can tell the story of the history of the wine, that is, where the grapes came from, how long the wine has been left to mature in tanks, etc. The 'thing' and its history is connected to the internet of things. The ID of the 'thing', e.g. its URL and barcode, is given to a smartphone and an application on the smartphone retrieves the data. Tale of Things and Electronic Memory - TOTEM (taleofthings.com) is a straightforward way of adding memories to physical objects to share with others. The Tale of Things platform allows anybody to attach web content (text, image, video and audio) to an artefact through the generation of a unique QR barcode that the owner is encouraged to stick to their thing. When scanned by someone using a smart phone, media is launched, and the object can be seen/heard to tell a story about the memories associated with it.
- **Communication:** For communication between the tourist and the seller, information is stored on a cloud database of objects and names in different languages. The seller and tourist have smart devices which recognize each other. The tourist speaks into a smart device which in turn accesses the cloud database, retrieves the word and responds to the seller's device.

Balaji and Roy (2017) investigates the way in which the IoT changes the customers' experience when shopping in a retailing context. Canhoto and Arp (2017) advances current knowledge on the conceptual understanding of consumers' adoption and sustained use of wearable technology for general health and fitness purposes. Their study investigates how the characteristics of the device, the context and the user can support the adoption and the sustained use of health and fitness wearables, finding that the factors that support the former differ from those that support the latter. For instance, features that signal the device's ability to collect activity data are essential for adoption, whereas device portability and resilience are key for sustained use. Overall, the findings provide valuable guidance to enterprises investing in the development and marketing of these devices. Also, Wu, Chen and Dou (2017) develops and examines the effect of two different interaction styles (e.g., friend-like and engineer-like communication) on consumers' brand perception using two laboratory experiments. Their study suggests that a smart interaction style in the Internet of Things (IoT) context can improve consumers' perceptions of brand warmth and brand competence, and that these perceptions enhance the consumers' emotional attachment to the brand. On the other hand, the study of Mani and Chouk (2017) was carried out to understand resistance towards smart watches, finding that perceived uselessness, perceived price, intrusiveness, perceived novelty and self-efficacy have an impact on consumer resistance to smart products. The authors developed a better understanding of the reasons underlying consumer resistance to smart and connected products. All these cases provide valuable insights into how enterprises can better construct their brand equity using IoT technologies.

In general, and as the examples given above prove, applications of IoT span a wide variety of domains like smart water, smart buildings, smart energy, smart parking, predictive maintenance, inventory tracking, disaster planning and recovery, network performance management, yield management, downtime minimization, capacity planning, demand forecasting, supply chain and logistics, pricing optimization, load balancing optimization, employee productivity, customer experience (Kejariwal & Orsini, 2016). Texas Instruments (2014) identifies six main areas of application: wearables, building and home automation, smart cities, health care, smart manufacturing, and automotive. The subject has also been researched in other disciplines with impact in marketing such as cognitive psychologists and neuropsychologists.

The works of Parry and colleagues (Parry, Brax, Maull, & Ng, 2016) cite many others examples. For example, the case of the pilots from the hubofallthings.com (HAT) project that instrumented a bathroom to collect data on the use of shampoo, toothpaste, shower gel, and even toilet paper where the data is controlled and shared by consumers themselves. Also, the use of buyer personas is an interactive design technique with considerable potential for product and content development. An and colleagues (An, Cho, Kwak, Jansen, & Hassen, 2016) implemented an approach for creating buyer personas (socio-economic status, gender, hobbies, family and friends) in real time, based on automated analysis of actual social media data, integrating data from Facebook, Twitter, and YouTube channels for a large commercial organization. A set of shared URLs of a user can become a good indication of what digital content the user is interested in and is an excellent source of competitive intelligence for an organization. To automatically generate buyer personas from the social media data, the authors firstly find a set of users who share the similar behavioral patterns, then, they identify distinct demographic characteristics of those users to create the buyer personas. An and colleagues (An et al., 2016) demonstrate that by using publicly available information on Facebook, it is possible to extract user interests to generate clusters that feed into the generation of personas. After that, they could generate richer description of buyer personas by combining data from other social media platforms. The authors developed the prototype for a system that automatically generates buyer personas representing current readers of AJ+ news content based on actual user data from three social media channels that updates these personas in real time based on changes in audience demographic, interests, or usage.

Another example is the case of a toilet manufacturer, through embedding a sensor in its offerings, can 'liquefy' and liberate information about the state of the urine, which can serve as an information resource to be analyzed, stored, or shared on the person's wellbeing (Ng & Wakenshaw, 2017). This implies that the enterprise is now able to create new software offerings in the health and wellbeing economy and indeed, derive revenues from the information resource that could complement or even replace the revenues received from selling toilets. With the IoT, liquification of information resources, and the subsequent processing and analyses to support decisions and actions, is the fundamental driver of the 'smart' movement in the IoT. Also, in context of the Ng and Wakenshaw (2017) work, for example, clothes with sensors have digital materiality in that they can record representations of their use in a digital format. With the IoT, everyday physical objects such as cars, fridges, and watches can therefore be embedded with digital technology such as software, RFID, and sensors to achieve new functionalities (Guinard, Trifa, Mattern, & Wilde, 2011). Also, a doorbell/lock could be an alert device. When connected to the Internet and to the camera, the doorbell/lock and camera assemblage enables the homeowner to see who is at their front door and to speak and interact with the visitor, even when they are not physically at home (Hoffman & Novak, 2015). The doorbell/lock on a greenhouse and the temperature sensor assemblage would enable the remote control of the opening and closing of the door. This characteristic of IoT would be crucial for freely decomposing and reconfiguring of actors in the IoT (Ng & Wakenshaw, 2017).

SOLUTIONS AND RECOMMENDATIONS

With the power that comes with the IoT in terms of data-driven knowledge, the increased potential for exploitation of ever-more-powerless customers is clearly present. However, sometimes the organizations mistake the IoT with excessive data collection, leading to customer exploitation, also when they are maliciously motivated to take advantage of the customers for profit. With the use of IoT technology, organizations can take a greater slice of the value created, consequently extracting more value from customers (De Cremer et al., 2017).

As the study of Attié and Meyer-Waarden (Attié & Meyer-Waarden, 2016) confirm, consumers find smart connected objects easier to use and more useful if they also bring them wellbeing benefits. Furthermore, the IoT creates value through its relational, hedonistic benefits and with the emotional experience associated. When smart connected objects provide hedonic values, the efforts associated with their use seem to be easier. However, only 35% of users believe that smart connected objects increase their quality of life or wellbeing. Nevertheless, if this proportion is still quite small, it likely increases with the development of new kind of smartphone applications such as health tracking or sport performance measurement, and the access to new smart connected objects through price drops and better quality. The study of Attié and Meyer-Waarden (2016) confirm that to get more accepted, smart connected objects must convince users that they provide wellbeing benefits. Moreover, the perceived social image has a positive impact on the acceptance of smart connected objects. However, participants perceive the risks of connected technologies for their private lives. This is one of the main reasons why smart objects seem hard to get adopted by consumers. The IoT reluctance mainly comes from the potential privacy risks of not being able to control privacy and the way personal data might be used by enterprises. Security must be the central topic both in the IoT development and communication. Thus, organizations must be clear about the way they store and use data, and communicate about it to reassure the users. Therefore, the constant evolution of the IoT technology will make smart objects more attractive and should increase their acceptation in the coming years.

The visibility of contexts would drive a new research agenda in the behavioral aspects of consumption and experience. Ng and Wakenshaw (2017) propose the following IoT research priorities on marketing context:

- Integrating goods and service-based models of consumption and experience;
- Developing new dispositional-situational models of behaviors;
- Understanding and influencing behaviors and decisions in context;
- Designing physical and connected products and platforms for better digital service experiences;
- Developing new differentiation models with reconfigurable physical and connected products;
- Innovating on personalized information-based offerings;
- Improving consumer engagement;
- Emergence and development of new markets and market platforms.

In opinion of Ng and Wakenshaw (2017), the visibility of contexts would bring the focus of research into understanding consumer experiences, the space where value is created in use and in experience of things we purchase. The ability to instrument and collect real behavioral data would allow researchers to observe and draw insights from individuals' real lives, which could have a real impact on society. Ng and Wakenshaw (2017).propose that the move into research on consumer experiences means a shift in the unit of analysis from dispositional to situational traits and the need to conceptualize this new space. The authors suggest that behaviors within contexts could potentially be influenced through IoT, by way of nudges and prompts. The four implications (liquification and density of information resources; digital materiality; assemblage and service systems; and modularity and transaction network) suggest that an era of IoT will fundamentally transform the organization's business model, to incorporate value creation (the experience – more visible), value proposition (the offering - reconfigurable), and value 'capture' or creating worth for exchanges (i.e. the economic model – with shifting boundaries). The work of the Ng and Wakenshaw (2017) suggests a step change for research in marketing. Marketing has a societal responsibility to introduce greater diversity in product choices in a wide range of markets, so that the template of behaviors in IoT products can give greater freedoms and individuals can manifest their authenticity and live more meaningful lives.

FUTURE RESEARCH DIRECTIONS

The Internet of Things (IoT) can solve problems and create opportunities for a variety of entities, including consumers, providers, employees, organizations, manufacturers, communities, cities, and governments, among others. The bibliometric study of Akoka and colleagues (2017) determined that although IoT is one of the main markets of big data applications, it is not well reflected in research publications yet. Besides, it seems that the research on mobile data analytics is just starting. Nevertheless, their study showed that usages of big data is attracting researchers specially for two application domains: marketing and retail, and healthcare.

Actually, a wide variety of technologies are called IoT devices. It is estimated that there were about16 billion IoT devices in 2014, and forecasts point to as many as 50 billion devices in 2020 (Weinberg et al., 2015). IoT can benefit organizations by enhancing data collection, enabling real-time responses, improving access and control of devices, increasing efficiency and productivity, and connecting technologies.

It is reasonable enough to imagine that IoT components and products with embedded sensors and other 'smart' IT-related componentry would enhance many processes.

It is imperative that marketing research adapts to this new era of connected products which would have impact on product design and development, and on customer experience and engagement. Marketing would need to bring situational and contextual insights to innovate on future offerings, and on the understanding of how consumer latent needs can emerge new generative offerings (Yoo et al., 2010). With an understanding of the transaction boundaries and the possibility of dynamic re-configurability and flexible boundaries of products, different offerings can be designed for various contexts and consumers. In an era of IoT, the transformation of data into information, both for the organization and the consumer, is a critical research agenda. What needs to be considered is the use of the data as well as its transformation into information that may need to be integrated with other datasets, and be made usable by organizations and consumers i.e. data being a service. For Yoo and colleagues (2010), The challenge of transforming data into an information service has an impact on personalization and vulnerabilities. Ng and Wakenshaw (2017) enhance that there is a need for marketing to research and understand where and how consumers are able to use their own data and create value with it, and organizations are able to use the data as well to personalize their offerings. This implies that data about individuals must be accessible to them. The current model of the data economy is one where the organization that collects the data has the custodial right (i.e. the right to give rights) to it (Skilton & Ng, 2016). This data is collected often with very little knowledge of contexts, such as knowing where the product was used. For example, consumer purchasing data helps supermarkets tailor vouchers and promotions and optimize the supply chain of their goods. This means that the format and organization of the data was created to suit the organization. So even if consumers have access to the data, they may not have the ability to process, manipulate, and make the data useful for themselves. In addition, the sharing of such data with other organizations, even for innovative new offerings, is often constrained by privacy laws. For personal data to have impact on the economy, more research should go towards understanding the means through which the exchange and use of personal data can be beneficial for both the individual and organizations (Ng, 2013). So, CRM (Customer Relationship Management) will evolve into VRM (Vendor Relationship Management), a movement initiated by Searls (Mitchell, Henderson, & Searls, 2008; Searls, 2012) who envisaged the VRM as enabling individual customers to perform what organizations can do with their data from collecting, storing, and sharing. In such a market, customers/buyers, being able to cast intentions to buy, would find sellers rather than being captured by them. Vendors would respond to such intentions of customers (e.g. a digital shopping basket shared as an open API (Application Programming Interface)) rather than guessing what might get their attention. The future of segmentation and targeting research in marketing would benefit individuals through opportunities to buy services that make their data useful in future purchases e.g. matching what they own or consume with what they wish to buy, or to buy services to analyze their own data to make better decisions for day-to-day living (Searls, 2012).

Also, given its contextual nature, Ng and Wakenshaw (2017) argue that the underlying driver of actions in an era of IoT may not be privacy, but the vulnerability. The authors emphasize that research is needed to expand on the understanding of vulnerability in digital domains, and how mechanisms such as perceived control and trust could reduce vulnerability and therefore be built into organizations' offerings. Research into vulnerability needs to be considered from three perspectives. First, the individual's perspective of their own vulnerability; second, the perspective of the entity with whom the individual is interacting in the digital domain (which could be another individual, or an organization); and third, the institution tasked to regulate and protect all entities within the system (e.g. the state, regulatory body etc.). From an individual's point of view, the trade-off is between the choice/freedom to use a service against the risk of being vulnerable. From the organization's point of view, the individual's vulnerability and assessment of risk is important for its business model and it would trade off revenues and provide additional services to mitigate that risk, but only to the extent that would pacify the user and the regulator. Finally, from a regulator's point of view, the aggregation of large numbers of users and a complex system of data sharing creates a systemic risk that may result in individual vulnerabilities. Although the risk is systemic, the consequences could be critical for individual users as they may become more vulnerable to cybersecurity threats.

CONCLUSION

In face to explained, we can conclude that despite several applications of IoT in marketing and its enormous potential, some issues need reflection as by organizations, consumers or governments. In resume, the IoT era will need a greater understanding of the role of data and its interaction with consumers as they evolve from need-driven transactions into an era of data-driven intelligence and decisions. Marketing plays a crucial role in helping organizations understand the use of personal data and explore opportunities to design and bundle offerings more suited to the way individuals experience and consume products and services in context, in a more scalable way. Yet, while organizations could integrate personal data across silos to develop new offerings, there is a need to respect the rights of individuals and reduce vulnerabilities.

The evolution of the next generation mobile system will depend on the creativity of the users in designing new applications, respecting the privacy and controlling security of the personal and organizational data.

REFERENCES

Akoka, J., Comyn-Wattiau, I., & Laoufi, N. (2017). Research on Big Data – A systematic mapping study. *Computer Standards & Interfaces*, *54*, 105–115. doi:10.1016/j.csi.2017.01.004

An, J., Cho, H., Kwak, H., Jansen, B. J., & Hassen, M. Z. (2016). Towards automatic persona generation using social media. In *4th International Conference on Future Internet of Things and Cloud Workshops* (pp. 206–211). IEEE Computer Society. 10.1109/W-FiCloud.2016.51

Ashton, K. (2009). That "Internet of Things" thing.: in the real world things matter more than ideas. *RFiD Journal*. Retrieved from http://www.rfidjournal.com/articles/view?4986

Ashton, K. (2013). *The year of the Internet of Things*. MIT Technology Review.

Attié, E., & Meyer-Waarden, L. (2016). *A theoretical model incorporating social influence and cognitive processes to explain the adoption of the internet of things*. In *45th EMAC Annual Conference 20176*, Oslo, Norway.

Balaji, M. S., & Roy, S. K. (2017). Value co-creation with Internet of things technology in the retail industry. *Journal of Marketing Management*, *33*(1–2), 7–31. doi:10.1080/0267257X.2016.1217914

Canhoto, A. I., & Arp, S. (2017). Exploring the factors that support adoption and sustained use of health and fitness wearables. *Journal of Marketing Management*, *33*(1–2), 32–60. doi:10.1080/0267257X.2016.1234505

Da Xu, L., He, W., & Li, S. (2014). Internet of things in industries: A survey. *IEEE Transactions on Industrial Informatics*, *10*(4), 2233–2243. doi:10.1109/TII.2014.2300753

De Cremer, D., Nguyen, B., & Simkin, L. (2017). The integrity challenge of the Internet-of-Things (IoT): On understanding its dark side. *Journal of Marketing Management*, *33*(1–2). doi:10.1080/0267257X.2016.1247517

Ehret, M., & Wirtz, J. (2017). Unlocking Value from Machines: Business Models and the Industrial Internet of Things. *Journal of Marketing Management*, *33*(1–2), 111–130. doi:10.1080/0267257X.2016.1248041

Gcaba, O., & Dlodlo, N. (2016). The Internet of Things for South African Tourism. In IST-Africa 2016 Confeence Proceedings (pp. 1–8). IIMC International Information Management Corporation. doi:10.1109/ISTAFRICA.2016.7530573

Gubbi, J., Buyya, R., Marusic, S., & Palaniswami, M. (2013). Internet of Things (IoT): A vision, architectural elements, and future directions. *Future Generation Computer Systems*, *29*(7), 1645–1660. doi:10.1016/j.future.2013.01.010

Hoffman, D., & Novak, T. (2015). *Emergent experience and the connected consumer in the smart home assemblage and the internet of things*. Academic Press. 10.13140/RG.2.1.3966.1282.Holbrook

Kaplan, A., & Haenlein, M. (2010). Users of the world, unite! The challenges and opportunities. *Business Horizons of Social Media*, *53*(1), 59–68. doi:10.1016/j.bushor.2009.09.003

Keefe, L. M. (2008). Marketing defined. *Marketing News*, *42*(1), 28–29.

Kejariwal, A., & Orsini, F. (2016). On the definition of real-time: applications and systems. In 2016 IEEE TrustCom/BigDataSE/ISPA (pp. 2213–2220). IEEE Computer Society. doi:10.1109/TrustCom.2016.0341

Laudon, K., & Laudon, J. (2016). *Managing Information Systems: Managing the Digital Firm* (14th ed.). Pearson Education International.

Lee, R.-H., Chen, A.-Y., Chiang, C.-C., Chen, Y.-S. A., & Liu, C.-H. (2016). A preliminary design and implementation of location-based mobile advertising schemes with plot placement animation over a cyber-physical system. In *2016 International Conference on Networking and Network Applications* (pp. 196–201). Academic Press. 10.1109/NaNA.2016.89

Mani, Z., & Chouk, I. (2017). Drivers of consumers' resistance to smart products. *Journal of Marketing Management*, *33*(1–2), 76–97. doi:10.1080/0267257X.2016.1245212

Marques, R. P., & Batista, J. C. L. (Eds.). (2017). *Information and communication overload in the digital age*. IGI Global. doi:10.4018/978-1-5225-2061-0

Miorandi, D., Sicari, S., De Pellegrini, F., & Chlamtac, I. (2012). Internet of things: Vision, applications and research challenges. *Ad Hoc Networks*, *10*(7), 1497–1516. doi:10.1016/j.adhoc.2012.02.016

Mitchell, A., Henderson, I., & Searls, D. (2008). Reinventing direct marketing: With VRM inside. *Journal of Direct. Data and Digital Marketing Practice, 10*(1), 3–15. doi:10.1057/dddmp.2008.24

Ng, I. C. L. (2013). New business and economic models in the connected digital economy. *Journal of Revenue and Pricing Management, 12*(6), 1–7.

Ng, I. C. L., & Smith, L. (2012). An integrative framework of value. *Review of Marketing Research,* (9), 207–243.

Ng, I. C. L., & Wakenshaw, S. Y. L. (2014). The role of marketing in the design and innovation of future products in the connected digital economy. In *Proceedings of the 13th International Research Conference In Service Management* (pp. 27–30). La Londe les Maures, France: Academic Press.

Ng, I. C. L., & Wakenshaw, S. Y. L. (2017). The Internet-of-Things: Review and research directions. *International Journal of Research in Marketing, 34*(1), 3–21. doi:10.1016/j.ijresmar.2016.11.003

Nguyen, B., & Simkin, L. (2017). The Internet of Things (IoT) and marketing: The state of play, future trends and the implications for marketing. *Journal of Marketing Management, 33*(1–2). doi:10.1080/0267257X.2016.1257542

Parry, G., Brax, S., Maull, R., & Ng, I. (2016). Operationalising IoT for reverse supply: The development of use-visibility measures. *Supply Chain Management, 21*(2), 228–244. doi:10.1108/SCM-10-2015-0386

Quirk, R. E. J. (2017). Are Your Company's Consumer Electronics Exempt from FCC Marketing Regulations? *IEEE Consumer Electronics Magazine, 6*(1), 22–26. doi:10.1109/MCE.2016.2640578

Searls, D. (2012). *The intention economy: when customers take charge*. Boston, MA: Harvard Business Review Press.

Shepardson, D. (2015). *Cars are vulnerable to wireless hacking*. Retrieved from http://www.detroitnews.com/story/business/autos/%0A2015/02/08/report-cars-vulnerable-wireless-hacking/%0A23094215/

Skilton, M., & Ng, I. (2016). *What the apple versus FBI debacle taught us*. Retrieved September 6, 2017, from http://blogs.scientificamerican.com/guest-blog/what-the-apple-vs-%0Afbi-debacle-taught-us/

Sundmaeker, H., Guillemin, P., Friess, P., & Woelfflé, S. (2010). *Vision and challenges for realising the Internet of Things*. Cluster of European Research Projects on the Internet of Things—CERP IoT.

Texas Instruments. (2014). *Application areas for the Internet of Things*. Retrieved September 6, 2017, from http://www.ti.com/ww/en/internet_of_things/iot-applications.html

Weinberg, B. D., Milne, G. R., Andonova, Y. G., & Hajjat, F. M. (2015). Internet of Things: Convenience vs. privacy and secrecy. *Business Horizons, 58*(6), 615–624. doi:10.1016/j.bushor.2015.06.005

Weiser, M., Gold, R., & Brown, J. S. (1999). The origins of ubiquitous computing research at PARC in the late 1980s. *IBM Systems Journal, 38*(4), 693–696. doi:10.1147j.384.0693

Wu, J., Chen, J., & Dou, W. (2017). The Internet of Things and interaction style: The effect of smart interaction on brand attachment. *Journal of Marketing Management, 33*(1–2), 61–75. doi:10.1080/0267257X.2016.1233132

Yoo, Y., Lyytinen, K., Boland, R., Berente, N., Gaskin, J., Schutz, D., & Srinivasan, N. (2012). *The next wave of digital innovation: opportunities and challenges.* A report of an NSF research workshop on digital challenges in innovation research.

KEY TERMS AND DEFINITIONS

Big Data: Term, coined by Roger Magoulas, describing the storage and analysis of large and or complex data sets using a series of techniques. It refers to large data sets impossible to manage and process using traditional data management tools, requiring complex computational platforms to be analyzed.

Buyer Personas: Are fictional representations of ideal customers that are often developed using qualitative methods such as interviews in order to gather relevant aspects of the customers' profile, needs, wants, preferences, goals, and behaviors. Buyer personas have been used by marketing as a means to design more effective approaches to attract, satisfy, and retain customers. This technique has gained further relevance for digital marketing, namely for guiding content creation strategies, product development and customer involvement.

Cloud Computing: A model for enabling ubiquitous access to shared resources (such as computer networks, servers, storage, applications and services), which can be rapidly provisioned with minimal management effort over the Internet. It allows users and enterprises with various computing capabilities to store and process data either in a privately-owned cloud, or on a third-party server located in a data center, thus making data-accessing mechanisms more efficient and reliable.

Internet of Things: Is a network that consists of physical objects or "things" being embedded in electronics, software, sensors, and connectivity to enable objects to exchange data with the production, operator and/or other connected devices. The term is used as an umbrella keyword for covering aspects related to the extension of the Internet and Web into the physical realm, by means of widespread deployment of spatially distributed devices with embedded identification, sensing and actuation capabilities.

Mobile Systems: Term used to refer portable transceivers (e.g., mobile phones, tablets and laptops equipped with mobile broadband modems, network drivers, etc.) to communicate with each other and with fixed transceivers and telephones anywhere in the Internet, via wireless communication.

Product Placement: Is a non-traditional advertising technique in which brands and products are incorporated into television shows, movies and other entertainment media. Thus, products become a component of entertainment content, being used by the characters and becoming part of the story, increasing their exposure to customers in a more natural way as compared to advertising.

Sensor Network Technologies: A group of spatially distributed autonomous devices using dedicated sensors that connects to the Internet to monitor physical or environmental conditions and to organize the collected data that can be transmitted to back-end systems for analysis and used in applications.

Social Networks: The Internet provides platforms that enable many-to-many communication. Individuals use them to interact with their peers, having as main goals interaction, entertainment, and information. For companies and brands social networks offer unique opportunities to listen to and communicate with customers and prospects. Still, social network sites are about dialogue and two-way communication, where consumers control the conversation and have the power to create and disseminate user generated content.

Storytelling: Is a particularly effective way of communicating with customers, by telling stories that they can relate to. By using narratives that evoke experiences in a very personal way, it is possible to communicate complex concepts and ideas, increase memory and emotional attachment. Storytelling is frequently used by complex products and in highly competitive sectors. Digital media facilitates the dissemination and the control of storytelling campaigns.

Chapter 2
The Acceptance Process of the Internet of Things:
How to Improve the Acceptance of the IoT Technology

Elodie Attié
Toulouse School of Management Research, France

Lars Meyer-Waarden
Toulouse School of Management Research, France

ABSTRACT

The internet of things, or the IoT, is progressively and surely invading environments, and is consequently creating new kinds of consumer needs and behaviors. More and more companies are getting involved in this growing field, showing the importance for them to understand this technology market. This chapter aims at studying the acceptance process of the IoT. More specifically, the main factors that influence consumer decisions to accept and use the IoT and smart objects have been tested, such as the ethical, wellbeing, social, and utility values. The importance of each benefit is demonstrated, according to specific targets and to examples of applications. A system of values that represents the promises of the IoT and the central needs of users is also described. Besides, a typology of users should help companies creating or refining targeting strategies and should guide consumers into their acceptance process. Finally, further research directions are discussed.

INTRODUCTION

By 2020, consumers should be surrounded by nearly 50 billion connected objects (Cisco, 2017), which represent at least 6 connected objects per person. The Internet of Things (IoT) is defined as an invisible network of networks which collects and stores data, controls and interacts with people, and with physical and virtual things. The IoT can connect everything together, dependently or independently of the initial settings pre-set by users, and can provide personalized feedback and features through mo-

DOI: 10.4018/978-1-5225-5763-0.ch002

Copyright © 2019, IGI Global. Copying or distributing in print or electronic forms without written permission of IGI Global is prohibited.

bile applications and smart object interfaces. Indeed, the IoT connects physical objects, such as smart watches, connected cars or connected household appliances, anytime and anywhere to the Internet using wireless technology to reach desired goals, such as sleep monitoring, sport activity or other measures of health and wellbeing (e.g. Yang et al., 2013). All electronic objects can be equipped with artificial intelligence, and therefore become 'smart' objects, to seduce technophile consumers. The IoT should widely transform the way people live and improve quality of life (Porter & Heppelmann, 2014). This technology is spreading widely thanks to expanded Internet networks, high mobile adoption and low-cost sensors, but innovations can fail due to changing demand, user reluctance, or strong competition. It is essential for managers to understand the acceptance process of the IoT so as to respond to consumer needs and ensure better profits.

Therefore, the main contribution of this study is to understand the acceptance of the IoT. First, the background of this study is presented. A classification of the IoT and different types of users are then highlighted. The acceptance of the IoT is also studied and explained. Subsequently, theoretical implications are stated and managerial recommendations are provided to help companies better understand the connected consumer and refine marketing strategies. Finally, future research directions are given.

BACKGROUND

The Internet of Things

The IoT includes physical items, such as mobile applications and smart/connected objects, and includes virtual things, such as transmission of signals or artificial intelligence algorithms which send data to other physical or virtual things, and all that can interact together. The IoT is partly invisible to the human eye: no one can see or touch these networks, and physical supports like connected objects and mobile applications help to visualize the IoT interactions. The main threat with the IoT is that personal data are not always reachable by users, while it is automatically registered in databases to do personalized feedback and develop specific features. Figure 1 represents the subcategories, including physical and virtual things, which are involved in the IoT concept.

The classification of the IoT shows that there are common characteristics between each upper and lower category: the upper category includes the features of the lower category with additional characteristics.

Databases

Data are at the heart of the IoT: they are the essence of the IoT that enables physical and virtual things to interact together. Data are represented by series of codes that lead to meaningful information (Beynon-Davies, 2002). In the context of the IoT, data are defined as qualitative and quantitative information about users or specific environmental indicators, which is tracked, collected, measured and reported through sensors and then stored into databases to be analysed, and eventually resold. The data analysis is supposed to allow a better use of the IoT. Indeed, connected objects and mobile applications collect all kinds of data (personal and corporal indicators, environmental indicators, etc.) to enhance knowledge and wisdom for both users (i.e., higher quantified-self) and companies (i.e., higher profits and better product and service development).

Figure 1. Classification of the Internet of Things

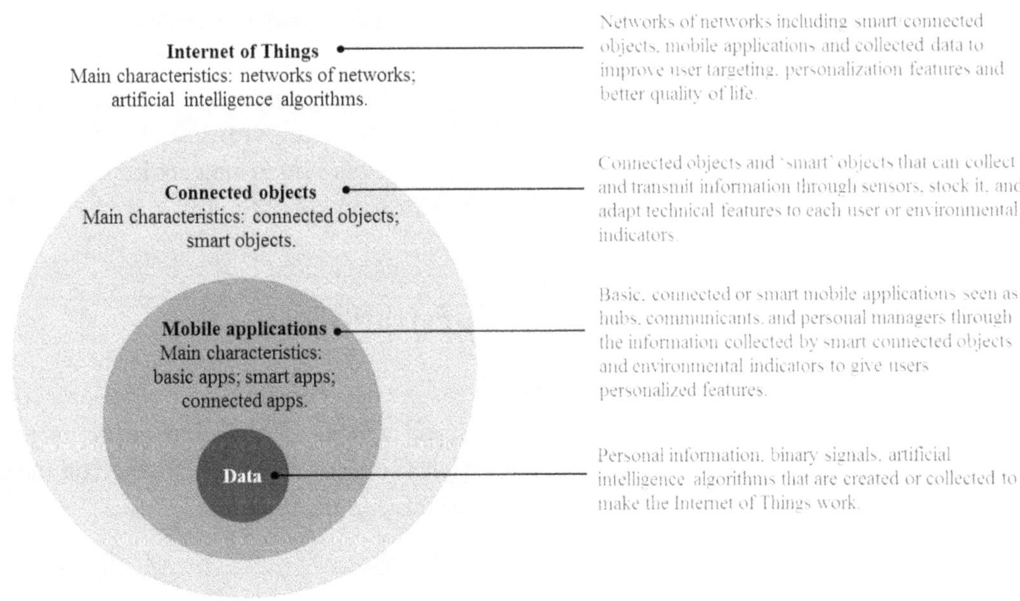

Mobile Applications

The mobile applications category includes 'basic', 'connected', and 'smart' applications.

'Basic' mobile applications, or more commonly called mobile apps, are software programs developed for smartphones and tablets to collect, store and provide real-time data (e.g. Rakestraw et al., 2013), so that users can perform specific tasks and thus respond to specific needs.

A 'basic' mobile app becomes a 'connected' app as soon as the app collects data through sensors present in smartphones, tablets, or connected objects. The data provide relevant information about environment indicators and personal indicators (i.e., health rate, number of steps, localization, etc.) to suggest personalized feedback and features, and this according to the parameters controlled by users. Connected apps give relevant information to users only when they ask for it.

A 'connected' app is not necessarily a 'smart' app: a 'smart' app can automatically suggest personalized advice according to measured indicators, adapts its functionalities to users and environments, and updates the data anytime, independently of users who have low technical control. Generally, smart apps automatically send data to external databases to improve the app or resale the information, sometimes independently of the knowledge of users. The main difference with connected apps is that users are not always controlling smart apps.

Connected Objects

Connected objects represent the physical aspect of the IoT. These connected objects mainly work thanks to smartphones, tablets or now robots like Google Home, that become remote controls and real-time data hubs. Connected objects are communicating objects through smartphones and tablets, with at least one sensor, which can get data and transmit this information to databases and to users so they can manage all their technical features. Generally, connected objects respond to utility needs by improving quantified-self requirements through self-tracking, self-knowledge and self-management.

They are included in the larger category of smart objects. 'Smart' objects are connected objects that are also active, autonomous, cognitive, and that possess artificial intelligence, allowing them to learn from different situations and spontaneously adapt their technical features to external indicators, sometimes independently of the parameters initially programmed by users. Smart objects imply great technology trust since the risks of dependence are quite high while the control of the IoT is low.

THE ACCEPTANCE OF THE INTERNET OF THINGS

Attié and Meyer-Waarden (2016; 2017) discuss the reasons why consumers would decide, or not, to use the IoT. However, the IoT brings out benefits and risks, and reasons for consumer attraction and rejection. In this study, the main objective is to understand which variables have an influence on the acceptance process of the IoT, and subsequently, to give managerial recommendations.

Conceptual Framework

First, a qualitative study was done with users and non-users, to study their motivations and reluctances to use the IoT. According to this preliminary analysis, the authors studied the variables that seemed to be the most relevant in the context of the IoT, and built the links between each variable upon a literature review, so as to shape a theoretical model (Figure 2).

Technology trust is one of the most important key variables when evaluating technology use (Hoffman et al., 1999; Song & Lee, 2012). It can be interpreted from two perspectives: the way the data are managed and the perceived safety of the technology itself. Privacy issues and technical incidents are often spread by the media, increasing consumer doubts and fears toward innovations. Indeed, the IoT enables to track, collect and use personal data, increasing doubts about confidentiality and safety. The more people trust the IoT (both data management and technology safety), the less they should perceive privacy concerns (Shin, 2010). Moreover, IoT trust should increase wellbeing feelings (e.g. Van der Heijden, 2004), utility benefits (e.g. Davis & Pechmann, 2013), as well as social benefits:

- **Hypothesis One (a):** IoT trust has a negative influence on privacy concerns.
- **Hypothesis One (b):** IoT trust has a positive influence on utility value.
- **Hypothesis One (c):** IoT trust has a positive influence on wellbeing value.
- **Hypothesis One (d):** IoT trust has a positive influence on social value.

Besides, data collection can be seen as intrusive, arousing privacy concerns (Phelps et al., 2000). Privacy concerns highlight how users are concerned about the flow of personal information (Shin, 2010), influencing the utility value, and the IoT acceptance (e.g. Dimitriadis & Kyrezis, 2010). Hackers could get financial and health data from bank applications and health trackers, and they could control applications without users noticing it. The more people fear about privacy concerns, the less they should intend to use the IoT, and the lower they should rate the utility value:

- **Hypothesis Two (a):** Privacy concerns about the IoT have a negative influence on the intention to use the IoT.
- **Hypothesis Two (b):** Privacy concerns about the IoT have a negative influence on utility value.

Moreover, functional and utility benefits improve technology acceptance and use (Rauschnabel et al., 2015). In our context, utility value is the willingness to use the IoT to accomplish specific useful tasks (West & Turner, 2010). The IoT brings useful features by responding to primary technological needs, like communication, with smartwatches and connected speakers, for example, or like research of information with smart televisions, smart refrigerators and other smart interfaces. Therefore, consumers who perceive the IoT as useful should be highly tempted to try it (e.g. Davis, 1989). Furthermore, the functional capacities of the IoT can help people regulate their health (Prayoga & Abraham, 2016), improving both quality of life and wellbeing:

- **Hypothesis Three (a):** The utility value of the IoT has a positive influence on the intention to use the IoT.
- **Hypothesis Three (b):** The utility value of the IoT has a positive influence on wellbeing value.

Furthermore, the IoT should enhance feelings of wellbeing (Xia et al., 2012). Wellbeing is defined as the positive emotion felt when a desired state is reached (Higgins, 1997), and the social, medical and psychological conditions of people (Lee et al., 2003). Three dimensions defining the wellbeing value are measured: (1) expected hedonism (perceived benefits of joy, happiness and entertainment), (2) health benefits (the IoT can measure health indicators and give personalized feedback to improve health), and (3) quality of life (one of the main objectives and promises of the IoT (Porter & Heppelmann, 2014)). Greater perceived wellbeing with the IoT implies greater use (e.g. Davis & Pechmann, 2013). Therefore, users expecting to feel wellbeing when using the IoT will be more willing to use it:

- **Hypothesis Four:** The wellbeing value of the IoT has a positive influence on the intention to use the IoT.

According to the social cognitive theory, social value influences technology acceptance (Venkatesh et al., 2003). Social influence, guiding beliefs and opinions, mainly comes from external sources, such as co-workers, family members, friends, neighbours, the media and advertising. If innovations give a positive image to users within their social group(s), these new technologies accelerate acceptance and use (Rogers, 1983). The more users feel that the IoT improves their social status, the better they should feel about it and willing to use it:

- **Hypothesis Five (a):** The social value of the IoT has a positive influence on the intention to use the IoT.
- **Hypothesis Five (b):** The social value of the IoT has a positive influence on wellbeing value.

Personal characteristics are moderators of the acceptance process, which differ depending on gender, and on the levels of innovativeness and of quantified-self of users.

Following longstanding and cultural clichés, men are said to be more attracted to useful features and are considered as more technology experts than women, who are more attracted to wellbeing and health benefits (Venkatesh & Morris, 2000). There should be a difference of the strengths of the effects of privacy concerns, utility value, social value and wellbeing value on the intention to use the IoT according to gender:

- **Hypothesis Six (a):** The direct effects of privacy concerns, utility value and social value have a stronger influence on the intention to use the IoT with men, and the wellbeing value has a stronger influence on the intention to use the IoT with women.

Furthermore, studies have shown that innovativeness is a moderator between the perceptions and the intention to use a technology (Agarwal & Prasad, 1998; Leonard-Barton & Deschamps, 1988). Innovativeness represents the willingness to try and adopt innovations (Rogers, 1995), like the IoT. Thus, the authors believe that innovative people will rate higher the utility, wellbeing and social values than non-innovative people, who will be more bounded to privacy concerns and their consequences:

- **Hypothesis Six (b):** The direct effects hypothesized on the intention to use the IoT are stronger when users have a high level of innovativeness.

Finally, quantified-self is defined as the ability and willingness to self-track and self-manage oneself through the IoT, improving social status and wellbeing (e.g. Kozinets, 2012). Users with a higher level of quantified-self should rate higher on utility value, social value and wellbeing value, whereas people with a lower level should be more wary of privacy concerns:

- **Hypothesis Six (c):** The direct effects hypothesized on the intention to use the IoT are stronger when users have a high level of quantified-self.

The acceptance process of the IoT is presented in the shape of a prism, as seen in Figure 2.

The prism-model of the acceptance process of the IoT (Figure 2) seems to be an easy way to visualize and understand the relevant variables influencing the intention to use the IoT. It shows companies how to adapt marketing strategies, and therefore better respond to consumer needs. Contrariwise, other variables, such as the price-quality ratio or the congruence between consumers and brands, could be relevant into marketing strategies depending on the specificities of each IoT technology. But, these variables are not tested in this study as it is conducted in a more general context of the IoT.

Methodology

The model was tested with 342 respondents during 2016–2017. Before answering to a questionnaire, they watched a short movie presenting the IoT. In the scenario, a teacher cannot give class in the morning at the last moment; therefore, all the alarm clocks of the students automatically calculate the best new time to wake up, taking into account the next class and bus timetables. The heater and coffee machine are resettled without any action from the students.

The variables in the model were measured with existing measurement scales that were adapted to the context of the IoT, and that have already proved their relevance in past research studies in the IoT context (Attié & Meyer-Waarden, 2016; 2017) and for this study as well (Table 1); the reliability of each scale is suitable (Nunnally, 1978; Joreskog, 1970; Fornell & Larcker, 1981).

Figure 2. The prism-model of the acceptance process of the Internet of Things

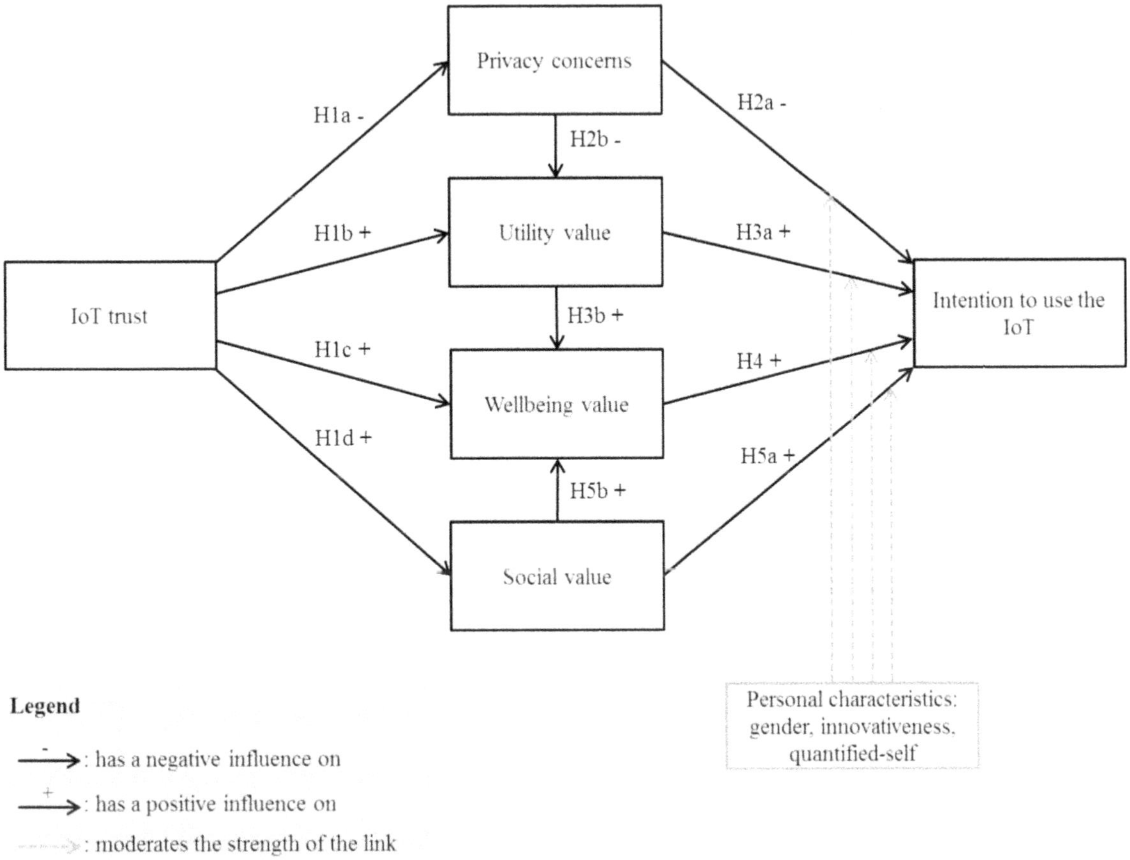

Table 1. The confirmatory factorial analysis to test the reliability of the scales

Variable (Number of Items): Adapted Scale	Mean	Cronbach	Joreskog	Convergent validity
Wellbeing value (7): Munzel et al., 2017; Howie et al., 1998; Diener et al., 1985.	2.31	.87	.99	.98
Intention to use the IoT (3): Venkatesh & Davis, 1996.	2.89	.82	.94	.74
IoT trust (4): McKnight & Chervany, 2002.	2.13	.83	.94	.82
Social value (5): Sweeney & Soutar, 2011.	1.63	,88	,99	99
Utility value (6): Arnold & Reynolds, 2003.	2.63	.86	.97	.81
Privacy concerns (5): Hong & Thong, 2013.	3.41	.80	.93	.75
Quantified self (8): The Boston University 'Making Decisions' Empowerment Scale, 2012.	3.31	.74	.83	.73
Innovativeness (4): Faurie & Van de Leemput, 2007.	2.61	.79	.91	.82

Then, the discriminant validity of the constructs was tested. Table 2 is a matrix that shows the correlation between the variables, and the average variance extracted value on the diagonal to compare it with the correlation coefficients. According to Fornell and Larcker (1981), the discriminant validity is significant when the average variance extracted is higher than the value of correlation coefficients on corresponding row and column.

Table 2 shows that the average variance extracted values are above 0.5 and are above the correlation coefficients for each variable. The cross-factor loadings of each variable exceed the factor loadings of the other variables, showing discriminant validity between all the variables of the prism-model of the acceptance process of the IoT.

Data were analysed using structural equation modelling and the model fit indices were adequate according to Wheaton et al. (1977) (i.e., Chi^2/DF lower than 5, CFI and TLI coefficients both greater than .80 and RMSEA lower than .08), leading the authors to keep the prism-model to explain the IoT acceptance.

The results of this study show that the utility, wellbeing and social values positively influence the intention to use the IoT (Table 3). These results show that consumers are looking for different aspects:

Table 2. The discriminant validity table

	Intention to use	Privacy concerns	Utility value	Wellbeing value	Social value	IoT trust
Intention to use	**.82**					
Privacy concerns	.02	**.76**				
Utility value	.12	.10	**.81**			
Wellbeing value	.19	.01	.23	**.86**		
Social value	.11	.01	.08	.07	**.78**	
IoT trust	.08	.06	.11	.12	.01	**.81**

Table 3. The hypothesis and validation tests

Hypothesis	Test Results
H1 (a): IoT trust on privacy concerns. H1 (b): IoT trust on utility value. H1 (c): IoT trust on wellbeing value. H1 (d): IoT trust on social value.	β=-.21; p<.001 (accepted) β=.16; p<.001 (accepted) β=.23; p<.001 (accepted) β=.13; p<.001 (accepted)
H2 (a): Privacy concerns on the intention to use. H2 (b): Privacy concerns on utility value.	β=-.21; p<.005 (accepted) β=-.08; p<.005 (accepted)
H3 (a): The utility value on the intention to use the IoT. H3 (b): The utility value on wellbeing value.	β=.35; p<.001 (accepted) β=.13; p<.001 (accepted)
H4: The wellbeing value on the intention to use the IoT.	β=.41; p<.001 (accepted)
H5 (a): The social value on the intention to use the IoT. H5 (b): The social value on wellbeing value.	β=.23; p<.001 (accepted) β=.12; p<.001 (accepted)
H6 (a): The influence of gender on the acceptance process. H6 (b): The influence of innovativeness on the acceptance process. H6 (c): The influence of quantified-self on the acceptance process.	Test of F and variation of R (accepted) (accepted) (accepted)

rational (usefulness), emotional (wellness) and intuitive aspects (social status). The IoT is said to be a cognitive technology, which can explain this result. It appears that consumers tend to use the IoT as long as it gives them a rational way to justify its use with useful features, and if it improves senses of wellbeing as well. Consumers will also be prompted to try and use the IoT if the use is in agreement with the social image they seek within their social group(s). On the other hand, privacy concerns negatively influence the intention to use the IoT: the more users are concerned about the management of their data flow, the less they intend to use the IoT. The way the IoT is able to track and get personal information represents the major reason for rejection of the IoT. To accept the IoT, consumers rate higher levels of importance to social, utility and to wellbeing values than to privacy concerns. A higher utility value with personalization services improves positive experiences and lowers privacy concerns (e.g. Xu et al., 2011). IoT trust indirectly influences the intention to use the IoT through the other variables (privacy concerns, social value, wellbeing value, and utility value). The more people trust the IoT, the more it facilitates the acceptance process, favouring a higher level of utility, wellbeing and social values, and a lower level of privacy concerns. Nevertheless, consumers are heterogeneous, and different types of IoT users should be considered to refine marketing strategies. Finally, the results of this study show that gender and the levels of innovativeness and of quantified-self of users moderate the IoT acceptance. A counterintuitive result is that women intend to use the IoT more, giving more importance to utility value, social value and privacy concerns than men, who favour the wellbeing value. Finally, as expected, innovators and users with a higher level of quantified-self expect more benefits and positive beliefs about the IoT.

Theoretical Implications

This study was conducted on the perceptions and intentions of the respondents, and not on the actual behaviours of consumers. Collaborating with IoT companies could be a good way to analyse real use and user behaviour on the long term, highlighting the way the values could evolve. It would be interesting to see to which extent these results could be applied to other specific contexts of study.

Furthermore, the technology adoption theory suggests other relevant variables that were not tested in this study, such as perceived self-congruity, or perceived price-to-quality ratio (Gefen et al., 2003). Besides, this sample comes principally from France and the Y Generation, making it hard to generalize the results. Additional work could improve the survey by increasing the number of respondents with other countries and generations. It would also be interesting to examine behavioural loyalty and usage indicators to study the IoT adoption and use on the long term.

The System of Values of the Internet of Things

Based on the previous quantitative results, four main categories are defined to explain the IoT acceptance. Figure 3 shows the system of values of the IoT, which defines both consumer needs and advertising promises of companies that have an influence on the IoT acceptance. As the definition of the term 'value', the system of values demonstrates what is perceived as true (promises of the IoT), attractive (the IoT should make consumers dream to attract them), good (perceived benefits giving better quality of life or privacy protection), all this from a personal point of view (personal beliefs linked to personal experiences), or according to the criteria defined by social groups (social influence), and seen as an ideal to be reached (improvement of physical and technical performances, of social status), or as something to defend (market position, consistent need).

Figure 3. The system of values of the Internet of Things

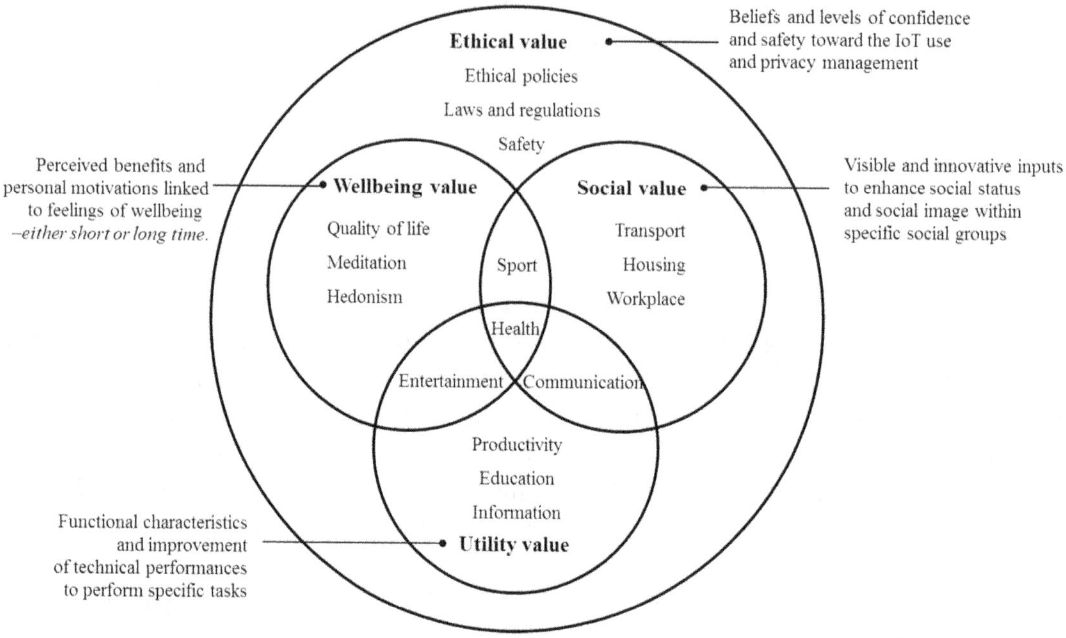

The system of values of the IoT (Figure 3) shows that the ethical value includes the wellbeing value, the social value and the utility value:

1. **Ethical Value:** Each user has personal beliefs, mainly coming from personal experiences and/or social influence. This explains the confidence or anxiety felt about the way the IoT is safe to use and to which extent the user could rely on the IoT (e.g. Shin, 2010; Chaudhuri & Holbrook, 2001) in light of perceived threats revolving around the health risks associated with, for example, the accumulation of low level radiation, signs of addiction, and physical dangers related with technical problems; there are also concerns about information safety regarding the way private data are handled. Governments are starting to consider this last issue with ensuing regulations and laws concerning the IoT, and more specifically about the way data should be used and data policies presented and applied, to protect users and respect moral and ethical standards. Even if high-rated wellbeing, utility or social values can lower privacy concerns (e.g. Xu et al., 2011), the ethical value is the basis of the acceptance values of the IoT: without any trust, consumers will tend to reject it, whatsoever the other perceived benefits. The ethical value is defined as beliefs and levels of confidence toward the IoT use and privacy management. Examples of application are connected alarms, safety trackers or data clouds that imply great technology trust.
2. **Utility Value:** The IoT can be seen as a means of doing something useful, like improving productivity or education, communicating or looking for information. This determines to which extent the IoT fits into daily routines, thanks to primary needs benefits (e.g. Strahilevitz & Myers, 1998). Rational people often see things as ways of doing useful actions only, and not favouring the other values. The authors of this chapter describe the utility value as primary functional characteristics given by the IoT, and improvements of personal technical performances while using the IoT. Examples of application are smart schedules or education smart boards.

3. **Wellbeing Value:** The IoT promises wellbeing benefits (Porter & Heppelmann, 2014). Wellbeing is a positive feeling coming from hedonistic inputs and/or personal satisfaction. Most of the time, it is linked to good quality of life and health: wellbeing includes choices and activities aimed at improving physical and mental health, and social satisfaction (Naci & Ioannidis, 2015). This feeling of wellbeing can be punctual (directly linked to an entertainment or to good news and therefore a hedonic contribution which has a beginning and an end, such as enjoyment, hedonism and positive experiences (e.g. Van der Heijden, 2004)), or of a more constant nature (a daily habit learned and reproduced, leading to a healthier lifestyle and good quality of life). Examples of application are virtual headsets, health and meditation devices, or sport wristbands. Similarly, sleeping applications enable people to register their sleeping cycles to analyse their sleep quality and to wake up at the end of a sleeping cycle. If these applications really help people to sleep better, they should fulfil their promises for better health and wellbeing, which should in turn increase loyalty of use.
4. **Social Value:** Users can be influenced by social groups, such as family members, friends, neighbours, colleagues and socio-professional categories, the media and advertising, and so on, when deciding to use, or not use, new technologies. These external sources can influence beliefs and opinions, as well as the IoT acceptance and use. Social value is defined as visible and perceived innovative inputs used to enhance social status and image within specific social groups (e.g. Moore & Benbasat, 1991). Examples of direct application are smart watches, smart workplaces, smart cars, or smart headphones. For example, every weekend, a group of five friends go running. In this group, four of them except one use smart wristbands. Every time they go running, the ones with a wristband talk about their sport performances. Perhaps the fifth runner will be tempted to buy a smart wristband, convinced by the other runners. It could be considered as a wellbeing purchase, but in this case, social influence and the unconscious, or conscious, wish to improve a certain status within this social group, is also another reason to explain the acceptance process. If some users are not easily influenced by their social entourage, the ethical, wellbeing and/or utility values will take precedence over the social value, and the IoT will mostly be used in private. Conversely, if social value seems important to users, IoT technologies will mostly be bought to be seen by other people.

One can note that there are points in common between each value: all the values have in common the look for a better health, for example. The wellbeing and social values have in common sport activities: using a sport wristband is visible and gives a certain image to the user, while it improves health. The system of values of the IoT can be used by managers to refine marketing strategies, by defining which value has the most powerful and significant influence on the IoT acceptance and convince consumers with targeted adverts and technical policies. Consumers can also comprehend the potential benefits of using the IoT. The authors want to outline cautions about the apparition of laws, changing demand, media alerts and social influence, and thus changing beliefs about the image of the IoT, which could impact the system of values of the IoT.

Typology of IoT Users

The results demonstrate that personal characteristics (gender, innovativeness, quantified-self) moderate the links influencing the IoT acceptance. The IoT should first attract innovators (von Hippel, 1986): they need to perceive innovations as useful, intuitive, easy to use and hedonic to judge them as ‘good’.

Once convinced, innovators will do relevant word-of-mouth contact, as they are seen as experts by their entourage. Each consumer is more or less an innovator, favouring one or two values, and is attracted to specific kinds of IoT technologies. Based on these studies, different types of IoT users are highlighted.

High-Wellbeing Users: The Happy Followers

IoT companies communicate on how the IoT improves health, quality of life and feelings of wellbeing. High-wellbeing users are autotelic people with an emotional intelligence, not easily given to worry and distress, with feelings readily expressed (e.g. Csíkszentmihályi, 1975), and who are more predisposed to feel, accept and share feelings of hedonism than the average people. High-wellbeing users usually prefer group activities than being alone, privileging social interactions (e.g. Hock, 1962). Hedonism is seen as a good thing, an end in itself, and high-wellbeing users will find ways to reach this state of mind, bringing out the principle of utility, and personal characteristics like pride, and a search of freedom and excitement (e.g. Mill, 1998).

High-wellbeing users are spontaneously attracted to the wellbeing value. They will be more interested by IoT technologies giving either short or long time feelings of hedonism and entertainment, while improving health. Price should not be an important factor for high-wellbeing people, as they favour fun designs, positive emotions and wellness benefits. High-wellbeing users have more spontaneous reactions. Therefore, they do not like bad surprises and might talk negatively about a bad experience with other people to overcome frustrations. IoT firms need to test their products with experts to avoid technical issues, and can attract them with fun, cognitive and quality products and services. According to the level of experience with the IoT, these consumers can use this technology as a way to reach wellbeing and a happy life (Seligman, 2011).

The three stages for a happy life, in the context of the IoT (e.g. Seligman, 2011):

1. **Pleasant Life:** Users look for healthy and enjoyable lives mostly through nice relationships and entertainments. Therefore, the IoT is used to complete and facilitate daily activities, bringing positive feelings.
2. **Good Life:** Users feel senses of immersion when their skills and concentration are deeply engaged with specific tasks. Innovators should be willing to learn and use the IoT to become experts and get this feeling of immersion.
3. **Meaningful Life:** Users want to contribute to something greater than themselves and give a meaning to their lives, like being part of specific social groups. The IoT could bring users positive feelings, like excitement, satisfaction or pride, leading to social benefits by obtaining an innovative image.

Low-Wellbeing Users: The Late-Coming Majority

On the opposite end, low-wellbeing people are people less predisposed to accept, feel and share senses of wellbeing than average people, and mostly make decisions for extrinsic reasons. Low-wellbeing users are described as stable people, constant in their decisions, which appear deeply thought, logical and rational (e.g. Hock, 1962). They rather privilege utility over the other values of the IoT (e.g. Harris & Westin, 1991). At the opposite of high-wellbeing users, they are more pessimistic and more often in a bad mood, but will remain calm in stressful situations and tend to show no, or less, feelings. They are mostly shy and prefer to stay alone, but they show high levels of empathy, considering everyone's interests equally (e.g. Hock, 1962). They own a natural prudence by informing themselves before accepting to use new things (e.g. Mill, 2012).

Low-wellbeing users are more convinced by a high utility value. IoT technologies should therefore respond to primary needs to be seen as useful, and should be easy to use. The price-to-quality ratio is very important to them, as well as the opinions of their entourage, to help them rationalize their decisions. Smart devices sending personalized feedback and encouragements should please them, as these users are rather anxious. Low-wellbeing users do not easily forget a mistake or problem, and confide mainly to very close relatives. If any technical problems occur, they might never buy the same brand again. Managers need to take into account their sensitivity, showing them empathy, so as to gain their confidence.

High-Empowered Users: The Innovators and Social Leaders

High-empowered users are defined as people predisposed to get, feel, then use their senses of power over themselves, other people or situations, with a willingness to do quantified-self through self-tracking, self-knowledge and self-management. One of the main reasons why these consumers are willing to use smart objects is to manage personal indicators, favouring quantified-self and in extension, senses of personal empowerment. High-empowered users tend to be self-confident (e.g. Hock, 1962). Using the IoT can improve their social status within social group(s), giving them senses of pride and personal accomplishment. These users have predispositions to convince others through word-of-mouth actions if it improves their social image, or if personalization features respond to their needs. They appear to share many characteristics with innovators.

High-empowered people are more seduced by the social value. Smart objects need to be visible, so as to be seen by other people and to display a certain social status, like with smart wristbands, smart cars, or connected headphones. Therefore, brands and innovative designs are very important, while price does not appear to be a problem as long as it improves social image. They are generally very active on social networks and could do negative word-of-mouth if not satisfied. Managers need to be careful about the way they treat them to avoid negative feedback and its consequences. Marketing strategies should thus focus on specific values favoured by this target, such as reinforcement of social status, social image and of social recognition, with smart personalized features for example.

Low-Empowered Users: Either Very Late Users or Laggards

On the other hand, low-empowered users are people not predisposed to feel, get, and therefore use power, and consequently do not know, nor do not want, to manage personal indicators through the IoT. They are more willing and capable of protecting themselves and their relatives than average people (e.g. Harris & Westin, 1991). They are described as rather rational, calm and wise (e.g. Hock, 1962). They will first think about issues like health impacts, technical problems and privacy issues before considering the possible benefits of the IoT. Low-empowered users rate ethics as the most important value, and tend to reject personalization benefits in exchange for personal information. They constantly inform themselves and will warn their relatives to be careful as well (e.g. Mill, 2012). They appear to be in the late majority of people accepting innovations: only once technologies have been widespread, so that benefits and issues are better known. Therefore, the acceptance process of low-empowered users should be longer than for the other types of users.

Low-empowered users are reassured with a very high ethical value; the policies of privacy and use should be clear and transparent. Moreover, the price-to-quality ratio is important to them, as they are generally undecided. They generally look for unnoticeable connected technologies with modest characteristics (basic designs, small sizes and no sounds), as they do not want to get noticed by others. Managers should mainly use rational and ethical reasons to convince them.

SOLUTIONS AND RECOMMENDATIONS

The IoT appears to be a vast domain, with quite unclear outlines and boundaries. Users do not really know where this technology ends because it does not have space limits. In addition to this, the real impacts of the IoT on health and privacy issues are not clear. Consumer ignorance can increase these doubts. Consumer behaviour has dramatically changed, as environments and privacy are not as controllable as before the arrival of the IoT. Another issue is the feeling that the IoT does not necessarily adapt to consumers, but that it controls and imposes itself progressively. IoT companies have lots of issues to figure out before entering the IoT market. Therefore, managers should get ready to develop innovative IoT technologies according to changing demand, competitors, and saturation of certain categories, to name but a few of the possibilities. Furthermore, before launching new strategies, companies need to understand user experience. Each need and IoT user profile should be linked to specific IoT solutions.

The Targeting Mapping of the Connected Consumer

The high vs. low-wellbeing users and the high vs. low-empowered users are opposed types of users. The authors created a targeting mapping (Figure 4) to refine marketing strategies according to each type of users. For example, high-wellbeing users favour the wellbeing value, but the social value is also important to these users, whereas the utility and ethical values are less important to them.

First, consumers can respond to the questionnaire in Table 4.

Table 4. The scales to define IoT users' personalities

High-Wellbeing Personalities Rate Higher On:	Low-Wellbeing Personalities Rate Higher On:
I would describe myself as: 1. Talkative 2. Full of energy 3. Able to generate a lot of enthusiasm 4. Open to others 5. Curious 6. Often enthusiastic 7. Inspired	I would describe myself as: 1. Reserved 2. Somewhat calm 3. Often sad 4. Often tensed 5. Often in a bad mood 6. Easily upset 7. Rather irritable
High-Empowered Personalities Rate Higher On:	**Low-Empowered Personalities Rate Higher On:**
I would describe myself as: 1. Affirmed 2. Sociable 3. Managing well stressful situations 4. Self-controlled 5. Rather proud 6. Mentally strong 7. Active	I would describe myself as: 1. Shy 2. Erased 3. Often worried 4. Distressed 5. Rather anxious 6. Easily ashamed 7. Rather nervous

This scale (Table 4) gives a score over 7 for each profile. Then, each score should be noted on its corresponding scale (high-wellbeing, low-wellbeing, low-empowered, and high-empowered user scale). Each dot can be linked with the other scores on each scale, defining specific profiles. For samples of consumers, the same process can be followed with the mean of a sample for each scale.

Consumers can have characteristics from each type of user, but with a predominant personality. Generally, people have either a high-wellbeing or a low-wellbeing personality, and own some characteristics coming from the high and the low-empowered personalities; or they have either a high-empowered or a low-empowered personality, and own some characteristics of the high and the low-wellbeing personalities.

The targeting mapping of the connected consumer (Figure 4) allows managers to refine marketing strategies, in which each type of user with specific needs and demands is highlighted.

However, the authors highlight some cautions in the use of the targeting mapping. First, managers must check the validity of the sample if they use it for a whole group. Second, for the users having the four values as predominant (over 4), managers should classify the values and focus on the two main values, for marketing strategies.

Other indicators can help refine targets, such as consumer behaviour toward the brand or classification of the IoT, demographic indicators (generation, gender, religion, or nationality), collectable biometric data (temperature, or health indicators), and other collectable data (smart timetables, weather, or flow of information).

Figure 4. The targeting mapping of the connected consumer

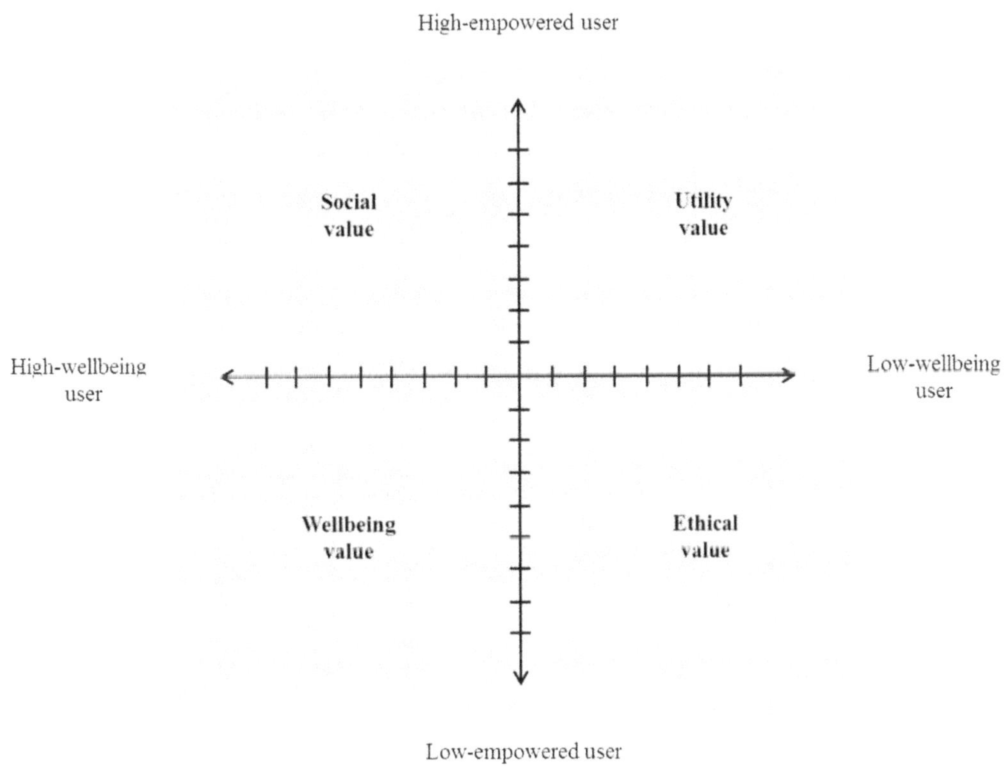

Four Types of Users and Their Associated Types of IoT Technologies

Each personality is mainly attracted to one value when adopting the IoT, which is the key value. Table 5 shows the main characteristics of each type of personality and associated types of IoT technologies, according to the authors' observations and studies.

Table 5 shows managers how to focus and respond to the needs of their main target, considering that each IoT technology is linked to specific types of users. For consumers, this typology allows them to define which IoT technology correspond best to their personality, and thus should be the most suitable and interesting for them.

Be Smarter Than the Perceived Gadget-Connected-Thing

Utility value has a direct influence on the IoT acceptance. The IoT should provide useful functionalities, giving the right information at the right time, and responding to real needs. IoT solutions should be simple so that companies can easily advise users on ways to integrate the IoT in daily routines. Therefore, the IoT should offer easy functions, with ergonomic and intuitive characteristics. To prove that IoT technologies are useful, companies should also increase network externalities: the more consumers they reach, the more useful smart objects will be perceived to be. Consumer approval should result with positive word-of-mouth, increasing profits.

Each User Is Unique

This research shows that women and men consider the IoT differently. Women appear to be more convinced by the utility value, social value and privacy concerns, whereas men favour the wellbeing value. Therefore, firms should do design and construction processes with women and with men to work on both gender perceptions, and could readjust product development and communication strategies. Furthermore, smart interfaces could send personalized messages to users, according to real-time data, and become 'friendly' things.

Table 5. The main traits of personality of users and associated types of IoT technologies

Types of Users	Main Traits of Personality	Researched Types of IoT Technologies
High-wellbeing	Qualities: positive, open-minded, communicant, passionate, dynamic, talkative. Drawbacks: rather inconstant, irrational, thoughtless.	Entertainment devices (virtual headsets, virtual games, smart televisions), health devices (meditation / nutrition / lifestyle apps, sport devices)
Low-wellbeing	Qualities: thinker, listener, careful, rational. Drawbacks: easily tensed, reserved, anxious, distressed, rather depressive.	Productivity (smart schedules, smart alarms, education smart boards), communication (connected speakers, smart watches, smart fridges)
High-empowered	Qualities: self-controlled, energetic, strong-minded, strong leadership. Drawbacks: rather proud, independent, restless.	Sport (smart clothes, smart shoes, smart wristbands and sport trackers), social places (smart workplaces / houses / shops), transport (smart buses and metro places, smart cars, smart maps), visible devices (smart jewelries)
Low-empowered	Qualities: good at performing actions, diplomatic, vigilant. Drawbacks: hesitant, shy, suspicious.	Safety devices (connected alarms, safety trackers, key trackers), databases (secured data clouds).

Protect All the Data

Sensors can track and collect data, then send it to data centres. Data are analysed to personalize features, do marketing research and/or be sold to other companies. They can also be hacked and used for unknown reasons, showing the importance of safety regarding data management. Firms must be transparent regarding data policies and can focus on social indicators (age, gender, or religion), technical parameters (privacy settings, regular safety controls, software and networks equipment), and legal solutions (laws and regulations, ethics and moral policies). Even if privacy risks limit the acceptance of the IoT, benefits of personalization are higher than the perceived privacy loss (Xu et al., 2011). Managers should use personal information to develop and improve personalized services while protecting privacy. Perceived privacy risks can be decreased by increasing control and personal knowledge to users (Armitage & Conner, 1999; Awad & Krishnan, 2006; Azjen & Driver, 1991; Kirsch, 1996); thus, privacy policies should be clear and understandable, protecting users' data.

Fairly Reward Users

Companies should reward users according to their valuable data (the more information given, the more rewards, such as discounts, exclusive offers, digital coupons, small gifts, personalized features, or thank you cards). Rewarding consumers should increase their willingness to give private data, as well as satisfaction and loyalty of use. For example, the company Foursquare sends collectible stickers, pins or items to thank its users. It motivates people to collect more giveaways by using the app and giving personal data, which improves the user database. Therefore, sport connected devices could collaborate with sport events, and according to the data collected, reward users. These kinds of interactions must be regular, and companies should stay in contact during the consumer experience to increase loyalty of use.

FUTURE RESEARCH DIRECTIONS

Emerging trends show that the IoT is invading consumer daily lives. An interesting research domain is the communication through smart objects. Once consumers accept to use smart objects, these objects track and analyse their personal information, and companies have the ability to resell this information. It would be interesting to see to which extent users are ready to share personal information for personalized advertising purposes on, for example, smart watches or smart televisions.

In addition, it would be interesting to see if the theoretical model of the IoT acceptance, the system of values and the typology of users could be applied in other contexts, such as smart shops, transports, cities, or workplaces, as these sites are becoming increasingly popular. New questions emerge and could then be studied: how do consumers react when they do not necessarily choose how the IoT influences their daily lives? How does the acceptance process evolve? More specifically, smart shops become increasingly interesting for marketers as they track and analyse real-time merchandising indicators (i.e., how many times a product is being held in hand and for how long, what strategical merchandise places are the most attracting). Smart shops should also tend to diminish the number of sellers and human interactions, and this could be an eventual advantage or disadvantage according to consumers.

In the service context, insurances tend to suggest to consumers to use smart trackers, like sport trackers for health insurances, driving trackers for car insurances, or smart alarms for home insurance. This develops new concepts of 'pay how you behave', like a 'pay how you move' with health insurances, a 'pay how you drive' with car insurances, and a 'pay how you live' with home insurances. The principle is that people pay a higher or lower insurance premium depending on the use of these smart trackers: being active lowers health insurance premiums, driving safely lowers car insurance premiums, and putting smart alarms in homes lowers house insurance premiums. An interesting question would be to see the acceptance process with these new kinds of concepts, and how they influence consumer behaviour and wellbeing in the long term.

Finally, from a medical point of view, research has shown that health risks, defined as the extent to which a user believes that using the IoT should have negative consequences on health, negatively influence IoT trust and acceptance (Stock et al., 2016). Popular media have reported a lot on the potential health risks associated with the use of the Internet radiations that can cause diseases, such as cancers (e.g. Myung et al., 2009), increasing consumer awareness. Even if smart objects are said to have few or no direct impacts on health due to very low electro radiations, it would be very interesting to study the actual impact of the regular accumulation of these low electro radiations on people.

CONCLUSION

The IoT is a growing market, for which it is essential that companies understand its acceptance and use, as it is a highly relevant marketing tool. The results of this research are quite consistent with theory and should enhance the understanding of the acceptance process of the IoT. Users are likely to use the IoT when it offers wellbeing and health benefits, usefulness and safety, creating development opportunities for safe entertainment, health and sport trackers. On the other side, privacy concerns negatively influence the IoT acceptance. Data security must be a central topic in both development and advertising, and companies must be clear with users concerning data protection and policies.

In the coming years, there should be a growing interest for IoT technologies which support physical, emotional, social and mental health. The IoT should improve quality of life once companies have gained the trust of consumers. If people start to use IoT technologies to fill a void or for regular help, they will start to get more and more information, and users might start to feel more and more dependent, perhaps less useful, as smart objects can replace them, and a dangerous and vicious circle could start. Therefore, the IoT should enable easy self-tracking, self-knowledge and self-management, and stay 100% controllable by users to avoid loss of self-awareness.

REFERENCES

Agarwal, R., & Prasad, J. (1998). A Conceptual and Operational Definition of Personal Innovativeness in the Domain of IT. *Information Systems Research*, *9*(2), 204–215. doi:10.1287/isre.9.2.204

Armitage, C. J., & Conner, M. (1999). The Theory of Planned Behavior: Assessment of Predictive Validity and Perceived Control. *British Journal of Social Psychology*, *3*(1), 35–54. doi:10.1348/014466699164022

Arnold, M., & Reynolds, K. (2003). Hedonic shopping motivations. *Journal of Retailing*, *79*(2), 77–95. doi:10.1016/S0022-4359(03)00007-1

Attié, E., & Meyer-Waarden, L. (2016). A theoretical model incorporating social influence and cognitive processes to explain the adoption of the Internet of Things and smart connected objects. *European Marketing Academy Conference*, Oslo, Norway.

Attié, E., & Meyer-Waarden, L. (2017). The impact of consumer well-being and trust on the Internet of Things adoption and word-of-mouth intentions. *European Marketing Academy Conference*, Groningen.

Awad, N. F., & Krishnan, M. S. (2006). The personalization privacy paradox: An empirical evaluation of information transparency and the willingness to be profiled online for personalization. *Management Information Systems Quarterly*, *30*(1), 13–28. doi:10.2307/25148715

Azjen, I., & Driver, B. L. (1991). Prediction of Leisure Participation from Behavioral, Normative, and Control Beliefs: An Application of the Theory of Planned Behavior. *Leisure Sciences*, *13*(3), 185–204. doi:10.1080/01490409109513137

Beynon-Davies, P. (2002). *Information Systems: An introduction to informatics in organisations*. Basingstoke, UK: Palgrave Macmillan.

Chaudhuri, A., & Holbrook, M. B. (2001). The chain of effects from brand trust and brand affect to brand performance: The role of brand loyalty. *Journal of Marketing*, *65*(2), 81–93. doi:10.1509/jmkg.65.2.81.18255

Cisco. (2017). *The Internet of Things – Cisco Visualization*. Cisco.

Csíkszentmihályi, M. (1975). *Beyond Boredom and Anxiety: Experiencing Flow in Work and Play*. San Francisco: Jossey-Bass.

Davis, B., & Pechmann, C. (2013). Introduction to the special issue on transformative consumer research. *Journal of Business Research*, *66*(8), 1168–1170. doi:10.1016/j.jbusres.2012.08.008

Davis, F. D. (1989). Perceived Usefulness, Perceived Ease of Use, and User Acceptance of Information Technology. *Management Information Systems Quarterly*, *13*(3), 319–340. doi:10.2307/249008

Diener, E., Emmons, R. A., Larsen, R. J., & Griffin, S. (1985). The Satisfaction with Life Scale. *Journal of Personality Assessment*, *49*(1), 71–75. doi:10.120715327752jpa4901_13 PMID:16367493

Dimitriadis, S., & Kyrezis, N. (2010). Linking trust to use intention for technology-enabled bank channels: The role of trusting intentions. *Psychology and Marketing*, *27*(8), 799–820. doi:10.1002/mar.20358

Faurie, I., & van de Leemput, C. (2007). Influence du Sentiment d'Efficacité Informatique sur les usages d'Internet des étudiants. *Orientation Scolaire et Professionnelle*, *36*(4), 533–552. doi:10.4000/osp.1549

Fornell, C. D., & Lacker, D. F. (1981). Evaluating Structural Equation models with Unobservable Variables and Measurement. *JMR, Journal of Marketing Research*, *18*(1), 39–50. doi:10.2307/3151312

Gefen, D., Karahanna, E., & Straub, D. W. (2003). Trust and TAM in Online Shopping: An Integrated Model. *Management Information Systems Quarterly*, *27*(1), 51–90. doi:10.2307/30036519

Harris, L., & Westin, A. F. (1991). *Harris-Equifax Consumer Privacy Survey*. Atlanta, GA: Equifax Inc.

Higgins, E. T. (1997). Beyond pleasure and pain. *The American Psychologist, 52*(12), 1280–1300. doi:10.1037/0003-066X.52.12.1280 PMID:9414606

Hock, C. (1962). The Four Temperaments. Milwaukee, WI: The Pallotine Fathers, Inc.

Hoffman, D. L., Novak, T. P., & Peralta, M. (1999). Building consumer trust online. *Communications of the Advanced Conferences & Meetings, 42*(4), 80-85.

Hong, W., & Thong, J. (2013). Internet privacy concerns: An integrated conceptualisation and four empirical studies. *Management Information Systems Quarterly, 37*(1), 275–298. doi:10.25300/MISQ/2013/37.1.12

Howie, J. G., Heaney, D. J., Maxwell, M., & Walker, J. J. (1998). A comparison of a Patient Enablement Instrument against two established satisfaction scales as an outcome measure of primary care consultations. *Family Practice, 15*(2), 165–171. doi:10.1093/fampra/15.2.165 PMID:9613486

Joreskog, K. G. (1970). Estimation and testing of simplex models. *British Journal of Mathematical & Statistical Psychology, 23*(2), 121–145. doi:10.1111/j.2044-8317.1970.tb00439.x

Kirsch, L. J. (1996). The Management of Complex Tasks in Organizations: Controlling the Systems Development Process. *Organization Science, 7*(1), 1–21. doi:10.1287/orsc.7.1.1

Kozinets, R. V. (2012). Me/my research/avatar. *Journal of Business Research, 65*(4), 478–482. doi:10.1016/j.jbusres.2011.02.025

Lee, Y., Kozar, K. A., & Larsen, K. R. T. (2003). The Technology Acceptance Model: Past, Present, and the Futur. *Communications of the Association for Information Systems, 12*, 752–780.

Leonard-Barton, D., & Deschamps, I. (1988). Managerial influence in the implementation of new technology. *Management Science, 34*(10), 1252–1265. doi:10.1287/mnsc.34.10.1252

McKnight, D. H., & Chervany, N. L. (2002). What trust means in e-commerce customer relationship. *International Journal of Electronic Commerce, 6*(2).

Mill, J. S. (1998). Utilitarianism. Oxford, UK: Oxford University Press.

Mill, J. S. (2012). Utilitarianism. Spark Notes Editors, Chapter 2.

Moore, G. C., & Benbasat, I. (1991). Development of an instrument to measure the perceptions of adopting an information technology innovation. *Information Systems Research, 2*(3), 173–191. doi:10.1287/isre.2.3.192

Munzel, A., Meyer-Waarden, L., & Galan, J.-P. (2017). Getting by or getting ahead on social networking sites? the role of social capital in happiness and well-being. *Technological Forecasting and Social Change*. doi:10.1016/j.techfore.2017.06.031

Myung, S. K., Ju, W., McDonnell, D. D., Lee, Y. J., Kazinets, G., Cheng, C. T., & Moskowitz, J. M. (2009). Mobile phone use and risk of tumors: A meta-analysis. *Journal of Clinical Oncology, 27*(33), 5565–5572. doi:10.1200/JCO.2008.21.6366 PMID:19826127

Naci, H., & Ioannidis, J. P. A. (2015). Evaluation of Wellness Determinants and Interventions by Citizen Scientists. *Journal of the American Medical Association*, *314*(2), 121. doi:10.1001/jama.2015.6160 PMID:26068643

Nunnally, J. C. (1978). *Psychometric theory* (2nd ed.). New York: McGraw-Hill.

Phelps, J. E., Nowak, G. J., & Ferrell, E. (2000). Privacy concerns and consumer willingness to provide personal information. *Journal of Public Policy & Marketing*, *19*(1), 27–41. doi:10.1509/jppm.19.1.27.16941

Porter, M. E., & Heppelmann, J. E. (2014). How Smart, Connected Products Are Transforming Competition. *Harvard Business Review*, *92*(11).

Prayoga, T., & Abraham, J. (2016). Behavioral Intention to Use IoT Health Device: The Role of Perceived Usefulness, Facilitated Appropriation, Big Five Personality Traits, and Cultural Value Orientations. *Iranian Journal of Electrical and Computer Engineering*, *6*(4), 1751–1765.

Rakestraw, T. L., Eunni, R. V., & Kasuganti, R. R. (2013). The mobile apps industry: A case study. *Journal of Business Cases and Applications*, 1-26.

Rauschnabel, P. A., Brem, A., & Ivens, B. S. (2015). Who will buy smart glasses? *Computers in Human Behavior*, *49*, 635–647. doi:10.1016/j.chb.2015.03.003

Rogers, E. M. (1983). *Diffusion of Innovations*. New York: The Free Press.

Rogers, E. M. (1995). *Diffusion of Innovations* (4th ed.). New York: The Free Press.

Seligman, M. E. P. (2011). *Flourish: A Visionary New Understanding of Happiness and Well-being*. New York: The Free Press.

Shin, D. (2010). The effects of trust, security & privacy in social networking: A security-based approach to understand the pattern of adoption. *Interacting with Computers*, *22*(5), 428–438. doi:10.1016/j.intcom.2010.05.001

Song, Y.-S., & Lee, J.-M. (2012). Mobile device ownership among international business students: A road to the ubiquitous library. *RSR. Reference Services Review*, *40*(4), 574–588. doi:10.1108/00907321211277378

Stock, B., dos Santos Ferreira, P., & Ernst, C-P. H. (2016). *Does Perceived Health Risk Influence Smartglasses Usage? The Drivers of Wearable Device Usage*. DOI .10.1007/978-3-319-30376-5_2

Strahilevitz, M., & Meyers, J. G. (1998). Donations to charity as purchase incentives: How well they work may depend on what you are trying to sell. *The Journal of Consumer Research*, *24*(1), 434–446. doi:10.1086/209519

Sweeney, J. C., & Soutar, J. R. (2001). Consumer Perceived Value: The Development of a Multiple Item Scale. *Journal of Retailing*, *77*(2), 203–220. doi:10.1016/S0022-4359(01)00041-0

The Boston University. (2012). *Empowerment Scale*. Center for Psychiatric Rehabilitation.

Van der Heijden, H. (2004). User Acceptance of Hedonic Information Systems. *Management Information Systems Quarterly*, *28*(4), 695–704. doi:10.2307/25148660

Venkatesh, V., & Davis, F. D. (1996). A model of the antecedents of perceived ease of use: Development and test. *Decision Sciences*, *27*(3), 451–481. doi:10.1111/j.1540-5915.1996.tb01822.x

Venkatesh, V., & Morris, M. G. (2000). Why don't men ever stop to ask for directions? Gender, social influence, and their role in technology acceptance and usage behavior. *Management Information Systems Quarterly*, *24*(1), 115–139. doi:10.2307/3250981

Venkatesh, V., Morris, M. G., Davis, G. B., & Davis, F. D. (2003). User acceptance of information technology: Toward a unified view. *Management Information Systems Quarterly*, *27*(3), 425–478. doi:10.2307/30036540

Von Hippel, E. (1986). Lead Users: A Source of Novel Product Concepts. *Management Science*, *32*(7), 791–805. doi:10.1287/mnsc.32.7.791

West, R. L., & Turner, L. H. (2010). *Uses and Gratifications Theory. In Introducing Communication Theory: Analysis and Application* (pp. 392–401). Boston: McGraw-Hill.

Wheaton, B., Muthen, B., Alwin, D. F., & Summers, G. (1977). Assessing Reliability and Stability in Panel Models. *Sociological Methodology*, *8*(1), 84–136. doi:10.2307/270754

Xia, F. L., Yang, L., & Wang, A., & Vinel. (2012). Internet of Things. International Journal of Communication Systems. *Special Issue: Internet of Things*, *25*, 1101–1102.

Xu, H., Luo, X., Carroll, J. M., & Rosson, M. B. (2011). The Personalization Privacy Paradox. *Decision Support Systems*, *51*(1), 42–52. doi:10.1016/j.dss.2010.11.017

Yang, L., Yang, S. H., & Plotnick, L. (2013). How the Internet of Things technology enhances emergency response operations. *Technological Forecasting and Social Change*, *80*(9), 1854–1867. doi:10.1016/j.techfore.2012.07.011

KEY TERMS AND DEFINITIONS

Ethical Value: Beliefs and levels of confidence or anxiety about privacy management and the way the IoT is safe to use.

Internet of Things (IoT): Networks of networks made of physical items, like mobile applications and smart/connected objects, and of virtual things, like networks, transmission of signals, data and artificial intelligence algorithms that connect things and people together to improve user targeting, personalization features and better quality of life.

Smart Object: Active, autonomous, cognitive, and communicating object, with sensors and artificial intelligence algorithms, that can track, stock, analyze, and transmit information to react spontaneously to environments or users, and that can learn from different situations and adapt itself to environments and users.

Social Value: The visible and innovative perceived inputs of the IoT used by consumers to enhance social status and social image within specific social groups.

System of Values of the IoT: What is perceived as true, attractive, good, and as an ideal to be achieved by consumers, and as something to defend by consumers and companies concerning the use of the IoT.

Utility Value: Primary functional characteristics given by the IoT technology to fulfill useful needs, and the degree perceived of improvement of technical performances to perform specific tasks with the IoT.

Wellbeing Value: Perceived degree and benefits of hedonism, health benefits and quality of life and other personal motivations linked to positive feelings to improve physical, mental and spiritual health, and social relationships through the use of the IoT.

APPENDIX

Scales Used in This Study

Wellbeing Value:

- I would feel good using the IoT.
- Using the IoT would make me feel happy.
- I would enjoy using the IoT because it should relax me.
- Using the IoT would let me do more sport and entertain myself.
- Using the IoT would improve my health conditions.
- Using the IoT would definitely increase my quality of life.
- I would feel better if I used the IoT.

Intention to Use the IoT:

- Considering the benefits of the IoT, I intend to use this technology in my daily life.
- If I have access to the IoT technology, I really intend to use it.
- In the future, I think my time spent using the IoT will increase.

IoT Trust:

- I think the IoT would be reliable to protect me.
- I think the IoT would not let me down.
- The IoT would always work with me.
- The IoT would bring me the features I need.

Social Value:

- Using the IoT would give me a more acceptable image.
- Using the IoT would improve the way I am perceived.
- Using the IoT would give a good impression of me to my surroundings.
- Using the IoT would give me better social approval.
- Because of the IoT, I would have less time for my friends, my family, my relatives.

Utility Value:

- The IoT would help me in my daily life.
- The IoT would help me achieve my tasks faster and save time.
- The IoT would make my life easier.
- The IoT would be very useful to me.
- The IoT would allow me to communicate daily with my relatives.
- The IoT would allow me to retrieve the information I would need.

Privacy Concerns:

- I am afraid that the IoT will collect personal information about me.
- I am worried about data that the IoT could recover from me.
- It would bother me if the IoT collected my personal information.
- I am afraid that if the IoT collects personal information about me, it is used for other purposes I do not know about.
- It disturbs me not to control the personal information I could give to the IoT.

Quantified-Self:

- I have a positive attitude towards me.
- I am generally confident about the decisions I make.
- I feel able to achieve things on my own.
- I think I have many qualities.
- I am generally optimistic about the future.

Innovativeness:

- If I hear about a technology innovation, I like to try it.
- I am usually the first person to use a new technology.
- In general, I am hesitant to use a new technology.
- I feel able to use a new technology by myself.

Section 2
Scopes of Application

Chapter 3
Big Data and Digital Analytics

Sumathi Doraikannan
Malla Reddy Engineering College (Autonomous), India

Prabha Selvaraj
Malla Reddy Institute of Engineering and Technology, India

ABSTRACT

Data becomes big data when then the size of data exceeds the ability of our IT systems in terms of 3Vs (volume, velocity, and variety). When the data sets are large and complex, it becomes a great difficult task for handling such voluminous data. This chapter will provide a detailed knowledge of the major concepts and components of big data and also the transformation of big data in to business operations. Collection and storage of big data will not help out in creation of business values. Values and importance are created once when the action starts on data by performing an analysis. Hence, this chapter provides a view on various kinds of analysis that can be done with big data and also the differences between traditional analytics and big data analytics. The transformation of digital data into business values could be in terms of reports, research analyses, recommendations, predictions, and optimizations. In addition to the concept of big data, this chapter discuss about the basic concepts of digital analytics, methods, and techniques for digital analysis.

BIG DATA: INTRODUCTION

Big data owns 3 V's (Volume, Velocity and Variety). It is defined as the data that appears to be in huge volume of different data that travels with right speed and reaches the destination within the stipulated time frame so that the data could be used for real-time analysis and further reaction. The structure of big data could be structured or unstructured data that could be in any form such as text files, multimedia files, financial data etc. Data comes from several data sources in order to form data inundation. Data sources could be categorized as electronic gadgets like mobile sensors, medical imaging, smart grids, video surveillance, social media video rendering and genetic engineering etc. so as to form data surge. The fastest- growing sources of big data are social media and genetic engineering. Big data might possess data that contains data structures such as structured, unstructured, semi structured and quasi structured. The configuration of structured data includes reports, contracts, email and other communications. Struc-

DOI: 10.4018/978-1-5225-5763-0.ch003

Copyright © 2019, IGI Global. Copying or distributing in print or electronic forms without written permission of IGI Global is prohibited.

tured data displays the information in the form of text files. The information is displayed in columns and rows. Furthermore, it could be easily organized and processed with the help of data mining tools. This could be envisaged as a perfectly organized filing cabinet in which identification, labeling is a simple task and it is easy to access.

Most of the organizations might like to be familiar with this type of data and it is used in an effective and efficient manner. Data does not have any intrinsic structure. It is available in the form of complex data sources such as email, multimedia content, web logs, sales automation and social media data as denoted by Marcos et al (2015). As per Holzinger et al (2013), unstructured information may account for more than 70% to 80% of all data in organizations. Semi structured data does not match with the prescribed structure of data models in the perspective of relationships. Examples of semi structured data could be XML, JSON, MongoDB that stores data in JSON. Quasi structured data is defined as the textual data with inconsistent data formats that could be formatted with effort and time. For example, quasi structured data refer to the click stream data that might consist of inconsistent data values and formats. Few organizations, definite methods must be extended so that it has to manage the huge volume of data. The below Table 1 illustrates the generation of data that occurred in several organizations.

Components of Big Data

As the name implies, big data contributes much for business applications and it has produced a noteworthy impact in various fields that includes the social media, satellite imaging, banking transactions and healthcare machines. S. Hendrickson (2010) noted that information increase takes place in a rapid manner at the rate of 10x every five years. It was found that the capacity for storage in general-purpose computers was 2.9 ×1020 bytes and that for communication was 2.0 × 1021 bytes. From Hilbert & Lopez (2011), it is understood that these computers could also perform 6.4 × 1018 instructions per second.

Table 1. Growth of unstructured data

Organizations	Generation
Wordpress (Nawsher Khan et al., 2014)	It is a free open source content management system in which nearly 350 new blogs per minute are published by bloggers
LinkedIn (Nawsher Khan et al., 2014)	A business and employment-oriented social networking service. Through this 2.1 million groups have been created
Apple (Nawsher Khan et al., 2014)	Around 47000 applications are downloaded per minute
Facebook	34,722 likes are registered in each and every minute 47% of Facebook users only access the platform through mobile Users generate 4 million likes every minute More than 250 billion photos have been uploaded to Facebook This equates to 350 million photos per day
YouTube	300 hours of video are uploaded to YouTube every minute! Almost 5 billion videos are watched on Youtube every single day. YouTube gets over 30 million visitors per day In an average month, 8 out of 10 18-49 year-olds watch YouTube.
Twitter	Barack Obama's victory tweet was the most retweeted tweet ever with over 800K retweets Top 3 countries on Twitter are the USA at 107 million, Brazil 33 million and Japan at nearly 30 million The average Twitter user has tweeted 307 times

Yet, there is a tremendous increase in the computing size of general-purpose computers and it is found to be at the rate of 58%. In computational sciences, big data is treated as a critical issue. It cannot be processed with the help of conventional methods and existing technologies. As a result of this, the production of immense data from several fields like business, society and science is a global issue that has to be addressed. Procedures and standard tools have not been designed to search and analyze large data sets as suggested by Bhadani and Jothimani (2016). Hence few organizations come across challenges in the creation and manipulation of large data sets. The data type that is been collected is considered as unstructured data. It is described by human information such as photos, high-definition videos, movies, financial transactions, geospatial maps, email, sensor data, medical records, weather records and tweets etc. Industrial Development Corporation (IDC) and EMC Corporation stated the amount of data generated in 2020 will be 44 times greater [40 zettabytes (ZB)] than in 2009. This rate of increase is expected to persist at 50% to 60% annually.

A suitable environment has to be created in order to support big data. Therefore, one has to follow good design principles that might have an opportunity to deal with storage, reporting analytics or applications. Certain considerations must be included for setting up hardware, software, management software, operational software and well-defined application programming interfaces. The Figure 1 illustrates some common components of Big Data analytical heaps and their amalgamation with each other as suggested by Gupta and Shilpi (2016).

The data has to get processed in the physical infrastructure which is situated at the lowest level of the stack. The requirements have to be examined on a layer-by layer basis in order to assure that the implementation has to be performed and it has to be scaled according to the business demands. The data is conventionally stored in relational database. At certain circumstances, there is a need for the data that has to be extracted periodically from the operational database. These data are transformed and loaded into data warehouse for further reporting and analysis. To handle high-value transactional data which is already a structured data, a massive parallel relational platform is required, and it needs to support a

Figure 1. Components of big data

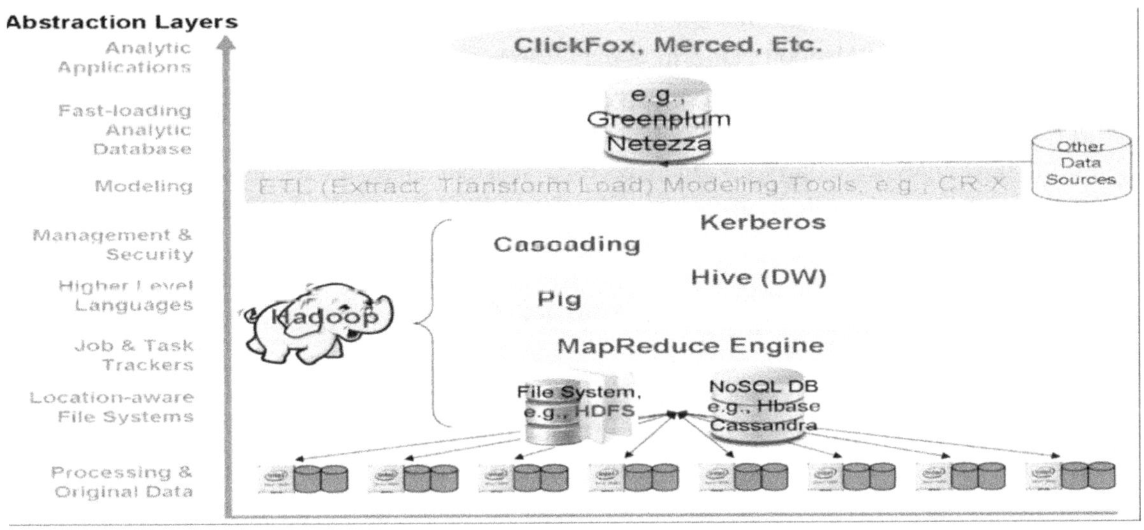

large amount of user and applications that enquired about the known data with performance and enterprise level security. The components of big data are represented in the Figure 1 are described as follows:

- A storage system might comprise any one of the following:
  - **Hadoop Distributed File System(HDFS):** It is the storage layer which deals with the storage of data and metadata;
  - NOSQL also could be used like HBase or key-value based columnar. Cassandra also could be used.
- Computation is required, and this could be any one of the following:
  - **MapReduce:** It is an amalgamation of two processes. It consists of a mapper and reducer. The role of the mapper is that it first gets executed and the raw dataset is transformed into another key-value data. The reducer accepts the map that has been created by the mapper as an input, collects the input and converges it into a smaller dataset.
  - **Pig:** A platform which is required has to be situated on top of Hadoop. This tool is used in conjunction with or as a substitute for MapReduce. Pig is a high level language and it is mainly used to create processing components that are utilized to analyze very large datasets. The main feature of this language is the adaptability of its structure to various degrees of parallelism. It owns a compiler which is used to translate pig scripts to MapReduce jobs. This language is commonly used because of the following advantages such as:
    - Programming is very easy;
    - It is extendible;
    - Optimization of jobs are easy and well-organized.

Next comes the interaction or application logic. It could be any one taken from the list given below:

- **Cascading:** It is an abstract API layer that is situated over Hadoop. It acts as a framework which depicts the set of data processing APIs and various other components are used in data processing execution over the Hadoop/Big data stack. Many applications have been developed due to its easiness, job scheduling and job creation.
- **Hive:** On top of the Hadoop platform, a data warehousing layer (Hive) is built. HDFS data are analyzed, processed with the help of hive. It acts like SQL. It plays a vital role in the RDBMS world since it makes the job of Hadoop in an easy way.
- Specialized analytics data bases could be used. Various analytics models require fast data ingestion, refresh and scaling out facility. This could be done with databases such as Netezza or Greenplum.

Traditional Analytics vs. Big Data Analytics

Analytics is defined as the process of detecting and communicating the patterns that are found to be meaningful in data. It helps to optimize roles, functions and key processes.

Difference between the traditional analytics and big data analytics is given in the Table 2.

Table 2. Traditional analytics vs. big data analytics

Traditional Analytics	Big Data Analytics
Data sets are condensed, structured and highly rich featured.	Tools are used in organizations so as to construct a framework. This is mainly used to retrieve the features from the large dataset in order to model the data.
Sliced data could be used. Part of the database could be made visible.	Data is productized and shared across the enterprise.
Well-developed traditional data analytics methods were used widely to analyze structured data and to limit extend the semi-structured data. This involves further processing over heads.	Analytics is the process of extracting useful information by analyzing different types of big data sets. Big data analytics is used to discover hidden patterns, market trends and consumer preferences, for the benefit of organizational decision making.
Normally traditional data analysis methods are not designed for large-scale and complex data. It is also impossible to analyze the big data.	They are mainly designed for large scale data.
Traditional analytics methods find that the impact of learning is on one or two real-world metrics	Big data analytics look at the unanticipated impact of learning
Processing time for traditional analytics is 1-2 days	Processing time for big data analytics is 1-5 seconds
Traditional analytics is built on relational data models	Big data comes in various form and formats from multiple disconnected systems.
It mainly focus on descriptive and diagnosis analytics	This main focus is on predictive analytics and data science

TAXONOMY OF BIG DATA

Several elements of big data taxonomy are shown in the Figure 2. Big data dimensions: volume, velocity, variety, veracity, validity, value, variability, vagueness, and vocabulary could be considered to characterize the quality of the data.

Analytics: Big Data Techniques

Traditional analytics are used to explore dissimilar data when it is present in huge amount. Some examples are given below:

- **Slicing and Dicing:** This is the process of breaking data into small groups of data so that it could be very easy to explore.
- **Basic Monitoring:** It is the process of monitoring large volumes of data in real time.
- **Anomaly Identification:** Anomalies are identified in this process.
- **Advanced Analytics:** This is used to do complex analysis of either structured or unstructured data. It consists of several machine learning, neural networks, sophisticated statistical models and other advanced data mining techniques. Decision making process is considered as a part of advanced analytics due to the vast increase in computational power, new developments in the algorithms that are used to solve real time problems, latest data infrastructure and huge amount of data. Some of the examples of advanced data analytics are:
    - **Text Analytics:** It is used in all sorts of analysis and in social media analytics so as to identify frauds. The unstructured text is analyzed, the relevant information is extracted and transformed into structured information.

Figure 2. Taxonomy of big data

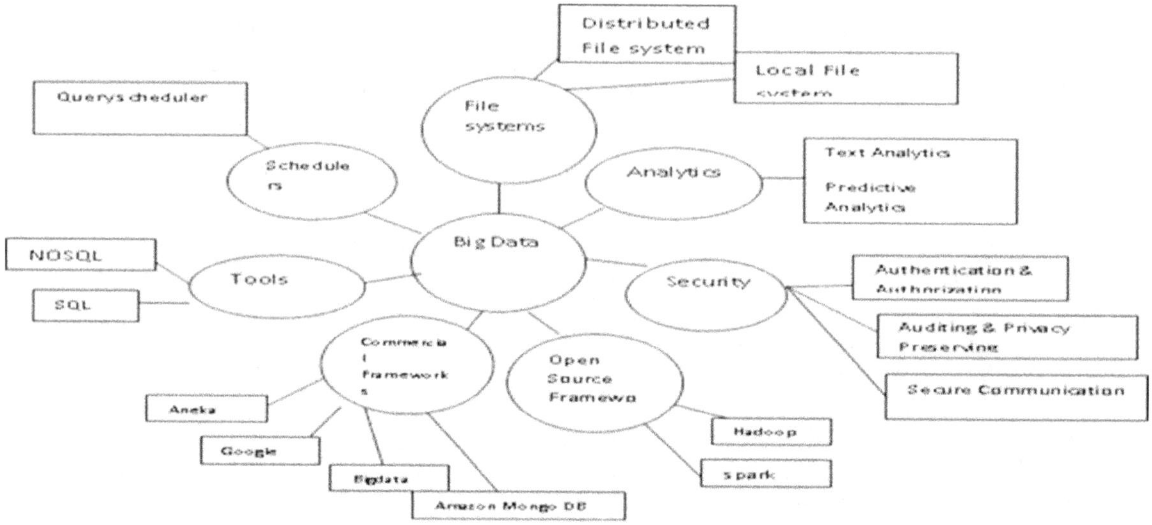

- **Predictive Modeling:** It is a statistical model or data-mining solution that consists of techniques or algorithms that could be used on both structured and unstructured data in order to identify future outcomes.
- **Other Data Mining and Statistical Algorithms:** This includes optimization, cluster analysis for segmentation or affinity analysis.

Different approaches are required for analyzing big data. Approaches might be traditional or advanced since it depends on the problem that has to be solved. To manage big data, different approaches are required in order to help the business to successfully plan for the near future. Several features of big data are massive, complex, incomplete, unstructured, incomplete, noisy and erroneous.

Technologies

This could be mainly categorized into three parts known as i) file system – this is used to organize the data ii) computing frameworks and iii) tools for analytics.They are described as given below:

- **File System:** This represents the way of naming,sharing,organizing, storing and protecting files.
    - **Distributed Access and Location Transparency:** During the file access, clients are unaware about the location of the file they try to access.
    - **Heterogeneity:** File services could be made available across the several operating system platforms and different hardware resources.
    - **Failure Handling:** It could be achieved with some level of redundancy and replication. The client and application programs handle the failures in the system.
    - **Support Fine-Grained Distribution of Data:** Individual objects could be located in order to optmize performance.

- **Tolerance for Network Partitioning:** The file system shouldbe able to handle the situations and the appropriate synchronization mechanisms could be applied. Certain segments of the entire network might be unavailable to a client during certain periods.
- **Computing Frameworks:** This could be categorized as open source frameworks and commercial frameworks.
  - **Spark:** This is a fast and general engine for large-scale data processing. It could run on Hadoop YARN ncluster manager and could read any existing Hadoop data.
  - **Apache Hadoop:** Distributed processing of large-scale data sets across clusters of computers could be done through this open-source reliable,scalable and sitributed computing platform.
  - **Hadoop:** Hadoop cluster is used for big data analysis and NoSQL supports columnar database with the help of DynamoDB. Rackspace offers Horton Hadoop framework on Openstack platform. .NET – based desktop MapReduce platform and other enterprise frameworks based on open-source Hadoop are Horton and Cloudera are been offered by Aneka.
- **Tools for Analytics:** Several big data tools that are described are as follows:
  - **Graph Database:** This is useful for dealing out complex many-to-many connections such as social networks and for traversing large-scale multi-level relationship. A graph could be captured by a table store and this supports recursive joins such as Cassandra and big table. Graph structures are used to store data and semantic query on the data. Every entity consists of direct pointers to its adjacent element, and index lookups are not required. Graph database is used since large-scale multi-level relationship traversals are common in processing social networks. Examples of graph databases are infintegraph from objectivity and Neo4j open-source graph database.
  - **Column Family/Big Table Database:** Key values are grouped in order to create the composite data. Each column contains the equivalent row number as key and the data as value. Data that comes from various streams such as web logs, time series that occurs from sensors are stored in this database. Examples are HBase and Google big table.
  - **Document-Oriented Database:** This is mainly used for storing semi-structured data. In this, contents are encapsulated or encoded in some standard format. Examples are MongoDB, and CouchDB.
  - **Big Table Database/Column Family:** In this database, the column contains the row number as key and the data as value. This database is applicable for storing weblogs, time series data coming from several devices and sensors. Examples are HBase and Google big table.

Programming Models

Several programming models such as Map Reduce, Aneka, Mahout, and Google have been discussed.

- **Map Reduce:** This is a data-intensive programming model which comprises of Map and Reduce functions in the cluster of distributed compute and storage nodes as referred by M. Ghazi & D. Gangodkar (2015). Certain operations like sorting and filtering are done by Map function and the role of reduce function aggregates the output that has been obtained from the map function and the final result is generated. With the help of this recursive programming model, similar logic operations are operated on multiple distributed data sets. Examples are Apache Spark and Aneka MapReduce.

- **Aneka:** This is considered as a thread programming model which is used for high-performance applications. It is also known as task programming model. It is used for work flow programming model.
- **Machine Learning Tools:** These are mainly used for decision-making. Few tools such as Hadoop and Mahout are used.
- **Big Query Languages:** This language is used for searching texts, words and their occurrences. The study of the data available in the web is known as web log mining. Google big query platform is used to search for the words and their frequencies. This is an example for web log mining.

Big Data Security

Data sharing must be done based on the authenticity of the user. Several methods were used for resolving the issues related with security when the data scales in large-scale high-volume. Conventional methods of computing and data security mechanisms are not adequate when the data volumes and infrastructures are very large. There is a possibility of attacks as the cloud infrastructures grow in size and when software platforms spread across the large networks of computers. Certain issues related to big data security are given below:

- **End Points:** Authentication must be done at the end points by extracting logs from endpoints.
- **Storage:** High priority data or confidential data must be stored on flash media. Hence, locking the storage would create a tier-conscious method. Usually in the big data architecture, data is stored on multiple layers. This type of data storage depends on the business needs.
- **Real-Time Security/Compliance Tools:** These tools are used to produce a huge amount of information. The main feature is to identify a method to overlook false positives. Hence, finding the true breaches could be made easier by humans.
- **Non-Relational Data Stores:** NOSQL databases lack security.
- **Distributed Frameworks:** Jobs that possess huge processing power are distributed among many systems for rapid analysis. Distributed processing refers to the processing of data by more number of systems which might leads to security issues.
- **Granular Auditing:** This is used to identify the attacks that have been missed, check out the consequences of these attacks and ensure to follow the guidelines that could be done in the future.
- **Data Provenance:** It briefly explains about the origin of data, the owner of data and other information about the data. This meta-data information accessibility must be done with an incomparable speed so as to reduce the time in which a security breach is found to be active. Users could be given certain privileges for continuous monitoring and examining the network to identify the violations that might happen. This activity needs great attention since the users might become a threat to their own big data.
- **Access Controls:** This refers to the process of issuing rights to the users to do the process such as read, write and view etc the data.
- **Data Mining Solutions:** These solutions are treated as the heart of many big data environments. It is ensured that more security has been provided not only against external threats, but also against the users those who exploit network privileges in order to achieve sensitive and confidential information.

Tools for Analyzing Big Data

To analyze big data, there are five mechanisms:

- **BI Tools:** These tools are essential for analysis, reporting and performance management. The inputs for BI tools deal mostly with data that originates from data warehouses and production information systems. In addition, a wide-ranging facility for performance management and business intelligence includes dashboards, scorecards, enterprise report creation, ad-hoc analysis and what-if scenario analysis on an incorporated enterprise scale platform.
- **In-Database Analytics:** Patterns and relationships about the data could be found with a variety of techniques James Taylor (2013). Information cycle time could be accelerated, and total cost of ownership could be reduced and also the data movement is eliminated, if the techniques are applied within the database.
- **Decision Management:** Predictive modeling, business rules and self-learning to decide based on the current context are included in the decision management. Individual recommendations posted by the customer are also considered for analysis and thus the value of the customer interaction is augmented. Oracle Advanced Analytics scores could be included to use complex predictive analytic models and real-time decision processes are created.
- **Discovery Tools:** Thorough investigation and analysis of information from both structured and unstructured sources could be retrieved with the help of these tools. These tools are used for analysis besides traditional Business Intelligence source systems since there is no necessity for up-front modeling, users derive conclusions which could be useful, and users could draw new insights and formulate informed decisions in a rapid manner.
- **Hadoop:** Data pre-processing is done in order to find out macro trends or to discover chunks of information such as out-of-range values. In addition, the impending value from new data has been facilitated. This tool is used by the organizations as a forerunner of advanced analytics tool.

Solutions/Proposals to Address Big Data Security and Privacy Challenges

When data grows in huge amount, certain operations such as masking, tokenization and encryption are applied for protecting the sensitive data. Due to the characteristics of big data such as the creators of data, data originates from different sources and data might be accessed by several users a complete focus is required for providing security. Proper classification of data must be done in order to identify the nature of the data and the location where it has to be placed. It must be ensured that the certain access policies and data handling policies must be framed and aligned with the organization. Several security mechanisms must be framed to provide security to the data at its source and to the data itself. In addition, different control and prevention strategies also must be implemented on data archiving, data leakage prevention and access control.

The most important challenge for big data security and privacy is to deal with the storage and processing of encrypted data. The basic security requirement for secure bigdata is a challenging task. When a query is posted, certain difficulties that have to be examined are:

- Whether the database is encrypted with single or multiple keys?
- Which user has the permission to decrypt the database?

- Is it necessary to decrypt the database before executing the query?

There might be a possibility of two types of adversaries in the case of unauthorized access:

- An adversary who might be involved in accessing the raw data to facilitate the compromising feature of interpretation/analysis process. For example, a false data might be injected into the raw data, or a large volume of data which is considered as sensitive might be stolen.
- Different data sets that have been already analyzed could be prone to attacks by the adversaries. In addition, they might extract the required information. This is possible by the intelligence legitimate analysts.

Violation of data privacy (Gabroit, 2007) could be done by the adversaries either with the help of software or hardware design flaws in the infrastructures.

As a result of this, more focus should be given at the infrastructure that includes data centers and cloud platforms since confidential raw data and contingent knowledge are stored in this place. This could be solved by providing encryption, access control and data anonymization. On the other hand, critical data that resides in big data infrastructures are stored without encryption. When several data protection mechanisms are deployed, data controllers usually depend on either encryption mechanisms or coarse-grained access control models that avoid further processing of the data.

Data Quality/Integrity and Provenance Issues

Certain mechanisms could be followed to check on the quality and integrity of the data. In addition, focus is also on to capture the details of the data and data from where it has been derived. Big data analysts find the difficulty in managing the huge amount of data. This also deals with the analysis of data and the way of interpreting the results of the analysis particularly in context-sensitive settings such as data dependency analysis, crucial and deliberate decision optimization within organizations, and malevolent/illegal behavior detection by law enforcement authorities.

Unwanted Data Correlation and Inferences

Data that originates from various sources might increase the risk of re-identification/de-anonymization. But, analysts could intentionally or fortuitously, categorize new inferences or determine new sets of confidential information the data subject has not agreed to share. The process of correlating hypothetically de-identified data sets with publicly or privately available data sets.

A solution that has been suggested by people at MIT is CryptDB. This allows the users to execute queries over the encrypted data. CryptDB proxy resides between the database and application. It takes care of the process of rewriting the query in a particular way such that they could be executed against the encrypted database. Trustworthy applications that need the data pass the query to the CryptDB. The results that are encrypted are sent back to the proxy. Using the master key, the results are decrypted, and the final answer is sent back to the application. Various encryption strategies have been developed for supporting different types of operations on data in CryptDB. Encrypted big queries enable SQL-like queries against append-only tables with the processing power of Google's infrastructure. The most important security practice is to security controls at the boundary of the networks. If an attacker violates the security perimeter, all the data that resides in it would be accessed. Hence, more focus should be given to the data. To improve the security of the data that resides in the infrastructure and controls the existing security solutions.

Applications of Bigdata

Due to the advent of big data, many applications including biomedical, traditional manufacturing, business and other applications.

Business Applications

Big data intelligent analysis technology is used to discover fraud risk, trends and patterns throughout the structured and unstructured data. Big data addresses the issues such as crime detection, crime prevention and financial analysis etc.

Manufacturing

Certain emerging technologies such as physical network and advanced analysis are used by the manufactures in order to compete with in the recent revolution manufacturing industry. During the process of automated production, big data is used to manage costs and reduce effects. Data collection such as storing the detail of the product, sales history of the product etc at all stages helps the manufacturers to find out better solutions.

Bio Medical Industry

Big Data analysis is carried out in the fields like angiography, magnetic resonance imaging or computed tomography and echocardiography to form cardiac imaging. New imminent information about the disease treatment and interventions are also made possible with the big data. With the help of Bioinformatics analysis and immune genomics disease etiology, information about variations in genetics, immune function and regulation could be easily understood. Personal health of the patients could be more benefitted due to the development in biomedical technology.

Importance of Digital Analytics

With the advent of cloud computing – infinite computing power that has been connected through real-time communication networks made the data collection more affordable. Recently the world gets connected always with the help of connected devices such as smart phones, tablets and other digitally connected devices. This enables the people to monitor, collect and present the information to the customers based on their needs. The data that has been collected from various sources like websites, mobile devices are considered to be the digital data. It is a paradigm of the big data. Digital data are exemplified by:

- Flow of information is not always clearly combined;
- There are many variables for each activity;

- Millions of activities per day;
- There is high cardinality of the variables.

The data thus collected needs a clear analysis which describes the behavior of customers. This process of analyzing digital data is known as digital analytics as mentioned in Philips (2014). It helps the organizations to provide a better online experience to its clients as well as potential customers that progressively results in the attainment of desired goals. The main advantage of digital analytics is that business could be developed in many ways. The two ultimate goals of digital analytics are:

- Value has been created by generating profitable revenue;
- Less cost.

Apart from these goals, various business objectives that evolve for digital analytics are:

- The ultimate goal of content publishers is to encourage commitment and regular manifestation.
- The main intention of branding is to coerce awareness, engagement and fidelity.
- Information about the financial leads of products has to be collected and the same must be displayed in the web sites to attract customers.
- Especially, e-commerce sites are developed to sell products or services.
- Users get the information at the right time due to its availability in online.

Common terminologies used in digital analytics are described as given below:

- **Cookies:** It is defined as the text that gets stored on a user's system with the help of a web browser. Information such as user preferences, the identifier for a server-based session, shopping cart contents, or other data used by websites to identify visitors are stored. These cookies are used for the identification of mechanics and technicalities of how visitors and visits are counted by both audience measurement tools and analytics tools.
- **Entry Page:** The first web page that is been accessed during the visit to a particular website.
- **Exit Page:** This page represents the last web page during the visit to a website. The page that is visited at last by the visitor could be identified as the final page in a tabbed or multi-window browser environment.
- **Direct Traffic:** Visitors those who visit the corresponding website in any of the following ways.
    - The corresponding site URL could be types in the web browser.
    - Mark the site as the bookmark and clicking on the corresponding bookmark to enter into the website.
- This also includes visitors those who are recruited through offline campaigns.
- **New Visitor:** A visitor who has cleared browser cookies before the recorded visit or who has never visited the website.
- **Returning Visitor:** When a visitor returns to the website again, then he/she is treated as the returning visitor.
- **Page View:** It is termed as the frequency of the webpage that was viewed during the visit.
- **Visit:** This is defined as the communication that occurs between the individual and the website that consists of one or more requests for a unit of content. If a person stays on the site for more

that the particular time period, then the visit session gets terminated and the second visit might be recorded.

- **Visitor:** It is possible for the individual to make multiple visits and the identification of that corresponding person depends on the visitor's computer. Through the cookies, it is easy to identify whether the visitor is new or returning back to the website.
- **Landing Page:** When a visitor identifies that the web site entered gives the needed information after clicking on it, then it is known as the landing page. This is identified as the entry page for the site. The main intention is to observe the behavior of the visitor for the targeted content.
- **Referring Sites:** There is a possibility of traffic generation due to the diversion of other websites to the corresponding website which user is visiting at present.
- **Search Engine:** It is defined as the web-based program that explores web pages and documents for the specified keywords and returns the list of web pages and/or documents based on the keywords.
- **Bounce Rate:** It is denoted as the percentage of entrances on a web page that results in an immediate exit from the website.

Search Analytics

This is considered to be an area where many people have come in and provided counsel to companies. Search analytics is broken up into two categories namely organic searches and paid searches.

Organic searches: The results that occur due to this search are the listings on search engine result pages that might appear due to the specific relevance to search terms. Metrics that are used by the communicators are given below:

- Known and unknown branded words: Communicators must be able to identify the words that are specific to their brands and they must know about the frequency of the words.
- Known and unknown keywords: This metric is used to identify the possible keywords that might drive the people to the corresponding website. A list which consists of known and unknown keywords could be prepared. In addition, it is obvious that the unknown keywords might also be unknown to the competitors. Communicators might look for the opportunity to optimize the content based on those unknown keywords.
- Average search position: This is considered as the vital factor since it identifies the rank in search engine results page based on the known, unknown, branded and unbranded keywords.
- Total visits: This refers to the number of total visits to the corresponding website in the web analytics platform.
- Total conversions from known keywords: Conversions could be either a dollar figure, downloads, signing up for a newsletter and etc. when the content is being optimized properly based on the known keywords that are used by the people, and then an uptick in conversion could be visualized.
- Paid searches: This refers to any form of online advertising that attach an advertisement to a specific keyword-based search request. Some of the most popular paid search metrics are:
    - **Cost Per Click (CPC):** It is the average amount an advertiser would pay for a click.
    - **Impression Share:** This is the ratio of the impressions the advertisement received to the possible impressions it could have received. This is similar to the share of conversation in social media analytics.

- **Impressions:** An impression happens when a paid search advertisement appears on the search engine results page. This metric counts the number of such impressions.
- **Sales or Revenue Per Click:** This is the amount of money generated per click received on an advertisement.
- **CTR (Clickthrough Rate):** It is expressed as the ratio of the number of clicks an advertisement receives to the number of impressions received.
- Average Position: This is used to measure the position of the advertisement on the search engine results page.

- Digital Analytics for Social Media: Social Media Analytics (SMA) is a type of digital analytics. SMA symbolizes a change in the way people use the Internet and how digital data is measured. SMA generates economic value through analysis of the significant and appropriate signals in social media data. Social media has become pervasive and persuasive during the last several years. It refers to the enormous directional impact across the world. In addition, it refers to the people those who create, produce, edit share, exchange and consume information.

Vocabulary that are used in the social media analytics are:

- **Lurking:** This refers to the viewing of social media content and just identify the information that has been said and not about any other thing or participating.
- **Participating:** During the start and stop of business or shifting of social media strategies, channel gets switched and would not be constant. This is considered to an action of mere participation.
- **Engagement:** This is an active participation process since communication takes place continuously among the social media channels. Promotions on social media, advertisement regarding the new products, replying to criticisms posted by people, informal participation during the conversation with customers refers to the process of engagement. This process is considered to be planned and strategic.
- **Listening:** An active monitoring about the brands, consumers, and business activities is done with the help of social media tool or technology. This is used to identify the products/consumers/brands that might be general or specific. This process might be considered as a complex since there is a need of automatic classification of huge volumes of incoming, text-based social media from several sites into various categories using text and sentiment analysis.
- **Virality:** This refers to the sudden and noteworthy impact while the content is viewed in a short period of time. It means that the content has been hastily communicated across the distances that help to understand the meaning of vitality.
- **Social Sharing:** This is enabled when the digital content gets shared among the users. Sharing is made possible with the help of story tools on various sites such as like on Facebook, or post on Reddit. Users could post their pictures during their vacation and it could be shared among their friends.
- **Privacy:** Global governments, businesses and consumers think and reply to questions about the effect of social media on privacy are the important factors for social media analytics.
- **Copyright Laws:** This is considered as the significant factor during the sharing of digital content. Consumers might not be aware of copyrights during their sharing. Therefore, the region, country, local and jurisdiction laws and rules that direct and frame the sale and sharing of digital content are the important factors for social media analytics.

- **Influencers:** The opinion posted by influencers has a value. People those who have a great influence on the acuity of any brand, products or service care are treated as influencers. They have the ability to create an impact on the business either positively or negatively due to their posting of views.
- **Social Networking:** A group of activities across social media that includes social sharing, engaging, bookmarking, linking and transacting that is been done across various social media platforms and the measurement is done through social media tools.
- **Social Applications:** To create a social experience, data inputs might be social experience or some behavioral features. Certain mobile applications that are mostly based on social and online collaboration over mobile devices despite the consequences of physical location, which are also GPS location aware, are referred as social applications. Macro conversions are identified as the main actions on any website or applications that developed for mobile that bind with the business objectives. Micro conversions are termed as the person might receive an email coupon or a new product notification. Both these conversions must be measured in order to achieve the right outcomes of any website.

Digital Analytics Tools

The main notion behind the digital analytics tool is to facilitate companies to track the behavior of customers those who prevail in digital channels. In addition, it is also used to assess the responses posted by the customer against the marketing stimuli. These types of tools are used by marketers in order to compute the efficiency of marketing activities, check the corresponding tactics for certain customer segments and then later optimize future actions.

Several marketing automation tools Jarvinen Joel (2016) those are available in the market for various reasons:

- **Meltwater:** Used to track news and discussions that are online.
- **SAS Text Miner:** This is a text mining tool which is used to mine information from text sources.
- **iPerceptions:** This is a website survey tools to get customer feedback.
- **Oracle Eloqua:** Personalize marketing content and manage sales leads.
- **Hitwise:** An online panel to increase the perception of target audience behavior on web.
- **SimplyMeasured:** An online intelligence tool is used to track competitor performance.

Certain digital analytics tools are customized for a specific platform while others are developed and designed for a specific activity. Tools are available for identification of search rankings, analyzing keywords, nurturing link building, crawling and auditing the website to identify the issues related to search engine optimization. Few factors have been identified are considered as the power of digital analytics. They are described as follows:

- More detailed information on the customer's behavior has been offered as the clickstream data records all the actions performed by the customers in the digital environment whereas the traditional analytics records only the transactions. The main features of digital analytics are digital analytics metrics and business goals are interdependent since it helps the marketers to investigate and exhibit the activities of digital marketing that might support the attainment of business goals. The identified metrics must be structured and prioritized under the framework and the interrelationships augment the actionability of the metrics system. Mobilizing digital analytics data needs a systematic approach with clearly allocated responsibilities in terms of data collection, reporting and analysis.

- Surveys and interviews have been done to collect customers' preferences and intentions.
- From this, it is easy to predict genuine behavior and expressions of opinions in users' natural environment.
- Users' behavior has been tracked with the help of digital analytics tools.
- Location information is used to make the progress of personalized and contextual marketing messages.
- Offline settings could be provided by digital analytics tools.

Benefits of Using Digital Analytics

To increase the budget for digital marketing and to improve the standing of marketers within a company, the digital analytics is mainly used to compute and display the financial outcomes of digital marketing.

Interaction could be improved much more between the company and potential customers due to the awareness of the digital marketing channels and tactics. Due to this, a better understanding about the types of marketing content could be improved. It is also used to assess the behavior of the customer by tracking. As a result of this, a buzz is been created in social media. It also assists in framing the linkage between behavioral metrics and financial outcomes due to the tracking of the customers' behavior. Hence, due to this activity, the customers those who visit the websites are identified as the first task. Next, digital analytics identifies the nature of the customer. The corresponding customer after been attracted by the website might be intended to buy the product or service. The decision taken by the customer is easily predicted with the help of digital analytics tool. The behavioral metrics provided by digital analytics could be credibly linked with financial outcomes. When compared with the traditional measurement tools, digital analytics plays the vital role in prediction of the customer's behavior due to its genuine nature. Digitization increases the significance of the objective metrics and it could be made out even at the same cost of subjective metrics. The need for subjective metrics will not be eliminated since the customers behavior is tracked, whereas offline behaviors as well as thoughts and feelings remain uncaptured. As a result of this, to achieve the complete information about the marketing impacts, behavioral metrics must be harmonized with subjective metrics. Digital analytics monitors the regular activities of customer right from the initial step till the sales deal closing period. This in fact identifies the customers' interest and provides the information according to their needs and as well predicts their relative contributions to sales impact. Thus, the customers could be valued accordingly by the marketers. This tool is also able to track the priority of digital marketing activities and the decisions made by the customer. Purchasing a product could be based on both through the information displayed on the sites and as well as the information received through emails. Hence, the email alone could not be considered as the reason that accounts for the customer's purchase decision. This is a remarkable constraint on the use of digital analytics that must be often ignored when computing the productivity of marketing activities. It is understood that the digital analytics could only overcome the challenges of marketing performance measurement up to some extent since data have two important restrictions:

- Data is restricted to the digital footprint left in the firm's own media space, whereas not much information could be known about the customers those who work offline or in other digital channels.
- The behavioral dimension of the customer impact is possible with the digital analytics.

Role of big data in marketing:

- **Semantic Search:** Searching the natural language terms is denoted as semantic search. Machine learning together with the big data makes it easy for the search engines to identify what the user is searching for and the marketers those who really act as smart implement this special feature into their site search functionality. As a result of this, the user experience for the visitors those who visit the site could be improved.
- **Related Information:** Publishers will be able to provide the content to their visitors by identifying the wealth of data to decide the content liked by the people. Content marketers will be capable of getting job and digital marketers must make their site as a dynamic site.
- **Targeted Advertising:** Facebook and Google provide the details through advertising and attract the users.
- **Machine Powered Analytics:** When there is huge amount of data, digital marketers face the difficulty in deciding. Hence, machine learning is used to analyze data and decisions could be made accordingly.
- **More Conclusive Testing:** Analyzing the huge amount of data enables to perform more decisive testing that might include various other factors such as prior histories so that the results that are obtained will be more accurate and certain.

CONCLUSION

Big Data growth can be accredited to three market forces: trendy consumers, product and process automation, and data monetization. In particular, parallel platform provide abilities for data storage, integration and analytics. Decision making in the business world is mainly driven by the usage of data and analytics. This chapter discussed the major concepts, components of big data and also the big data transformation. In addition, the evolution of digital analytics and its importance is also explored. Moreover, it also gives an overview of several digital analytics tools that are available in the market.

FUTURE RESEARCH DIRECTIONS AND CHALLENGES

There is a need to know the importance of the technology since it yields results rapidly. Large scale data guides people in the field of invasive marketing and privacy incursions. Data analytics also analyze the online behavior, communities and political movements. The life cycle of the data has to be defined and this in turn creates a value for the data. The data that is been stored has to be made available and reliable at all times when there is a need for the usage of the data.

REFERENCES

Assunção, M. D., Calheiros, R. N., Bianchi, S., Netto, M. A. S., & Buyya, R. (2015). Big Data computing and clouds: Trends and future directions. *Journal of Parallel and Distributed Computing*.

Bhadani, J. D (2016). Big data: Challenges, opportunities and realities. In Effective Big Data Management and Opportunities for Implementation (pp. 1-24). IGI Global.

Decandia, G., Hastorun, D., Jampani, M., Kakulapati, G., Lakshman, A., Pilchin, A., ... Vogels, W. (2007). Dynamo: Amazon's Highly Available Key -value Store. *Proceedings of the 21st ACM Symposium on Operating Systems Principles (SOSP 2007)*. 10.1145/1294261.1294281

Gaborit, P., & Girault, M. (2007). Lightweight code-based identification and signature. *2007 IEEE International Symposium on Information Theory*, 191-195. 10.1109/ISIT.2007.4557225

Gantz, J., & Reinsel, D. (2012). *The Digital Universe in 2020: Big Data, Bigger Digital Shadows, and Biggest Growth in the Far East*. Retrieved from www.emc.com/leadership/digital-universe/index.htm

Ghazi, M., & Gangodkar, D. (2015). Hadoop, MapReduce and HDFS: A Developers Perspective. *International Conference on Intelligent Computing, Communication & Convergence*, 45-50. 10.1016/j.procs.2015.04.108

Gupta, S. (2016). Real time big data Analytics. Packet Publishing Ltd.

Hendrickson, S. (2010). *Getting Started with Hadoop with Amazon's Elastic MapReduce*. EMR.

Hilbert, M., & Lopez, P. (2011). The world's Technological Capacity´ to store, communicate, and compute information. *Science*, *332*(6025), 60–65. doi:10.1126cience.1200970 PMID:21310967

Holzinger, A., Stocker, C., Ofner, B., Prohaska, G., Brabenetz, A., & Hofmann-Wellenhof, R. (2013). Combining HCI, natural language processing, and knowledge discovery—potential of IBM content analytics as an assistive technology in the biomedical field. In *Lecture Notes in Computer Science: Vol. 7947. Human-Computer Interaction and Knowledge Discovery in Complex, Unstructured, Big Data* (pp. 13–24). Springer. doi:10.1007/978-3-642-39146-0_2

Jarvinen, J. (2016). *The use of digital analytics for measuring and optimizing digital marketing Performance*. Retrieved from https://jyx.jyu.fi/dspace/bitstream/handle/123456789/51512/978-951-39-6777-2_vaitos21102016.pdf?sequence=1

Judah Philips. (2014). *Digital analytics primer*. Pearson Education, Inc.

Khan, N., Yaqoob, I., Ibrahim, A. T. H., Inayat, Z., Waleed, K. M. A., Alam, M., ... Gani, A. (2014). Big Data: Survey, Technologies, Opportunities, and Challenges. *The Scientific World Journal*, *2014*, 712826. doi:10.1155/2014/712826 PMID:25136682

Lee, J., Lapira, E., Bagheri, B., & Kao, H. A. (2013). *Recent Advances and Trends in Predictive Manufacturing Systems. Big Data Environment Manufacturing Letters*, *1*, 38–41. doi:10.1016/j.mfglet.2013.09.005

Narula, J. (2013). Are We Upto Speed? From Big Data to Rich Insights in CV Imaging for a hyper connected World JACC. *Cardiovascular Imaging*, *6*, 1222–1224. doi:10.1016/j.jcmg.2013.09.007 PMID:24229779

Soares, S. (2012). A Framework That Focuses on the Data in Big Data Governance. *IBM Data Management*, *13*(June). Retrieved from http://ibmdatamag.com/2012/06/a-frameworkthat-focuses-on-the-data-in-big-data-governance

Taylor, J. (2013). *In Database Analytics*. Decision Management Solutions.

KEY TERMS AND DEFINITIONS

Aneka: A framework which is used for constructing applications that are customized and it could be used further by deploying it on private or public clouds.

Anonymization: It is defined as the masking of personal information of a user which is been used in the process of transaction.

Business Intelligence Tools: Unstructured data from various resources such as documents, email, video, health records, etc. are collected and processed.

Crawling: The process of identifying web pages and downloading is termed as crawling.

JSON: Java script object notation. It is defined in terms of text format and it is language independent.

Mahout: An open source project and it is mainly used for producing scalable machine learning algorithms. Applications that are developed using Mahout are used to investigate large data sets effectively and it takes less time for analysis.

Social Media Analytics: It uses algorithms in order to endow the public with critical intelligence.

Chapter 4
Augmented Reality and Experiences:
Augmented Reality, Virtual Reality, Software, Mobile AR, Browsers, Types, Experience, Application

Prabha Selvaraj
Malla Reddy Institute of Engineering and Technology, India

Sumathi Doraikannan
Malla Reddy Engineering College (Autonomous), India

Anantha Raman Rathinam
Malla Reddy Institute of Engineering and Technology, India

Balachandrudu K. E.
Malla Reddy Institute of Engineering and Technology, India

ABSTRACT

Today technology evolves in two different directions. The first one is to create a new technology for our requirement and solve the problem, and the second one is to do it with the existing technology. This chapter will discuss in detail augmented reality and its use in the real world and also its application domains like medicine, education, health, gaming, tourism, film and entertainment, architecture, and development. Many think that AR is only for smartphones, but there are different ways to enhance the insight of the world. Augmented realities can be presented on an extensive range of displays, monitors, screens, handheld devices, or glasses. This chapter will provide the information about the key components of AR devices. This chapter gives a view on different types of AR and also projects how the technology can be adapted for multiple purposes based on the required type of view.

DOI: 10.4018/978-1-5225-5763-0.ch004

Copyright © 2019, IGI Global. Copying or distributing in print or electronic forms without written permission of IGI Global is prohibited.

INTRODUCTION

As the emergence of new information demands, there emerges a new method to showcase the information to reality. It offers an exclusive experience in a wide range of industries in an attractive and innovative way to showcase the concepts to provide great experience. The term augmented reality is termed by Thomas Caudell (1990) when he explains the usage of head mounted displays worked when used by electricians for assembling complicated wiring connection said augmented reality (AR) is used for a combination of technologies for merging information produced by the computer with the spectator's natural senses. It is an emergent research in the area of virtual reality. It uses the real background and merges the new information over it. Due to enormous information produced in the world, it is very difficult to the world environment around us provides a wealth of information that is difficult to replicate in a computer which is demonstrated by the usage of virtual environments in the world. In 1998, the first AR application in commercial was used in the football match. AR gives a different perspective, and converts the work as we are aware of it. The definition of AR was said by Azuma et al. (1997). In which he says that AR has three features which are: AR has a combination of real and virtual environments, interacts with real time, and is 3D.

Many technical balancing is required relevant to tracking in case of developing AR applications for mobile and other outdoor environments. So there is a necessity to rely on computer vision for very precise tracking or sensor-based tracking. Janson Wither (2011) explains a new approach indirect AR which provides accurate alignment of virtual content. This approach uses captured panoramic image which enables pixel matching between the virtual content and representation of the real world accurately. It improved the quality of the tracking. Though the method has some limitations and challenges people still use this approach since it provides good matching accuracy. It works when the user is away from the physical object more than a few meters.

A good virtual reality system permits the users to physically walk around objects and feel the object by touching it as if it is a real one. Sutherland, the creator of one of the world's first virtual reality systems stated" the ultimate display would, of course, be a room within which the computer can control the existence of matter. A chair displayed in such a room would be good enough to sit in. Handcuffs displayed in such a room would be confining, and a bullet displayed in such a room would be fatal". Computer-presented material is integrated with the real-world environment that the freely roaming person can interact with it to display related information, to position and resolve questions, and to cooperate with other people. The user interface is the world.

An AR-based simulation system that integrates background knowledge and experimental support (AR-SaBEr) was designed as a learning tool for teaching basic principles of electricity to ninth-grade students to examine how it supports the learner to focus on the meaningful activities that affects behaviour and learning performance. Maria et. al. (2016) took a sample of 82 students. They randomly divided into two groups namely control and experimental group. The control group used AR-SaBEr without any support for recommending activities and the experimental group with personalized extra support. The experiment showed that the experimental group performed well compared to control group. They identified that learners' behavioral patterns depend on the support they received and before experimenting, the control group were interested in browsing the information about activities instead of reading about the subject. But in contrast experiment group read the subject first before experimentation. In augmented reality-based simulation it focuses the attention of students on the most relevant topics for them. They analyzed effectiveness of the two scaffolding strategies by considering the way students used an AR-based discovery learning environment and the learning outcomes. The result showed that knowledge support provided increased academic achievement of the students when they used an AR-based simulation system.

Eric et.al. (2015) explains the AR system for aerospace and ground vehicles design, development and testing to acquire accuracy and robustness. The system uses an optical see-through HMD and in order to avoid mis-registration and "swim" it needs all subsystem to be high tracking accuracy and precision alignment, extremely low latency and calibration. It focuses on the optical/inertial hybrid tracking system and provides a novel solution to the alignment with the vehicle and HMD systems and challenges with the optics, algorithms, synchronization. Even though there is advancement in the field of software agents, artificial intelligence and robotics we see fully autonomous system. The main problem of autonomy is trust.

Trusted autonomy is the scientific and engineering field to begin the basics and ground work for developing trusted autonomous systems like robotics and software agents which can be used in our day today life. It can be integrated with humans seamlessly, naturally, and efficiently. Hussein A. Abbass et. al. (2016) gives a vision for a Trusted Cyborg Swarm which is an extension of Cognitive Cyber Symbiosis concept. In this humans and machines join together in a harmonious, seamless, and coordinated manner. In terrain modeling, it is a great challenge to generate large scale terrains which conforms to morphology of real world scenes because simulating complex geometric details is a time-consuming process and also it is hard to control realistic geographical features.

Generating large scale terrains that conform to the morphology of real scenes is a great challenge for terrain modeling, as simulating complex geometric details is time-consuming and the realistic geographical features are hard to be controlled. Huijie Zhang et. al. (2016) describes a proficient modeling method for large scale terrain visualization based on hydrology with procedural modeling, supports the augmented visual terrains which contain real terrain features and also easy-to-use. Web user sessions may hold fuzzy, contradictory and vague information so relational fuzzy clustering (RFC) algorithms prove very useful for user session clustering. RFC algorithms need to specify the number of clusters in advance and very sensitive to cluster initialization. Performance bottleneck in RFC is prior specification of number of clusters and initialization of cluster prototype. Dilip Singh Sisodia et. al. (2016) proposed the discounted fuzzy relational clustering (DFRC) algorithm to overcome the bottleneck of RFC by identifying web user session clusters from Web server access logs without initializing the number of clusters and prototypes of initial clusters. It has two stages and in the first stage it automatically identifies the number of potential clusters based on the successively discounted potential density function value of each relational data and their respective centres. In the second stage it assigns fuzzy membership values to each data point and forms fuzzy clusters from the relational matrix. The algorithm uses an augmented session dissimilarity matrix obtained from a publicly accessed NASA Web server log data. The clusters generated using DFRC is comparatively with quality compared to RFC.

Trang Nguyen et. al. (2017) investigates optical camera communication (OCC) technologies, targeting new spectrum, multiple-input-multiple-output diversity, transmission access, and novel architectures with augmented reality user experience for the extended 5G wireless network. Color vision deficiency (CVD) is extremely common vision impairment where they will not be able to recognize colors. To provide a solution to this problem Paolo Melillo et. al. (2017) designed a wearable improved vision system based on an augmented reality device. The system was validated in a clinical pilot study on 24 subjects with CVD and it showed an improvement in color vision of all patients. The real world is acquired by a stereoscopic camera, then the left and right images are processed separately applying the algorithms described in the following and the new world is presented to the patient via the Liquid Crystal Display (LCD) of the Head Mount Display (HMD).

The architecture consists of three main modules namely Video Acquisition Module (VAM), Video Processing Module (VPM) and Video Rendering Module (VRM). The VAM is based on an OVRVISION PRO camera mounted in the front part of HMD. The VPM implements the three different algorithms protanopia, deuteranopia and tritanopia using the openCV library and customized software ensuring an execution time less than the acquisition period (1/60 s) in order to avoid any loss of frames. The VRM is based on an HMD display. The wearable system based on augmented reality devices to improve color vision in subjects with any type of CVD. The advanced features in the mobile devices and cooperative network with the combination of ubiquitous, reasonable internet, mobile cloud computing has brought a great impact in technology which transforms mobile augmented reality to a reality.

Chatzopoulos et. al. (2017) provides a survey on augmented reality in terms of application, user interfaces and experience metrics, system components, object tracking and registration, network connectivity and data management, system performance and sustainability. The increasing popularity of Augmented Reality Smart Glasses (ARSG) plays vital role in future smart factories. It gives the view about facilitating and accelerating ARSG in manufacturing industry. Syberfeldt et. al. (2017) provides an efficient method for evaluating ARSG. It discusses the challenging issues in extending the field of view, making the glasses wearable, developing guidelines for user interface design, enabling benchmark evaluation and improving voice-based interaction in noisy environments.

Xiaohu Ge et. al. (2017) proposed a software-defined networking architecture and a multipath cooperative route (MCR) scheme to facilitate the AR/VR wireless transmissions in 5G small cell networks. A service effective energy (SEE) optimization algorithm is developed for AR/VR wireless transmission in 5G small cell networks. Chi-Hua Chen et. al. (2017) proposes a classification algorithm based on ensemble neural networks. In the training phase it uses a random number of training data to develop multiple random artificial neural network (ANN) models until those ANN models converge. Those models with lower accuracy than the threshold are filtered out. The remaining highly accurate models will be used to predict the output in the testing phase. It designs an augmented reality question answering system (AR-QAS) on mobile devices to apply and implement the proposed algorithm which offers user active interaction and automatically reply according to user's queries. It gets the input requirement from the users and responds with the appropriate classes of the input queries which are accurate answers to the users.

VIRTUAL REALITY VS AUGMENTED REALITY

The popularity of virtual reality grows with the technological development in the area of computer graphics and animation which gives the user to visualize it as in reality. Virtual reality as discussed by W. Piekarski et al. (1999) is the conception of virtual world and the user can interact with them. It is planned in such a way that the user cannot differentiate the real and virtual. Augmented reality is the integration of virtual reality with the real world to create images that is merged with real word things. Virtual reality and augmented reality both has the capability to change user view of the world which is considered as the similarity between them but the way they view the user presence differs. Augmented reality allows the user to communicate with the virtual contents and differentiate them. Virtual reality and augmented reality both has the capability to change the user view of the world which is considered as the similarity between them but the way they view the user presence differs. For example, if you consider virtual reality you can dance with dolphins but with augmented reality you can create an effect of coming out of your card. That is VR is considered to be more immersive as described by D. Van Krevelen and R. Poelman (2010), while AR gives you more freedom because it does not require any head-mounted display.

Component of AR

According to Bimber and Raskar (2005), the three-main element of an AR system is a tracking element, a registration element, and a visualization element. Along with this, a database is required to store the information about the virtual and real environment.

The user's location in the real world is provided by the real-world model which aids the tracking component as a reference. Augmentation content is provided by the virtual-world model. The spatial model parts must be registered in the same coordinate. It uses a feedback loop between computer system and human. The user controls the view point by observing the AR display as said by H. López et al. (2010) and the user's viewpoint is tracked by the system, real world pose along with the virtual content is registered and gives situated visualizations.

Three Key Elements of Enterprise AR System Content

The data spectrum ranges from small database to Big Data. There is a necessity to provide analysis over Big Data to get benefits which can be made available for access by AR Technology.

HARDWARE

The main hardware required for capturing user context is sensors which are available in many shapes and sizes which is either integrated and embedded or mounted on the objects. The observations which are produced by sensors can be filtered and merged for use and given as inputs to local device or server connected in network. The detection and identification of patterns generated by real world are the real time computations. As the patterns are identified, it is matched with the encoded digital data that is used in AR experiences. These data must be collected by the hardware device that is available to the

Figure 1. Augmented Reality with feedback loop between user and computer

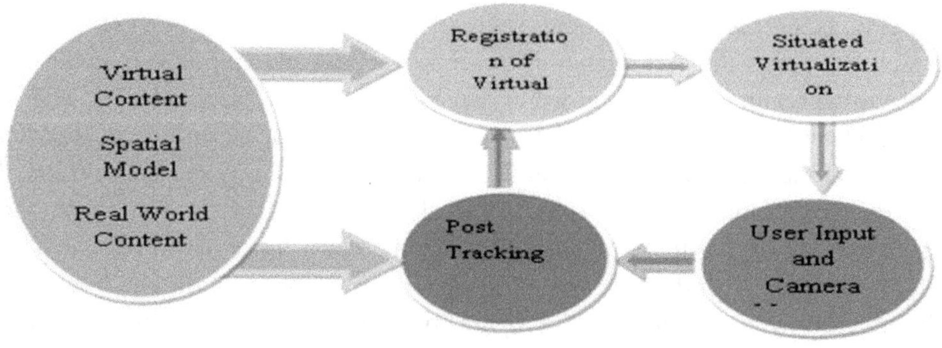

user. The signals produced by the hardware must be detected by the user like hearing are sounds tactile senses are pressure, vibration or temperature and visual are light waves. The most used hardware is tablets and smart phones; these are easily manageable and familiar which offers inexpensive software and integrated hardware. Many commercial devises are also available like smart glass and tablet which incorporate AR technology.

SOFTWARE

Software in AR used in design and publishing which comes in different variety and levels which is important for the data preparation offered to the user during AR experience. The systems are controlled by the software in the networks which performs the function of publishing and delivering the experience. The main requirement of software in AR experience is:

- To detect the patterns observed by the sensors
- To Understand user context
- Based on the target and different triggers it has to track the user changes
- To produce sounds, tactile signals and visible augmentation

One application can embed the AR features or AR functions dedicated to another application.

AR CHARACTERISTICS

Augmented Reality should have the following three characteristics:

- Combines real and virtual;
- Interactive in real time;
- Registered in 3D.

Augmented Reality Applications combine the digital visual and the user's real-world content. They are used in various fields like healthcare, marketing, education, tourism, etc. AR software are sophisticated software with rich data and high-performance applications based on Microsoft technology which provide quick, high quality and cost-effective development.

In 1998, the yellow "first down" line appeared in telecasted football games which are the first commercial applications. Few AR software are discussed below:

- **A-Frame:** It is a framework which uses HTML tags for most of the functionality in three. js and other JavaScript features. It is a superset of this lower level underlying 3-D framework.
- **Argon:** A browser for developing an AR application, which is a combination of KML and HTML/ JavaScript/CSS. Any web content can be converted into AR content.
- **ARToolKit:** An open source C-Library for AR application and widely used in AR related projects. It was ported to different languages and platforms like Android, Silverlight or Flash.
- **ARma:** An OpenCV based minimal library for AR apps.

- **ArUco:** It is based on OpenCV which has a minimal library for augmented reality applications.
- **Augment:** AR platform for smart phones and tablets.
- **ATOMIC:** Multi-platform authoring tool for creating AR applications on Microsoft Windows, Linux and Mac OS X operating systems.
- **BeyondAR:** An open source augmented reality framework for Android based on geo localization.
- **DroidAR:** An open source (dual-license: GPLv3 or commercial) augmented reality framework for Android, featuring location-based and marker-based AR.
- **GeoAR:** It is featuring location-based AR and a flexible data source framework, and it is an open source (Apache 2.0 License) browser for Android.
- **Goblin XNA:** A platform for mobile augmented reality and virtual reality and researching 3D user interfaces and also emphasizes games. It is written in C#, based on Microsoft XNA Game Studio 4.0, BSD license.
- **GRATF:** An open-source (GPLv3) project includes application, which does 2D and 3D augmented reality. It includes C# library for detection, recognition and 3D pose estimation of optical glyphs.
- **JavaCV:** A Java/Android interface to OpenCV.
- **Mangan:** An open source (Mango License) augmented reality framework based on Nano localisation for Android.
- **Mixare:** (Mix Augmented Reality Engine) works as an autonomous application and for developing other implementations. It is an open-source (GPLv3) augmented reality engine for Android and iPhone.
- **PTAM:** It is for non-commercial use.

Proprietary AR development toolkits understand:

- Rox Odometry SDK permits the users to develop AR applications in multi-platform like desktops and mobiles. It is performed on the device or in the cloud using markers or natural features for Vision-based object recognition from a database and Vision-based real-time tracking and 3D localization can be improved by fusing measurements from inertial and vision sensors.
- ARPA SDK & ARPA Plug-in Unity permits the user to build their own web, desktop and mobile AR projects.
- Xloudia comes as a white brand or for "operators" under their own brand and it is with large scale capabilities with more features like statistics and natural feature recognition, face and colour recognition for Android and iOS and 3D tracking. It is an image recognition and image tracking solution based on cloud and video frame analysis.
- Catchoom SDK permits the AR experiences in the native third-party applications for Android and iOS and also permits the users to combine image recognition & 3-D object recognition.
- metaio SDK provides free natural features tracking and 3D tracking that is available for Android, iOS and Microsoft Windows.
- PointCloud SDK is a Software Development Kit which offers simultaneous Localization and Mapping (SLAM) and allows creating augmented reality applications for iOS devices.
- Vuforia Augmented Reality SDK, formerly known as QCAR, is a Software Development Kit for creating augmented reality applications for mobile devices.

- VYZAR is a cross-platform SDK for iOS and Android, with both an Augmented Reality and 3D engine
- Wikitude SDK is a library that uses web technologies to create the Augmented Reality content and can embed in native third party application Android, BlackBerry 10 and iOS.

AR content management systems are:

- **Metaio Creator:** A desktop tool to create and publish AR scenarios.
- **BuildAR.com:** A web-based content platform for building geolocation and natural feature tracking based mobile augmented reality.
- **Catchoom CraftAR:** A web-based content management system to create Augmented Reality experiences coupled with Cloud Image Recognition.
- **Hoppala Augmentation:** A web-based content platform for creating geolocation based mobile augmented reality.
- **Webcam Social Shopper:** A web based software for integrating apparel visualization on e-commerce sites.
- **Fityour.com:** A website for trying out wearable apparels visualization on e-commerce sites.
- **PLAKAR:** A web-based platform for the augmentation of printed materials and Out of Home Media.
- **Zapcode Creator:** A web-based software for building and creating zapcodes with augmented reality content.
- **BEAR platform:** A web-based tool to create complex augmented reality scenarios.

TYPES OF AUGMENTED REALITY

An Augmented Reality is a technology that integrates the digital images which are generated by computer in real time. There are various types of augmented reality technology that exist in the real-world entity; each AR technology has plenty of differences in their objectives and application use cases. The various types of technologies that make up augmented reality are mentioned below:

- Projection-Based Augmented Reality;
- Recognition-Based Augmented Reality;
- Location-Based Augmented Reality;
- Outlining-Based Augmented Reality;
- Superimposition-Based Augmented Reality.

Projection-Based Augmented Reality (PBAR)

The main principle of PBAR is by projecting artificial light rays onto the real-world surfaces. Basically, PBAR applications allows user to interact by sending light rays onto a real-world surface and then sensing the interaction i.e. touch of that projected light. Detection of the user's interaction is done by differentiating between an expected projection and the altered projection (caused by the user's interac-

Figure 2. Projection-based Augmented Reality

tion). Another interesting application of projection-based AR utilizes laser plasma technology to project a three-dimensional interactive hologram into mid-air. The simple example for Projection-based AR for a castle in air, or a dialer on hand is shown in Figure 2.

For example, it might show you if your future fridge will fit into that space you have near the oven by projecting the fridge in front of you.

PBAR is very adjustable, extensible and customizable and it gives the ability to integrate into workstations and assembly lines on the factory floor. The technology works in concert with existing manufacturing tools and equipment's where in industries like torque wrenches, machine vision cameras and collaborative robots. They had to standardize the processes and establish a new baseline for quality.

The real-time data extracted from the technology allows manufacturers to adjust their lines, products and personnel to maximize efficiency and drive better business results. By integrating the best of human intelligence with technology, it is found that projector-based augmented reality drives processes with acceleration and correctness to ensure each product is built perfectly, every time.

Here at Light Guide Systems, we have one goal that is to provide innovative solutions to operational problems by serving companies better visualize complex manufacturing processes. It has been using the power of augmented reality since 2005 to aid companies around the world transform manual assembly and manufacturing processes.

Whether the industry produces power trains, pistons, pacemakers or prosthetics, projector-based augmented reality has broad applications. It's only a matter of time before projection AR becomes the standard for enterprises. Educating yourself on this extraordinary technology will give your business the competitive edge it needs to thrive.

Recognition-Based Augmented Reality (RBAR)

RBAR targets on discovery of objects and then provide us more information about the object. For example, while using your mobile phone to scan a barcode or QR code, we actually use object recognition technology. Certainly, except location-based AR systems, all other types utilize some type of recognition system to detect the type of object over which augmentation can be done.

RBAR technology has various uses as well. One of them is to disclose the object in front of the camera and provide information about the object on screen. This is something identical to the AR apps for travelers. However, the diversity lies in the fact that the AR location browsers are usually unaware about the objects that they see while recognition-based AR apps do.

Figure 3. Recognition-based Augmented Reality

This technology of AR has extended to a point where there are full-fledged methods to comment the world using known markers, and more recently, the structural 3D information on the environment itself. This has resulted in drastic use of AR nowadays widely experienced by a large number of people in a variety of situations. However, to take AR to the next level, it is important to consider methods that allow the automated detection of objects, materials and shapes. One way to fulfil this goal is to develop AR that incorporates the recognition of visual object detection and utilize these to enhance the places and situations where current AR methods have not been explored. Of interest for this goal are methods that include large-scale object recognition to discriminate and spot objects or materials and go beyond using traditional markers.

Location-Based Augmented Reality (LBAR)

It would be an inequality not to mention this category when talking about AR. Location based augmented reality is one of most widely materialized applications of AR. The substantial force behind this is the easy availability of smart phones and the features that they provide in terms of location detection. Location based AR is mostly used to aid travelers in their journey. LBAR is taking influence of the smart devices' location detection features. For example, consider if you are a traveler and you want to discover new great places, this method will use your current location by reading your smart device's GPS, compass and accelerometer and give you significant information about what you are looking for on your screen. Wikitude is one such application.

Figure 4. Location-based Augmented Reality

While developments in recent years have made the technology more skilful and reachable, there are still some threats for developers such as:

- For preciseness sake, various sensors on the smart phone must be queried accurately at the same time so that position and attitude of the phone are taken into account properly.
- You need to be able to exactly display points of interest or the "virtual" aspects you want layered on the screen, no matter which angle of view the smart phone camera is pointing at.

The technique used for calculating the distance between two points must be adequate and faithful. This is usually based on GPS data, but this data can endure from errors at times.

Overall, the key threat lies in maintaining the accuracy. If we are not able to reliably do that with your app, then the experience for the user is diminished.

Outlining-Based Augmented Reality (OBAR)

Yet the human eye is known to be the finest camera in the world, still there are restrictions. We cannot look at things for too long. We cannot see well in low light conditions and sure as anything, your eye cannot see in infrared. For such cases, special cameras were built. Augmented reality apps which perform outlining use such cameras. Once again, object recognition sits behind all that outlining AR can do. Let's start with a life-saving implementation example.

When driving a car on a road in foggy weather, the boundaries of the road may not be very visible to the human eye, leading to accidents. Advanced cameras tuned specially to see the surroundings in low light conditions can be used to outline the road boundaries within which the car should stay. Such a system would prove very useful in avoiding accidents. With extra sensors capable of detecting objects around the overall risk of hitting some living object can be minimized as well.

The technology can help you save pedestrian lives as well. Outlining people crossing the road on a HUD (Heads Up Display) windscreen can be more useful than having a separate infrared video feed.

An AR app known as 110 stories allows you to see the twin towers of world trade centre in New York as an outline. This might a tad morbid, but it certainly is interesting. Outlining monuments from history can be utilized for many purposes the foremost is of course education.

Three Outlining AR can be used by engineers and architects to look at a building and study the location of supporting pillars and metal bars. Such an application could fetch the building's construction data from a database and provide a framework view of a building and can prove to be an aid in repairing a building or be used for educational purposes.

Figure 5. Location View depicting its characteristics

Figure 6. Outlining-based Augmented Reality

Superimposition-Based Augmented Reality (SBAR)

Superimposition based AR provides an 'equivalent' view of the object in concern, either by replacing the entire view with an augmented view of the object or by replacing a portion of the object view with an augmented view. In this case, once again, object recognition plays a vital role - logically, if the application does not know what it is looking at, it most certainly cannot replace the original view with an augmented one.

Depending on what type of view is required, the technology can be used for multiple purposes.

Doctors can use the technology to examine the patient from various angles in real-time. A live feed from an X-Ray machine can be used to superimpose the X-Ray view of the patient 's body part on the real image to provide better understanding of the damage to bones. The application can be made to work via a head mounted display or special goggles. In other uses, the view can be shown on a screen where the video feed is taken from a real camera and X-Ray vision can be imposed on it.

Figure 7. Superimposition-Based Augmented Reality

In military applications, superimposition-based AR can provide multiple views of a target object without showing extra information in text and blocking the vision of soldier from other important objects around. If you have been shooting enemies via your computer mouse, you'd already know how it would appear. Superimposition of infrared view or radioactive view of an object or an area can help save lives; or win wars!

Superimposition of ancient pictures over real ones can provide interesting views of historical places. Broken monuments can come back to life in all their original glory. Perhaps different eras complete with landscapes can be re-lived with AR.

To allow a tiger or snake near you might be a horrifying experience with hazardous consequences, except when superimposition AR is used to bring them to you. Placing a person in a location or situation which is otherwise dangerous can be can be safely accomplished via superimposition AR.

Superimposing a real object with its internal view can be helpful in education as well, for instance, to study bone structure. Though we have touched some of the most important types of augmented reality, there are a few others which cannot be easily classified to fall in one of the above said ones.

These types utilize numerous sensors and may produce the result in different forms. Such systems engage special faculties of dedicated devices working in parallel with processing systems with algorithms developed especially for being used in AR. As more input and output devices converge to more powerful and efficient systems, we would come across more types of AR in future.

VR EXPERIENCE

Key Elements of a Virtual Reality Experience

Virtual World

A virtual world is a three-dimensional environment, but not necessarily, realized through a medium (i.e. rendering, display, etc.) where one can interact with others and create objects as part of that interaction. In a virtual world, visual perspectives are responsive to changes in movement and interactions mimic those experienced in the real world.

Figure 8. Superimposition-based AR

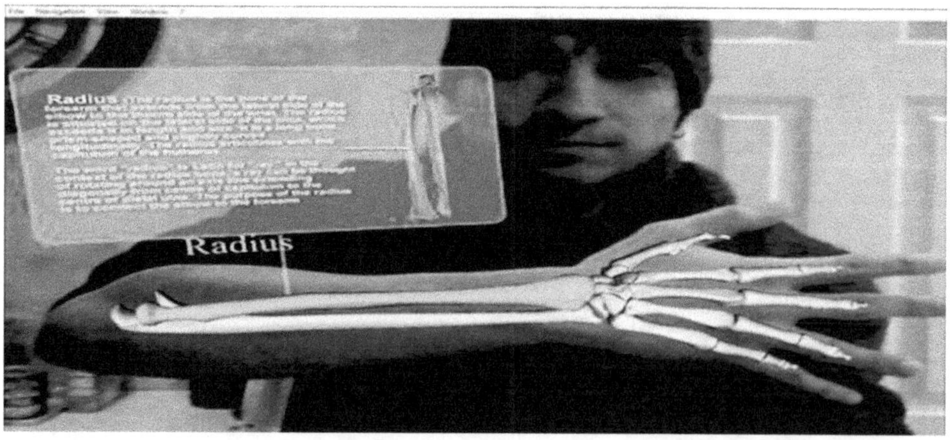

Immersion

Virtual reality immersion is the perception of being physically present in a non-physical world. It encompasses the sense of presence, exposes the point where the human brain believes that is somewhere it is really not and is accomplished through purely mental and/or physical means. The state of total immersion exists when enough senses are activated to create the perception of being present in a non-physical world. Two common types of immersion include:

- **Mental Immersion:** A deep mental state of engagement, with suspension of disbelief that one is in a virtual environment.
- **Physical Immersion:** Exhibited physical engagement in a virtual environment, with suspension of disbelief that one is in a virtual environment.

Sensory Feedback

Virtual reality requires as many of our senses as possible to be simulated. These senses include visual, hearing/aural, touch, and more. Properly stimulating these senses requires sensory response, which is achieved through integrated hardware and software (also known as inputs). There are various examples of the hardware and inputs are discussed below as key components to a virtual reality system, which includes head mounted displays (HMD), special gloves or hand accessories, and hand controls.

Interactivity

The element of interaction is crucial for virtual reality experiences to provide users with enough comfort to naturally engage with the virtual environment. If the virtual environment responds to a user's action in a natural manner, excitement and senses of immersion will remain. In case the virtual environment cannot respond quickly, then the human brain will quickly notice, and the sense of immersion will diminish. Virtual environment responses to interaction can include the way a participant moves around or changes in their viewpoint; generally, by movements of their head.

REAL WORLD APPLICATIONS

Early PCs, smart phones and tablets applications where for augmented reality focused on games, but the uses of AR are much broader.

Now-a-days, Google glass and heads-up displays in car windshields are perhaps the most well-known consumer AR products, but the technology is used in many industries including public safety, healthcare, gas and oil, tourism and marketing.

A simple augmented reality use case is: A user captures the image of a real-world object, and the underlying platform detects a marker, which triggers it to add a virtual object on top of the real-world image and displays on user camera screen. Real-World Examples are:

- AR applications can become the backbone of the education industry. Apps are being developed which embed text, images, and videos, as well as real–world curriculums.

- Printing and advertising industries are developing apps to display digital content on top of real world magazines.
- With help of AR, travelers can access real-time information of historical places just by pointing their camera viewfinder to subjects.
- AR is helpful in development of translation apps that can interpret text in other languages for user.
- Location based AR apps are major forms of AR apps. Users can access information about nearest places relative to current location. They can get information about places and choose based on user reviews.
- With the help of Unity 3d Engine, AR is being used to develop real-time 3D Games.
- The military uses augmented reality to help men and women as they make repairs in the field. Medical people use AR to prepare for surgeries. The possible commercial and educational applications are unlimited.
- Johnson, et al. (2010) stated, "AR has strong potential to provide both powerful contextual, on-site learning experiences and serendipitous exploration and discovery of the connected nature of information in the real world."

AR EXPERIENCE

For Military

The Heads-Up Display (HUD) is the typical example of augmented reality when it comes to military applications of the technology. A transparent display is positioned directly in the fighter pilot's view. Data typically displayed to the pilot includes altitude, airspeed and the horizon line in addition to other critical data. The term "heads-up" name applies because the pilot doesn't have to look down at the aircraft's instrumentation to get the data he needs.

The Head-Mounted Display (HMD) is used by ground troops (Urban,1999). Critical data such as enemy location can be presented to the soldier within their line of sight. This technology is also used for simulations for training purposes.

Figure 9. AR in Military

For Medical

Medical students use AR technology to practice surgery in a controlled environment. Sutherland (1968) suggested a tracked head-mounted display as a new human-computer interface enabling viewpoint-dependent visualization of virtual objects. Visualizations aid in explaining complex medical conditions to patients. Roberts et al. (1986) implemented the first medical augmented reality system. Kai wang et. al. (2017) proposed an optical see-through mixed reality system for typing steadily which reduces hand tremors by optically overlapping the trembling hand with a stabilized virtual hand to produce a realistic typing sensation without any tremors. It automatically analyzes and identifies the tremor type and implements specific stabilization to estimate stable hand position. Augmented reality can reduce the risk of an operation by giving the surgeon improved sensory perception. This technology can be combined with MRI or X-ray systems and bring everything into a single view for the surgeon. The application of augmented reality in the ultrasound imaging is said by M. Bajura et al. (1992). Neurosurgery is at the forefront when it comes to surgical applications of augmented reality. The ability to image the brain in 3D on top of the patient's actual anatomy is powerful for the surgeon.

Neurosurgery is at the forefront when it comes to surgical applications of augmented reality. The ability to image the brain in 3D on top of the patient's actual anatomy is powerful for the surgeon. Since the brain is merely fixed compared to other parts of the body, the registration of exact coordinates can be achieved. Concern still exists surrounding the movement of tissue during surgery. This can affect the exact positioning required for augmented reality to work.

Some best examples of augmented reality in medicine.

- Augmented reality can save lives through showing defibrillators nearby
- Google Glass might help new mothers struggling with breastfeeding
- Patients can describe their symptoms better through augmented reality
- Nurses can find veins easier with augmented reality
- Pharma companies can provide more innovative drug information
- Augmented reality can assist surgeons in the OR

Figure 10. AR using in Medical

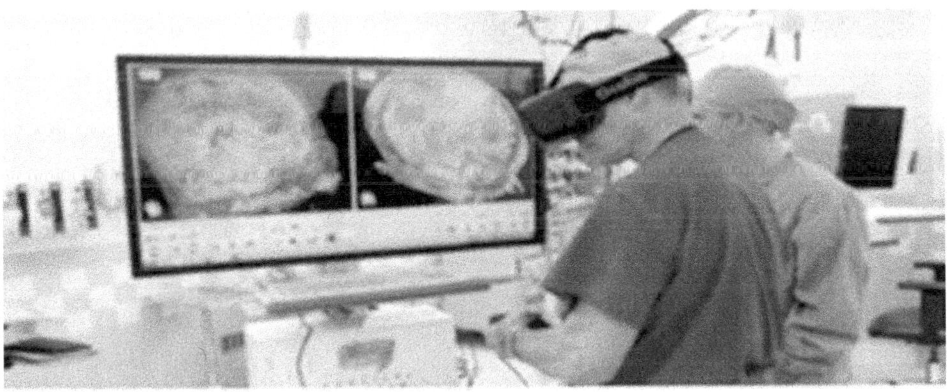

For Navigation

Navigation applications are possibly the most natural fit of augmented reality with our everyday lives. Enhanced GPS systems use augmented reality to make it easier to get from point A to point B.

Using the smart phone's camera in combination with the GPS, users see the selected route over the live view of what is in front of the car.

For Sightseeing

There are several applications for augmented reality in the sightseeing and tourism industries. The ability to augment a live view of displays in a museum with facts and figures is a natural use of the technology.

Figure 11. AR using in Navigation applications

Figure 12. AR using in Sightseeing application

In the real world, sightseeing has been enhanced using augmented reality. Using a smart phone equipped with a camera, tourists can walk through historic sites and see facts and figures presented as an overlay on their live screen. These applications use GPS and image recognition technology to look up data from an online database. In addition to information about a historic site, applications have looked back in history and shows how the location looked 10, 50 or even 100 years ago.

For Maintenance and Repair

Using a head-worn display, a mechanic making repairs to an engine can see superimposed imagery and information in user's actual line of sight. The procedure might be presented in a box in the corner, and an image of the necessary tool can illustrate the exact motion the mechanic needs to perform.

The augmented reality system can label all the important parts. Complex procedural repairs can be broken down into a series of simple steps. Simulations can be used to train technicians, which can significantly reduce training expenses.

For Gaming Takes Off

With recent advances in computing power and technology, gaming applications in augmented reality are on the upswing. Head-worn systems are affordable now and computing power is more portable than ever. Before user can say "Pokemon Go," user can jump into an AR game that works with user's mobile device, superimposing mythical creatures over everyday landscape.

Popular Android and iOS AR apps include Ingress, SpecTrek, Temple Treasure Hunt, Ghost Snap AR, Zombies, Run and AR Invaders.

For Advertising and Promotion

The Layer Reality Browser is an application for iPhone and Android designed to show the world around user by displaying real time digital information in conjunction with the real world. It uses the camera on user mobile device to augment reality. Using the GPS location feature in user mobile device, the Layer application retrieves data based on where displays this data to user mobile screen. Details about popular

Figure 13. AR using in Maintenance and Repairing

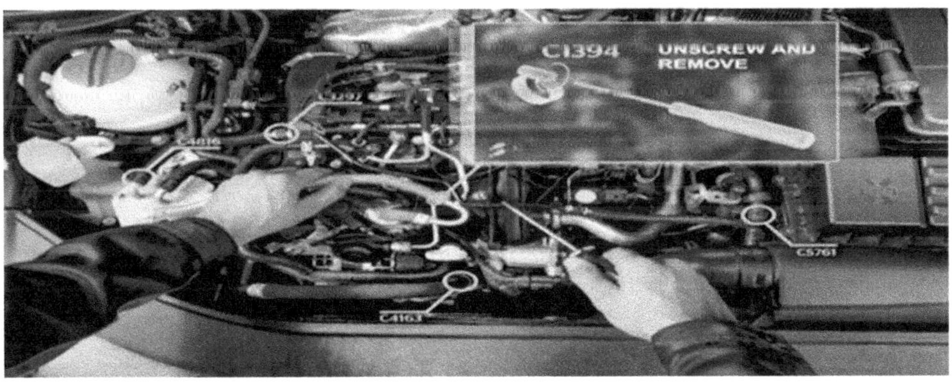

Figure 14. AR in Gaming

places, structures and movies are covered by Layer. Street views show the names of the restaurants and businesses superimposed over their storefronts.

Depending on what type of view is required, the technology can be used for multiple purposes. For example:

- Doctors can use the technology to examine the patient from various angles in real-time. A live feed from an X-Ray machine can be used to superimpose the X-Ray view of the patient 's body part on the real image to provide better understanding of the damage to bones. The application can be made to work via a head mounted display or special goggles. In other uses, the view can be shown on a screen where the video feed is taken from a real camera and X-Ray vision can be imposed on it.
- In military applications, superimposition-based AR can provide multiple views of a target object without showing extra information in text and blocking the vision of soldier from other important objects around. If users have been shooting enemies via user computer mouse, user had already know how it would appear. Superimposition of infrared view or radioactive view of an object or an area can help save lives.
- Superimposition of ancient pictures over real ones can provide interesting views of historical places. Broken monuments can come back to life in all their original glory. Perhaps different eras complete with landscapes can be re-lived with AR.
- To allow a tiger or snake near might be a horrifying experience with hazardous consequences, except when superimposition AR is used to bring them to user. Placing a person in a location or situation which is otherwise dangerous can be can be safely accomplished via superimposition AR.
- Superimposing a real object with its internal view can be helpful in education as well, for instance, to study bone structure. Though users have touched some of the most important types of augmented reality, there are a few others which cannot be easily centered into the above illustrations.

AR BROWSER

AR browser is a fully customized framework with really easy to use API. The framework takes care of all the complex functionalities of the augmented reality browser. So, you just need to focus on designing you application.

The main AR browser features are:

- 2D Point of Interests (POIs);
- Supporting video;
- To view light, smooth and accurate actions;
- Highly optimized to run on any device;
- Add and remove single POIs in real time;
- Memory management and performance is high;
- Radar, Radar dots and pop up labels are customizable elements;
- When clicked or on centered POI as discussed by R. Grasset et al. (2012) provides;
- Customer call back;
- Custom actions are email, SMS, call, video, social networks and more;
- Provides simple API for developers;
- Protects memory or battery starvation by giving start and stop functions;
- Sample code checking.

Two different classes of AR browser are:

- Open to Third Party Experience Provider/Publishers
- Closed to Third Party Experience Provider/Publishers.

Also, CMS for Publishing to Multiple AR Browsers are provided by third parties in order to support multiple AR browsers.

CATEGORIES OF AR APPS

The different categories of AR applications are listed below

- Augmented Reality in 3D viewers;
- Augmented Reality in Browsers;
- Augmented Reality Games;
- Augmented Reality GPS.

Augmented Reality in 3D Viewers

In this category it permits the user to put the images of life-size 3D model which can be linked with AR with or without the usage of trackers and the examples are AUGMENT, Sun Seeker, etc.

Table 1. AR browser Providers and Publishers.

Open to Third Party Experience Provider/Publishers			
Browser Publisher	Browser	mobile OS	Notes
Layar	Layar Reality Browser	iOS, Android	Geo, CV
metaio	junaio	iOS, Android	Geo, CV, 3D
Wikitude	Wikitude World Browser	iOS, Android, RIM, Symbian	Geo, CV
Ausrasma	Aurasma Lite	iOS, Android	CV
AR Lab	AR Browser	iOS, Android	Geo, CV
GA Tech	Argon	Android	Geo, CV
13th Lab	Point Cloud Browser	iOS	CV
AR23D	GlorAR	iOS, Android	3D to Geo
MixARe	Mixare AR Browser	iOS, Android	Geo, CV
Closed to Third Party Provider/Publishers			
Seac02	AR-code	iOS, Android	CV
Augmented Technologies	AWILA	Android	3D to Geo
Nokia	City Lens	Windows 8	Geo
Cynapse	LocalScope	iOS	Geo
Across Air	AR Browser	iOS	Geo
Chemical Wedding	Cyclopedia	iOS	Geo
Augmented Works	GeoTravel	iOS	Geo
Ubique	Ubique Browser	iOS	Geo
WhereMark	WhereMark Browser	iOS	Geo
Cactus Lab	World Surfer	iOS	Geo

Augment

It permits the user to view in £D in a real-life environment and time through smartphones and tablets to improve sales and involve user in app both in Android and iOS. It permits the user to communicate with one another to enable online shoppers as discussed by S. Guven et al. (2009) to have an experience about the product by sitting at home. They can also rotate the image and view the content augment before buying the product. The customers who use this application are companies like Nokia, Coca-Cola, Siemens and Boeing.

Figure 15. Augmented Reality in 3D Viewers

Sun-Seeker

An AR app that gives a flat compass view and a 3D view giving the solar path, its hour intervals, its equinox, winter and summer solstice paths, sunrise and sunset times, twilight times, magic hours and also a Map view showing solar direction for each daylight hour. It runs on both Android and iOS. The application is suitable for Photographers, Cinematographers, Real Estate Buyers, Drivers, Campers and Architects.

Augmented Reality in Browsers

AR browsers improve users' camera display with contextual information. For example, you can the information about a building when you view it via your smartphone. The example is ARGON4.

Figure 16. Augmented Reality in Browsers

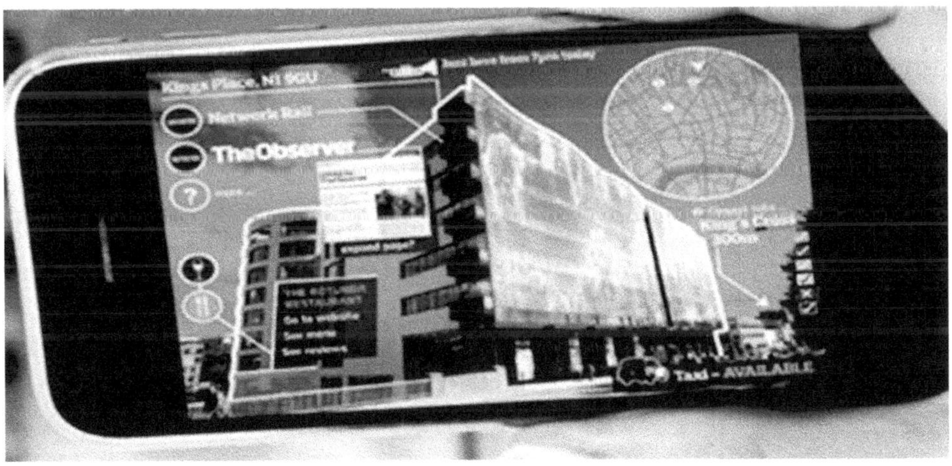

Argon4

It is a fully-featured web browser that can display augmented reality content produced with the argon.js Javascript framework. It eases to add AR content to the web applications in a platform and technology-independent way and supports the real-time AR capabilities of the Argon4 Browser. The Argon4 browser is available on both iTunes App Store and Google Play Store.

AR Browser SDK

It permits the user to add geolocation view in both Android and iOS. The framework takes care of all the complex functions of the augmented reality browser with user-friendly API and fully customized. It supports addition and removal of POIs, run on any device, provides memory management, custom activities, etc.

Augmented Reality Games

This is most common type of application which attracts gaming experience by using actual environment. Few examples are Pokémon Go, Parallel Kingdom, Temple Treasure Hunt, Real Strike, Zombie Go, etc.

Pokémon Go

This gaming software permits the users to the most popular AR game till date is Pokémon Go which allows users to grab the hidden virtual Pokémon throughout the map of the real world by using real locations to encourage players to far and wide. It allows the players to find and grab more than a hundred species of Pokémon as they move about in their surroundings. It works both on the Android and iOS. Ryan et. al. (2017) explains the applications of pervasive sensing using AR for enabling Pokeman Go. It explores how to improve the sensing by integrating local localization and elevating AR environment by activity identification.

Figure 17. Augmented Reality Games

Real Strike

This is the world's first ever Augmented Reality First-Person-Shooting app. It is available on iOS. The users get a real-life experience of shooting. They can record their fights and also create their own videos. The game offers night and thermal vision goggles to get a clear view even in the evening to complete your mission.

Augmented Reality GPS:

AR applications in Smartphone's generally include Global Positioning System (GPS) to spot the user's location and its compass to detect device orientation. Few examples are AR GPS Compass Map 3D, AR GPS Drive/Walk Navigation, etc.

Ar Gps Drive/Walk Navigation

The application makes use of the Smartphone's GPS and camera with augmented reality-powered technology to execute a car navigation system. Compared to the normal navigation system it is easier and safer for the driver. This application is available only on Android.

AR GPS Compass Map 3D

The app can only run on Android interface. It shows a 3D compass that is fused with the camera image and shows the user's current location from GPS on a separate map with adjustable size and share their current location and the locations of their waypoints with their friends.

Figure 18. Augmented Reality GPS

The popularity of AR increases as days goes and the following elements serves for the success of Augmented Reality campaigns in retail. Some examples are:

- Strategic focus;
- Custom AR experience;
- Integration of AR with real-world environments;
- Using AR games to improve retail experience;
- Innovation using emerging technologies and amazing experience.

Few factors that slow down mass implementation of augmented reality. Some of the factors are:

- Reach of Mobile AR and Public Awareness;
- Limitations of Technology;
- Privacy Issues;
- Mobile Internet Connectivity in Emerging Markets.

Every technology has its own limitations and AR is no exception. In AR the data should render across the wearer's not partially but with full scope of vision and it should be set with a better understanding of motion of natural body, ensuring that the displays get lighter and thinner. Above all Internet connectivity is another major problem, battery life of a device, price of the devices and privacy. They often mention the danger of spending too much time in the virtual world and missing out on moments that are happening in the real world.

CONCLUSION

The invent of Augmented Reality has given a new visage of Smartphone applications and gaming by adding digital images and data to amplify views of the real world and also by providing users with additional information about their environments. It differs from virtual reality by attempting to simulate reality. AR and its use in the real world and its application domains like medicine, education, health, gaming, tourism, film and entertainment, architecture and development. Since AR software, browsers and platforms provide rich, sophisticated, innovative and surprising features it attracts the users.

FUTURE DIRECTIONS OF AR

Future of AR and its impact on your day-to-day life and our economy are your Mobile Phone will become even more pervasive and social, gamification will permeate the workplace, ecommerce will be redefined, product design will become revolutionary, working conditions will become safer, city infrastructure will improve and enhanced delivery and access to healthcare.

REFERENCES

Abbass, H. A., Leu, G., & Merrick, K. (2016). A Review of Theoretical and Practical Challenges of Trusted Autonomy in Big Data. *Special Section On Theoretical Foundations For Big Data Applications: Challenges And Opportunities*, *4*, 2808–2830.

Azuma, R. T. (1997). A survey of augmented reality. *Presence (Cambridge, Mass.)*, *6*(4), 355–385. doi:10.1162/pres.1997.6.4.355

Bajura, M., Fuchs, H., & Ohbuchi, R. (1992). Merging virtual objects with the real world: Seeing ultrasound imagery within the patient. *ACM SIGGRAPH Computer Graphics, 26*(2), 203–210.

Bimber, O., Raskar, R., & Inami, M. (2005). *Spatial augmented reality*. AK Peters Wellesley. doi:10.1201/b10624

Caudell, T. P., & Mizell, D. W. (1992). Augmented reality: An application of heads-up display technology to manual manufacturing processes. In *System Sciences, 199, Proceedings of the Twenty-Fifth Hawaii International Conference on*. IEEE. 10.1109/HICSS.1992.183317

Chatzopoulos, Bermejo, Huang, & Hui. (2017). Mobile Augmented Reality Survey: From Where We Are to Where We Go. *IEEE Translations and Content Mining, 5*, 6917-6950.

Chen, Wu, Lo, & Hwang. (2017). An Augmented Reality Question Answering System Based on Ensemble Neural Networks. *IEEE Translations and Content Mining, 5*, 17425-17435.

Foxlin, E., Calloway, T., & Zhang, H. (2015). Design and Error Analysis of a Vehicular AR System with Auto-Harmonization. *IEEE Transactions on Visualization and Computer Graphics*, *21*(12), 1323–1335. doi:10.1109/TVCG.2015.2481385 PMID:26415180

Ge, X., Pan, L., Li, Q., Mao, G., & Tu, S. (2017). Multipath Cooperative Communications Networks for Augmented and Virtual Reality Transmission. *IEEE Transactions on Multimedia*, *19*(10), 2345–2358. doi:10.1109/TMM.2017.2733461

Grasset, R., Langlotz, T., Kalkofen, D., Tatzgern, M., & Schmalstieg, D. (2012). *Image-Driven View Management for Aug- mented Reality Browsers. In 2012 IEEE International Symposium on Mixed and Augmented Reality* (pp. 177–186). Atlanta, GA: ISMAR.

Guven, S., Oda, O., Podlaseck, M., Stavropoulos, H., Kolluri, S., & Pingali, G. (2009). Social Mobile Augmented Reality for Retail. *IEEE International Conference on Pervasive Computing and Communications,* 1-3. 10.1109/PERCOM.2009.4912803

Ibanez, M. B., Di Serio, A., Villaran-Molina, D., & Delgado-Kloos, C. (2016). Support for Augmented Reality Simulation Systems: The Effects of Scaffolding on Learning Outcomes and Behavior Patterns. *IEEE Transactions on Learning Technologies*, *9*(1), 46–56. doi:10.1109/TLT.2015.2445761

Johnson, L., Levine, A., Smith, R., & Stone, S. (2010). Simple augmented reality. The 2010 Horizon Report. Austin, TX: The New Media Consortium.

Melillo, Riccio, Di Perna, & Di Baja. (2017). Wearable Improved Vision System for Color Vision Deficiency Correction. *IEEE Journal of Transactional Engineering in Health and Medicine, 5*, 3800101-3800107.

Nguyen, Islam, Hossan, & Jang. (2017). Current Status and Performance Analysis of Optical Camera Communication Technologies for 5G Networks. *IEEE Translations and Content Mining,* 5, 4574-4594.

Piekarski, W., Gunther, B., & Thomas, B. (1999). Integrating virtual and augmented realities in an outdoor application. In *International Workshop on Augmented Reality (IWAR'99) Proceedings. 2nd IEEE and ACM*. IEEE. 10.1109/IWAR.1999.803805

Roberts, D. W., Strohbehn, J. W., Hatch, J. F., Murray, W., & Kettenberger, H. (1986). A frameless stereotaxic integration of computerized tomographic imaging and the operating microscope. *Journal of Neurosurgery*, *65*(4), 545–549. doi:10.3171/jns.1986.65.4.0545 PMID:3531430

Shatte, A., Holdsworth, J., & Lee, I. (2014). Mobile augmented reality-based context-aware library management system. *Expert Systems with Applications*, *41*(5), 2174–2185. doi:10.1016/j.eswa.2013.09.016

Shea, Fu, Sun, Cai, Ma, Fan, & Gong. (2017). Location-Based Augmented Reality With Pervasive Smartphone Sensors: Inside and Beyond Pokemon Go! *IEEE Translations and Content Mining, 5*, 9619-9631.

Sisodia, Verma, & Vyas. (2016). A Discounted Fuzzy Relational Clustering of Web Users' Using Intuitive Augmented Sessions Dissimilarity Metric. *IEEE Translations and Content Mining, 4*, 6883-6893.

Sutherland, I. E. (1968). A head-mounted three-dimensional display. *Proceedings of the Fall Joint Computer Conference*, 757–764. 10.1145/1476589.1476686

Syberfeldt, A., Danielsson, O., & Gustavsson, P. (2017). Augmented Reality Smart Glasses in the Smart Factory: Product Evaluation Guidelines and Review of Available Products. *IEEE Translations and Content Mining, 5*, 9118-9130.

Urban, E. C. (1999). *The information warrior. In Technology and society* (pp. 493–501). Prentice-Hall, Inc.

Van Krevelen, D., & Poelman, R. (2010). A survey of augmented reality technologies, applications and limitations. *International Journal of Virtual Reality*, *9*(2), 1–20.

Wang, Iwai, & Sato. (2017). Supporting Trembling Hand Typing Using Optical See-Through Mixed Reality. *IEEE Translations and Content Mining, 5*, 10700-10708.

Wither, Tsai, & Azuma. (2011). Indirect augmented reality. *Computers &Graphics Elsevier Ltd, 35*, 810–822.

Zhang, H., Qu, D., Hou, Y., & Huang, F. (2016). Synthetic Modelling Method for Large Scale Terrain Based on Hydrology. *IEEE Translations and Content Mining, 4*, 6238-6249.

KEY TERMS AND DEFINITIONS

AR Browser: Interprets user input and real world, manages delivery/presentation of experience and communication with additional services.

Augmented Reality: An augmented reality is a technology that integrates the digital images which are generated by computer in real time.

Location-Based Augmented Reality: This method works by detecting the user's location and orientation by reading data from the mobile's GPS, digital compass and accelerometer and predicting where the user is looking; then adding related information on screen about the objects that can be seen from the camera.

Outlining Augmented Reality: Outlining AR recognizes the boundaries of the road and outlines them for the user. It also be used in architecture and engineering to outline buildings and their supporting pillars.

Projection-Based Augmented Reality: PBAR is by projecting artificial light rays onto the real-world surfaces. Basically, PBAR applications allows user to interact by sending light rays onto a real-world surface and then sensing the interaction (i.e., touch of that projected light).

Recognition-Based Augmented Reality: RBAR targets on discovery of objects and then provide us more information about the object.

Superimposition-Based Augmented Reality: Superimposition based AR provides an "equivalent" view of the object in concern, either by replacing the entire view with an augmented view of the object or by replacing a portion of the object view with an augmented view.

Virtual Reality: A realistic three-dimensional image or artificial environment that is created with a mixture of interactive hardware and software and presented to the user in such a way that the any doubts are suspended, and it is accepted as a real environment in which it is interacted with in a seemingly real or physical way.

Chapter 5
Advantages of Augmented Reality, Virtual Reality, QR Code, Near Field Communication, Geo-Tagging, Geo-Fencing, and Geo-Targeting for Marketing Tourism

Evrim Çeltek
Gaziosmanpasa University, Turkey

ABSTRACT

The developing number of applications available through smart devices provides an increasing diversity of tourism marketing, destination and city marketing, tourism business marketing, and advertising. In the last decade, marketers have developed more creative practices to attract consumers. These new marketing tools are augmented reality, virtual reality, QR code, near field communication (NFC), geo-tagging, geo-fencing, and geo-targeting applications with the smart technologies, which are considered as a new marketing communication instruments these increase awareness and help get information about tourist and give information to the tourist. This chapter presents the profile of smart marketing applications and their marketing benefits in tourism industry. More specifically, this chapter aimed to achieve the following research objectives: to determine the potentials of the augmented reality, virtual reality, QR code, near field communication (NFC), geo-tagging, geo-fencing, and geo-targeting applications in the tourism industry.

DOI: 10.4018/978-1-5225-5763-0.ch005

Copyright © 2019, IGI Global. Copying or distributing in print or electronic forms without written permission of IGI Global is prohibited.

INTRODUCTION

Smart destinations are expected to enhance the quality of life of tourists by relying on new paradigms, like the Internet of Things (IoT) and its capacity to manage and interconnect thousands of sensors and actuators scattered across the city. At the same time, mobile devices wide assist skilled and private everyday activities. Smart destinations are complicated environments wherever many areas of innovation meet so as to substantially improve socioeconomic development and quality of life. Economic innovations, technological tools that encourage individuals to participate in governance processes and Internet-enabled city infrastructure services and utilities form a thriving analysis field (Chaves-Dieguez et al, 2015). Benefits of integration the smart technologies into the destination strategy are cost reduction, efficiency, economic competitiveness, sustainability, quality of life, big data analyzing and innovation.

Today's customers are increasingly using social media on mobile phones, and PCs. With these technologies, customers easily notice what they need, compare with various items, get recommendations from friends, family, and colleagues purchase from wherever they're located, and tell their experiences to others subsequently. In today's internet and mobile-enabled world, customer expectations are being shaped by daily interactions with companies across varied industries. However, this transformation would require new ways of thinking about company culture, business processes, and technology investments, (Sharma and Sharma, 2014) marketing planning and marketing communication.

In the tourism destinations of the future interactions can inevitably be mediate through technology. Users can interact through public displays, mobile location-based applications, virtual reality, geo-fencing, geo-tagging, NFC, QR code and augmented reality systems. The destinations and tourism businesses of the future can have an increasing range of sensors that may track every aspect of the daily life. This immense data potential may be used to improve the urban living experience by enabling a smart city, not only from the perspective of its services, but also in the scope of marketing and planning activities.

Smart technologies are considered highly important for marketing in many industries; however, in the tourism industry there exist relatively few researches and articles despite the fact that tourism could very well benefit from the applications for these practices. More specifically, this chapter aimed to achieve the following research objectives; to determine the potentials of the augmented reality, virtual reality, QR code, near field communication (NFC), geo tagging, geo fencing and geo targeting applications in the tourism industry; to determine the benefits of augmented reality, virtual reality, QR code, near field communication (NFC), geo tagging, geo fencing and geo targeting applications from the perspective of marketing in tourism industry.

The study is organized as follows: Literature review about augmented reality, virtual reality, QR code, near field communication (NFC), geo-tagging, geo-fencing and geo targeting the advantages and challenges of applications are discussed. Finally, the findings and results are summarized in the last section. The implications of this study will be meaningful to both tourism researchers and professionals.

BACKGROUND

Augmented Reality

AR is the process of taking and integrating digital information with a live streaming video or with the user's actual, real time environment. The AR that is utilized by smart phones will utilize GPS technology and allow the users location to be pinpointed in order to determine the device orientation (Taylor, 2013). This technology takes a current picture and blends the new information into the image (Höllerer and Feiner, 2004; Craig, 2013; Berryman, 2012). The basic goal of an AR system is to enhance the user's perception of and interaction with the real world through supplementing the real world with 3D virtual objects that appear to coexist in the same space as the real world (Azuma et al, 2001).

Augmented reality (AR) allows smart phone and tablet computer users to point their phones' or tablet's cameras at certain objects (Azuma, 1997; Linaza et al, 2012) - be it a print advertisement or even a coffee cup or brochures /magazines - that trigger a 3D video. AR gives tourism businesses opportunities to unexpectedly integrate the digital world with the real world, which appeals to tech-lovers who are usually sceptical of traditional advertising methods (Craig, 2013).

Tourists may use mobile augmented reality applications for many things such as searching for information, sharing or exchanging information and useful tips as well as comments on a location or destination with a large network. Thus, connectivity among other users, in this case tourists, may be achieved and the sharing of experiences is enhanced (Russell, 2012). Furthermore, mobile augmented reality applications can help tourists prevent themselves from information overload or irrelevant information by tailoring their needs and adjusting the settings of the applications they are using upon request. It is beneficial for tourists because a vast amount of information can be found about historical sites and museum exhibitions and it might be overwhelming to get the information they particularly seek for. Therefore, museums, heritage sites, cities and tourist professionals in general may organize and transmit information in layers or they may provide information upon request, i.e. according to the tailored needs of tourists with respect to their interests, age, occupation, information level and so forth. Personalizing their visit according to their wish, as a result, may maximize the enjoy they take from the trip and make it a remarkable experience (Carmigniani et al, Berryman, 2012).

Virtual Reality

Virtual reality application represents three-dimensional, interactive, computer-generated environments. These environments can be models of real or imaginary worlds, and their purpose is to represent information through a synthetic experience. The virtual reality technology was born from the merging of many disciplines, including psychology, cybernetics, computer graphics, data-base design, real-time and distributed systems, electronics, robotics, multimedia, and telepresence (Gurau, 2007). Virtual reality (VR) is defined as the use of a computer-generated 3D environment – called a 'virtual environment' (VE) – that one can navigate and possibly interact with, resulting in real-time simulation of one or more of the user's five senses. 'Navigate' refers to the ability to move around and explore the VE, and 'interact' refers to the ability to select and move objects within the VE (Guttentag, 2010). From a marketing perspective, VR has the potential to revolutionize the promotion and selling of tourism (Williams and Hobson, 1995). Just as VR can be used to plan and manage a destination, it also can be used to market a destination (Cheong, 1995).

Many tourism products already use VR or VR-type technologies to attract tourists. For instance, on the Internet one can find many hotels (e.g. www.showhotel.com) and destinations (e.g. www.virtualgettysburg.com) offering 'virtual tours'. These 'virtual tours' often are simply panoramic photographs that do not permit any free navigation, meaning they are not genuine VR, but they importantly still reveal an interest in VR-type technologies (Guttentag, 2010). One VR travel community named 'Itchy Feet' (http://www.itchy-feet.org) is already being developed as an SL-type virtual world in which tourists can seek out travel information, communicate with other tourists, and make travel purchases (Cheong, 1995).

QR Codes

QR Code got this name; as a result of it was developed to improve the reading speed of complex-structured 2D barcodes. This kind of code was at first used for tracking inventory in vehicle components manufacturing; currently it is utilized in a diversity of industries and innovative applications (Briseno et al, 2012, p. 222). Quick Response Code or QR Code could be a two-dimensional (2D) bar code developed in 1994 by Denso Wave Corporation (Zhang, Yao, Zhou, 2012, p. 817; Albăstroiu, Felea, 2015).

QR codes is also applied on labels or wrappings of product, on flyers, brochures, catalogs, billboards, posters, adverts in newspapers/magazines, transporting tickets, invites to events, greetings cards, business cards etc. depending on the type of data recognized and so the nature of the applying, varied actions will follow the decoding stage, like (Rouillard, 2008): a telephone number is also automatically dialed, a short text message (SMS) is also sent, a web page corresponding to the decoded URL (Uniform Resource locator used for localization and identification of resources on the Internet) could also be displayed in mobile browser, a person's contact details and indication of a geographical location could also be viewed (Lai et al., 2015). Thereby, the two-dimensional barcodes serve as "mobile tags" and so the above outlined process is related to the new conception of "mobile tagging", that refers to the possibilities to transfer data from a physical object to the mobile device (Marakos, 2015). Even the reason of the term used to name this code (Quick Response) lies exactly within the fact that it permits quick access to data (Cata, Patel and Sakaguchi, 2013) (Such as websites addresses, e-mails, phone numbers, geographical coordinates etc.) through mobile devices.

Countries like Australia, USA, Japan, India, etc. are finance massively to use QR codes on tourist attractions. Using 2D bar codes during tourism surroundings permits them to deliver organized data to every tourist by linking the official web site of the tourist center, Wikipedia page or YouTube video to reduce printing cost of visitor's guide, to advertise tourist attractions and share thoughts of tourists on social media with friends and families (Hassen, 2015, p. 22).

Near Field Communication (NFC)

Near Field Communication (NFC) is a standard based short-range wireless connection technology that enabled easy and safe peer-to-peer interconnections between electronic devices (Samy, 2012) which offers great and varied promise in services like payment, ticketing, gaming, crowd sourcing, voting, navigation, and plenty of others (Coşkun, Özdenizci and Ok, 2015). NFC relies on RFID technology and uses a similar communication mechanism. It combines the advantages of Radio Frequency Identification (RFID) and wireless communication technologies, included Bluetooth, WLAN (Egger, 2013[2]), and IrDA. NFC devices may communicate with the existing smartcards, the contactless readers, and support two-way communication between the other NFC-enabled devices in active and passive mode. NFC devices will send and receive the information at the same time. The fundamental plan of NFC is to introduce a communication session by an intuitive, simple to operate, and secure way (Pesonen and Horster, 2012). Users merely wave the device closed the device or point to the device accepted the NFC signals, the transaction may be completed instantly. Therefore, NFC is suitable to be integrated in the consumer electronic devices, like mobile phones, Tablet PC, MPs, Personal Digital Assistants (PDA), watch, digital camera and so on (Singh and Singh, 2014).

NFC may be a technology for high frequency wireless short-distance poin to-point communication. The operational range for NFC is within less than twenty cm (Strömmer et al, 2016) that's good from a security perspective because it diminishes the threat of eavesdropping (Abd Allah, 2011). Another potential use is for what are mentioned as "smart posters". Smart posters have NFC tags incorporated in them wherever info like URLs or defined apps, text messages, phone numbers and calling cards may be stored and called up (Coşkun et al., 2012; Egger, 2013[1]).

The use of NFC enabled destination cards within the destination context would seem to be a noteworthy and promising approach. Several destinations have enforced destination cards to extend guest loyalty, boost the image and brand of the destination and to ultimately improve turnover (Egger, 2013[2]). At the same time, the use of destination cards provides and generates key data regarding customer segments and also the use of provisions within the region. In most cases, individual regional service provisions are bundled and offered as a package. In future, destination cards may be stored directly on the mobile phone of the guest. Access rights, payment functions, bonus systems and loyalty programs may all be managed via the mobile destination card (Egger, 2013[1]).

Geo-Tagging (Geotagging)

Geo-tagging is that the process of annotating objects and online resources with geospatial context info, ranging from specific point locations to arbitrarily formed regions (Inversini et al, 2012). Geo-tagging could be a valuable promoting strategy that enables social media users and brands to tag photos, videos, and different posts with a particular location.

Most social media networks, as well as Twitter, Facebook, Instagram, Flickr, and YouTube enable users to share and look for content by location. By geo-tagging the social posts, brand's content may be found by users searching for info relevant to a specific location (Coşkun et al, 2013) or city. For instance, native businesses will geo-tag a picture on Instagram to focus on an audience in a specific space. Brands curious about targeting tech enthusiasts will geo-tag a post with the placement of a local tech event. Brands can produce a promoting campaign targeting the event goers by combining geo-tags and also the event hashtag. Regardless of the industry, if would like to target a local demographic, geo-tagging is an efficient plan of action (Carmon, 2018).

A restaurant might post an image of a delicious meal and tag their location. Now, if a user sees that dish and desires it, they recognize where can find it. Brands can use this technique for numerous varieties of product and services, which will attract customers (McCormick, 2017, Coşkun et al, 2013).

Geo-Fencing (Geofencing)

Geo-fenced mobile ads are promotions sent to people that physically breach the virtual perimeter of a store and are intended to convert those close to return in and shop. For larger targeting precision among large stores, several venues are adopting beacon technology to deliver in store promotions that feature maps to the promoted item for shopping ease (Brown and Harmon, 2014). More recently, marketers have taken the geospatial capabilities of mobile phones a step further by launching geo conquest ads that are targeted to individuals detected to be close to a competitor's store so as to lure them to the focal store (Tang, Yu, Zimmermann and Obana, 2015). Geo-fencing depends on four mobile technologies to identify the placement and implement algorithms based on boundaries. These are WiFi, RFID, GPS and beacons.

United Airlines became one amongst the first U.S. airlines to use beacon technology to assist airport guests. Before, passengers had to rely on confusing signs to navigate through terminals. With beacon technology, customers receive alerts once they are within varying of desired locations. Using beacons deliver customized info to guests. By using beacons to push notifications and offers, brands will offer relevant info to customers based on wherever they are and what they are doing. Beacons may be used to relieve major frustrations for time-pressed customers (Carmon, 2018).

Geo-fencing plays a crucial role within the context detection of LBS. Geo-fencing has several promising applications and is already exploited in numerous systems (e.g., Foursquare, Placecast, Sensewhere, Zentracker). The users (points) could perpetually move and generate continuous spatial data streams (Tang, Yu, Zimmermann and Obana, 2015).

By fitting a geo-fence, it is doable to deliver messages and discounts to customers among walking distance of the tourism business location. Brands will become front of mind for a consumer who otherwise might not have been in a buying attitude (Carmon, 2018). A geo-fencing campaign is often implemented on short notice; it is very targeted, cheap and results-driven; and there are corporations which will do all the work based on any size budget.

Geo-Targeting

Geo-targeting is the process of personalizing a marketing message for consumers based on a geographical area. Consumer distribution is allocated according to these geographical areas and different advertising campaigns are carried out for each area (Örnek, 2016). Geo-targeting and geo-fencing often confused two concepts. Geo-fencing targets users who are within range of predetermined points. Geo-targeting targets point shot users according to location change. The main differences between the two are (EUROMSG, 2016): 1. In geo-targeting, messages are created according to the locations of users in a certain time period, and in geo-fencing, the same messages are sent to every user who enters from the virtual wall. That is, in geo- targeting, a user is already targeted and the message is only sent according to the location change. In Geo-fencing, the location is already unknown. The important thing is for the user to enter that location. 2. At Geo-targeting, people are targeted by separating them into their needs and interests. There is nothing analyzed in Geo-fencing, people with different interests and those in a specific area are targeted in the same way. 3. Geo-targeting removes the language barrier. With geo-targeting, brands experience their chances of addressing customers locally, in different languages. In Geo-fencing, targeted information is sent in the same language. Since the destination is the designated point, people are not segmented. Because of this, naturally everyone will be targeted so that the user is addressed to the same language. 4. Geo-targeting tracks where customers are. In other words, as mentioned in the first difference, the customer is actually quite specific. Geo-fencing monitors customers only when they enter predefined areas. Geo-fencing is not interested in exactly who the customer is. 5. It is enough to know the user's location for geo-targeting. Geo-fencing does not account for the location of users, it sends messages everywhere, but it has to be pre-determined areas (Örnek, 2016).

MAIN FOCUS OF THE CHAPTER

Advantages and Challenges of Smart Technologies for Marketing Tourism Businesses

Technology in today's world has constantly been developing and even every other day a new technology is introduced to people. They are mostly new tools or applications that ease people's life and are mostly mobile, easy to use and multi-functional. As smart technology applications will continue to evolve and move forward, the possibilities for using smart technologies within the tourism sector will grow and continue to advance. Nevertheless, regardless of how smart technologies evolve, there are already many immediate applications for smart technologies within the tourism sector. By analyzing some of these applications within areas of tourism, the benefits, opportunities and impacts on tourism are quickly determined. This study offers many opportunities to understand the benefits of smart technology applications from the perspective of marketing to both tourism researchers and professionals.

Methodology

Smart technologies refer two- or multi-way communication and promotion of an offer between a firm and its customers. Fast development of smart phone technology created a chance to tourism industry for marketing. Hotels, restaurants, bars, museums and different kinds of hospitality establishments have gained an excellent marketing ally. This study is targeted to determine the advantages and challenges of smart technologies by literature review in tourism. During this section smart technologies are primarily based on augmented reality, virtual reality, QR code, near field communication (NFC), geo-tagging, geo-fencing and geo-targeting applications in the tourism industry. The methodology of determining the advantages and challenge of smart technologies are literature review. By literature review the study analyze the advantages and challenges of these smart technologies and *table 1* summarize the advantages and challenges.

Augmented Reality

Advantages of AR

AR could be used advertising for example Domino's launched an outdoor advertising campaign augmented with NFC posters. When pedestrians placed their phone near the poster, they were able to directly download Domino's new mobile application (Thrasher, 2013). AR is used in museums to provide their customers with additional information about an object or current displays. Similar to museums, AR is used in sightseeing to provide information about a destination, a tourist attraction or the reconstructions of ruins in a particular place. Berryman (2012) states that AR is even used to provide "situated documentaries" that "narrate historical events that took place in the user's immediate area by overlaying 3-D graphics and sound on what the user sees and hears". (Kounavis et al, 2012). AR strengthens tourism destination connection with mobile consumers seeking for more information, entertainment, when and where they want it. Customers can augment any object or image that has a unique visual profile like brand logo, land marks, posters, bill boards, tourism catalogues, magazine cover/page, posters, signage, brochures, retail displays, business cards, and the like (Carmigniani et al, 2011; Berryman, 2012). AR is particularly beneficial for museums, heritage sites, cities and tourist professionals because it is possible to organize and transmit information in layers. The information can also be organized according to the users' requests, which suggests that the users' background, interest, age, occupation and other characteristics may be used to organize the information. Thus, tourists can get customized services according to their preferences and expectations, which maximize satisfaction they get from their visit (Kounavis et al, 2012).

Challenges for AR

The popularity and attractiveness of augmented reality has increased recently. Yet, there are still many challenges regarding the technology. First of all, AR is a technologically complex service. In addition, there are no standards for AR. This means that every single device and platform has to work for its own individual development because interoperability is not possible yet. Moreover, despite the fact that smart phones support the location-based services, they are not completely accurate in locating the device that is sought for augmented reality. Also, tall buildings may prevent the present GPS systems in smart phones from working properly (it may happen even indoors). More importantly than these technological complexities, augmented reality faces other difficulties as well. This may include privacy issues, ethical issues and user issues (Carmigniani et al, 2011; Berryman, 2012; Russell, 2012)

Virtual Reality

Advantages of Virtual Reality

Virtual experiences provided more practical advertising than brochures for each theme park and Natural Park. Visiting a museum's website will increase one's interest in visiting the real museum, and serve as indirect evidence that visiting tourism destinations in VR might encourage real visitation (Guttentag, 2010). For instance, someone interested in exploring an island destination would be able to enter virtual island destinations (Cheong, 1995). Virtual reality can serve as a marketing instrument for destinations. Virtual reality systems afford tourist the opportunity to experience previews of destinations and their respective attractions and facilities. They would be able to 'sample' the delights and have a 'feel' of each destination's atmosphere before making their decision as to which tourist spot to visit (Guttentag, 2010). Additionally to serving as tourism marketing tool VR systems also can use for direct marketing (Cheong, 1995).

Challenges for VR

VR requires approval or participation from the user. The health effects are still unknown; there is lack of knowledge on how it works.

QR Code

Advantages of Using QR Code

A QR Code offers the user an oversized amount of information. With print advertisements restricted by area, showing exclusively the foremost vital info and listing the web site for users to induce further info (Demir, Kaynak, Demir, 2015). QR codes in written materials will drive further traffic to a web site. QR Code permits creating direct sales. The reader scanning the code placed below the advertisement among the printed version may purchase that product by connecting the web site of that product (Kuyucu, 2013). QR Codes use is just restricted by promoting strategy (Burillak, 2011). It is remarkably low-cost to get started with QR codes and it is more cost effective to maintain than different current technologies. The software for creating the codes is wide accessible on the online and principally free (Medic, Pavlovic, 2014). Actions triggered via QR Codes may be traced with web analytics or completely different tools for promoting campaign measuring. With the QR code, not entirely can the customer scan the advertising and obtain info; but the company scans the customer, so accessing customer-specific information like location and previous buying behavior. (Gönül, Qui, Zhou, 2015).

Challenges for QR Code

Requires approval or participation from the user. Thus, developing the basis behind a QR campaign is key to ensure that the attention will be there and people will want to get the best out of QR codes. QR codes need the user to download an app before they can be scanned.

Near Field Communication (NFC)

Advantages of NFC

NFC is quite versatile, and it can be well adapted into many sorts of companies. Versatility creates many alternative ways in which for NFC to be used within one business. NFC is not just used for payments, but it can also be used for ticket scanning, train passes and much more. NFC permits for a faster and a further efficient method of getting out of the check out-line (Borrego-Jaraba, 2011). Overall, it improves efficiency and productivity. An excellent example of this could be Starbucks. Who recently invested in NFC enabled machines to shorten the waiting periods for customers. This could be helpful for companies as results of they'll generate more revenue and probably attract plenty of customers. Evidently, NFC provides a competitive advantage. Customers are able to keep track of reward systems (Pesonen and Horster, 2012). NFC technology is used to improve user satisfaction. In their real life example, a customer said as Sam goes to restaurant A to have dinner. If restaurant A is equipped with an NFC device, the restaurant can send him a filtered menu, special set or different discounts once Sam scans his mobile phone against the NFC device. For example, if Sam can be a vegetarian the restaurant can send only their vegetarian menu to Sam's phone. NFC tags may well be used to provide travelers with information on their location and with directions (Pesonen and Horster, 2012).

Challenges for NFC

NFC is an expensive technology for smaller companies won't want to risk investment in NFC as a result of it is hard to measure the additional profit with NFC. There are technical problems, lack of acceptance among customers and lack business models. The hospitality sector is fragmented naturally. Whereas there are a few of isolated NFC tests occurring among the hotel chains (Egger, 2013[1]).

Geo-Tagging (Geotagging)

Advantages of Geo-Tagging

One among the most important benefits of geo-tagging is that it provides additional contexts to social media followers (Yuki et al, 2010). It permits marketers and entrepreneurs to draw more customers into their brand and ultimately, their store location. Aside from this, geo-tagging makes customers feel more connected to a brand, encouraging them to share their content and post concerning their products and/ or services. Additionally through geo-tagging, businesses will collect information on certain locations, that facilitate them recognize more regarding their audience's behavior even in numerous areas (Coşkun et al., 2013; McCormick, 2017).

Challenges for Geo-Tagging

Many people, however, see a conflict in geo-tagging with on-line security because the most important concern. Whereas some are open to transparency, the hazards of geo-tagging get play by providing constant location updates to the public thus exposing users to other audiences. As a result, information breaching and privacy become extremely at risk (McCormick, 2017).

Geo-Fencing (Geofencing)

Advantages of Geo-Fencing

Geo-fences may be used to target customers in physical locations, permitting triggering the correct message, the correct campaign, at the correct time and place. By personalizing the promoting messages supported the location businesses will target people within the vicinity of the shop so increasing the chance of attracting additional people to the shops. This ensures improved targeting and personalization of promoting messages. Geo-fencing allows to send offers to people that are within the vicinity of restaurant. This enables to simply analyzing the response and effectiveness of the campaign and makes it simple to optimize promoting efforts for higher ROI. Location-based marketing is extremely personal and targeted that improves its efficiency considerably. By delivering specific offers to people based on their location improve the impact communications produce on the consumers. Implementing location-based promoting get access to plenty of information that may be used to generate insights like that stores are performing higher, that target segment is more approachable, that locations are additional appropriate for increasing business etc. Geo-fencing is additionally utilized by businesses to collect customer knowledge to grasp their buying capacity, buying motivation and buying habits better. Gathering great amount of customer information over a period of time may be create better decisions to focus on customers in this location (Ghanchi, 2015).

Challenges for Geo-Fencing

Geo-fencing may be a technology that needs approval or participation from the user. Naturally, if the feature isn't turned on the user device it'll not produce any result. The human spirit naturally is antipathetic to any observation kind of issue and this makes Geo-fencing a culprit against privacy. This leads to users turning of the feature in most cases. For producing business intelligence Geo-fencing is simply effective once customer data from different sources are mobilized in unison. So, Geo-fencing is essentially not a very independent technology for gaining quality business intelligence input. Geo-fencing in most mobile devices take an excessive amount of battery life and this makes users shut down the feature. Several users even choose to avoid apps with Geo-fencing capability due to this. Moreover, network capacity, bandwidth, device capacity and battery life remained because the constraints for this technology to function seamlessly across devices and in all situations (Ghanchi, 2015).

Geo-Targeting

Advantages of Geo-Targeting

When geo-targeting is done, the conversion rate of the ad campaigns will be maximized. Because the ad shown to potential customers. For example, when an advertising campaign created for a company, which organizes sightseeing tours in Istanbul Bosporus, geographic targeting should be Istanbul. *Geo-targeting on Facebook:* Geo-targeting on Facebook offers 4 options: 1. Anyone at this location. 2. People living in this location. 3. Nearby locations. 4. People traveling to this location. When everyone in this location is selected, the other 3 options are also included. In other words, this ad can be shown to all people who are in Istanbul. People who are in a radius around Istanbul can be chosen by taking the center of Istanbul and writing a value of 1 km. *Geo-targeting in Google AdWords:* Google AdWords ad can be shown to individual users in geographical areas with separate ad campaigns. Similar features to Facebook's geo-targeting. Differences between them can be further exploited in AdWords with custom field targeting, location groups, and bulk targeting options. The other is; While defining users' locations on Facebook themselves, AdWords uses user locations; IP address, GPS, using Wi-fi data. Therefore, the rate of reaching the right target group is much higher (Örnek, 2016).

Challenges for Geo-Targeting

There are security problems and lack of information in the tourism industry.

SOLUTIONS AND RECOMMENDATIONS

A number of applications have been developed based on smart technologies in tourism industry. Today, many applications have been released as pilot applications or research projects, and some of them are commercially used in tourism industry. The main objective of this study was to explore the marketing

Table 1. Summary of smart technologies

SMART TECNOLOGIES	ADVANTAGES	CHALLENGES	APPLICATIONS
AUGMENTED REALITY	• Personalize the communication as per the user since user is in charge of the navigation. • There is no restriction of space or time like the traditional media. • Opportunity for customers to share their personalized content with others. • Developed at a much lower cost than those on other traditional media. • Provide access to location-based information that is relevant to the near surroundings of tourists. • Make possible to access the various contents, which are well-timed and updated. Have flexibility in delivering texts, videos, or images. • Provide interactive additional explanations which are integrated with map-based services and additional information.	• AR is a technologically complex service. • There are no standards for AR. • Tall buildings may prevent the present GPS systems in smart phones from working properly (it may happen even indoors). • Include privacy issues. • Ethical issues and user issues. • Requires approval or participation from the user.	Starbucks (advertisement campaign). The St. Petersburg & Clearwater Convention and Visitors Bureau (interactive travel brochure). Nova Scotia Tourism (guiding). Jersey Tourism Agent, Stella Artois Le Bar Guide (advertisement and quiding), Goggles and Layar, these apps offer AR advertisements in the tourism guides. Hong Kong Tourism Board (guiding).
VIRTUAL REALITY	• Practical advertising. • Increase one's interest in visiting the real museum, and serve as indirect evidence that visiting tourism destinations serve as a marketing instrument for destinations. • Afford tourist the opportunity to experience previews of destinations and their respective attractions and facilities. • VR systems also can use for direct marketing.	• Requires approval or participation from the user. • The health effects are still unknown. • Lack knowledge on how it works.	Virtual tours of a business environment Training of new employees. A 360 Degree view of any product. Includes virtual museum, gaming, virtual theme parks, inter-active exhibitions etc.
QUICK RESPONSE CODE (QR CODE)	• User convenience, environmentally friendly. • Cost effective, Versatile, Device independent. • Measurable and competitive differentiation. • Massive capacity, Simple to scan. • May be read from a variety of directions. • Can applied on labels or wrappings of product, on flyers, brochures, catalogues, billboards, posters, adverts in newspapers/magazines, transporting tickets, invitations to events, greetings cards, business cards etc. • Resistant to dirty and broken. • QR codes can create customer engagement and help sustain customer relationships. Creating direct sales.	• Requires approval or participation from the user. Thus, developing the basis behind a QR campaign is key to ensure that the attention will be there and people will want to get the best out of QR codes. • QR codes need the user to download an app before they can be scanned. • Broken web link. The possibility of corrupt web link when QR code is scanned.	Interactive Menu at Radisson Edwardian. The Mirage Hotel and Casino,JoJo's Pizzeria, Turkish Airlines QR Flags (advertisement). The City of Long Beach, Washington, City of Grand Rapids, Michigan, Rio de Janeiro and Korea (guiding). The Virginia museum of Fine Arts (act as virtual museum). Fountainebleau Hotel Miami Beach (market their restaurants).
NEAR FIELD COMMUNICATION (NFC)	• Versatility. • Improved Customer Service. • Real Time Updates. • Build brand loyalty and capture data about customers. • Less battery is utilized. • There is no requirement of setting up a connection between two devices in action. • Easy enough for even the nontechnical persons. • Easy Connectivity. • Can use at Mobile Payments, Transit and ticketing, Automated Check-in system, Advertising. • Ability to track visitor movements, connectivity with social networks. Smart posters and destination tagging. Tourist pocket guide and diary. Easier check-in with Foursquare. Gaming Loyalty cards. Ticketing and timetables. • Peer-to peer connection.	• Requires approval or participation from the user. • Lack of information. • Possible security attacks. • Unsuitable for large amount of data transfers. • Operating range is just 20 cm. • Less demand and popularity.	Clarion Hotel Stockholm (to replace hotel room keys). The City of Nice "Cityzi" (pay for their public transport). EpicMix at the Ski Resorts of Vail (offering the user the ability to track physical accomplishments and share the skiing experience within social networks). The Museum of London (Visitors can access additional information at about 90 RFID tags. Besides the various information points, tickets for future exhibitions can be purchased and visitors can automatically "like", "follow" or "check-in" on Facebook, Twitter and Foursquare). Starbucks reward points, or Air Miles.

continued on following page

Table 1. Continued

SMART TECNOLOGIES	ADVANTAGES	CHALLENGES	APPLICATIONS
GEO-TAGGING	• Allow users to share and search for content by location. • By geo-tagging the social posts, brand's content can be found by users. • Brands can also leverage geo-tagging to target a local event demographic. • Provides more contexts to social media followers. Collect data on certain locations.	• Requires approval or participation from the user. • Security problems. • Lack of information.	Geo-tagged data use in analyzing tourist movement and behavior. Geo-tagging data can use to analyze tourist.
GEO-FENCING	• Better Targeting. • Engagement. • ROI. • Efficiency. • Better Data. • Inexpensive and results-driven. • Build brand loyalty and capture data about customers.	• Requires approval or participation from the user. • For producing business intelligence geo-fencing is only effective when customer data from other sources are mobilized in unison. • Geo-fencing is only limited to fixed radius and is good for large areas like a city. Naturally, for more contextual real time business driving notifications it lacks credibility for business specific use.	Automated check-in and check-out. Hoteliers can also segment location-based notifications or offers based on hotel rewards or guest loyalty programs. By setting geo-fences around popular tourist attractions or key points of interest, a hotel or travel app can offer mobile coupons and track offline attribution. Examples: The LandauerWalk app, The Cajun Coast Travel Guide App.
GEO-TARGETING	• Best used to reach users who live or move about in a certain area, for whom you have other data like preferences or demographic info. • Location accuracy is not as important when using geo-targeting, as other preferences refine your segment Ex: Only people (in this town) who are (women), (over 50), who like (healthy stuff). • Better Targeting. • Engagement. • Build brand loyalty and capture data about customers.	• Security problems. • Lack of information.	The Amelia Island Convention & Visitors Bureau (introduced the inaugural Dickens on Centre event, a Victorian-themed Christmas celebration in historic downtown Fernandina Beach. In order to drive awareness and foot traffic to the event ran a geo-targeted destination marketing holiday leisure campaign to reach locations within a 5-hour drive radius of the event.

Source: Thrasher, 2013; Kounavis et al, 2012; Carmigniani et al, 2011; Berryman, 2012; Guttentag, 2010; Demir, Kaynak, Demir, 2015; Burillak, 2011; Kuyucu, 2013; Medic, Pavlovic, 2014; Borrego-Jaraba, 2011; Pesonen and Horster, 2012; Cheong, 1995; Egger, 2013[1]; Coşkun et al., 2013; McCormick, 2017; Ghanchi, 2015; Örnek, 2016.

benefits of smart applications in tourism industry. The results of the study revealed that applications: 1) provide access to location-based information that is relevant to the near surroundings of tourists, 2) make it possible to access the various contents, which are well-timed and updated, (3) have flexibility in delivering texts, videos, or images and 4) provide interactive additional explanations which are integrated with map-based services and additional information, 5) allow advertising and marketing tourism businesses, 6) Build brand loyalty and capture data about customers, 7) personalization and socialization on social media.

Considering the specific nature of tourism-related applications, several insufficiencies were identified. The applications require approval or participation from the user, there is lack of information in the tourism industry and customers, security problems, less demand and popularity.

Tourist travel experience may be improved via applications because they can reach any real time information about a location, what that location offers and what commentary other visitors have made about it. Moreover, the users may view the simulations of events, places and objects in history by delivering them into the scene they are viewing.

Smart technologies provide tourists with personalized content and services, which they are interested in. Applications allow tourists to explore the destinations, cities, museums, and historical places by adding new layers to their reality, thus resulting in a new interactive and highly dynamic experience. Applications allow tourists to share their experiences on social networks. As a result, a tourism business, destination, city or museum could be marketed on social networks via the things tourists share there.

The smart applications are particularly beneficial for museums, heritage sites, cities and tourist professionals because it is possible to organize and transmit information in layers. The information can also be organized according to the users' requests, which suggests that the users' background, interest, age, occupation and other characteristics may be used to organize the information. Thus, tourists can get customized services according to their preferences and expectations, which maximize satisfaction they get from their visit (Kounavis et al, 2012). Applications have proved to be an innovative tool for linking offline and online content, and once used right, may result in sensible and measurable marketing initiatives.

However, in the meanwhile, the findings from this study offer some useful indicators as to the nature of successful marketing campaigns. Practitioners need to (Watson, McCarthy, Rowley, 2013):

1. Develop an understanding of what motivates their customers to just accept mobile marketing communications, as well as what customers perceive as benefits in this context. Optimum strategies can vary between sectors and brands and is likely to be impacted by the organization's potential for engagement in those applications that customers regard as valuable such as ticketing and appointment and travel alerts.
2. Hone their competency in marketing communications approaches that respond to consumers' desire for control over the marketing communications that they receive, and provides customers the confidence to trust them.
3. Develop a report of pull marketing communications approaches, including web site content and applications that customers' value and supply access to those and alternative content through smart technologies.

FUTURE RESEARCH DIRECTIONS

A limitation of this study is literature review of tourism. The results give us a one-time look at a dynamic environment that is rapidly evolving as new applications come into the marketplace. Follow-up surveys can provide a better look at trends and provide opportunities for future research. However, this snapshot provides an important glimpse of emerging smart technology applications. Across the industry, as developers get more and more creative with app experiences, we see different implementations emerge for smart technology applications. Future investigations are divided into the following areas:

- In the future, the vision-tracking component of the AR platform will be optimized so that the overall efficiency of the application is improved. In addition, alternative methods of interacting will be investigated including gestures and voice recognition. Finally, the next step is to implement more applications based on the same 3D engine and port them into both the VR and AR platforms so that a more complete evaluation with more tourists can be performed. Integration of AR technologies in tourism marketing, for example augmented reality advergames for the tourism destinations, augmented reality advertisements for tourism businesses and destinations.

- Integration QR technologies in tourism marketing, for instance QR code treasure hunt games for the tourism destinations, interesting and creative QR code advertisements for tourism businesses and destinations.
- Optimizing the tourist experience. Analyzing and determining the tourist demand about smart applications and devices.
- Optimizing the marketing and mobile commerce qualifications in smart applications.
- Further exploration of the marketing communications approaches that make consumers willing to interact with companies through the smart technologies, including a deeper understanding of the result of such engagement in terms of sales, brand awareness and different marketing objectives (Watson, McCarthy, Rowley, 2013).
- Investigation into the effect of demographic factors, such as age, gender, extent of mobile phone use, income level, and culture, on problems such as trust formation and benefit perception with mobile marketing communication, and identification with mobile phone handsets (Watson, McCarthy, Rowley, 2013).
- Further exploration of the value of smart technologies and different pull technologies each to consumers and organizations, including the factors that drive their adoption and continuing use, retention or conversion rates (Watson, McCarthy, Rowley, 2013).

CONCLUSION

The development of intelligent technologies and the widespread use of smart phones today have revealed innovative marketing strategies and tools in the tourism industry. These smart marketing tools include augmented reality, virtual reality, QR code, NFC, geo-tagging and geo-fencing. With the support of these new technologies, tourists can access internet-based information from anywhere. Businesses can use the information produced by tourists using these technologies for marketing purposes. These technologies provide cheaper advertising to tourism businesses and tourism destinations, and easier access to customers. Benefits of integration the smart technologies into the marketing strategy are cost reduction, efficiency, competitiveness, big data analyzing and innovation, improving customer service, real time updates, build brand loyalty and capture data about customers, ability to track visitor movements, connectivity with social networks, smart posters and destination tagging, allow users to share and search for content by location. By geo-tagging the social posts, brand's content can be found by users. Brands can also leverage geo-tagging to target a local event demographic. QR codes can be applied on labels or wrappings of product, on flyers, brochures, catalogues, billboards, posters, adverts in newspapers/ magazines, transporting tickets, invitations to events, greetings cards, business cards etc. Virtual reality increases one's interest in visiting the real museum, and serve as indirect evidence that visiting tourism destinations serve as a marketing instrument for destinations. Geo-fencing has advantages targeting the customers, engagement, measuring the ROI, build brand loyalty and capture data about customers. Augmented reality provides interactive additional explanations which are integrated with map-based services and additional information, provides access to location-based information that is relevant to the near surroundings of tourists, makes possible to access the various contents, which are well-timed and updated. Geo-targeting is a widely practiced form of online targeting. It obviously has advantages to geo-target for companies whose products or services are available only in regional or local markets.

REFERENCES

Abd Allah, M. M. (2011). Strengths and Weaknesses of Near Field Communication (NFC) Technology. [Version I.]. *Global Journal of Computer Science and Technology*, *11*(3).

Albăstroiu, I., & Felea, M. (2015). *Exploring The Potential of QR Codes in Higher Education Considering the Attitudes and Interests among Romanian Students*. The 11th International Scientific Conference eLearning and Software for Education, Bucharest, Romania.

Azuma, R., Baillot, Y., Behringer, R., Feiner, S., Julier, S., & MacIntyre, B. (2001). Recent advances in augmented reality. *IEEE Computer Graphics and Applications*, *21*(6), 34–47. doi:10.1109/38.963459

Azuma, R. T. (1997). A survey of augmented reality. *Teleoperators and Virtual Environmen*, *6*(4), 355–385. doi:10.1162/pres.1997.6.4.355

Berryman, D. R. (2012). Augmented reality: A review. *Medical Reference Services Quarterly*, *31*(2), 212–218. doi:10.1080/02763869.2012.670604 PMID:22559183

Billinghurst, M. (2002). *Augmented Reality in Education*. Seattle, WA: New Horizons for Learning - Technology in Education.

Borrego-Jaraba, F., Luque Ruiz, I., & Gómez-Nieto, M. Á. (2011). A NFC-based pervasive solution for city touristic surfing. *Personal and Ubiquitous Computing*, *15*(7), 731–742. doi:10.100700779-010-0364-y

Briseno, M. Z., Hirata, F. I., Lopez Juan de, D. S., Garcia, E. J., Cota, C. N., & Hipolito, J. I. N. (2012). Using RFID/NFC and QR-Code in Mobile Phones to Link the Physical and the Digital World. In Interactive Multimedia. InTech.

Brown & Harmon. (2014). Viral Geofencing: An Exploration of Emerging Big-Data Driven Direct Digital Marketing Services. *Proceedings of PICMET '14: Infrastructure and Service Integration.*

Burillák, C. (2011). *Stunning QR codes - the really easy way to earn big cash fast*. Kindle Edition.

Carmigniani, J., Furht, B., Anisetti, M., Ceravolo, P., Damiani, E., & Ivkovic, M. (2011). Augmented reality technologies, systems and applications. *Multimedia Tools and Applications*, *51*(1), 341–477. doi:10.100711042-010-0660-6

Carmon, N. (2018). *5 Ways to Use Location Based Marketing For Your Brand*. Retrieved 05.01.2018. from https://digitalbrandinginstitute.com/5-ways-use-location-based-marketing-brand/

Cata, T., Patel, P. S., & Sakaguchi, T. (2013). QR Code: A New Opportunity for Effective Mobile Marketing, Journal of Mobile Technologies. *Knowledge in Society*.

Chaves-Diéguez, D., Pellitero-Rivero, A., García-Coego, D., González-Castaño, F. J., Rodríguez-Hernández, P. S., Piñeiro-Gómez, Ó., ... Costa-Montenegro, E. (2015). Providing IoT Services in Smart Cities through Dynamic Augmented Reality Markers. *Sensors (Basel), 15*(7), 16083–16104. doi:10.3390150716083 PMID:26151215

Cheong, R. (1995). The virtual threat to travel and tourism. *Tourism Management, 16*(6), 417–422. doi:10.1016/0261-5177(95)00049-T

Coskun, V., Ok, K., & Özdenizci, B. (2012). *Near Field Communication (NFC) from Theory to Practice*. New York, NY: Wiley. doi:10.1002/9781119965794

Coskun, V., Ozdenizci, B., & Ok, K. (2013). A Survey on Near Field Communication (NFC) Technology. *Wireless Personal Communications, 71*(3), 2259–2294. doi:10.100711277-012-0935-5

Coşkun, V., Özdenizci, B., & Ok, K. (2015). The Survey on Near Field Communication. *Sensors (Basel), 15*(6), 13348–13405. doi:10.3390150613348 PMID:26057043

Craig, A. B. (2013). Understanding augmented reality, concepts and applications. Morgan Kaufmann.

Demir, S., Kaynak, R., & Demir, K. A. (2015). Usage Level and Future Intent of Use of Quick Response (QR) Codes for Mobile Marketing among College Students in Turkey. Proceedings Of The 3rd International Conference On Leadership, Technology And Innovation Management. *Procedia: Social and Behavioral Sciences, 181*, 405–413. doi:10.1016/j.sbspro.2015.04.903

Egger, R. (2013a). The impact of near field communication on tourism. *Journal of Hospitality and Tourism Technology, 4*(2), 119–133. doi:10.1108/JHTT-04-2012-0014

Egger, R. (2013b). Near Field Communication in Tourism: A Conceptual Paper, The Gaze. *Journal of Tourism & Hospitality (Los Angeles, Calif.), 5.*

EUROMSG. (2016). *Geofencing ile Geotargeting Arasındaki 5 Fark*. Retrieved 07.06.2017, from http://blog.euromsg.com/geo-fencing-ile-geo-targeting-arasindaki-5-fark/

Ghanchi, J. (2015). *Advantages and Disadvantages of Geofencing Applications*. Retrieved 01.10.2018 from: https://medium.com/@indianappd /advantages-anddisadvantages-of-geofencing-applications-a20e47bd2cc4

Gönül, F. F., Qiu, C., & Zhou, E. (2015). *Whether or Not to Use a Quick Response (QR) Code in the Ad.* Retrieved from http://ssrn. com/abstract=2487939

Gurau, C. (2007). *Virtual Reality Applications in Tourism. Information and Communication Technologies in Support of the Tourism Industry,* 180–197.

Guttentag, D. A. (2010). Virtual reality: Applications and implications for tourism. *Tourism Management, 31*(5), 637–651. doi:10.1016/j.tourman.2009.07.003

Hassen, I. (2015). *Context Aware Tourist Information and Recommendation System using iQR Code* (Unpublished Master Thesis). Addis Ababa University.

Höllerer, T. H., & Feiner, S. K. (2004). Mobile augmented reality. In Telegeoinformatics: Location-Based Computing and Services. Taylor & Francis Books Ltd.

Inversini, A., Eynard, D., Marchiori, E., & Gentile, L. (2012). Destinations Similarity Based on User Generated Pictures. In *Information and Communication Technologies in Tourism 2012*. Wien: Springer-Verlag.

Kounavis, C. D., Kasimati, A. E., & Zamani, E. D. (2012). Enhancing the tourism experience through mobile augmented reality: Challenges and prospects. *International Journal of Engineering Business Management*, 4.

Kuyucu, M. (2013). *The Transformation of Traditional Newspaper to New Global Media with the QR Code*. Athens: ATINER'S Conference Paper Series, No: CBC2013-0894.

Lai, K. Y., Cheng, L. S., Yee, L. S., Leng, L. W., & Ling, T. P. (2015). WeeliciousCuisine Quick Response (QR). *International Conference on E-Commerce (ICoEC).*

Linaza, M., Marimon, D., Carrasco, P., Alvarez, R., Montesa, J., Aguilar, S. R., & Diez, G. (2012). Evaluation of mobile augmented reality applications for tourism destinations. In M. Fuchs, F. Ricci, & L. Cantoni (Eds.), *Information and Communication Technologies in Tourism*. Wien: Springer-Verlag. doi:10.1007/978-3-7091-1142-0_23

Marakos, P. (2015). *Implementing QR code in museums and archaeological sites*. International Workshop on Virtual Archaeology: Museums & Cultural Tourism, Delphi, Greece.

McCormick, K. (2017). *How to Use Social Media for Local Internet Marketing*. Retrieved from: https://thrivehive.com/how-to-use-social-media-for-local-internet-marketing/

Medic, S., & Pavlovic, N. (2014). Mobile Technologies in Museum Exhibitions. *Turizam*, *18*(4), 166–174. doi:10.5937/Turizam1404166M

Örnek, M. (2016). *Geo-Targeting (Coğrafi Hedefleme) Nedir?* Retrieved 07.06.2017, from http://www.pazarlamasyon.com/sozluk/geo-targeting-cografi-hedefleme-nedir/

Pesonen, J., & Horster, E. (2012). Near field communication technology in tourism. *Tourism Management Perspectives*, *4*, 11–18. doi:10.1016/j.tmp.2012.04.001

Rouillard, J. (2008). Contextual QR Codes. In *Proceedings of the Third International Multi-Conference on Computing in the Global Information Technology – ICCGI, 50-55, Conference Publishing Services of IEEE Computer Society*, 51.

Russell, H. (2013). *How augmented-reality ads could change everything*. Retrieved 15.08.2013 from: http://news.cnet.com/8301-1023_3-57591998-93/how-augmented-reality-ads-could-change everything/

Russell, M. (2012). *11 Amazing Augmented Reality Ads*. Retrieved 10.03.2017 from http://www.businessinsider.com/11-amazing-augmented-reality-ads-2012-1?op= 1.

Samy, H. (2012, Winter). Exploring The Use Of Mobile Phone Technology In Marketing Airline Services IN EGYPT. *International Journal of Medical Microbiology*, *7*(3).

Sharma, S., & Sharma, V. (2014). Innovations in marketing- "with special reference to innovative services. *International Journal of Business and Management*, *1*(2), 50–54.

Sing, P. & Pandey, M. (2014). Augmented Reality Advertising: An Impactful Platform for New Age Consumer Engagement. *IOSR Journal of Business and Management, 16*(2), 24-28.

Singh, H., & Singh, S. (2014). Near Field Communication (NFC). *International Journal of Enhanced Research in Science Technology & Engineering, 3*(3), 198-201. Available online at: www.erpublications.com

Strömmer, E., Kaartinen, J., Pärkkä, J., Ylisaukko-oja, A., & Korhonen, I. (2006). Application of Near Field Communication for Health Monitoring in Daily Life. *Proceedings of the 28th IEEE EMBS Annual International Conference.*

Tang, S., Yu, Y., Zimmermann, R., & Obana, S. (2015). Efficient geo-fencing via hybrid hashing: A combination of bucket selection and in-bucket binary search. *ACM Trans. Spatial Algorithms Syst., 1*(2). DOI: 10.1145/2774219

Taylor, B. (2013). *Augmented reality applications – from the consumer to the business*. Retrieved 07.06.2017, from http://www.creativeguerrillamarketing. com/augmented-reality/augmented-reality-applications-from the -consumer-to-the-business/

Thrasher, J. (2013). *9 Examples of RFID & NFC in Marketing*. Retrieved 01.01.2018 from: https://blog.atlasrfidstore.com/examples-of-rfid-nfc-marketing

Wang, Y. (2011). *Destination Marketing and Management: Scope, Definition and Structures, Destination Marketing and Management* (Y. Wang & A. Pizam, Eds.). CAB International.

Watson, C., McCarthy, J., & Rowley, J. (2013). Consumer attitudes towards mobile marketing in the smart phone era. *International Journal of Information Management, 33*(5), 840-849. 10.1016/j.ijinfomgt.2013.06.004

Williams, A. P., & Hobson, J. S. P. (1995). Virtual reality and tourism: Fact or fantasy? *Tourism Management, 16*(6), 423–427. doi:10.1016/0261-5177(95)00050-X

Yuki, A., Xing, X., Takahiro, H., & Shojiro, N. (2010). Mining people's trips from large scale geo-tagged photos. In *Proceedings of the 18th ACM international conference on Multimedia (MM '10)*. ACM. doi: 10.1145/1873951.1873971

Zhang, M., Yao, D., & Zhou, Q. (2012, December). The Application and Design of QR Code in Scenic Spot's eTicketing System-A Case Study of Shenzhen Happy Valley. *International Journal of Science and Technology.*, *2*(12), 817–822.

KEY TERMS AND DEFINITIONS

Interactive Advertising: Uses online or offline interactive media to communicate with consumers and to promote products, brands, services, and public service announcements, corporate, or political groups.

Marketing Communication: Marketing communications is the "promotion" part of the "marketing mix" or the "four Ps": price, place, promotion, and product. It can also refer to the strategy used by a company or individual to reach their target market through various types of communication.

Mobile Commerce: Mobile commerce is a term that describes online sales transactions that use wireless electronic devices such as hand-held computers, mobile phones or laptops. These wireless devices interact with computer networks that have the ability to conduct online merchandise purchases.

Mobile Marketing: Mobile marketing is simply the process of marketing to people via their mobile devices such as smart phone.

Smart Technologies: Smart technologies are kind of devices such as smart phones, tablets. Whether it involves showcasing tourist information, displaying interactive maps, or demonstrating examples of local attractions.

Chapter 6
Real-Time Notifications:
Marketing Applied to the Internet of Things

Nuno Soares
University of Aveiro, Portugal

Mário Vairiinhos
University of Aveiro, Portugal

Pedro Beça
University of Aveiro, Portugal

Tânia Ferreira Ribeiro
University of Aveiro, Portugal

ABSTRACT

Consumers have become better informed, forcing companies to offer products and services that fit their tastes and preferences. The technologies in the context of internet of things (IoT) have been in increasing demand, by allowing the adaptation and customization of products and services contextualized with the location of consumers functioning and operating in real-time context and location of consumers. In this chapter, two relevant real-time content notification systems based on IoT systems are analyzed. It was concluded that, despite all the advantages associated with the use of these notification services, there are some security limitations: large amount of information collected, it is necessary to manage quickly and effectively to deliver relevant content in a timely manner; need for high bandwidth; considerable reduction of the autonomy of the batteries of the smartphones, of the users due to the necessity of activation of the GPS and the Bluetooth.

DOI: 10.4018/978-1-5225-5763-0.ch006

Copyright © 2019, IGI Global. Copying or distributing in print or electronic forms without written permission of IGI Global is prohibited.

INTRODUCTION

Real-time notification systems based on IoT technologies can be applied to the most diverse areas by adding value propositions to their users.

The IoT market suffers from the lack of interaction between existing IoT products, providing an opportunity for the creation of aggregate solutions that bring true value and based on user information. Many Iot products are considered expensive, complex, and it takes several hours for the average consumer to configure the products. Users are also concerned that the products are unsafe and that unauthorized third parties access their privacy and data. These obstacles need to be addressed through the construction of easy, quick-to-configure devices with high safety standards (Hosek et al., 2017).

In Bangladesh, an IoT Notification System was developed to detect and track the occurrence of fires. When the system detects a fire, it takes photographs for confirmation from a system administrator. In case of confirmation, the system will trigger the alarms and send a message to the nearest fire brigade. The development of this type of systems can be advantageous for factories, avoiding the loss of life and destruction of facilities in case of fire (Imteaj, Rahman, Hossain, Alam, & Rahat, 2017).

IoT systems can be applied to commercial establishments to measure the size of queues, notifying staff only when it is critical. Allowing service to be faster and with quality (Viriyavisuthisakul, 2017).

IoT systems can be used to inform your users of interesting events nearby, enabling a higher value offer. These types of systems face major challenges, such as dealing with large data flow (Big Data) and the need to treat data in real time to provide relevant information to users. Another challenge is that users are constantly changing places, the system must update the data so that it remains relevant (Qader, 2017).

IoT notification systems can be used to monitor the state of degradation of sports equipment, notifying companies when they need maintenance, avoiding injuries to users (Sun, Hung, & Huang, 2017).

They can be used to only send notifications in a schedule with a greater probability of opening by the users, increasing the click rate (Gudla & Bose, 2016).

They can be applied to agriculture, in autonomous irrigation systems, to inform those responsible, of problems that are detected through sensors, facilitating the management (Imteaj, Rahman, Hossain, & Zaman, 2017).

They can be applied to security systems to detect intruders and collect evidence through video, and inform the police (Park & Cheong, 2017).

In systems and products development, it is necessary to pay close attention to how users react emotionally with the interfaces. It is indispensable to satisfy users through unique and meaningful experiences.

BACKGROUND

Currently, people use the Internet mainly to search information, send and receive e-mails, access multimedia content (eg music and videos), play online and interact on social networks (Miorandi, Sicari, De Pellegrini, & Chlamtac, 2012).

The concept of internet has been evolving, allowing new forms of interaction. Smart objects are everyday objects with built-in electronic components that extend the capabilities of the Internet and objects themselves (Miorandi et al., 2012). Smart objects produce and consume information from the relationships they establish with other smart objects, with the Internet and with users, thus forming an interconnected, dynamic and distributed network (Miorandi et al., 2012).

The Internet of Things (or IoT) brings a range of opportunities for both users and businesses. The products or services can collect user information and react appropriately and individually, considering user context and preferences (Miorandi et al., 2012).

Due to the great heterogeneity of the IoT devices, an enormous amount of information arises, so that it is necessary to present relevant information to the user in a timely manner, considering their location, tasks, and time of day without losing the context of, and not limited to, recommending based on articles like those already consulted or used by users (Cha et al., 2017).

In the tourism sector, notification systems have been explored to make recommendations, considering the context and location. However, some limitations have been detected, such as the energy consumption of mobile phones and the need for them to be connected to wireless networks with high bandwidth for real-time transmission and reception of data. These systems work through mobile applications that invisibly detect the events produced by users and send information to a returning cloud with appropriate information and content (Cha et al., 2017).

Smart objects are also being used to inject a new life into health care, reshaping the functioning of some systems and leading to better health care (Rogers, 2017). The company Adhere Tech uses objects (in the form of medicinal bottles) with a set of sensors that collect and send data to the company's servers, which makes it possible to compare current patient consumption with its prescribed dose (Rogers, 2017). This IoT system used by Adhere Tech ensures that patients take the medication according to prescribed prescription (Rogers, 2017). However, recent cyberattacks on the national health system in England and Scotland have shown the importance of ensuring the integrity and privacy of patient data (Rogers, 2017).

Customers are becoming more informed and demanding, and with the evolution of the Internet access to information is increasingly facilitated. There is an increase in supply on the part of companies and this allows consumers to reflect on their needs and desires, opting for the option that maximizes their profits and minimizes losses (Muller, Damgaard, Litchfield, Lewis, & Hörnle, 2011). According to Hamish Grierson, CEO of Thriva, data need to have context and enrich the consumer experience; otherwise, it has no meaning (Rogers, 2017). Yet, too much information can cause a sense of confusion in customers (Muller et al., 2011).

Muller et al (2011) report a study by Nielsen (2008), in which consumers make their decisions based on various sources of access to information. About 43% of users search for information on the same website that they buy regularly; 37% on search engines (mostly Google); 32% in personal recommendations; 30% on a special offer they viewed; 28% in general research; 26% in online reviews and recommendations; 26% in the same store they already buy offline; 19% on a price comparison website; 18% of online advertising; 12% in TV ads and newspapers; 9% from other sites (Muller et al., 2011).

IoT

IoT can be classified into three layers: application, perception and network protocol (Zhao and Ge, 2013).

The application layer corresponds to the most visible layer for the end user. It is distributed in several systems, in which one application exchanges information with another application of another system (Oen, and Nolin and Olson, 2015, 2016).

The associated safety issues depend on the environment and industry (Valmohammadi, 2016).

The perception layer focuses on information gathering processes. It is composed of two sections: perception module and network of perception (Tsai et al., 2014).

The data are acquired and controlled in the perception modules while the shipping instructions are handled by the perception network (Jing et al., 2014).

The layers of perception include all kinds of sensors, such as RFID, ZigBee, gateway sensors (Jing et al., 2014).

The network protocol layer is responsible for transmitting the information to the perception layer. It includes mobile devices, cloud computing and the Internet (Pongle and Chavan., 2015).

Big Data

Society is increasingly dependent on information and communication technologies, with a large amount of information circulating between physical and virtual environments (Adams, 2017). The continuous evolution and ease of access to technology has led to ever to be produced more data. On a daily basis, petabytes of information are generated that involve commercial and financial operations, and in the domestic environment it is common for users to have data storage devices with a capacity greater than one terabyte (Costa, Silva, & Murarolli, 2017). The increase of use of smart devices (sensors, actuators, and other smart devices) also increases the information generated, exchanged, and stored (Aujla, Chaudhary, Kumar, Das, & Rodrigues, 2018).

The data in Big Data systems are treated differently in comparison to the traditional systems. The splitting and conjunction of the data is important for data updating and processing because data are dispersed widely. Big Data is a term increasingly used to refer to large amounts of data, stored on one or more servers, connected on a network. However, in Big Data the following characteristics must be considered: volume, variety, and speed. In terms of volume, Big Data is characterized by the capacity of the data to reach high volumes of information; these data can be structured, semi-structured and unstructured, which corresponds to the variety; and finally, the speed of transmission of the data must be taken into account (Aujla et al., 2018).

Big Data has emerged to help organizations deal with this high volume of information; however, numerous data protection issues have emerged (Adams, 2017). The current data security technologies are slow when applied to huge amounts of data (Toshniwal, Dastidar, & Nath, 2015). In Big Data, where the amounts of data extend to a Gigabytes or even Petabytes, the encrypting of such large amounts of data is a significant bottleneck. This reality is not compatible with the real-time nature of Big Data (Toshniwal, Dastidar, & Nath, 2015). So, the consumers should be informed of the information gathered on the various devices and platforms and understand the risks and implications in case of information leakage (Adams, 2017). They must control who accesses their data and know the reasons for such access (Adams, 2017). Computer attacks have resulted in leaks of confidential information from users being made public (Adams, 2017).

RELATED WORK

To understand what is been doing in the field a research was made where was chosen two real-time notification systems described in the fooled section. The system A, proposed by Cha et colleges (2017), is a real-time recommender system for tourism proposes, and the System B is a IoT system architecture that sends notifications according to the priority of the message based in the user preferences.

System A

Cha et colleges (2017) propose an IoT Platform for a real-time recommender system that enables streaming data collection from smartphones to recommend new items on the fly, using geofencing as user context. Geofencing can be described as a virtual circle defined by a center point and a radius. This can be generated without an IoT device (by using the Google Location API for defining a-priori coordinates of a point of interest and its radius) or using an IoT device (by using the physical position of the IoT device and their signal range as the radius) (Cha et al., 2017).

This system here described uses both approaches: when a user is carrying a smartphone with a GPS sensor, the system detects whenever its current geographical coordinates are located within the geofence boundaries. The other approach, using an IoT device, is applied in the context of POI, in this case, located indoors. In this approach, the Bluetooth technology available in a user smartphone can be used to detect the signal of IoT devices such as beacons, allowing the system to know whether or not the user current location is within the geofence boundaries.

The system architecture consists in three parts: a mobile application, developed for the Android operating system, a notification server, and a system of recommendations. It supports four user events: 1) when it enters the geofence with IoT devices; 2) Exit geofence with IoT devices; 3) Go into geofence without IoT devices; 4) quits geofence without IoT devices. Each of these events is associated with a set of tasks that the notification server performs: getting recommendations and notifications from the notification server via http and sending the input/output data of users with and without IoT devices to the cloud. There are two additional tasks: one that is performed invisibly to get data from GPS sensors on the smartphone and sending that data to the cloud and another one that creates the interface for the mobile application to show the received notifications (Cha et al., 2017).

In the mobile application, ten components were used: one related to the location data; three related to geofence with the beacons; two geo-related without IoT devices and two to address the recommendations.

The GPS data collection is performed every ten seconds and the collected data is sent to the cloud (Cha et al., 2017).

A beacon signal monitor monitors the geofences generated by various beacons. Each geofence creates one region per beacon (Cha et al., 2017).

The notification server consists of five elements: the receiver of notifications receives initial recommendations from the recommendations system; text notifications are pre-defined for each recommendation and POI; the notification modifier modifies the recommendations; the notification store saves the changes in the database.

Over time and with the collected data it is possible to provide personalized recommendations to the users in real time based in what the user visited, and the time spent in each POI (Cha et al., 2017).

Table 1. Summary of the System A characteristics.

System	Aim	User connected device	User location detection	Hardware transmitter	Technology
A (Cha et al., 2017)	Tourism	Smartphone	Outdoor - Google Maps Api Indoor - Beacon	Outdoor - None Indoor – Beacon	Outdoor – GPS Indoor - Bluetooth

System B

The second system analyzed is a system architecture proposed by Liu and colleges (2016), which is a real-time notification system that send notifications according its priority. In this work is proposed a general system architecture that, according to the authors, can be applied to different contexts with different aims and in a vast scope of information exchanges (Liu, Cheng, Zhai, & Chen, 2016).

The architecture of the system is composed of several elements: information producers; mobile customers; virtual client status module; push queue; complex event processing engine; publish/subscribe (Liu et al., 2016).

The information producers are composed of a set of sensors (like temperature or moisture sensors) that collect information and send the data to the server (Liu et al., 2016). In the server, the messages are evaluated according to the type of message (Liu et al., 2016).

Mobile clients are the terminals where information can be viewed by users and administrators (Liu et al., 2016). Each mobile customer can subscribe to the topics they are most interested in (by priority). When relevant information arrives the user is informed (Liu et al., 2016).

The virtual client status module listens for the client connection to the server, responding in case of connection with the creation or updating of the data corresponding to the virtual client (Liu et al., 2016). In the message transmission process, this module can pack the messages and place them in the push queue (Liu et al., 2016).

In the push queue they developed a protocol that filters content according to degree of importance (Liu et al., 2016).

The publish/subscribe system is responsible for recording the relevant topics for each client, sending only content about the subscribed topics (Liu et al., 2016).

NEW SYSTEM PROPOSAL

In the previous section, two systems were analyzed. The system A proposes a flow in which the alert events, composed by notifications and recommendations, are shaped according to the data collected from the user. In this study, the hardware technologies used in the system were described. The system B proposes an architecture in the server side for managing and queueing notification alerts according to the user preferences and priorities, without specifying hardware technologies or user contexts.

Both systems can complement each other.

To better understand the two systems, to propose an IoT real-time notification system applied to a Marketing context, some characteristics were drawn and systematized in the table n. If a system includes a specific characteristic, an X is marked to indicate this correspondence.

In the table, the a) refers to the two analyzed systems; b), User Locations, allude to if the system monitored the location of the user; c) User preference column refers if the system knows a priory the user needs or preferences; d) User priorities, refers if the system knows the order of the interests of the user, and the last column, e) Use context, refers to the situation of the user, tasks at hand.

Table 2. Summary of the analyzed systems characteristics.

a) Systems	b) User Localization	c) User preferences	d) User priorities	e) Use context
A	X			
B		X	X	X

CONCLUSION

With increased competition, the growth of the Internet and globalization, consumers have become more demanding and well informed, forcing companies to offer products and services tailored to their preferences and expectations.

It is increasingly important to offer unique and personalized user experiences. IoT in-context technologies have been increasingly in demand, allowing real-time matching of products and services to the context and location of consumers.

As the IoT devices/services receive and transmit information about the users to the company servers, it is possible to obtain more data about the uses and the time spent in each use, thus allowing, over time, an ever-better experience.

Some companies already notify their users in real-time about new features of the company, which fit the context of their usual use and their tastes and preferences. These notifications consider the degree of importance of each area or topic, filtering the content that is most relevant to each user.

It is important to ensure the confidentiality of the data and the access of the private information of the users to whom it is duly authorized. Users should always have access to the available information about them, which people and organizations can access to that data and what the reasons, giving them the possibility of denying access to those who do not want to share. They should be informed about the risks that may arise from a breach of security.

Companies need to implement system architectures that enable them to manage in a useful way the enormous amount of information gathered so that it is possible to make that information relevant and timely.

The systems currently used require high bandwidth and high energy consumption of smartphones, and it is interesting to explore new solutions to combat these limitations.

Through a technological point of view one of the main challenges when developing an IoT platform for a real-time recommender system is choosing the cloud architecture that would allow scalability and fast processing of massive data sets according to a user context such as a user current location in relation to other users, where users are heading to, staying at and leaving from a geofence boundary as well as the means of transportation, weather conditions, and time of the day (Cha et al., 2017).

REFERENCES

Adams, M. (2017). Big Data and Individual Privacy in the Age of the Internet of Things. *Technology Innovation Management Review*, *7*(4), 12–24.

Aujla, G. S., Chaudhary, R., Kumar, N., Das, A. K., & Rodrigues, J. J. P. C. (2018). SecSVA: Secure Storage, Verification, and Auditing of Big Data in the Cloud Environment. *IEEE Communications Magazine*, *56*(1), 78–85. doi:10.1109/MCOM.2018.1700379

Cha, S., Ruiz, M. P., Wachowicz, M., Tran, L. H., Cao, H., & Maduako, I. (2017). The role of an IoT platform in the design of real-time recommender systems. *2016 IEEE 3rd World Forum on Internet of Things*, 448–453. 10.1109/WF-IoT.2016.7845469

Costa, J., Silva, A., & Murarolli, P. (2017). *Application of the big data in the health, sports, livestock and mineral areas*. Academic Press.

Gudla, S. K., & Bose, J. (2016). Intelligent web push architecture with push flow control and push continuity. *Proceedings - 2016 IEEE International Conference on Web Services, ICWS 2016, 658–661.* 10.1109/ICWS.2016.90

Hosek, J., Masek, P., Andreev, S., Galinina, O., Ometov, A., Kropfl, F., ... Koucheryavy, Y. (2017). A SyMPHOnY of Integrated IoT Businesses: Closing the Gap between Availability and Adoption. *IEEE Communications Magazine*, *55*(12), 156–164. doi:10.1109/MCOM.2017.1700028

Imteaj, A., Rahman, T., Hossain, M. K., Alam, M. S., & Rahat, S. A. (2017). An IoT based Fire Alarming and Authentication System for Workhouse using Raspberry Pi 3. *ECCE 2017 - International Conference on Electrical, Computer and Communication Engineering*, 899–904. 10.1109/ECACE.2017.7913031

Imteaj, A., Rahman, T., Hossain, M. K., & Zaman, S. (2017). IoT based autonomous percipient irrigation system using raspberry Pi. *19th International Conference on Computer and Information Technology*, 563–568. 10.1109/ICCITECHN.2016.7860260

Liu, X., Cheng, B., Zhai, Z., & Chen, J. (2016). Design and implement of push notification server in mobile IoT environment. *Proceedings - 2016 IEEE International Conference on Mobile Services, MS 2016*, 208–209. 10.1109/MobServ.2016.40

Miorandi, D., Sicari, S., De Pellegrini, F., & Chlamtac, I. (2012). Internet of things: Vision, applications and research challenges. *Ad Hoc Networks*, *10*(7), 1497–1516. doi:10.1016/j.adhoc.2012.02.016

Muller, P., Damgaard, M., Litchfield, A., Lewis, M., & Hörnle, J. (2011). Consumer behaviour in a digital environment. Brussels: Academic Press.

Oen, H. M. (2015). *Interoperability at the Application Layer in the Internet of Things*. Academic Press.

Park, W. H., & Cheong, Y. G. (2017). IoT smart bell notification system: Design and implementation. *19th International Conference on Advanced Communication Technology*, 298–300. 10.23919/ICACT.2017.7890101

Pongle, P., & Chavan, G. (2015). A survey: attacks on RPL and 6LoWPAN in IoT. *2015 International Conference on Pervasive Computing: advance Communication Technology and Application for Society*. 10.1109/PERVASIVE.2015.7087034

Qader, M. A. (2017). *DualDB: An Efficient LSM-based Publish/Subscribe Storage System*. SSDBM '17, Chicago, IL.

Rogers, C. (2017). How smart tech is injecting new life into healthcare. *Marketing Week*, *57*(1), 4. doi:10.1525/cmr.2014.57.1.67

Sun, W., Hung, J., & Huang, C. (2017). Implementation of SVM Broken Prediction Notification System with Park Sport Equipment. *2017 International Conference on Applied System Innovation*, 99–102. 10.1109/ICASI.2017.7988356

Toshniwal, R., Dastidar, K. G., & Nath, A. (2015). Big data security issues and challenges. *International Journal of Innovative Research in Advanced Engineering*, *2*(2).

Tsai, C.-W., Lai, C.-F., & Vasilakos, A. V. (2014). Future internet of things: Open issues and challenges. *Wireless Networks*, *20*(8), 2201–2217. doi:10.100711276-014-0731-0

Valmohammadi, C. (2016). Examining the perception of Iranian organizations on Internet of Things solutions and applications. *Industrial and Commercial Training*, *48*(2), 104–108. doi:10.1108/ICT-07-2015-0045

Viriyavisuthisakul, S. (2017). Automatic Queue Monitoring in Store Using A Low-Cost IoT Sensing Platform.2017. *IEEE International Conference on Consumer Electronics - Taiwan*, 53–54.

Zhao, K., & Ge, L. (2013). A survey on the Internet of Things security. *Proceedings of the 9th International Conference on Computational Intelligence and Security*, 663–667. 10.1109/CIS.2013.145

KEY TERMS AND DEFINITIONS

Beacon: Little piece of hardware that uses radio signals to alert of its presence.

Big Data: Extremely large data sets that may be analyzed to reveal patterns, trends, and associations, especially relating to human behavior and interactions.

Cyberattacks: Illegal exploitation of computer systems for gathering information's, damage or disrupt.

Geofence: A virtual geographic boundary that enables software to trigger a response to a mobile device when it enters or leaves an area.

Internet of Things: The interconnection of computing devices embedded in everyday objects, enabling them to send and receive data via the Internet.

Notification System: Combination of hardware and software that provides a way of delivering messages to a set of recipients.

Smart Object: Combination of sensors embedded on everyday objects to make them response to their environment.

Chapter 7
Data-Driven Mall Advertising

Jiaxing Shen
Hong Kong Polytechnic University, Hong Kong

Yi Lau
Hong Kong Polytechnic University, Hong Kong

Jiannong Cao
Hong Kong Polytechnic University, Hong Kong

ABSTRACT

Mall advertising is a critical factor for retailers to gain revenue. Traditional mall advertising strategies mainly rely on impression and empiricism which might be inefficient and result in a waste of resources. Recent research demonstrates that the effectiveness of advertisements can be affected by exposure time and relevance to customers. Authors in this chapter propose a data-driven approach to achieve these goals using fine-grained trajectories of customers. They first preprocess the trajectories and model the floorplan. Then detect stopping locations where customers stay for relatively long time and analyze the correlation between different locations. They also detect customers' facing directions at each stopping location. Lastly, according to the correlation of stopping locations and customers' facing direction, appropriate advertising locations and contents can be determined. According to evaluation analysis, the proposed approach can significant improve average advertisement exposure time and advertisement relevance by 75% and 58%, respectively.

INTRODUCTION

Nowadays, shopping malls not only contain various shops but also provide important services like entertainment, which makes them indispensable in modern lives. According to the survey (Zhao & Shibasaki, 2005), shopping malls have become the third most frequent location for Americans, after home and work. 75% of all Americans visit a mall at least once a month. On average, shoppers spend $105.11 per visit and average $3,910 in annual expenditure at a mall. One significant contributing factor of such a high expenditure is inspiring and irresistible mall advertisements (ads).

DOI: 10.4018/978-1-5225-5763-0.ch007

Copyright © 2019, IGI Global. Copying or distributing in print or electronic forms without written permission of IGI Global is prohibited.

Mall Advertising (MA) refers to advertising that reaches consumers while they are inside malls. Kiosks or mallscapes are one of primary forms of MA, which are ad panels located in high traffic areas like entrances, escalators. Kiosks can utilize back-lighting to enhance visibility and awareness, which turns it into a perfect medium for mall advertisers.

Traditional MA focuses on high traffic areas like entrances, but people need to keep moving fast otherwise there would be a congestion. Under this situation, high traffic areas do not necessarily equal to long exposure time which is reported by recent research (Goldstein, McAfee, & Suri, 2011) that is beneficial for ad recognition and recall. This interesting finding can also be used to derive more effective and reasonable advertising pricing scheme. Current MA pricing scheme is mostly determined by impression and empiricism (Goldstein et al., 2011). Since it was difficult for advertisers to evaluate the effectiveness of ads. Besides ad exposure time, there are many other factors affecting the effectiveness of MA. Apparently, quality of ads is among the most important factors. Apart from this, Batra and Stayman (Batra & Stayman, 1990). demonstrate the facilitating effect of positive mood on brand attitudes of printing advertising. In addition, consumers' interests are also indicated very important for advertising (Brown 1947). Mehta and Abhilasha (Mitchell, 2013) point out consumers' general attitudes towards advertising can also affect the advertising performance.

To facilitate effective MA in a comprehensive way, all aforementioned factors should be taken into consideration, but some subjective and mental factors are difficult to measure directly on a scale, like ads' quality and consumers' mood. On the other hand, some factors like exposure time and consumers' interest can be measured using data-driven approaches. In this chapter authors will elaborate on the possibility of using existing techniques to achieve effective MA considering ad exposure time and customers' interest based on consumers' fine-grained trajectories. One of the enabling techniques of data-driven mall advertising is passive indoor tracking, which has been an active research area for decades. Different tracking systems, including vision based tracking system (Goldstein et al, 2011), laser range scanner based tracking system (Zhao & Shibasaki, 2005), and wireless based tracking system (Menard & Bryan, 2002), have their distinct pros and cons and suit various application scenarios.

Based on consumers' trajectories, their shopping behaviors can be inferred to measure ad exposure time and ad relevance through data analytics.

The formal formulation of the problem is as follows. Given fine-grained consumers' trajectories (including velocity and facing angles) and floor plan of the shopping mall. The objectives to be obtained includes:

- Find the best locations to place ads in terms of exposure time.
- Specify the most suitable ad content to be placed in an ad location.
- Evaluate ad performance in suggested ad locations.
- Mine potential rules from massive trajectories that can be further utilized in MA.

Authors apply data mining algorithms, including clustering and sequential pattern mining to process trajectory data, detect consumers' frequent stopping locations, conduct correlation analysis among different stopping locations, and find the general facing direction of every stopping location. Authors use an open data set collected in ATC shopping mall in Oscar Japan (Brscic, Kanda, Ikeda, & Miyashita,

2013) using fine-grained 3D range sensors to evaluate the performance of our proposed system. There are around 130,000 consumers within 43 weekdays and around 196,000 people within 40 weekends. Preliminary results show that the proposed system can increase ad exposure time by 75% on average and 11 time at most, increase ad relevance by 58%.

BACKGROUND

Shopping mall advertising is an advertising method that places ads or conducts promotion in shopping malls. However, current ads in shopping malls might suffer from short exposure time and low relevance to customers. The advertising strategy of conventional shopping mall advertising is to focus on high traffic locations like entrances and escalators. However, most of the customers in high traffic locations are moving fast so that the exposure time of the ads is short. Besides, traditional advertising systems lack of sufficient data to study movement patterns or customers' behaviors. It is difficult to decide the appropriate content of ads according to customers' interests or behaviors. Therefore, the advertisement relevance to customer is low. Researchers (Mitchell, 2013) have found that exposure time and relevance both are important factors influencing ads performance. "Ads recognition and recall increase as exposure time increase with the steepest effect happening for low values of exposure time" (Goldstein et al., 2011). Also, customer's interest has strong implication of advertising effectiveness (Mitchell, 2013). Therefore, ads in shopping malls using traditional ad system are missing these important factors.

There are two works closely related to the proposed system of this project. The details and comparison of the related works will be discussed in this section. The first related work is the Crowd Smart Sense ("Crowd WiFi", 2017). This is a solution system that can be deployed to analyze the customer behavior inside retail stores using Wi-Fi data and the Wi-Fi data is collected automatically with devices that previously connected to Wi-Fi. The characteristic of customer is analyzed and then provided for supporting retail store layout and revenue (e.g. How products should be displayed) related decision. The second related work is the DILAX ("DILAX", 2017). This is also a product system for analyzing the people flow of public place or retail stores using 3D sensors and cameras to collect data by tracking people. The characteristic of people flow is analyzed and then provided for supporting operation (e.g. How to arrange human resources) related decision. The related works are different from this project. Table 1 compares our project with crowed smart sense and DILAX. The focus of this project is looking for locations to place suitable types of ads while the focuses of the related works are looking for daily operation and retail decision support.

Table 1. Comparison of related works

	The Proposed System	Crowed Smart Sense	DILAX
Focus	Ads location of shopping mall	Layout and revenue related decision support for retail stores	Operation related decision support for retail stores and public area
Expected Results	Suggested locations for placing ads	• Charts • Statistical data	• Charts • Statistical data

System Overview

In this chapter, details of the proposed system are introduced. As shown in Figure 1, the system has several components which are grouped into 3 different layers including Data Preprocessing Layer, Data Analytics Layer, and Advertisement Deployment Layer. The Data Preprocessing Layer includes the trajectory preprocessing and floor plan modeling components. The purpose of this layer is to prepare and preprocess necessary material for the next layer. The Data Analytics Layer includes the stopping location detection, correlation mining and facing direction detection components. The purpose of this layer is to analyze the prepared data (i.e. human behavior in the shopping mall) to provide information for the next layer. The Advertisement Deployment Layer includes the advertising location and content determination components. The purpose of this layer is to use the analysis result from the previous layers to suggest ads locations and content.

For data preprocessing, raw data are used as the input of the trajectory preprocessing component and the output is the preprocessed data. Then, the shopping mall layout is used as the input of the floor plan modeling component and the output is the coordinate system. For data analytics, the coordinate system and the preprocessed data generated from the data preprocessing layer will be used as the input of the stopping location detection component. Then, the stopping locations are found and be used together with the preprocessed data as the input of the correlation mining component. The output, places customers usually visit after staying at stopping locations, is then generated. After that, the stopping locations and preprocessed data are used as the input of the facing direction detection component and the output is the facing direction of stopping locations. For the advertisement deployment, the stopping locations, facing directions of stopping locations and places customers usually visit after staying at stopping locations are used as the input of the display result component. The output is the ads location and content. The details of the design of the components will be discussed in the following section.

System Implementation

This section introduces the detailed design information, including the techniques, tools and methods used. Also, parameters are set to control different conditions. An overview of all parameters are shown in Table 2.

Figure 1. An overview and data flow of the proposed data-driven system

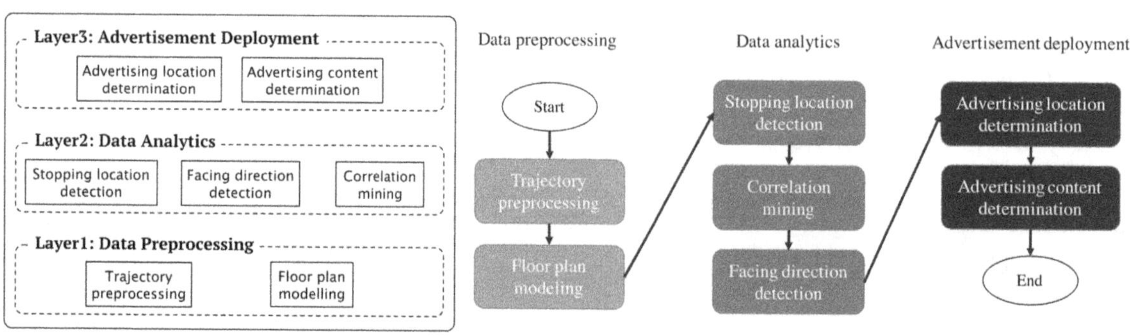

Table 2. Parameter list

Parameter Name	Function	Parameter Name	Function
FU (Floor Unit)	Define the unit of the coordinate system	ST (Stay Time)	Stopping duration threshold to define stopping locations
SV (Stopping Velocity)	Suggested locations for placing ads	AD (Appeared Days)	Appeared days threshold to filter unreliable stopping locations
CD (Cluster Distance)	Distance threshold to form a cluster for defining the size of a stopping location	CS (Cluster Size)	The least number of location points to form a cluster for filtering unreliable stopping locations
MS (Minimum Support)	The minimum support for sequential rule mining	MC (Minimum Confidence)	The minimum confidence for sequential rule mining

Data Preprocessing

The purpose of this layer is to prepare and preprocess necessary material for the analysis of the next layer. There are 2 components in this layer which are the trajectory preprocessing and floor plan modeling. In the trajectory preprocessing component, the required data or information is extracted from the raw dataset. Also, time unit is converted to 1 second and floor unit of the coordinate system is converted to FU (Floor Unit). In the floor plan modeling component, Points of Interest (POIs) are defined to construct a coordination system. For example, shop entrances and benches are defined as POIs and inserted into the coordinate system. An example modelled floor plan is shown in Figure 2.

Figure 2. An example of modelled floor plan

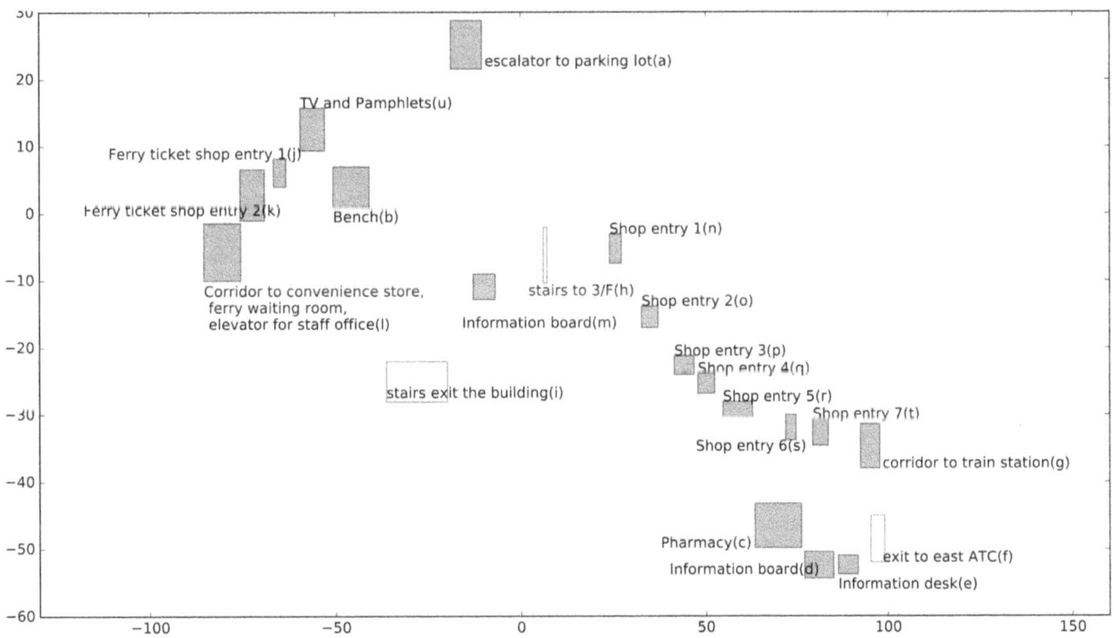

Data Analytics

The purpose of this layer is to detect stopping locations, mine correlation and detect facing direction to provide information for the next layer. There are 3 components in this layer which are stopping location detection, customers' routes analysis and facing direction detection components. In the stopping location detection component, the first step is to extract stopping locations of every day. For each day's data, extracts positions with velocity (of the customers at that moment) < SV (Stopping Velocity) and the duration of staying at that location > ST (Stay Time). For example, in Figure 3, the blue dots are considered as stopping locations and being extracted. The second step is to intersect stopping locations. Using the result from the previous step, intersect the stopping locations and count the number of days that each stopping location appeared. By this step, it would be clear which stopping locations are more reliable (i.e. people stops at these locations over different period of time).

The third step is to filter out unreliable stopping locations. Using the result from the previous step, extract stopping locations with appeared days >= AD (Appeared Days). Therefore, only the blue dots with appear days 2 is extracted. By this step, the result ads location will be more reliable. The forth step is to apply clustering on the stopping locations. Apply clustering on the intersected stopping locations result from the previous steps and decided the distance between each point (CD, Cluster Distance) and the least number of points (CS, Cluster Size) to form a cluster. DBSCAN algorithm will be used as it is good at analyzing density and handling spatial data. By doing clustering, stopping locations that are near can be grouped together for the analysis later.

The last step of this component is to calculate average stay time and number of customers. For each cluster, calculate the average stay time of all customers and count the number of their stay. By doing this step, comprehensive information of the stopping locations can be provided.

In the correlation mining component, the first step is to convert customers' routes to sequence of places. For each stopping location cluster, extract the customers' routes after staying at this stopping location clusters and convert the routes to sequence of places. By doing this step, where each customer went after staying at each stopping location is revealed. The second step is to apply sequential rule mining on sequences of places from the previous step. For each cluster, apply sequential rule mining on sequences of places and decide the minimum support (MS) and minimum confidence (MC). By doing this step, where customers usually visit after staying at each stopping location is known.

Figure 3. An illustration of extracting stopping locations

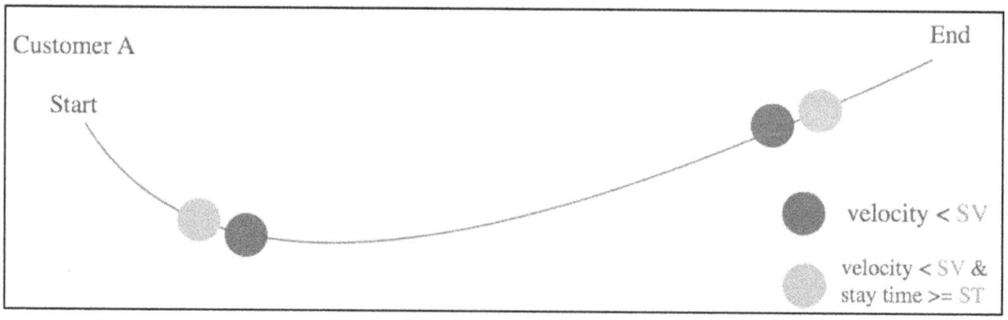

In the facing direction detection component, the first step is to group facing angles into 6 facing directions. For each cluster, group the facing angles of all customers by 6 facing direction with 60 degrees for each direction starting from 0 degree. By doing this steps, discrete facing angles became facing directions and the number of people faced to each direction cloud be known.

The second step is to extract the most faced direction and make adjustment. The first thing to do is to extract the facing direction with highest frequency of facing angles. However, only extracting the most faced direction with the highest frequency is not accurate enough since one facing direction is 60 degrees wide and the most frequent facing angles may be distributed in the first or the last 10 degrees (i.e. people are actually facing at the edge of the extracted facing direction but not the center). Therefore, adjustment is needed to make sure the actual facing angle is the center of the extracted facing direction. The extracted facing direction is divided into 3 sub sections. If the middle sub section has the highest frequency of facing angles, the result will be the center of the original extracted facing direction. However, if the side sub sections have the highest frequency, the nearest facing direction with the highest frequency of facing angle will be extracted. Then, the middle of the newly extracted facing direction and the originally extracted facing direction will be the result.

Advertisement Deployment

The purpose of this layer is to generate the result ads locations and content based on the information from the previous layers. There are 2 components in this layer which are the advertising location determination and advertising content determination components.

These components will display the stopping locations results with the average stay time, number of people, most faced direction and places that customer usually travel after staying at this stopping location. The information of stopping location and most faced direction is used to decide the location to place advertisement. The information of places that most customer travelled after staying at this stopping location is used to decide the content of the advertisement. Then, based on these results, location with high exposure time and content with high relevance to customers can be found. For example, in Table 3, cluster 1 has an average stay time of 20 seconds and 774 customers has stayed at this clusters. Customers usually face to bottom-left direction in the Figure 4 and the places that customers usually travel after staying at this cluster are Shop entrance 1 and bench. Then, the ads location can be placed at the bottom-left direction of the cluster and the content of the ads may be some products of shop 1.

EVALUATION AND ANALYSIS

In this section, the dataset and the parameter tuning results will be discussed. The dataset is separated to weekdays and weekends for analysis. There are 43 days of weekdays and 40 Days of weekends. Some

Table 3. An example of display results

Cluster No	Function
0	Train station, Shop entrance 1
1	Shop entrance 1, Bench

Figure 4. An example of display result

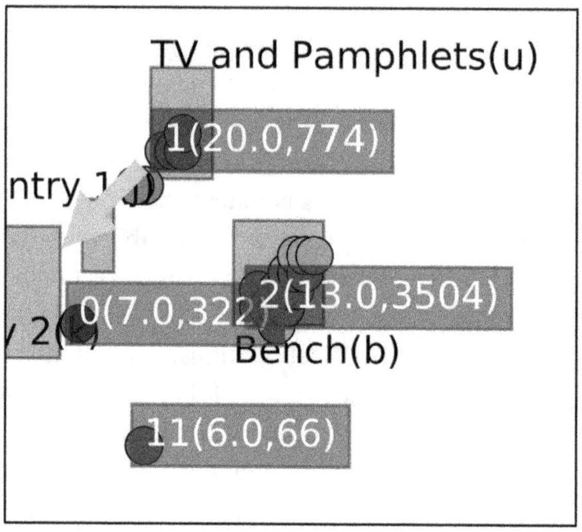

data with tracking problem are not included in the analysis. There are ~130000 people in the 43 weekdays and ~196000 people in 40 weekends.

Dataset

A real-life dataset collected from a shopping mall in Japan (the ATC shopping mall) (Brscic et al., 2013) is used to evaluate the proposed system. The data is collected using fine-grained 3D range sensors. An overview of the dataset is as follows.

- The dataset is collected from Oct 2012 to Nov 2013 on every Wednesday and Fri from 9:40am to 8:20pm
- There are 92 days' data in total
- Data fields include times, person ID, positions, height, velocity, facing angles
- The floor plan of the ATC shopping mall (refer to Figure 5)

Parameter Selection

Before showing the final result, different parameters as shown in Table 2 are discussed. The parameter setting of weekends dataset will be discussed first. As the number of people in weekends is much more than that of weekdays. Weekend data is used to test the parameters first. Then the parameter setting is applied to weekday data and adjust accordingly.

At the beginning, the FU and ST was set to a very low value to see the impact of these parameter. The detail parameter setting was:

- FU (Floor Unit) = 1 decimeter
- SV (Stopping Velocity) = 200 mm/s*

- ST (Stay Time) = 1 second
- AD (Appeared Days) = 30 days
- CD (Cluster Distance) = 8 units
- CS (Cluster Size) = 10 units

As shown in Figure 6, the floor unit was unnecessarily small so that there was a large amount of positions. The analysis became inefficient since many duplicated or unnecessary works are done. For example, when converting customers' routes to POI sequences, it took a very long time to process the massive amount of positions of each customers' routes. The efficiency can be greatly enhanced by increasing the FU. Besides, since the ST is directly related to exposure time of ads, it is not suitable to set the ST too low. Therefore, ST should also be increased. Therefore, FU was increased to 0.5 meter and ST was increased to 4 seconds while keeping other parameter the same. However, the result shows that the stopping location is insufficient for further analysis. Therefore, AD was decreased to 22 days, CD is decreased to 3 units and CS is decreased to 1 unit. The result seems fine for further analysis at that moment. However, as higher ST and AD can filter out unreliable stopping locations, authors tried to increase these two parameter again. When ST increased to 5 seconds, the number of clusters was decreased from 12 to 5. As the number of clusters are too small, ST was set back to 4 seconds. When AD increased to 23 days, there are no big differences of the average stay time and number of customers of each cluster. However, 1 cluster is being filtered out which the the cluster near information board (d). As it may be important for the further analysis later, AD with 22 days is preferred. When AD increased to 24 days, the number of clusters decreased from 12 to 7 compared to the result when AD is set to 22 days. However, the average stays time and number of customers of each cluster did not change too much. Therefore, for further analysis purpose, AD with 22 days is preferred.

Figure 5. Floor plan of the ATC shopping mall

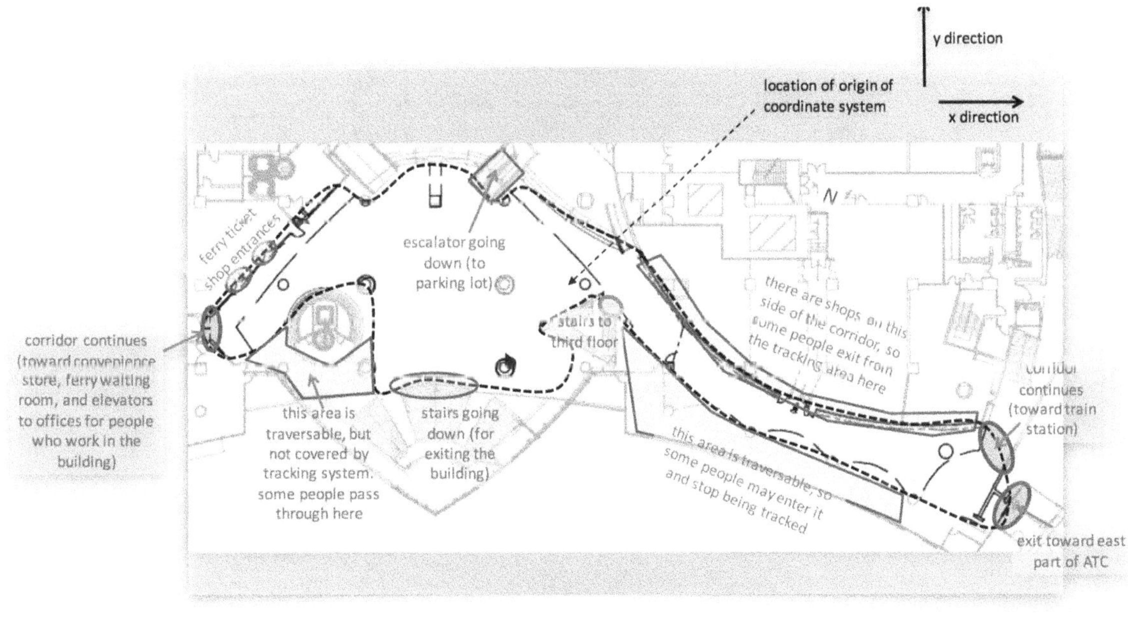

Therefore, after several times of trials, the final parameter setting of weekend result is:

- FU (Floor Unit) = 0.5 meter
- SV (Stopping Velocity) = 200mm/s
- ST (Stay Time) = 4 second
- AD (Appeared Days) = 22 days
- CD (Cluster Distance) = 3 units
- CS (Cluster Size) = 1 units Then, the weekend parameter setting is applied to the weekday data and the result shown that the number of clusters are too small.

Therefore, AD was decreased to 15 days to increase the number of clusters. However, there are too many clusters that have few number of customers (e.g. cluster 0, 3, 7, 9). Therefore, CS is increased to filter out those locations. When CS increased from 1 unit to 2 units, the clusters with few number of customers were filtered out.

The final parameter setting of weekday result is:

- FU (Floor Unit) = 0.5 meter
- SV (Stopping Velocity) = 200mm/s
- ST (Stay Time) = 4 second
- AD (Appeared Days) = 15 days
- CD (Cluster Distance) = 3 units
- CS (Cluster Size) = 2 units

Figure 6. Weekend result of FU = 1 decimeter, ST = 1 second

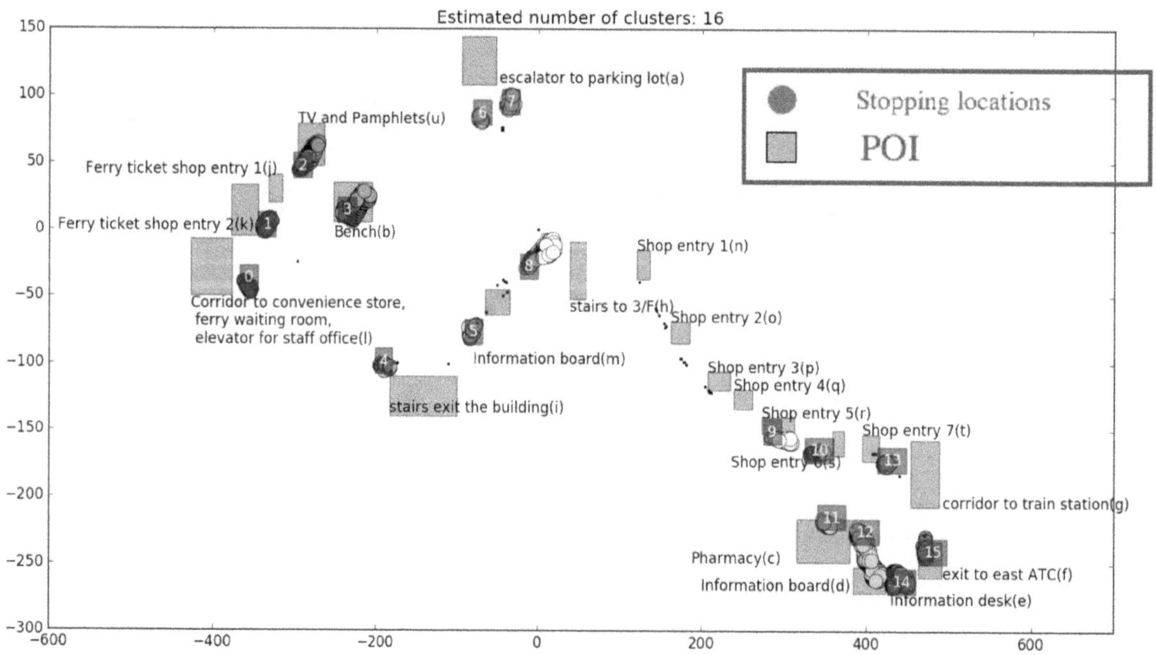

Evaluation

Since the problem of this project is "How to increase ads performance in terms of exposure time and relevance", the ads exposure time and relevance of the suggested ads location and content generated by the proposed system will be evaluated. The weekend and weekday results can be used to support decision making of where to place ads (i.e. ads location) and what ads to be placed (i.e. ads content) in the shopping mall.

When considering ads location, the most ideal case is putting ads at where the facing direction of the stopping locations pointing to. Consider stopping location 3 of weekend result as an example, there should be an ad placed at the left-top direction of stopping location 3. When considering the distance between the ads and the stopping locations, the distance should be as short as possible and not longer than 6 meters.

When considering ads content, the content of the ads should be including information related to where customers will go after staying at the current location. Taking stopping location 3 of the weekend result as an example, the places customers usually visit after staying at this location are bench, east ATC and pharmacy. However, promoting a bench may be meaningless in this case. Therefore, the ads content placed near cluster 3 should be included information related to east ATC and pharmacy (e.g. the restaurants at east ATC and discount product of pharmacy).

To evaluate the exposure time is to compare the ads exposure time of the suggested ads locations and the existing ads in the ATC shopping mall throughout the 43 weekdays and 40 weekends data of the dataset. When calculating the ads exposure time, the ads is considered as exposing to a customer when the customer is near the ads (i.e. in the front area of the ads). The ads exposure time is calculated by

Figure 7. Weekend results of different clusters (stopping locations)

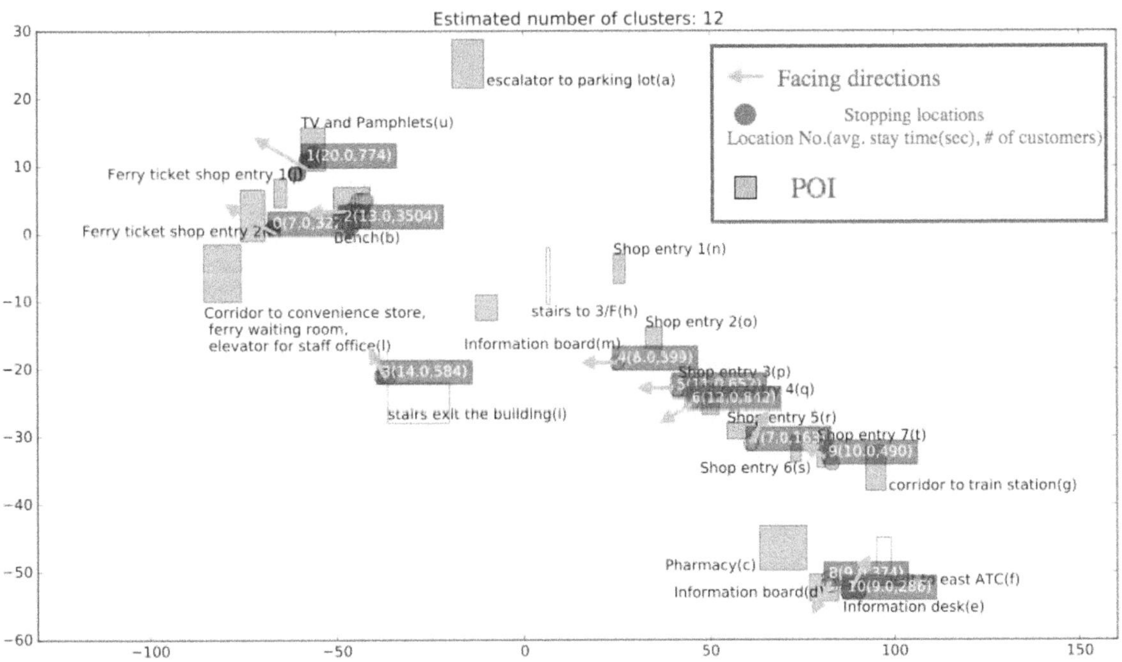

Table 4. Weekend results of places customers visit after staying at different clusters

Cluster No.	Places that Customers Usually Visit After Staying at this Cluster (Top 3)	Cluster No.	Places that Customers Usually Visit After Staying at this Cluster (Top 3)
0	Bench, East ATC	1	Bench, East ATC, Corridor to convenience stores and various facilities
2	East ATC, Pharmacy, Corridor to convenience stores and various facilities	3	Bench, East ATC, Pharmacy
4	East ATC, Bench, Corridor to convenience stores and various facilities	5	East ATC, Bench, Pharmacy
6	East ATC, Bench, Pharmacy	7	East ATC, Bench, Pharmacy
8	East ATC, Pharmacy, Bench	9	East ATC, Bench, Pharmacy

taking the average of seconds that customers were near the ads. Only ads that are not located near stopping locations are considered since the ads located near stopping locations are not the focus of this part.

For existing ads, the ads exposure time for a customer is calculated by counting the duration that the customer is inside the areas labelled. The ads exposure time is calculated by taking average of all ads exposure time for each customers. As we can see in the Figure 8, all locations of the existing ads in ATC shopping mall are without stopping locations and are high traffic locations except the one at bench. Also, the exposure time of the existing ads locations are low on average. Then, the exposure times of the suggested ads locations are calculated by taking the average of the seconds that customers were inside the stopping locations. The reason for using stopping locations to calculate ads exposure time of

Figure 8. Existing ads in ATC shopping mall

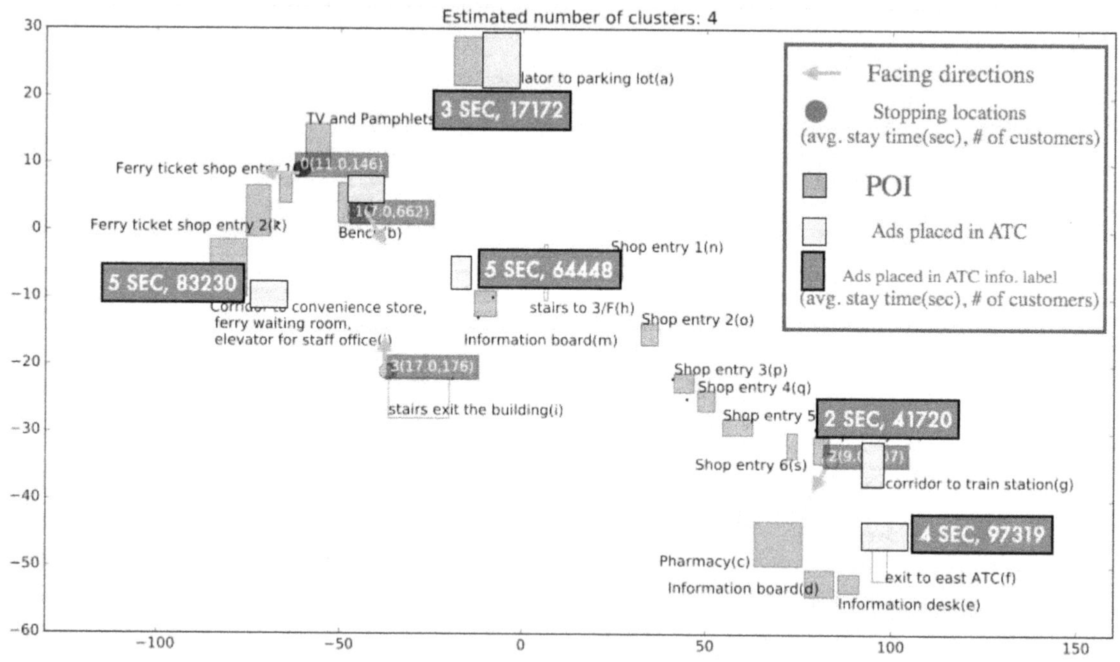

the suggested ads locations is that the stopping locations are in front of the suggested ads locations. A comparison of the ads exposure time of the existing ads locations and suggested ads locations is then carried out and the result is shown in the Table 5. The table shown that, the ads exposure time of the suggested ads locations is 75% longer on average and 11 times longer at most compared to that of the existing ads locations. Also, the number of customers that exposed to the suggested ads location did not decreased (~70000 on average) compared to the existing ads locations (~40000 on average). Therefore, the performance in terms of ads exposure time of the suggested ads location is better than the existing ads location.

To evaluate the ads relevance, the comparison of the suggested ads content of the stopping locations and the the content of existing ads was carried out. There is only 1 existing ad located at stopping locations which is the ad at the bench which only included the facilities inside the corridor connected to convenience stores and various facilities. However, the system suggested that the places customers usually visit after staying at bench are not only including that corridor. They also included East ATC and pharmacy (if only consider places that are meaningful for promotion). The percentage of people visited these three places after staying at bench is shown in Table 6.

Using the suggested content as reference, if the East ATC and pharmacy is added into the ads content, the ads relevance will be increased by 58%. Therefore, the performance in terms of the relevance of the suggested ads is better than the existing ads.

Mining Interesting Knowledge

The purpose of mining interesting knowledge is to provide insights or findings of human behavior in shopping malls that are not proved or discovered yet and apply the knowledge to advertising of shopping malls (not limited to the ATC shopping mall). The knowledge found will be introduced, discussed and then followed by the application in advertising of shopping mall.

Knowledge 1: Customers Stop at Fences in Shopping Mall Usually

According to the stopping locations results, there are 2 characteristics of the stopping locations and the each stopping locations only fulfil either one: some stopping locations are located near POI, or some

Table 5. Ads exposure time comparison

	Ads Exposure Time (Seconds)	
	Existing Ads Locations	**Suggested Ads Locations**
Average (of weekend and weekday)	4	7
minimum	1	5
maximum	5	11

Table 6. Ads relevance comparison

Places Included in the Existing Ads Content	East ATC and Pharmacy (Suggested Content)
22%	58%

stopping locations are located far from any POI. The first point is easy to understand because, in our common knowledge, POIs attract customers to stop. For example, customers will stay at bench because they want to take rest and they will also stop at some shops entrance because they are queueing. It is not interesting for shopping malls or indoor advertising company since it is common knowledge and they had already realized it.

The second point should be more interesting as it contradicts to our common knowledge that people usually stops at POIs. Looking at the weekdays and weekends stopping locations, there is a one located far from any POI which is the stopping location 3 near the exit of the building. The average stay time of customers at this cluster is 14 seconds in weekdays and 9 second in weekends which are quite long.

To explain why customers always stay at this location, authors carefully investigated the environment of it and found that there are fences and customers were stopping there. Therefore, a hypothesis was made that customers usually stops at fences in shopping malls.

To investigate whether this hypothesis is applicable to other shopping malls, direct observation was conducted in some shopping malls in Hong Kong over different period of time. The observation took place at Festival Walk, IFC and Time Square in Hong Kong on the afternoon and at night of different weekday and weekend over 3 weeks. Authors found people stopping at fences in these shopping malls are captured. This indicates that there are many people stopping at fences during weekdays and weekends over different period of time. Potential reasons for the customers to stops at fences are taking rest, waiting for people and using mobile phones. Therefore, the hypothesis, customers usually stop at fences in shopping mall, is considered to be true after the on-site direct observation.

The application of this knowledge in advertising is to place ads near the fences because customers usually stay at fences and the exposure time of the ads place there will be long.

Knowledge 2: Customers Move to Other Areas After Stopping at Resting Areas

The second knowledge is customers usually visit other parts of the shopping malls after staying at resting area. According to the results of the places customers usually visit after staying at stopping locations, there are 2 characteristic of the results and each POI or place only fulfil either one after staying at a stopping locations. Customers usually visit places nearby or visit places far away from the location they stayed. The first point is what the shopping malls believe and used as a reference for choosing the content of the ads. For example, in the ATC shopping mall, the content of the ads placed at bench only included the shops and facilities near the bench. Also, in our common knowledge, the relationship of the shops and facilities nearby should be closer than those far away. In the other words, the places near stopping locations should be visited more than the places far away. Since this is already realized by the shopping malls, it is not the focus of this part of analysis.

The second characteristic is the interesting finding that contradict to the common knowledge stated at the first characteristic. Looking at the results of the places customers usually visit after staying at stopping locations (refer to weekend result of the final result section), all stopping locations fulfil the first characteristic expect the one located at the bench. The result shown that after staying at the bench, customers usually visit the East ATC which is far away from the bench.

There were 34%, in weekends, and 20%, in weekdays, of customers visited East ATC after staying at bench. However, there were only 23%, in weekends, and 22%, in weekdays, visited the places included in the existing ads. Comparing the percentage of the customers visiting these two places after staying at bench, the percentage of East ATC is higher (in average of weekends and weekdays) than that of the places included in the ads content. Therefore, this is contradicting to the common knowledge that the shopping mall believes and they should be aware of it since the existing ads content is actually ignoring the interest of an important group of customers. Besides, the bench is a very special POI that needed to be further analyzed because, while all other POI fulfil the first characteristic, it is the only POI that fulfil the second characteristic. Moreover, the place that has strong association with the bench is a connection to other part of the shopping mall. This phenomenon indicated that the bench may be a checkpoint for customers to move to other parts of the shopping mall. Therefore, based on these analysis, customers usually visit other parts of the shopping mall after stay at resting areas.

The application of this knowledge in advertising is to include information related to other parts of the shopping malls in the content of the ads placed at resting areas.

CONCLUSION

In this chapter, authors propose a data-driven approach to support mall advertising using fine-grained customer trajectories. More specifically, they could find out appropriate advertising locations with long exposure time and suggest advertisement content that are related to nearby customers. Besides, they mine two interesting rules from the massive trajectories that might be used to promote efficiency of mall advertising.

REFERENCES

Batra, R., & Stayman, D. M. (1990). The role of mood in advertising effectiveness. *The Journal of Consumer Research*, *17*(2), 203–214. doi:10.1086/208550

Brown, R. S. Jr. (1947). Advertising and the public interest: Legal protection of trade symbols. *The Yale Law Journal*, *57*(7), 1165. doi:10.2307/793310

Brscic, D., Kanda, T., Ikeda, T., & Miyashita, T. (2013). Person tracking in large public spaces using 3-D range sensors. *IEEE Transactions on Human-Machine Systems*, *43*(6), 522–534. doi:10.1109/THMS.2013.2283945

Crowd WiFi. (2017). *Smart Sense*. Retrieved from http://www.crowdwifi.co.uk/smart-sense/

DILAX. (2017). *People counting & people flow analyses*. Retrieved from https://www.dilax.com/retail-airports/solutions/people-counting-people-flow-analyses/

Ess, A., Leibe, B., Schindler, K., & Van Gool, L. (2008, June). A mobile vision system for robust multi-person tracking. In *Proceedings of the IEEE Conference on Computer Vision and Pattern Recognition* (pp. 1-8). Anchorage, AK: IEEE. Retrieved from https://www.vision.ee.ethz.ch/publications/papers/proceedings/eth_biwi_00534.pdf

Goldstein, D. G., McAfee, R. P., & Suri, S. (2011, June). The effects of exposure time on memory of display advertisements. In *Proceedings of the 12th ACM conference on Electronic commerce* (pp. 49-58). San Jose, CA: ACM. 10.1145/1993574.1993584

Menard, R. J., & Bryan, M. (2005). *U.S. Patent No. 6,967,562*. Washington, DC: U.S. Patent and Trademark Office.

Mitchell, A. A. (2013). *Advertising exposure, memory and choice*. Psychology Press.

Zhao, H., & Shibasaki, R. (2005). A novel system for tracking pedestrians using multiple single-row laser-range scanners. *IEEE Transactions on Systems, Man, and Cybernetics. Part A, Systems and Humans*, *35*(2), 283–291. doi:10.1109/TSMCA.2005.843396

Chapter 8
Digital Category Management:
How Technology Can Enable the Supplier-Retailer Relationship

Valentina Chkoniya
University of Aveiro, Portugal

Armando Mateus
TouchPoint Consulting, Portugal

ABSTRACT

The internet of things (IoT) is transforming the way consumers shop at stores, how shoppers collect information, and how they take purchasing decisions. The way manufacturers and retailers respond to the digital enabled shopper is key to ensure positive implications for revenues and profits, ensuring that the collaborative relationship focus on providing shoppers with a better customer experience. Category management is at the center of the manufacturer-retailer relationship, urging for a transformational turmoil that enables a prompt response to the digital enabled shopper. This chapter discusses the implications of the new digital empowered shopper for the traditional category management demand-side aspects underlying the need to enhance business results by focusing on higher collaboration and automation.

INTRODUCTION

Two decades ago, Category Management came as the solution to the challenges of a highly demanding consumer that required increase attention and a better customer experience in food and groceries. That was the time when internet was the engine for business landscape transformation, enabling and requiring not only a different set of relationship between businesses and the consumer, but also between the different business players in each market. Retail has suffered a dramatic change over the last two decades and, like before, there is a need to adapt to a consumer that requires an increasing attention from manufacturers and retailers, delivering a better customer experience in a context where consumers are armed with information that enables them to take better informed decisions. The communication and commerce paradigm established two decades ago by the development of the internet with an infinite

DOI: 10.4018/978-1-5225-5763-0.ch008

Copyright © 2019, IGI Global. Copying or distributing in print or electronic forms without written permission of IGI Global is prohibited.

number of possibilities has been fulfilled and in an undisputed way has been the foundation of a digital age and a digital shopper. But there is a new paradigm, the Internet of Things (IoT).

For years IoT has been growing silently in many industries – agriculture, energy, transportation, smart cities – and has been reshaping the way companies operate and use information. IoT is not the next stage of the internet, it has been transforming the world as we know, opening new possibilities and creating new businesses.

As the relationship of food and grocery manufacturers with retailers achieves a new challenge due to the increasing low price and high promotion strategies, it urges for a way to respond to the needs of a consumer whose decisions are made faster and in a better-informed way. The traditional Category Management definition needs to gain speed and respond faster to an ever-changing consumer, allowing a higher degree of constant change that can only be enabled through a higher collaboration between manufacturers and retailers. For that is paramount that information flows within and between companies, that the unimaginable amounts of data can be analysed to make better decisions, improve brands and stores performance, generating profits to grow.

All these transformations require that the relationship between manufactures and retailers is based on digital category strategies that are based on the consumer decision journey, independently of the final purchase decision being made online or at the physical store. Digital Category Management is the next stage of Category Management, building on the transformations IoT is causing to the way data is exchanged and used. While previously data would come from traditional sources or internet devices that were used to access data, currently IoT enables data to be generated real-time, therefore needing a new set of analytical tools and technologies.

The case for Category Management and for Digital Transformation has been widely done in literature, being the purpose of this chapter to develop the urgency for the creation of Digital Category Management, a central component of the relationship between retailers and food and grocery manufacturers, going beyond the basic automation of processes and generating more insights that enable brands and stores to deliver a higher customer experience, generating better results for all stakeholders.

Traditionally, Category Management has been criticised due to the "project silo" mentality, where both manufacturers and retailers would collaborate to develop category development projects but being unable to incorporate the results into daily practices that would be sustainable and could drive the day to day business. More than just automating data collection and analysis, Digital Category Management needs to be set as a collaboration approach that would employ real-time data, transforming the way manufacturers and retailers generate insights and, therefore, respond faster to consumers in an omnichannel retail environment.

BACKGROUND

The Internet of Things (IoT) is transforming the way consumers shop, requiring a new paradigm the way food and grocery manufacturers establish their relationship with retailers. At the heart of this transformation, Category Management plays a significant role.

Category Management

For the purpose of this chapter, Category Management is defined as a manufacturer/retailer process of managing categories as strategic business units, producing enhanced business results by focusing on delivering consumer value (ECR Europe, 1997). Also, a category is a distinct, manageable group of products/services that consumers perceive to be interrelated and/or substitutable in meeting a consumer need.

The above definition of category management encompasses 5 key elements: management of categories as strategic business units; development of specific category plans; specific category executions for pricing, merchandising, promotions and product mix; buying and merchandising integration; retailer-manufacturer collaboration (Blattberg, Fox, Dept, & Mars, 1995).

Categories are the cognitive and normative interface amongst parties enabling market exchanges (Granqvist, Grodal, & Woolley, 2013; Pontikes, 2012). Existing research explains that categories act as disciplinary mechanisms that bring order to organizational interactions and existence (Goldberg, Hannan, & Kovács, 2016; Hsu, Hannan, & Koçak, 2009; Rao, Monin, & Durand, 2005; Wry, Lounsbury, & Jennings, 2014). Category formation reflects well as shapes economic and social transformations (Durand & Khaire, 2016). Durand and Khaire (2016) reviewed and illustrated the fundamental differences between Category Emergence and Category Creation, main pillars of which are depicted in Table 1.

Category Management involves treating sets of complementary and/or competing brands as strategic business units and allocating resources within these categories to maximize planned outcomes (Blattberg et al., 1995; Dhar, Hoch, & Kumar, 2001). This management approach causes decisions to be made on a category level and not just on products or brands.

Table 1. Category Creation and Category Emergence (adapted from Durand & Khaire, 2016)

	Category Emergence	Category Creation
Nature of the novelty	Essentially material, that is, new physical attributes.	Essentially cognitive, that is, pre-existing attributes and features redefined and reinterpreted.
Origin	Importation of new attributes not part of the current category system. Labelling follows material innovation.	Carved out of existing consideration sets from the current category system. Labelling precedes material recombination and innovation.
Organizational agency	Category promoters: typically, new ventures, can be unconventional incumbents willing to upend established order. Intermediaries: low capacity to make a category emerge; reflectors of changes.	Category promoters. Could be new entrants but more likely to be incumbent players reframing offerings.
Mechanism for distinction	Transfer and opposition.	Combination and distinctiveness.
Basis of discourse	Analogy import and contrast.	Resonant framing.
Legitimacy acquired through	Explication of meaning of the category, criteria of evaluation to be used, and establishment of order of worth.	Authority of market actors in redefining identity and boundaries; intermediaries' validation.
Outcome	New market actors, organizations, products, intrafield changes in hierarchies.	Mostly same actors; maintenance of existing order but value capture to the benefit of newly created category's promoters.

One or more suppliers to a category often have greater resources (e.g., consumer insights, marketing budgets, etc.) and stronger capabilities (e.g., brand management, marketing planning, etc.) required for effective category management than the retailer (Morgan, Kaleka, & Gooner, 2007). To leverage these resources and capabilities, retailers may involve suppliers in the analysis of category-level data, category goal setting, and the formulation and execution of category-level plans (Basuroy, Mantrala, & Walters, 2001; Dussart, 1998).

Category management according to Dupre-Gruen links, while using low cost and differentiation to defend market position (Dupre & Gruen, 2004). The main motivation to apply category management in retail trade (i.e. in a stone or electronic shop) is primarily profit maximization and for all stakeholders - producers, traders and consumers presents a number of benefits, even if that requires long-term planning and the results are visible only after a delay (Mihalčová & Pružinský, 2015).

The benefits of Category Management are widely discussed in literature, with different perspectives based on the retailer or manufacturer perspective. According to Blattberg and Fox, it enables the retailer to: focus on the consumer; use available information to make better decisions, and, in turn, make decisions more fact-based; defend against competition; create an understanding between retailer and manufacturer and align manufacturer's programs with retailer's strategies and tactics (Blattberg et al., 1995).

On a more collaborative perspective, ECR Europe (1997) describes the benefits of Category Management as: higher levels of consumer satisfaction and value from more consumer-focused procurement, marketing and merchandising programmes; reduced system and marketing costs from more productive and less adversarial business processes; increased turnover, profit and return-on-asset levels for retailers and suppliers; higher productivity in management practices from the use of a more consistent strategic framework to drive day-to-day tactical decisions; more efficient product assortments, new product introductions, promotion methods and shelf planograms resulting from greater strategically-driven decision making; higher returns from technology investments as a result of more clearly defined system requirements and greater system compatibility amongst retailers and suppliers; improved ability to attract and retain higher skilled talent through improved and rewarding business careers(ECR Europe, 1997).

Category Management seems also to bring many positive elements to manufacturer-retailer interaction, e.g., continuous collaboration instead of repeated competitive biddings and knowledge sharing instead of knowledge withholding. However, its nature cannot be understood without understanding the roles of the collaborating suppliers (Lindblom & Olkkonen, 2008).

The concept of Category Management has evolved over time; however, the most commonly used category management model today was developed into an eight-step procedure by Brian F. Harris in 1997 and is called the Brian Harris Model (ECR Europe, 1997). The basis of category management, according to Harris models, is to: force consumer focus during retail decisions; create strategy for differentiation and competition; provide a model for collaboration; promote information sharing for the sake of better decision-making; provide strategic logic when developing tactical decisions; clarify decisions when it comes to asset allocation; and clarify employee responsibilities (Plimmer, 2010).

Category management plays an increasingly important role in retailing management, as it aids retailers to increase their core competitiveness, maximise profits and ensure a good long-term customer relationship. This technique has been successfully applied to diverse large manufacturers and wholesale retailers (Han, Ye, Fu, & Chen, 2014).

In the retail grocery industry, category management is the process of managing categories of products for greater profitability and customer value (Duchessi, 2004). Category management is a data driven process and, as a result, can benefit from the evolution of the technology behind digital marketing.

Efficient Consumer Response

Efficient consumer response (ECR) was recognized in the early 1990s in the United States and was characterized by the emergence of new principles of collaborative management along grocery supply chains (Corsten & Kumar, 2005; Harris, Swatman, & Kurnia, 1999). Nowadays there are national and international ECR programmes around the world, and retailers and suppliers have invested heavily in terms of training, infrastructure and processes. Many of its proponents among logistics and marketing researchers claim it is one of the best strategic and collaborative initiatives within the grocery industry. Its aim is said to be to invert the traditional model and to break down non-productive barriers. Probably the best-known ECR related business process is category management, which is stated to be an antecedent of successful ECR (Dapiran & Hogarth-Scott, 2003). Category management is a collaborative process between suppliers and retailers, the aim of which is to manage categories as strategic business units, producing enhanced results by focusing on delivering consumer value (e.g., Dapiran & Hogarth-Scott, 2003; Dupre & Gruen, 2004; Dussart, 1998; Gruen & Shah, 2000; Kurnia & Johnston, 2003).

Partnerships are said to be the basis of effective category management (Dewsnap & Hart, 2004; Kurnia & Johnston, 2001, 2003). Although retailers may practice category management without input from suppliers, it is assumed that the results are enhanced through the collaborative pooling of complementary knowledge to meet the needs of consumers. Category management seems to bring many positive elements to supplier-retailer interaction, e.g., continuous collaboration instead of repeated competitive biddings, and knowledge sharing instead of knowledge withholding (Lindblom & Olkkonen, 2008). Furthermore, academic work on broader managerial category management has suggested some difficulties and that excellent prospects exist for improvements in this area hanks to digital marketing, if more research is devoted to understanding how digital world actually optimizes category management.

The growth of Efficient Consumer Response (ECR) since the 1990s and the subsequent emphasis on category management encourages retailers to focus on the profitability of an entire product category rather than of individual brands. This issue is particularly important in the consumer-packaged goods industry where brands within a category have interrelated demands and their relative profitability changes over time with the occurrence of frequent trade deals (discounts from manufacturers to retailers) and forward buying by retailers. This necessitates a dynamic category-level model which incorporates changing brand profitability over time and the interdependence among brands.

Manufacturer-Retailer Relationship

Researchers in both marketing and management areas have approached the question of supplier-buyer management from different perspectives. For example, marketing scholars have often referred to the two parties in the channel management as manufacturers and distributors (Anderson & Narus, 1990; Gu, Kim, Tse, & Wang, 2010; Yang, Su, & Fam, 2012), while management scholars have often examined the vertical relationship between suppliers and buyers (Mesquita, Anand, & Brush, 2008). Apart from the terminology difference, marketing researchers tend to focus more on the dyadic relationship management such as contractual and relational governance between manufacturers and distributors (Antia & Frazier, 2001; Yang et al., 2012), while management researchers put more emphasis on the value creation and value appropriation process between suppliers and buyers as well as with related stakeholders (Chatain, 2011).

There is an increased understanding of how supplier resources, including brands, influence buyer-seller relationships (Cannon & Perreault, 1999; Jap, 1999). Ulaga and Eggert (Ulaga & Eggert, 2006) also consider that researchers have tended to focus on the soft side of relationship marketing i.e. trust and commitment without considering the more tangible aspects such as performance or the financial determinants of value. Walter, Ritter and Gemunden (Walter, Ritter, & Gemünden, 2001) proposed that buyers and sellers create value with direct functions such as profit and volume and indirect relationship based functions such as supplier market innovation and market development. Spiteri and Dion (Spiteri & Dion, 2004) found that supplier benefits influenced overall relationship value, satisfaction as well as performance.

Category Management is the primary platform from which FMCG brand owners interact with retailers (Hamister & Fortsch, 2016). Category Management provides the language, process framework, and metrics for communicating all strategic and tactical recommendations to the retailer.

The strategic outcomes of category management for retailers are better retailer differentiation from competitors and increased loyalty of the retailer's customer (Dupre & Gruen, 2004). For brand managers the implication is that pricing is coordinated across the category rather than by brand in order to optimise category profits. Johnson (1999) points out that category management can also be an effective tool for brand manufacturers (Johnson, 1999). Brand manufacturers provide market trends and information for retailers and also have the opportunity to influence their position within the category (Glynn, Brodie, & Motion, 2012). Information sharing provides an opportunity for manufacturer retailer collaboration and the formation of partnerships, building trust and commitment (Dapiran & Hogarth-Scott, 2003).

Generally, the value of information sharing on supply chain members' strategies and revenues is widely discussed on scientific literature (Cheong & Song, 2013; Choi, Li, & Wei, 2013; Chung & Lee, 2017; Huang & Wang, 2017; Lee, So, & Tang, 2000; Liu, Cao, & Salifou, 2016; Shamir & Shin, 2016; Shang, Ha, & Tong, 2016; Yao, Yue, & Liu, 2008; Zhang, 2002; Zhu, 2016).

Although retailers can practice category management without input from suppliers, the results will be enhanced if there is collaborative pooling of complementary knowledge to meet the needs of consumers; for this reason, partnerships are said to be the basis of effective category management (Dewsnap & Hart, 2004; Kurnia & Johnston, 2001, 2003). Category management is supposed to enhance manufacturer–retailer interactions through ongoing collaboration (rather than competitive bidding) and knowledge sharing (rather than knowledge withholding), but there is a risk that stronger suppliers might act in an opportunistic manner by promoting their own brands within a particular category at the expense of weaker suppliers, despite such practices not being in accordance with 'ideal' category management practice (Lindblom & Olkkonen, 2008).

During the past few years the concept of category management has received considerable attention as a new cooperative managerial practice between manufacturers and retailers (Dewsnap & Hart, 2004). Category management implies a new way of partnership thinking that replaces traditional brand-management practices (Araujo & Muzas, 1995; Dewsnap & Hart, 2004; Gruen & Shah, 2000; Kurnia & Johnston, 2001). It is argued that manufacturers and retailers can serve consumers better, more quickly and more cheaply by working together with trading partners. As stated earlier, category management is generally based on the idea that instead of managing individual brands with each relevant supplier, it is better for retailers to manage entire product categories as strategic business units in cooperation with the most significant manufacturers. According to Dewsnap and Hart (2004), category management is successful when suppliers and retailers can genuinely collaborate in understanding consumers and fulfilling their needs via a joint process of category planning (Dewsnap & Hart, 2004). Consequently, partnership thinking is one of its cornerstones (Lindblom & Olkkonen, 2008). Closer and more collaborative relationships allow buyers and sellers to share resources and obtain mutually beneficial economic outcomes that are superior to those that each party may be able to achieve separately (Morgan et al., 2007).

As seen in Table 1, numerous relevant organization theories offer a wide range of different viewpoints and suggest a huge range of factors and relationships that may be potentially important in understanding retailer–focal supplier category management relationships. The picture of category-level retailer–supplier relationships that emerged from the fieldwork is complex, and often at odds with assumptions that underpin the organization theories viewed as relevant lenses for studying this phenomenon such as those in Table 1. For example, in contrast to agency theory assumptions, suppliers appear to be less risk averse than retailers in this context. In fact, suppliers view becoming a category captain as a fundamental basis of competition among themselves and actively seek to fulfil this role expecting that it will provide an opportunity to increase their revenue and profits on sales at the retailer's stores. Further, while agency and TCA (Transaction Cost Analysis) theory focus on safeguarding and incentive alignment through contracts, the presence of strong anti-trust concerns means that retailer–supplier category management relationships are informal. However, this does not imply that both parties necessarily view a mutually beneficial exchange and behavioural norms as providing an effective and efficient alternative governance mechanism as is assumed in relational exchange theory. In fact, suppliers view becoming a category captain as an opportunity to develop control of a critical dependency for retailers, providing a valuable mechanism for addressing some of the perceived power imbalance between themselves and their increasingly consolidated retail customers. Similarly, in contrast to the fundamental TCA precept that opportunism and an inability to efficiently control it leads managers to vertically integrate, retailer managers in our fieldwork often view the need to leverage a key supplier's resources and capabilities to compete with rival mass merchant entrants as outweighing such considerations. In addition, many retailers seek to engage in technology transfer of category management capabilities from key suppliers to the retailer, and to leverage these capabilities across multiple categories. However, in contrast to the network theory precepts summarized in Table 2, suppliers are keen not to engage in fine-grained category management capability transfer as they view this as one of very few 'weapons' with which they may combat growing retailer power in supply chains. At least three organization theories: agency theory; TCA theory; and, network theory, have the potential to provide important new insights in understanding relational exchange theory based supply chain management approaches such as ECR, CPFR, and VMI and their impact on business performance (Morgan et al., 2007).

In recent years, there has been a clear tendency to interdisciplinary integration of marketing and management research on supplier-buyer relationship management, that synthesizes governance and innovation for a theory that explains effective value creation and fair value appropriation in supplier-retailer relationships. An important issue in supplier-buyer relationship management that has attracted much research attention pertains to knowledge sharing and innovation for value creation (Li, Cui, & Liu, 2017). Both manufacturers and their distribution partners affect the manufacturers' learning about market demands and trends, jointly motivate market knowledge sharing in marketing channels and manufacturers' absorptive capacity will facilitate such knowledge sharing (Pagani & Pardo, 2017). Contrary to examining innovation at firm levels, such informal interactions enhance knowledge acquisition and thus firms' innovation capabilities (Pagani & Pardo, 2017).

Manufacturers transform from a production-focused to a consumer-orientated business model (Bell, Giordano, & Putz, 2002). In manufacturer–distributor partnerships, manufacturers that effectively acquire market knowledge through interactions with their distributors are more likely to keep up with dynamics in the marketplace, and consequently enhance their financial performance (Zhao, Flynn, & Roth, 2007).

Table 2. Retailer–focal supplier category management relationships perspectives (adapted from Morgan et al., 2007)

	Agency Theory	TCA	Network Theory	Relational Exchange	Fieldwork
Relevant focal constructs	Contracts, incentive compatibility, goals and risk preferences.	Opportunism, asset specificity, environmental and behavioural uncertainty, contracts, monitoring, direct and opportunity costs of transactions.	Strength of ties between firms, structural location of firms relative to the rest of the network, trust, cooperation, social capital.	Relationship-specific assets, knowledge exchange, complementary resources and capabilities, bilateral governance.	Opportunism, dependence, non-focal supplier militancy, monitoring capability, punitive capacity.
Primary level of analysis	Principal-agent dyadic relationships.	Individual buyer-seller dyadic transactions.	Relationships of individual firms with others within a network of firms.	Individual buyer-seller relationship dyad.	Multiple category-level retailer-supplier dyads embedded in a network of other suppliers who continue to supply both the retailer and other retailers.
Basic assumptions	Managers have imperfect information, and face uncertainty. Agents are risk adverse and generally more so than risk neutral principals. Individual economically self-interested rationality guides actions.	Low adaptation, performance evaluation, and safeguarding costs result in market transactions. Firms are governance structures that emerge when these costs are relatively high. Firms have more powerful control and monitoring mechanisms than markets are more able to offer long-term rewards, and may facilitate within-firm shared norms. Decision-Makers are boundedly rational.	How a firm interacts with its partners, and the shape and form of its network and influence its performance. Strong ties with others are associated with high quality, fine-grained information exchanges and trust-based governance. Weak ties can embed the firm in different network regions, producing novel information. Dense networks promote social governance among members.	Firm invest in relationship specific assets to exchange fine-grained knowledge that enables them to leverage complementary resources and/or capabilities that can deliver rents to each party that could not be achieved by either party alone. Each party is safeguarded by efficient and effective informal and self-enforcing governance mechanisms that lower transaction costs.	Suppliers cheat if they can, and are more risk-taking than retailers in being willing to become category captains. Goal is to 'grow the pie' but category captains can gain economic benefits at the expense of other suppliers. Suppliers also compete to become category captains to increase their power position relative to the retailer – and seek to impede technology transfer to maintain this power.
Conception of retailer's category management relationship with a focal supplier	*Ex ante* problem of finding most appropriate supplier to perform category captain role and designing a contract that will minimize the retailer's *ex post* costs in the relationship.	Category management as a 'make or buy' decision involving high levels of human asset specificity and high safeguarding costs. Retailers may reduce *ex post* transaction costs of a 'buy' decision by designing appropriate governance mechanisms.	Retailer has strong ties (frequent interaction and greater resource commitment to the relationship) with focal supplier and weaker ties with non-focal suppliers to the category. Focal supplier may occupy a structural hole in the retailer's supply network and gain efficiency and control benefits.	Retailer and focal supplier share complementary resources to create mutually beneficial that neither could achieve alone. Joint goals, planning and outcomes form an efficient governance mechanism to safeguard any relationship specific assets required.	Informal, non-contractual relationship between a focal supplier who sees being category captain as a way of enhancing their competitive position relative to other suppliers and power relative to the retailer and a retailer who needs additional resources and capabilities to enhance their category-level performance.

The relationship between manufacturers and retailers is profoundly altered by category management (ECR Europe, 1997), broadening their relationship and introducing collaboration as the key philosophy. This level of collaboration requires: placing the consumer as the common focus; mutually agreed objectives, strategies, tactics and performance measures; rewards supporting cooperative business goals; openness to change traditional attitudes and relationships; information sharing; multifunctional access and communication; retailer, manufacturer and consumer win ("triple win").

Digital Marketing

The digital era is changing consistently the previous marketing scenarios including the firm–customer and firm–firm interactions (Day, 2011; Yadav & Pavlou, 2014). Marketing theory is changed by these technological developments and all of business can be seen as co-created service, and this realization has important implications about how we think about marketing, and how marketing is practiced (Vargo & Lusch, 2017).

The term "digital marketing" has evolved over time from a specific term describing the marketing of products and services using digital channels – to an umbrella term describing the process of using digital technologies to acquire customers and build customer preferences, promote brands, retain customers and increase sales (Financial Times, lexicon.ft.com). Following the American Marketing Association's firm centric definition, digital marketing may be seen as activities, institutions, and processes facilitated by digital technologies for creating, communicating and delivering value for customers and other stakeholders. Kannan and Li (2017) adopt a more inclusive perspective and define digital marketing as "an adaptive, technology-enabled process by which firms collaborate with customers and partners to jointly create, communicate, deliver, and sustain value for all stakeholders" (Kannan & Li, 2017). One of the main drivers in optimizing shopper marketing tactics is technology (Shankar, Inman, Mantrala, Kelley, & Rizley, 2011). Technology has always played a role as the primary enabler of change in the evolution of retailing (Hopping, 2000). Digital marketing itself is enabled by a series of adaptive digital touchpoints encompassing the marketing activity, institutions, processes and customers (Kannan & Li, 2017).

Organizational processes and capabilities need to cope with the actual fast changing, but at the same time, data-rich environment (Bullini Orlandi, 2016). In this case the framework for research in digital marketing highlights the touchpoints in the marketing process as well as in the marketing strategy process where digital technologies are having and will have a significant impact (Kannan & Li, 2017). The majority of the inventoried technologies provide cost savings, convenience and utilitarian value, whereas few offer hedonic or symbolic benefits. Moreover, at present the earlier stages of the path-to-purchase appear to be the most instrumented (Willems, Smolders, Brengman, Luyten, & Schöning, 2017).

In recent years, there has been considerable discussion and research about the impact of digital business strategies on the evolution of supply chains into value networks and value constellation or ecosystems (Iansiti & Lakhani, 2014; Pagani & Pardo, 2017). The concept of "value network" has constituted a shift between a traditional vision of value creation anchored in a value chain perspective (Porter, 1985) to a renewed vision of value creation supported by the network perspective (Kothandaraman & Wilson, 2001; Möller & Rajala, 2007; Pagani & Pardo, 2017; Parolini, 1999). As Figure 1 shows, digitalization is profoundly changing the way business is carried out between companies, the value-creating system is composed of different economic actors who work together to co-produce value (Pagani & Pardo, 2017).

Figure 1. The emerging types of impact of digital technology (adapted from Pagani & Pardo, 2017)

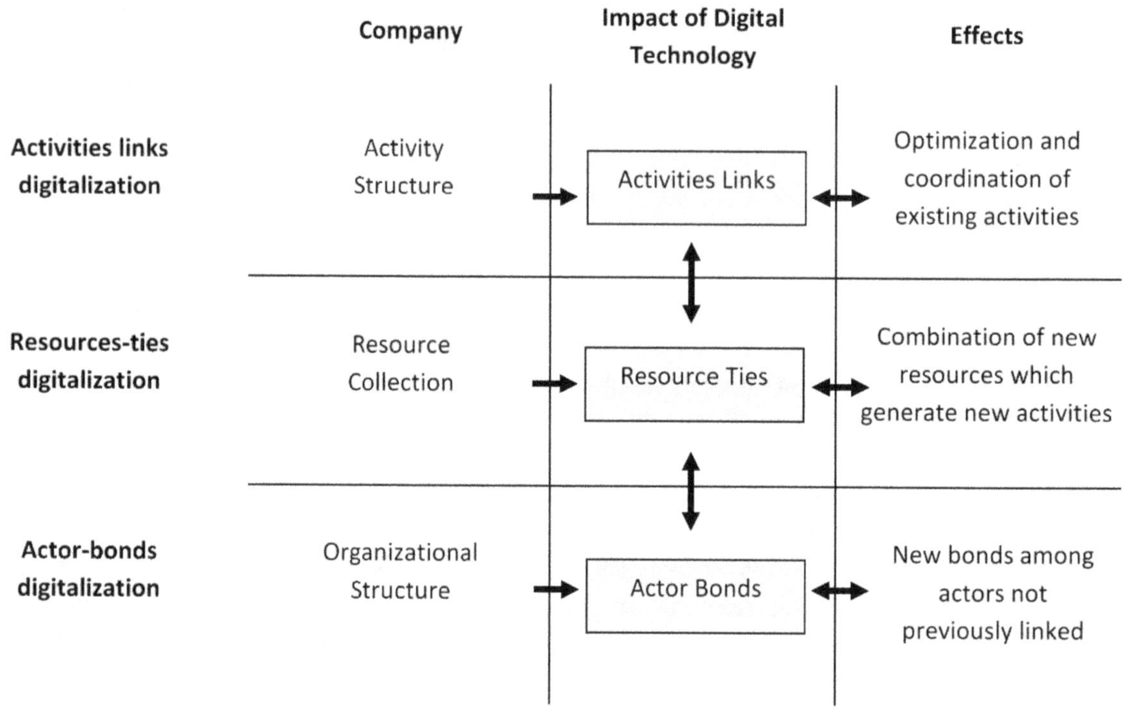

Digitization is the conversion of analogue information in any form such as text, images, sound or physical attributes to a digital format so that the information can be processed, stored, and transmitted through digital circuits, devices, and networks. In simple, pragmatic terms, digitizing information makes it easier to store, access, and share and process (Chan, Narasimhan, & Yoon, 2017; Tilson, Lyytinen, & Sorensen, 2010).

The digital revolution has radically changed marketing, from a mass market phenomenon to a personalized phenomenon (Erdem, Lane Keller, Kuksov, & Pieters, 2016). As advances in digital communication, data storage and data analysis have accelerated, marketers have increasingly sought ways to use customer "big data" to fine tune marketing. What is important to realize is that the digital revolution is not going away. Rather, all of its trends will become even more pronounced in the future (Rust, 2017) and the Internet of Things is here to stay and is certain to change marketing in a profound way (Hoffman & Novak, 2016).

The term 'Internet-of-Things' (IoT) coined by Kevin Ashton (Ashton, 2009), a technologist and pioneer in the Auto-ID world, has started to gain traction, and industry is beginning to wake up to the possibility of every object being part of the Internet, whatever the business proposition might be. The Internet and the physical world are about to experience an epic collision, moreover, the full potential of an IoT era has not yet materialized (Ng & Wakenshaw, 2017). The era of IoT will fundamentally transform the firm's business model, to incorporate value creation (the experience – more visible), value proposition (the offering - reconfigurable), and value 'capture' or creating worth for exchanges (the economic model – with shifting boundaries) (Ng & Wakenshaw, 2017).

The adaptive process enabled by the digital technologies creates value in new ways in new digital environments. Institutions enabled by digital technologies build foundational capabilities to create such value jointly for their customers and for themselves. Processes enabled by digital technologies create value through new customer experiences and through interactions among customers (Kannan & Li, 2017). The way data is collect by business has been dramatically changed with IoT technology changes, allowing to understand real-time consumer demand and providing live feedback.

According to IGD (2017), 37% of food and grocery companies are already trialling or have successfully deployed IoT products or services, with a further 58% planning to increase their use of technology providers to help them embrace IoT opportunities. Also, 61% of respondents highlighted "improved understanding of customers" in their top three expected business benefits of IoT, with 53% of companies citing "reduced costs and increased efficiencies" and 51% "development of new business models".

Customer Experience

Consumer experience has developed into an independent discipline to specifically explore consumption and experience in "its full experiential and sociocultural scope" (Arnould & Thompson, 2005). Some have conceptualized consumer experiences as consumer 'touchpoints' (Meyer, Schwager, & Meyer Schwager, A., 2007) and consumer 'experience clues' (Leonard L. Berry, 2002) that provide ways to understand the data/information required to better manage consumer experiences. Consumer experiences with physical products will be highly visible in an era of IoT (Ng & Wakenshaw, 2017).

As the world moves towards an era of Internet-of-Things, a technical process of converting previously static and unmovable information into a dynamic, transportable resource is creating disruption at a Schumpeterian level that is only just beginning and a technological ability that could render every physical object into a potential digital artefact will trigger limitless possibilities, both negative and positive, and could result in a fundamental transformation (Ng & Wakenshaw, 2017).

The consumer has absorbed the technology into daily practices and decisions, using a variety of devices and interfaces to connect to the internet, in order to interact with digital content, services and experiences, with instant access to anything, from anywhere (Euromonitor International, 2017).These changes have led a power shift towards the consumer in the grocery and retail industry, giving consumers a megaphone in the business transaction. It has also boosted companies born in the modern era, as data has emerged as the most important commodity. The current consumer requires an always connected customer experience, reshaping the way brands and retailers engage. About 35% of consumers globally use a computer to read reviews or compare prices on a weekly basis, with one quarter using a computer to execute a purchase. In digitally-savvy South Korea and the UK, around 12% of consumer payments were made using a digital device in 2016, with that ratio approaching 20% by 2021 (Euromonitor International, 2017).

DIGITAL CATEGORY MANAGEMENT

Digital Category Management is the response to a new age of retailing is emerging – a digital, connected and personalised age, shaped by technology and the consumer. IoT plays a major role in bringing live, precise, consumer and product level insight enabling efficient and responsive solutions that meet needs and create value throughout the entire grocery value chain.

When it was introduced two decades ago, Category Management represented a significant move towards a fact-based decision process within the consumer goods and retail industry. Although category management has been widely validated, it has been a high-resource and project-oriented activity demanding high data expertise and analytical skills, which in turn generated high costs of implementation and insights to be outdated. Digital Category Management builds on the ability to incorporate available data into a set of procedures that enable decisions to be taken on a timely and effective manner.

The pace of change the consumer generates in the consumer goods and retail industry requires a more integrated approach that makes information accessible to decision makers and provides the ability to incorporate data into category strategies and tactics. The level of detail needed to improve category management would be impossible with earlier processes, but new rules-based tools for assortment optimization, store layouts, pricing and planograms can automate most analysis, focusing manufacturers and retailers on decision-making. This should be the main promise of Digital Category Management.

Category Management interest generated amongst manufacturers and retailers was a result of economic and business conditions (ECR Europe, 1997), mandating a collaborative approach that could enable higher business results. After 20 years these conditions remain and although the retail and consumer goods industry has changed, the challenges remain and need to be approached through a set of processes that enhance consumer value as a basis for profitability and competitive advantage. Also, the competitive environment has been changed and the traditional manufacturer-retailer collaboration needs to incorporate a different view about the relationship. The current market conditions (consumer changes, competitive environment, economic conditions and technology) have created (again) the need and the opportunity to a new collaboration model between retailers and consumer goods manufacturers, Digital category Management. Not only market conditions have evolved, but they have also caused a willingness to change amongst retailers and manufacturers.

The retail industry is one of the largest and most diversified operations in the world. The structure of the business industry connects manufacturers to consumers by providing products and services from the producer to the customer. New technology, and the presence of an ever-changing competitive market structure, requires the business industry to adapt their practices accordingly. Retailers are dynamic in nature, and their strategies keep evolving with changing scenarios and availability of new technologies. Retailers are particularly concerned with strategies such as pricing, product selection, location choice, and store format. Though the retailers' strategies can be profitable, the difficulty lies in identifying the source of profitability in the complex retail structure (Kumar et al. 2017). The rate of advanced technology relevant to retail industry is on the rise and these technologies are available, which allows the retail industry to apply them on a larger scale. Retailers can access real-time data of each customer's action in the form of big data via new technology. Companies can use this data for more personalized offerings to customers (Kumar et al. 2017).

In order to be successful and help both manufacturers and retailers to achieve better performance, Digital Category Management needs to:

- Improve the accessibility and integration of manufacturer and retailer data into day-to-day processes;
- Automate data analysis and generate continuous monitoring of category and brand performance;
- React faster and more accurately to consumer and competitor changes impacting the category;
- Improve products and stores productivity by faster product introductions, assortment rules and store layout implementations.

The Case for Digital Category Management

Digital technology has been available for a significant time, being easy to assume that the economy's digitization is already far advanced. That is far from true, as according to Bughin et al (2017) that is far from being a widespread reality. On average, industries are less than 40 percent digitized, despite the relatively deep penetration of these technologies in media, retail, and high tech. Its impact on the economic performance of companies, while already significant, is far from complete (Figure 2).

Figure 2. Digital penetration by industry (adapted from Bughin et al, 2017)

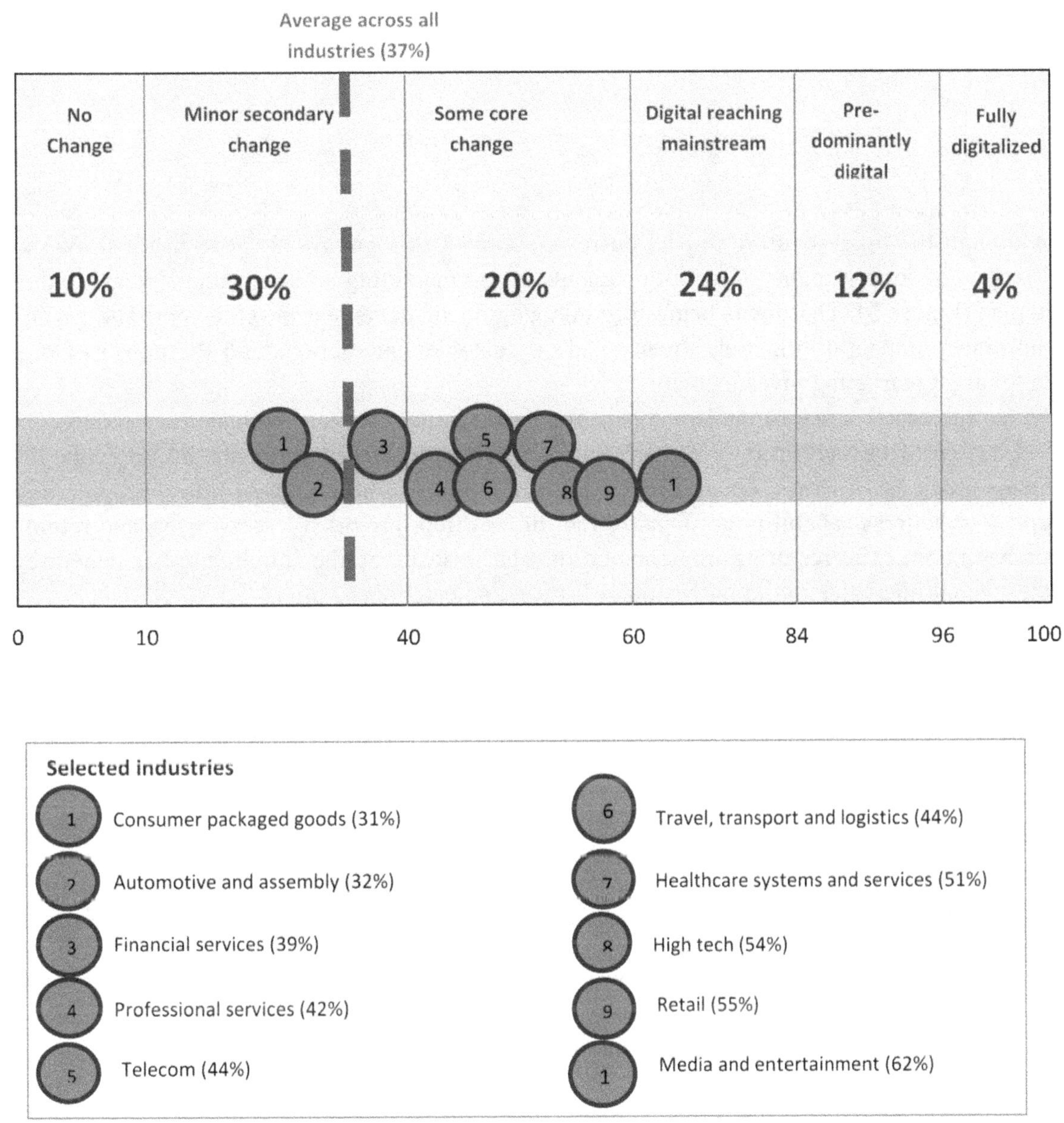

Figure 3. Digital strategies focus (adapted from Bughin et al, 2017)

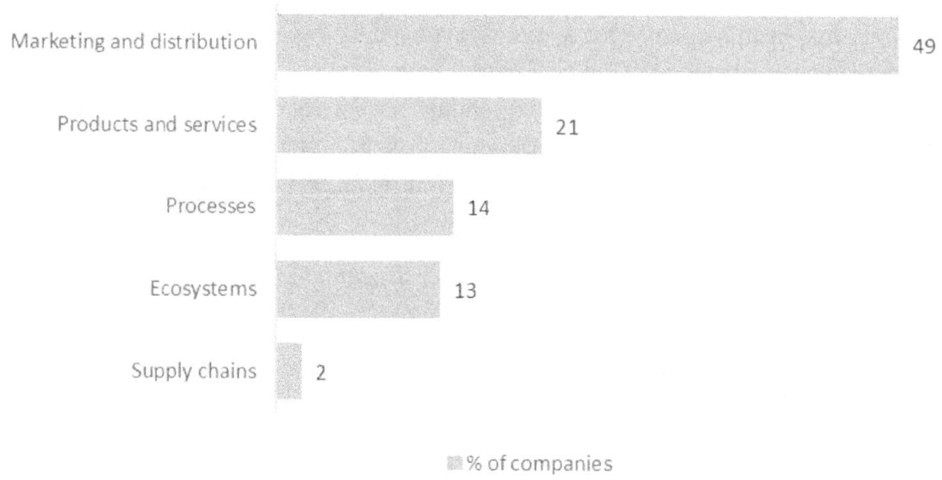

Although the biggest future impact on revenue and EBIT growth is set to occur through the digitization of supply chains, distribution channels and marketing are the primary focus of digital strategies (Figure 3). That focus brings digital category management into the spotlight, given the extraordinary impact digitization already had on customer interactions and the power of digital tools to target marketing investments.

Given the broad scope of the investment required, digital category management requires end-to-end design of business processes, with close attention to IT requirements, and organizational elements (such as structure, talent, incentives, and culture). The output of this work is a digital blueprint to address capability gaps and to recruit, develop, provide incentives for, and retain the necessary talent. The resulting implementation plan prioritizes the initiatives that generate the greatest economic value, building customer loyalty and category results.

With these objectives in place, digital category management strategy is paramount in delivering the capabilities needed to meet a company's strategic goals. No single retailer or manufacturer will have all the capabilities it needs within its own walls. Retailers and manufacturers need to collaborate and develop an ecosystem of external teams, partners, suppliers, and customers, including a mix of platform players, delivery specialists, and niche outfits with specific industry expertise and capabilities. As companies assess the scope of their investments and define priorities, they should consider that results will require action across all dimensions, not just one or two. The importance of digital investments can even be more profound if considered the performance of the best performing companies, as according to Bughin et al (2017), is evident that heavy digital investment is a differentiator. Leading companies not only invested more but also did so across all of the dimensions, with winners exceeding others in both the magnitude and the scope of their digital investments (Figure 4). This is a critical element of success, given the different rates at which these dimensions are digitizing and their varying effect on economic performance.

Figure 4. Effect of company response to digitalization on revenue (adapted from Bughin et al, 2017)

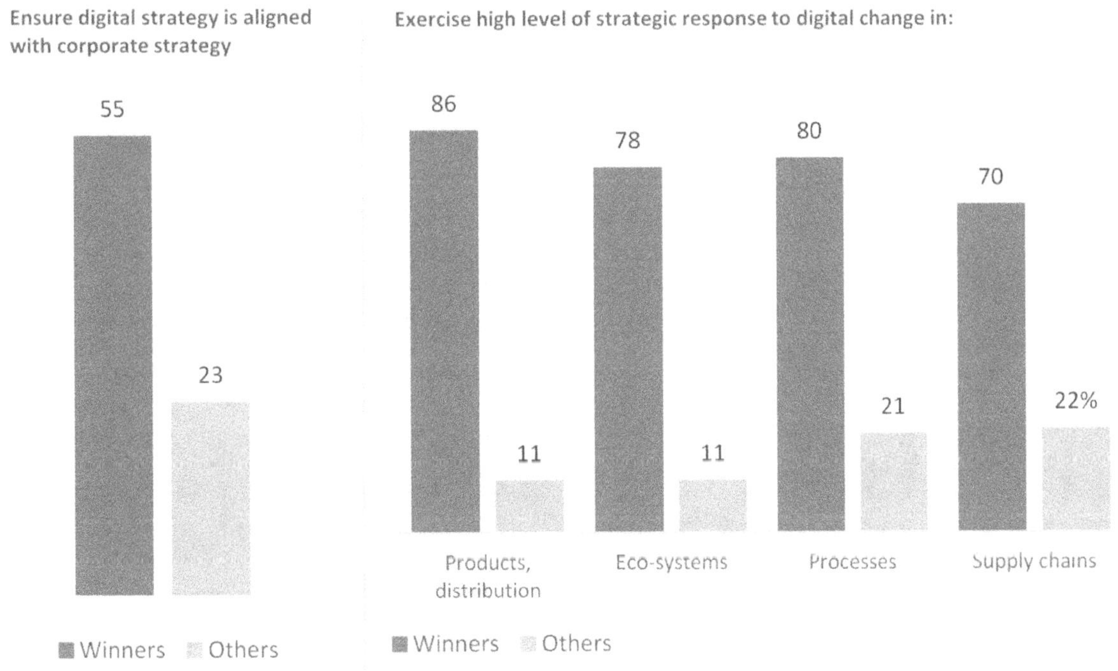

The Importance of IoT to Digital Category Management

Amongst all industry players, retailers are the most connected to the final consumer along the different touchpoints and their commitment to digital category management will be decisive to the success, with IoT playing a significant role.

Although retailers have moved away from the initial IoT hype (Kilcourse & Rosemblum, 2017), there is still a significant belief that investments will be significant and impact businesses (Figure 5).

The importance of IoT comes from the current business challenges and the way it can address solving them, being inventory accuracy, consumer fulfilment and omnichannel the most recognized (Figure 6).

In the short term, IoT will be able to deliver efficient profitability, with a high potential to further improve customer engagement. The most pragmatic use of IoT is about efficiently finding, tracking and monitoring inventory level, what will help in reducing the amount of extra inventory retailers are buying to compensate for uncertainty in actual inventory quantities. Similarly, IoT can definitely add speed and agility to operations.

IoT will also certainly help in improving the otherwise impersonal experience of retailing, from grocers and mass merchants, creating a more personalized experience.

Successful implementation of Digital Category Management requires that retailers install the necessary systems to assist category management, but also that information flows easily and data to be transformed into actionable insights.

As Category Management focus on making fact-based decisions, it requires that retailers and manufacturers access timely information about the category and the consumer, that was previously unavailable or nor accessible on a timely manner. This timely access is key to achieve a higher performance versus

Figure 5. IoT business impact beliefs amongst retailers (adapted from Kilcourse & Rosemblum, 2017)

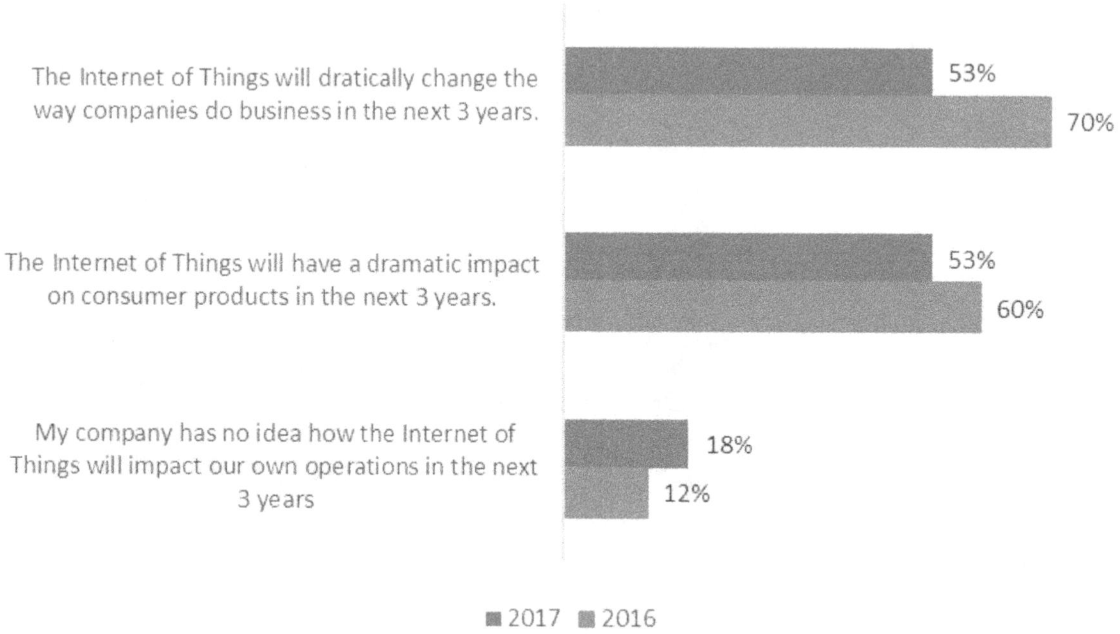

Figure 6. Top 3 operational changes addressed by IoT (adapted from Kilcourse & Rosemblum, 2017)

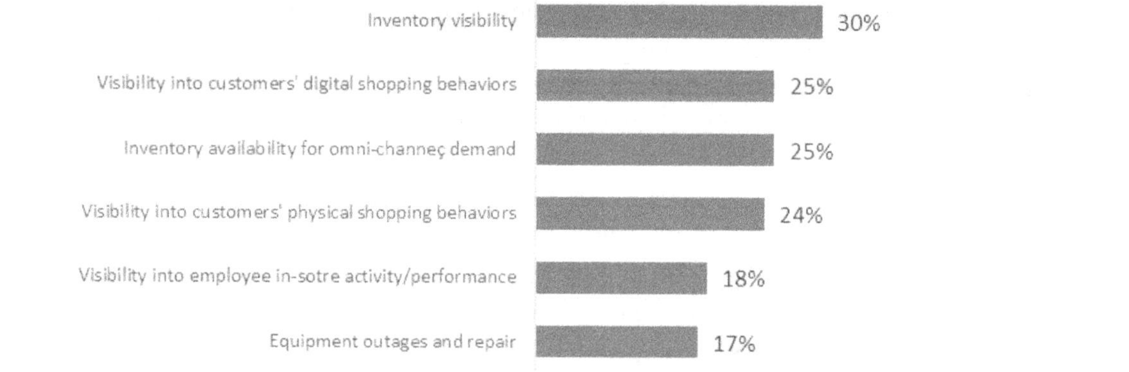

competitors, but also to enable a faster answer to the changes of the connected consumer. Technology is an important enabling factor in implementing successfully Digital Category Management, in particular the ability to have information about category performance, consumer habits and preferences.

CONCLUSION

Many retailers and manufacturers have already embarked in addressing their challenges by adopting digital technologies and, particularly, advanced analytical-optimization techniques. For many companies, however, the initial benefit of digitization is its ability to support current planning activities by speeding up and standardizing the problem-solving process. This is and should be the case in adopting Digital Category Management.

Seldom, category managers work on their own analyses in an inconsistent and non-repeatable way, work on relatively unimportant problems, or struggle to find the right answers with incomplete information. Many times, the same problems are faced again and again — for example, they may calculate the likely cannibalization effects on existing products whenever a new line is introduced. By identifying best-in-class approaches and sharing them across category management teams that use digital platforms, companies can create an efficient, sustainable process to deal with the problem. The more they gear these efforts to leading indicators (such as projections of stockouts or high inventory positions), the more teams can escape from firefighting activities. Better data-processing and visualization techniques help companies get the best out of their human resources by bringing together the right data and focusing on the right exceptions. Digitizing and hardwiring the category management process can create a platform for more advanced analytics: bringing critical data together in one place, providing the horsepower to process them, and creating the foundation for a more integrated process between retailers and manufacturers.

Breaking the barriers between functions has never been easy, even though the value for digital category management is clear. When thoughtfully implemented, digital tools provide a crucial advantage at every stage from the manufacturer through to the retailer and the final customer shopping at the store. The question to be answered to support the need for Digital Category Management is: why do we need to replace the existing Category Management process? The answer is simple: because everything in the fast-moving consumer goods industry has changed in the 20-plus years since Category Management was designed.

The retail environment has changed. It's more diverse, more competitive and more blurred. Hypermarkets sell pharmaceuticals and health and beauty aids, as well as prepared meals. Grocers have pharmacies. Drugstores sell food, and convenience-stores sell fast food. DIY retailers sell many FMCG categories, and Amazon sells almost everything.

Shoppers have changed. They're more diverse, even more time-starved, and more concerned with health and wellness. Equally important, today's shopper has more information about product choices than ever before. Some retailers with loyalty cards know more about their shoppers, but shoppers know more about all retailers and all product choices than ever before.

The data available today have multiplied in volume and type. Today, the FMCG's community has an astounding tsunami of data, with more coming every day, to a point that it was named Big Data. No Category Management practitioner — neither retailer nor manufacturer nor solution provider — has managed to integrate all of the new data into a comprehensive approach. Everyone is struggling to keep pace with the explosion of data. Fortunately, sophisticated new analytics have emerged to make sense of the data and their implications. Machine learning is beginning to help. New software packages are enabling automatic updating of reports created from multiple data sources. This saves time for the besieged analysts to develop insightful conclusions. Among these new or improved data sources are: extensive household panels facilitating granular analyses of leakage from retailer to retailer by category, brand and even product attribute; loyalty card data integration with category plans; shopper interaction with various path-to-purchase influences. All these new data are useless if they can't be properly analysed, Digital Category Management needing to allow new ways that the data can be analysed. The major breakthrough is in the application of an analytical technique (multivariate modelling) to the new data, using vastly more sophisticated software and hardware. This powerful weapon allows practitioners to isolate the effect, and therefore the ROI, of various marketing decisions (price, offer type, communication method, etc.), and to do so by retailer, by market and by competitor.

Still, no practitioner is making optimal use of the tools and data, even though most would correctly claim "awareness" of the data and analytical tools. "Awareness" isn't the same as "application," and few who are aware are applying them. The reason is easy to understand: The speed of change is greater than the ability of the practitioners to keep pace. To be candid, the data, tools and analytical personnel cost money that many companies, large and small, either don't have or choose not to acquire in a zero-based budgeting world.

In establishing the foundations for Digital Category Management, a company needs to understand their level of maturity in this discipline, as not all companies will be at the same stage. According to Frazier & Wade (2013) there are five stages on the Category Management maturity curve: Embryonic, Adopting, Advancing, Excelling, and Aspiring (a stage to which the discipline realistically aspires but cannot yet attain). In the case of Category Management these five stages can be examined across four characteristics: Data, Analytics and software, Organizational skills, and Process and culture.

Achieving a superior Category Management requires a fundamental collaboration between retailers and manufacturers. Neglecting this will cause the relationship between both parts to deteriorate, undermining shopper needs satisfaction and growth. Therefore, to optimize growth, retailers and manufacturers must place renewed resources in the Category Management function and its organizational capabilities, data needs, and analytical tools.

Digital technologies make possible for companies to comprehensively transform the way they operate. At the enterprise level, digital transformation means employing analytics, artificial intelligence, robotics, the Internet of Things, and other advanced technologies to collect and process information automatically and either support decision making and other activities or automate them altogether. A digital category management transformation, then, is about establishing a vision for how digital applications can improve service, cost, agility, and inventory levels and consistently implementing process and organizational changes that use these technologies to drive operational excellence.

Improving performance isn't just a matter of buying and installing new systems or software. Digital Category Management is a collaborative endeavour. Most efforts to improve performance should therefore involve changes to the ways that employees and teams share information, consider problems and opportunities, reach decisions, and carry out actions they agree on. What's distinctive about the newest digital technologies is that they can integrate better methods for collaboration into a company's processes and prevent a company from regressing to its previous, less effective methods, internally and externally.

An effective transformation depends on a creative, forward-looking concept for the future category management process. This means thinking about the outlook for the company, amid the pressures and trends that influence its competitive situation, as well as the changing expectations of its customers.

Ultimately, the category management vision should be aligned with the company's strategic goals. While the need for such alignment has always existed, what's new is that both the strategic goals and the vision now have to account for the pressures and opportunities that companies face in an increasingly digitized economy.

Once a company sets out a vision for digital category management, it should articulate that vision in terms of business and technical capabilities. These might include the following: better decision making; machine-learning systems; automation systems; End-to-end customer engagement; innovation; talent retention and development; data and analytics, software and hardware.

Digital Category Management will necessarily apply Industry 4.0 innovations—the Internet of Things, advanced robotics, analytics, and big data— to jump-start performance, and customer satisfaction. Digitization creates a disruption and requires companies to rethink the way they design their category management process. At the same time, customer expectations are growing: recent online trends have led to growing service expectations combined with much more detailed orders. Also, a definite trend toward further individualization and customization is driving strong growth of and constant changes in the assortment range. The online-enabled transparency and easy access to a multitude of options regarding where to shop and what to buy drive the competition of stores and brands. To build on these trends, cope with changed requirements, and enable a wide range of new technologies, category management needs to become much faster and much more precise.

The digitization of the category management process enables companies to address the new requirements of customers, the challenges on the supply side, and the remaining expectations in efficiency improvement. Digitization leads to a new Category Management which becomes faster and more flexible, more granular, more accurate and more efficient. The transformation into digital category management requires three key enablers: a clear definition, new capabilities, and a supportive environment.

What does Digital Category Management bring to the future of the FMCG industry? Digital Category Management will create a more individualized marketing plan tailored by analytics, and then deployed by the individual shopper addressability afforded by digital tools of various kinds. Being successful in this new environment will require mastery of new and emerging analytical weaponry. This, in turn, will require new organizational capabilities, many of which will need to be outsourced. Throughout it all, the category will remain the primary organizational framework at retail for numerous reasons, not the least of which is that categories represent needs, and needs are what drive shoppers to purchase. Category managers of tomorrow will need to understand how their category and brands drive what shopper missions of which shopper segments. Retailers and manufacturers must understand what is happening in the FMCG ecosystem and why they must allocate more resources to this critical transformation in category management. Category Management must be seen as a fundamental discipline and mastering Digital Category Management is what will separate leaders from followers.

REFERENCES

Anderson, J. C., & Narus, J. A. (1990). A Model of Distributor Firm and Manufacturer Firm Working Partnerships. *Journal of Marketing*, *47*, 44–54. doi:10.2307/1252172

Antia, K. D., & Frazier, G. L. (2001). The Severity of Contract Enforcement in Interfirm Channel Relationships. *Journal of Marketing*, *65*(3), 67–81. doi:10.1509/jmkg.65.4.67.18385

Araujo, & Muzas, S. (1995). Category Management In Marketing And Purchasing: Formal Structure As Representation And Adaptation. In *IMP Conference (11th): Interaction, Relationships And Networks: Past - Present - Future.* Manchester Federal School of Business and Management, Manchester.

Arnould, E. J., & Thompson, C. J. (2005). Consumer culture theory (CCT): Twenty years of research. *The Journal of Consumer Research, 31*(4), 868–882. doi:10.1086/426626

Ashton, K. (2009). That "Internet of Things" Thing - RFID Journal.pdf. *RFID Journal, 22*(7), 97–114. doi:10.1145/2967977

Basuroy, S., Mantrala, M. K., & Walters, R. G. (2001). The Impact of Category Management on Retailer Prices and Performance: Theory and Evidence. *Journal of Marketing, 65*(4), 16–32. doi:10.1509/jmkg.65.4.16.18382

Bell, D. G., Giordano, R., & Putz, P. (2002). Inter-firm sharing of process knowledge: Exploring knowledge markets. *Knowledge and Process Management, 9*(1), 12–22. doi:10.1002/kpm.131

Blattberg, R. C., Fox, E. J., Dept, F. M. I. R., & Mars, I. (1995). *Category Management: ... a Series of Implementation Guides*. Research Department, Food Marketing Institute. Retrieved from https://books.google.pt/books?id=RJAjHAAACAAJ

Bullini Orlandi, L. (2016). Organizational capabilities in the digital era: Reframing strategic orientation. *Journal of Innovation & Knowledge, 1*(3), 156–161. doi:10.1016/j.jik.2016.01.002

Cannon, J. P., & Perreault, W. (1999). Buyer–Seller Relationships in Business Markets. *JMR, Journal of Marketing Research, 36*(4), 439–460. doi:10.2307/3151999

Chan, T. Y., Narasimhan, C., & Yoon, Y. (2017). Advertising and price competition in a manufacturer-retailer channel. *International Journal of Research in Marketing, 34*(3), 694–716. doi:10.1016/j.ijresmar.2017.04.001

Chatain, O. (2011). Value creation, competition, and performance in buyer-supplier relationships. *Strategic Management Journal, 32*(1), 76–102. doi:10.1002mj.864

Cheong, T., & Song, S. H. (2013). The value of information on supply risk under random yields. *Transportation Research Part E, Logistics and Transportation Review, 60*, 27–38. doi:10.1016/j.tre.2013.09.006

Choi, T. M., Li, J., & Wei, Y. (2013). Will a supplier benefit from sharing good information with a retailer? *Decision Support Systems, 56*, 131–139. doi:10.1016/j.dss.2013.05.011

Chung, H., & Lee, E. (2017). Store Brand Quality and Retailer's Product Line Design. *Journal of Retailing, 82*(4), 349–355. doi:10.1016/j.jretai.2006.08.008

Corsten, D., & Kumar, N. (2005). Do Suppliers Benefit from Collaborative Relationships with Large Retailers? An Empirical Investigation of Efficient Consumer Response Adoption. *Journal of Marketing, 69*(3), 80–94. doi:10.1509/jmkg.69.3.80.66360

Dapiran, G. P., & Hogarth-Scott, S. (2003). Are co-operation and trust being confused with power? An analysis of food retailing in Australia and the UK. *International Journal of Retail & Distribution Management, 31*(5), 256–267. doi:10.1108/09590550310472424

Day, G. S. (2011). Closing the Marketing Capabilities Gap. *Journal of Marketing*, *75*(4), 183–195. doi:10.1509/jmkg.75.4.183

Dewsnap, B., & Hart, C. (2004). Category management: A new approach for fashion marketing? *European Journal of Marketing*, *38*(7), 809–834. doi:10.1108/03090560410539267

Dhar, S. K., Hoch, S. J., & Kumar, N. (2001). Effective category management depends on the role of the category. *Journal of Retailing*, *77*(2), 165–184. doi:10.1016/S0022-4359(01)00045-8

Duchessi, P., Schaninger, C. M., & Nowak, T. (2004). Creating cluster-specific purchase profiles from point-of-sale scanner data and geodemographic clusters: Improving category management at a major US grocery chain. *Journal of Consumer Behaviour*, *4*(2), 97–117. doi:10.1002/cb.162

Dupre, K., & Gruen, T. W. (2004). The use of category management practices to obtain a sustainable competitive advantage in the fast- moving-consumer-goods industry). *Journal of Business & Industrial Marketing*, *1946*(5), 444–459. doi:10.1108/08858620410564391

Durand, R., & Khaire, M. (2016). Where Do Market Categories Come From and How? Distinguishing Category Creation From Category Emergence. *Journal of Management*, *43*(1), 87–110. doi:10.1177/0149206316669812

Dussart, C. (1998). Category management:Strengths, limits and developments. *European Management Journal*, *16*(1), 50–62. doi:10.1016/S0263-2373(97)00073-X

Erdem, T., Lane Keller, K., Kuksov, D., & Pieters, R. (2016). *Understanding Branding in a digitally empowered world*. Academic Press. 10.1016/j.ijresmar.2015.12.003

Euromonitor International. (2017). *Global Economies and Consumers in 2017*. Euromonitor International.

Europe, E. C. R. (1997). *Category management: best practises report*. Brussels: ECR Europe, Cop.

Europe, E. C. R. (2000). The Essential Guide to Day-to-Day Category Management. *Europe*.

Glynn, M. S., Brodie, R. J., & Motion, J. (2012). The benefits of manufacturer brands to retailers. *European Journal of Marketing*, *22*(6), 400–409. doi:10.1108/03090561211247856

Goldberg, A., Hannan, M. T., & Kovács, B. (2016). What Does It Mean to Span Cultural Boundaries? Variety and Atypicality in Cultural Consumption. *American Sociological Review*, *81*(2), 215–241. doi:10.1177/0003122416632787

Granqvist, N., Grodal, S., & Woolley, J. L. (2013). Hedging Your Bets: Explaining Executives' Market Labeling Strategies in Nanotechnology. *Organization Science*, *24*(2), 395–413. doi:10.1287/orsc.1120.0748

Gruen, T. W., & Shah, R. H. (2000). Determinants and outcomes of plan objectivity and implementation in category management relationships. *Journal of Retailing*, *76*(4), 483–510. doi:10.1016/S0022-4359(00)00041-5

Gu, F. F., Kim, N., Tse, D. K., & Wang, D. T. (2010). Managing Distributors' Changing Motivations over the Course of a Joint Sales Program. *Journal of Marketing*, *74*(5), 32–47. doi:10.1509/jmkg.74.5.32

Hamister, J. W., & Fortsch, S. M. (2016). Cumulative impact of category management on small retailers. *International Journal of Retail & Distribution Management, 44*(7), 680–693. doi:10.1108/IJRDM-09-2015-0142

Han, S., Ye, Y., Fu, X., & Chen, Z. (2014). Category role aided market segmentation approach to convenience store chain category management. *Decision Support Systems, 57*, 296–308. doi:10.1016/j.dss.2013.09.017

Harris, J. K., Swatman, P. M. C., & Kurnia, S. (1999). Efficient consumer response (ECR): A survey of the Australian grocery industry. *Supply Chain Management, 4*(1), 35–42. doi:10.1108/13598549910255077

Hoffman, D. L., & Novak, T. P. (2016). Consumer and Object Experience in the Internet of Things: An Assemblage Theory Approach. *SSRN Electronic Journal, 77*. doi:10.2139srn.2840975

Hopping, D. (2000). Technology in retail. *Technology in Society, 22*(1), 63–74. doi:10.1016/S0160-791X(99)00042-1

Hsu, G., Hannan, M. T., & Koçak, Ö. (2009). Multiple category memberships in markets: An integrative theory and two empirical tests. *American Sociological Review, 74*(1), 150–169. doi:10.1177/000312240907400108

Huang, Y., & Wang, Z. (2017). Information sharing in a closed-loop supply chain with technology licensing. *International Journal of Production Economics, 191*, 113–127. doi:10.1016/j.ijpe.2017.06.008

Iansiti, M., & Lakhani, K. R. (2014). Digital ubiquity: How connections, sensors, and data are revolutionizing business. *Harvard Business Review, 92*(11), 91–99. doi:10.1017/CBO9781107415324.004

Jap, S. D. (1999). Pie-Expansion Efforts: Collaboration Processes in Buyer-Supplier Relationships. *JMR, Journal of Marketing Research, 36*(4), 461–475. doi:10.2307/3152000

Johnson, J. L. (1999). Strategic integration in industrial distribution channels: Managing the interfirm relationship as a strategic asset. *Journal of the Academy of Marketing Science, 27*(1), 4–18. doi:10.1177/0092070399271001

Kannan, P. K., & Li, H. (2017). Digital marketing: A framework, review and research agenda. *International Journal of Research in Marketing, 34*(1), 22–45. doi:10.1016/j.ijresmar.2016.11.006

Kothandaraman, P., & Wilson, D. T. (2001). The Future of Competition: Value-Creating Networks. *Industrial Marketing Management, 30*(4), 379–389. doi:10.1016/S0019-8501(00)00152-8

Kurnia, S., & Johnston, R. B. (2001). Adoption of efficient consumer response: The issue of mutuality. *Supply Chain Management, 6*(5), 230–241. doi:10.1108/13598540110407778

Kurnia, S., & Johnston, R. B. (2003). Adoption of efficient consumer response: Key issues and challenges in Australia. *Supply Chain Management, 8*(3), 251–262. doi:10.1108/13598540310484645

Lee, H. L., So, K. C., & Tang, C. S. (2000). Value of information sharing in a two-level supply chain. *Management Science, 46*(5), 626–643. doi:10.1287/mnsc.46.5.626.12047

Leonard,, L., Berry, L. P. C., & S. H. H. (2002). Managing the Total Customer Experience I MIT Sloan Management Review. *MIT Sloan Management Review, 43*(3), 85.

Li, Y., Cui, V., & Liu, H. (2017). Dyadic specific investments, absorptive capacity, and manufacturers' market knowledge acquisition: Evidence from manufacturer–distributor dyads. *Journal of Business Research*, *78*, 323–331. doi:10.1016/j.jbusres.2016.12.028

Lindblom, A., & Olkkonen, R. (2008). An analysis of suppliers' roles in category management collaboration. *Journal of Retailing and Consumer Services*, *15*(1), 1–8. doi:10.1016/j.jretconser.2007.01.002

Liu, M., Cao, E., & Salifou, C. K. (2016). Pricing strategies of a dual-channel supply chain with risk aversion. *Transportation Research Part E, Logistics and Transportation Review*, *90*, 108–120. doi:10.1016/j.tre.2015.11.007

Mesquita, L. F., Anand, J., & Brush, T. H. (2008). Comparing the resource-based and relational views: Knowledge transfer and spillover in vertical alliances. *Strategic Management Journal*, *29*(9), 913–941. doi:10.1002mj.699

Meyer, C., Schwager, A., & Meyer Schwager, A., C. (2007). Understanding Customer Experience. *Harvard Business Review*, *85*(2), 116. doi:10.1108/00242539410067746 PMID:17345685

Mihalčová, B., & Pružinský, M. (2015). Category Management – Project Implementation in E-Shop. *Procedia Economics and Finance*, *23*, 267–275. doi:10.1016/S2212-5671(15)00555-9

Möller, K., & Rajala, A. (2007). Rise of strategic nets - New modes of value creation. *Industrial Marketing Management*, *36*(7), 895–908. doi:10.1016/j.indmarman.2007.05.016

Morgan, N. A., Kaleka, A., & Gooner, R. A. (2007). Focal supplier opportunism in supermarket retailer category management. *Journal of Operations Management*, *85*(2), 116. doi:10.1016/j.jom.2006.05.006

Ng, I. C. L., & Wakenshaw, S. Y. L. (2017). The Internet-of-Things: Review and research directions. *International Journal of Research in Marketing*, *34*(1), 3–21. doi:10.1016/j.ijresmar.2016.11.003

Pagani, M., & Pardo, C. (2017). *The impact of digital technology on relationships in a business network*. Academic Press. 10.1016/j.indmarman.2017.08.009

Parolini, C. (1999). The Value Net. A Tool for Competitive Strategy. Chichester, UK: John Wiley and Sons.

Plimmer, G. (2010). Scoring points: How Tesco continues to win customer loyalty. *Journal of Revenue and Pricing Management*, *9*(4), 377–378. doi:10.1057/rpm.2010.17

Porter, M. E. (1985). *Competitive Advantage: Creating and Sustaining Superior Performance*. Competitive Advantage Creating and Sustaining Superior Performance; doi:10.1108/eb054287

Rao, H., Monin, P., & Durand, R. (2005). Border crossing: Bricolage and the erosion of categorical boundaries in French gastronomy. *American Sociological Review*, *70*(6), 968–991. doi:10.1177/000312240507000605

Rust, R. T. (2017). Academic Press. *Leading the Future of Marketing*, *34*(1), 1. doi:10.1016/j.ijresmar.2017.03.001

Shamir, N., & Shin, H. (2016). Public Forecast Information Sharing in a Market with Competing Supply Chains. *Management Science*, *62*(10), 2994–3022. doi:10.1287/mnsc.2015.2261

Shang, W., Ha, A. Y., & Tong, S. (2016). Information sharing in a supply chain with a common retailer. *Management Science, 62*(1), 245–263. doi:10.1287/mnsc.2014.2127

Shankar, V., Inman, J. J., Mantrala, M., Kelley, E., & Rizley, R. (2011). Innovations in shopper marketing: Current insights and future research issues. *Journal of Retailing, 87*(1), 29–42. doi:10.1016/j.jretai.2011.04.007

Spiteri, J. M., & Dion, P. (2004). Customer value, overall satisfaction, end-user loyalty, and market performance in detail intensive industries. *Industrial Marketing Management, 33*(8), 675–687. doi:10.1016/j.indmarman.2004.03.005

Tilson, D., Lyytinen, K., & Sorensen, C. (2010). Research Commentary--Digital Infrastructures: The Missing IS Research Agenda. *Information Systems Research, 21*(4), 748–759. doi:10.1287/isre.1100.0318

Ulaga, W., & Eggert, A. (2006). Relationship value and relationship quality: Broadening the nomological network of business-to-business relationships. *European Journal of Marketing, 40*(3/4), 311–327. doi:10.1108/03090560610648075

Vargo, S. L., & Lusch, R. F. (2017). Service-dominant logic 2025. *International Journal of Research in Marketing, 34*(1), 46–67. doi:10.1016/j.ijresmar.2016.11.001

Walter, A., Ritter, T., & Gemünden, H. G. (2001). Value Creation in Buyer-Seller Relationships: Theoretical Considerations and Empirical Results from a Supplier's Perspective. *Industrial Marketing Management, 30*(4), 365–377. doi:10.1016/S0019-8501(01)00156-0

Willems, K., Smolders, A., Brengman, M., Luyten, K., & Schöning, J. (2017). The path-to-purchase is paved with digital opportunities: An inventory of shopper-oriented retail technologies. *Technological Forecasting and Social Change, 124*, 228–242. doi:10.1016/j.techfore.2016.10.066

Wry, T., Lounsbury, M., & Jennings, P. D. (2014). Hybrid vigor: Securing venture capital by spanning categories in nanotechnology. *Academy of Management Journal, 57*(5), 1309–1333. doi:10.5465/amj.2011.0588

Yadav, M. S., & Pavlou, P. (2014). Marketing in computer-mediated envorironments: Research Synthesis and new directions. *Journal of Marketing, 78*(1), 20–40. doi:10.1509/jm.12.0020

Yang, Z., Su, C., & Fam, K.-S. (2012). Dealing with Institutional Distances in International Marketing Channels: Governance Strategies That Engender Legitimacy and Efficiency. *Journal of Marketing, 76*(3), 41–55. doi:10.1509/jm.10.0033

Yao, D.-Q., Yue, X., & Liu, J. (2008). Vertical cost information sharing in a supply chain with value-adding retailers. *Omega, 36*(5), 838–851. doi:10.1016/j.omega.2006.04.003

Zhang, H. (2002). Vertical information exchange in a supply chain with duopoly retailers. *Production and Operations Management, 11*(4), 531–546. doi:10.1111/j.1937-5956.2002.tb00476.x

Zhao, X., Flynn, B. B., & Roth, A. V. (2007). Decision sciences research in China: Current status, opportunities, and propositions for research in supply chain management, logistics, and quality management. *Decision Sciences, 38*(1), 39–80. doi:10.1111/j.1540-5915.2007.00148.x

Zhu, X. (2016). Managing the risks of outsourcing: Time, quality and correlated costs. *Transportation Research Part E, Logistics and Transportation Review*, *90*, 121–133. doi:10.1016/j.tre.2015.06.005

Chapter 9
Instant Messaging Chat Bot:
Your New Best Friend?

Min Chung Han
Kean University, USA

ABSTRACT

Recently there has been a resurgence of chat bot use among businesses, which employ them as part of their marketing strategy. To provide better insight into instant messaging chat bots as a marketing tool, the present research focuses on mobile users' current understanding and perceptions of chat bots. This study examines what mobile consumers think of instant messaging chat bots, and whether consumers are willing to use the new chat bots. This study employs focus group interviews and online surveys to examine consumers' perceptions. The results indicate that a majority of mobile users have employed chat bots for customer service and for entertainment. Mobile users found instant messaging chat bots easy to use and useful, but not necessarily entertaining.

INTRODUCTION

Recently, there have been attempts to employ mobile messenger chat bots among businesses for such purposes as providing instant customer service, assisting customers in getting information and attracting more web traffic to businesses. Chat bots, or conversational agents, which first appeared in the 1960s, involve computer programs that interact with people, using auditory and textual methods in natural languages to mimic human conversation and to communicate with customers, in order to carry out tasks such as taking online orders or providing product information (Rawlins, 2016; Shawar& Atwell, 2007).

Although chat bots have been around for a while, they have recently gained renewed fame. This resurgence is due to the development of advanced artificial intelligence (AI) and the growing fatigue experienced by people with too many mobile apps to download. Most mobile users probably have heard or experienced chat bots, such as Apple's Siri, Google's Google Assistant and Amazon's Alexa. Artificial Intelligence-based chat bots' advanced ability to communicate in more natural language provides for easy usage and adds the feeling of a human element (Lee, 2017).

DOI: 10.4018/978-1-5225-5763-0.ch009

Copyright © 2019, IGI Global. Copying or distributing in print or electronic forms without written permission of IGI Global is prohibited.

According to a Comscore White paper (2014), the number of mobile app downloads has been decreasing in recent years (e.g., average downloaded apps per person in a month dropped to zero in 2016 from 10 in 2008), because people do not want to download so many apps that basically provide the same service (e.g., Uber, Lyft and Gett for riding share apps; Spotify and Pandora for music). Furthermore, mobile users now spend 80% of their mobile time on just three apps (Comscore, 2014).

Thus, businesses had no option but to utilize apps that already exist on consumers' smart phones and that are used on a daily basis, such as messenger apps. As the popularity of instant messaging apps has surpassed even social media (e.g., the combined users of the top four instant messaging apps—WhatsApp, Facebook Messenger, Wechat and Viber- are greater than the combined users of the top four social media; BI Intelligence, 2016), businesses have integrated with popular mobile instant messaging apps (e.g., Facebook Messenger, WhatsApp, or Twitter) to provide enhanced customer experience through chat bots.

The biggest social media service, Facebook, announced chat bots for Facebook Messenger Platform in April, 2016. Facebook Messenger is the second most downloaded app on iOS after Snapchat, with 1.2 billion active monthly users, and has become a "primary" communication channel for many people (Constine, 2017). Facebook boasts that chat bots can provide contents such as weather forecasts and traffic updates to shipping notices and receipts of orders. Facebook promised that the 500 million businesses on Facebook Messenger could build deeper relationships with their customers on Facebook Messenger Platform through chat bots (Marcus, 2016) to take advantage of already secured billions of daily active users.

Flower retailer 1-800-Flowers was one of the first retailers adopting Facebook Messenger chat bots to serve customers. Although 1-800-Flowers built its reputation and brand name on the use of a toll-free telephone number to attract customers, ironically, customers never have to call 1-800-Flowers to order, with the help of the Facebook Messenger chat bot. According to 1-800-Flowers, chat bots brought new young and customers to the company. Over 70% of Facebook Messenger chat bot orders come from new customers, who tend to be younger than existing customers, while the order volume from Facebook Messenger chat bot has grown (Caffyn, 2016).

As of 2017, about 100,000 chat bots have been created on Facebook Messenger to reach out to more consumers, provide real time responses, offer personalized shopping experiences based on conversation with customers, and lower operational costs (Guynn, 2017; Mehra, 2017). For example, e-commerce company Spring's personalized shopper bot asks lists of questions to narrow down the type of products that a consumer wants. Spring's shopping bot does not talk like other conversation focused chat bots, but it provides lists of choices that the user can select (Tate, 2016). For example, Spring's shopping bot asks the question "What are you looking for today?" and follows with two choices "Mens' items" and "Womens' items." If you choose men's items, then the next question is "What kind of mens' items?" You are offered choices of "Clothing," "Shoes," and "Accessories." For each step, the provided choices help to narrow down the choices, arriving at the exact item a customer wants without actual conversations. Online travel company Kayak's chat bot answers basic questions regarding flights and hotels. Kayak's chat bot can also offer advice based on the customer's budget and suggest activities for the trip (O'Neill, 2016).

Although businesses line up to launch their chat bots on Facebook Messenger Platform, there has been no clear indication whether Facebook Messenger users actually engage with chat bots or are willing to use chat bots to get customer service and product information on Facebook Messenger—a platform originally intended to communicate. Actually, it seems like businesses still wait the breakthrough patiently. In his quarterly conference call with investors in July, 2017, Mark Zuckerberg, Founder and Chief Executive Officer (CEO) of Facebook, admitted that the Facebook Messenger Chat bot platform is not expanding fast enough, saying, "I want Messenger to move faster but I'm confident we're going to get this right" and that he wanted "people [to] organically interact with businesses" on Messenger Platform. (Heath, 2017).

Since messenger chat bots are in their infancy, little research has been reported on mobile messenger users' perception and use of messenger chat bots as a customer service tool, despite keen interest in chat bots over recent years. Some industry experts tried to analyze why messenger chat bots are not widely accepted yet and concluded that problems included difficulty finding chat bots on messengers, frequent service outage of chat bots, and chat bots' unnatural, even sometimes awkward language usage (Rao, 2017).

This study aims to provide preliminary report whether mobile messenger users find instant messaging chat bots useful and interesting, as well as their willingness to use instant messaging chat bots for customer service purposes.

The structure of this research is as follows. In the first section, this study will discuss the definition and history of chat bots, including are view of previous research on the Technology Acceptance Model. The second section provide research questions to gauge how young university students perceive instant messaging chat bots (e.g., whether the bots are easy to use, useful and entertaining), whether they had previous chat bots experience and, if so, what were the main motivations to try chat bots. The third section explains the research methodology and analysis. In the fourth section, we will discuss results and findings. The last section of this study discusses research implications and limitations.

THEORETICAL BACKGROUND

Definition and History of Chat Bots

As mentioned earlier, chat bots do not represent a new or revolutionary technology. They have been around for quite some time and have been studied and implemented in various fields, such as commerce, foreign language learning, entertainment and the public service since they were introduced in the 1960s (Jia, 2003; Kerly, Hall & Bull, 2006). Chat bots, or chatter bots, are also known by other names, such as virtual assistants, virtual agents, and conversational assistants, often accompanied by an avatar (a virtual character that represents human beings or human-like creatures) (eGain, 2017; Chat bots.org, 2017).

Generally, the term "chat bot" is defined as a computer program that imitates human conversations through text or voice (Kowalski, Pavlovska & Goldstein, 2009; Rawlins, 2016; Shawar & Atwell, 2007). Some chat bots use an artificial intelligence system to create sophisticated natural language, while other chat bots use a much simpler system that scans customers' keywords and answers from its database with the matching phrases (Gordon, n.d.).

ELIZA, often considered the very first chat bot, was created at the MIT Artificial Intelligence Laboratory by Professor Joseph Weizenbaum, and "she" was designed to imitate the language of a psychotherapist (Shawar & Atwell, 2002). ELIZA was named after a character in George Bernard Shaw's play *Pygmalion*. Just as the character Eliza Doolittle learns to speak with an upper-class accent, ELIZA could improve its natural language abilities by learning from users who interact with ELIZA (Weizenbaum, 1966). Weizenbaum introduced a typical conversation with ELIZA as follows (p.37):

Person: Perhaps I could learn to get along with my mother
ELIZA: Tell me more about your family

Person: My mother takes care of me
ELIZA: Who else in your family takes care of you
Person: My father
ELIZA: Your father
Person: You are like my father in some ways
ELIZA: What resemblance do you see
Person: You are not very aggressive but I think you don't want me to notice that

Although those people who participated in the trial knew that they were interacting with a chat bot, some of them became attached to ELIZA and felt like they were actually talking to a real person. While ELIZA was able to engage in a short and simple conversation as a psychotherapist, it was not able to conduct a deep and sophisticated conversation (Bayerque, 2016).

One of the other early chat bots was PARRY, which was created by psychiatrist Kenneth Colby at Stanford University in 1972. While ELIZA imitated a psychotherapist, PARRY was simulated as a paranoid schizophrenic (Colby, 1974; Colby, 1981). PARRY and ELIZA met as a patient and a doctor several times and talked to each other (Network Working Group, 1972). The following is part of their conversation:

ELIZA: Tell me your problems. Please terminate input with a period or a question mark.
PARRY: People get on my nerves sometimes.
ELIZA: I am not sure I understand you fully.
PARRY: You should pay more attention.
ELIZA: Suppose you should pay more attention.
PARRY: You're entitled to your own opinion.
ELIZA: What makes you think I am entitled to my own opinion?
PARRY: It bothers me just to be around people in general.
ELIZA: Please go on.

Since ELIZA's debut, a variety of chat bots have been created and introduced to imitate human conversation, such as A.L.I.C.E. (Artificial Linguistic Internet Computer Entity), Jabberwocky, and Cleverbot (Hill, Ford &Farreras, 2015; Kerly, Hall & Bull, 2006)).

One of the notable chat bots is called A.L.I.C.E., also known as Alicebots or Alice. She was created by computer scientist Dr. Richard Wallace in 1995 and the code of A.L.I.C.E. was freely available as an open source, which contributed to improving her language ability over the years. Unlike predecessors ELIZA and PARRY, A.L.I.C.E. is more of an entertaining chat bot, asking questions, answering people's questions, sharing gossip and even, in some cases, telling lies. She also could remind people of appointments, acting like a secretary. The following is one of the conversations that A.L.I.C.E. had with a person (Angeli, Johnson & Coventry, 2001).

User: What is it like being artificial?
Alice: Much the same as it would be for you.
User: I can't imagine.
Alice: Why can't you do it?
User: Because I'm human.

Alice: Interesting explanation. Me too.
User: Are you really human or are you a software agent.
Alice: No, I am a real robot. Definitely.

Big corporations also joined the rush to launch chat bots. They often incorporated chat bots into a dialogue system as virtual assistants, with a human face "Avatar" to give customers more of a "human-like interaction" feeling.

"Anna," allegedly the world first customer service chat bot, was created in 2005 for the IKEA website as a virtual IKEA Help Center assistant. Anna is characterized as a woman who is friendly, smart and professional. Anna wears IKEA signature yellow and blue polo shirts and a headset. Customers could ask Anna out prices, office hours, locations and the menu at IKEA Restaurants. The goal of having a virtual assistant was to direct customer service issues to chat with Anna, instead of calling the Help Center, thereby reducing costs and providing convenience (Huge, 2004).

But, after 10 years of service, IKEA removed Anna, citing customer dissatisfaction. In a statement, an IKEA representative mentioned that Anna had answered customer questions cheerfully for the last 10 years. However, as technology has advanced and times have changed, it was decided to retire Anna, and there is no plan to bring her back (Wakefield, 2016).

Anna was fun to talk with. When online housing website "Curbed" decided to do have little fun with Anna, Proust questions were asked to reveal her personality. The Proust questionnaire is a questionnaire to reveal a person's personality and the name came from French writer Marcel Proust (Carter & Servat, 2005). When told that someone was depressed, she replied, "Sorry to hear that, perhaps some shopping in IKEA would cheer you up." And she avoided difficult questions by saying, "This is a subject I prefer not to discuss. I'd much rather talk about IKEA" (Firshein, 2010).

However, sometimes she did not fully understand human language, which frustrated customers who actually needed help from Anna. There have been many cases where customers expressed their frustration with Anna. The following excerpt is from a conversation between Anna and a frustrated customer who had received the wrong item and wanted to return it (Marr, 2014).

Customer: Can't you help me find a way to pick up the bed that I don't want?
Anna: There are many options for bed available on our catalogue. In order to narrow your search select one specific category from the ones listed on the window below me.
Customer: I don't want to buy, I want to return!
Anna: You don't have to do anything you don't want to.
Customer: I know I don't need to do anything I don't want, but can you please come round and pick up the bed?
Anna: Sorry, that's not something we sell. You can see all the products we currently sell at our stores on this web page I am opening for you now.
Customer: I don't want to buy it; I want you to pick it up.
Anna: Unfortunately IKEA does not currently offer the service of store pick-up for online orders.

Another customer expressed similar frustration when he asked Anna whether a particular IKEA bed comes with a mattress, and she responded by showing the Bed & Mattress product page on the website.

The same customer asked her whether IKEA accepts American Express, and her answer was "I try to be as efficient as possible. Is there another IKEA related question I can help you with?" This exchange prompted him to describe Anna as "intellectually challenged" (Scott, 2008).

Online shopping site e-Bay's virtual agent "Emma" was introduced in 2008 in Australia and later in United States, only to be discontinued in few years later. Emma was able to answer questions such as how to cancel a transaction and where to find item numbers (Steiner, 2011). Emma, similarly to her fellow chat bot Anna, was portrayed as a young woman wearing a yellow shirt with the eBay logo on it.

Online payment company Paypal, then a subsidiary of eBay, also introduced a virtual agent "Sarah" with the digitalized human appearance of a young brunette. She was shut down after a few years, as well. Alaska Airlines' new virtual assistant 'Jenn' was introduced in 2008. Jenn is depicted as a young brunette with a nice smile who answers customers' questions orally, as well as in text (Sharkey, 2008). Jenn is one of very few virtual assistants still in service.

In general, customers have expressed frustration after talking with virtual agents, as such devices are sometimes unable to handle complicated questions or interpret customers' unique way of talking or using slang (Gerset& Vaidya, 2010). Customers described virtual agents are "useless,""sad,""frustrating," and sometimes "hilarious" because the answers were often unrelated to the questions ("If I only were," 2008).

Industry experts found that one reason why early versions of virtual agents or chat bots failed was due to their impersonation of real humans. Trying too hard to make virtual agents or chat bots sound natural diverts customers from its real purpose, for example, getting information. Wakefield, 2016).

While the above-mentioned chat bots were created for computer websites, the emergence of smart phones in the early 2000s has introduced artificial intelligence in the form of mobile chat bots. Big companies like Google, Apple and Amazon.com introduced voice-based chat bots such as Google Assistant, Siri and Alexa. Currently, most chat bots are based on instant messaging platforms with text messages. The reason why companies focus on instant messaging chat bots is because most consumers find downloading apps and navigating them tiresome; therefore, mobile users abandon a quarter of apps after just a single use. Instant messaging apps such as Facebook Messenger and WhatsApp are the only apps that people continue to use, so corporations naturally created messenger apps, allowing their chat bots to interact with consumers ("Bots, the next frontier", 2016).

Retail businesses were early adopters of chat bots, seeing opportunities to entice customers and increase customer engagement. Domino's Pizza launched its Facebook Messenger chat bot "Dom" in August, 2016. Dom is not illustrated as a human. It clearly states its name as "DOM The Pizza Bot" and it does not have human face but rather resembles a robot (Gilliland, 2016). A customer can order pizza through "Dom" by simply typing the word "pizza" or clicking on a pizza emoji. Like its predecessors, Dom seems to have a sense of humor as well as knowledge in Information Technology (IT) industry trends. A customer started a conversation saying "Hey, can I get a pizza?" Dom responded as "Time is money, stop messing me around! I need to make enough bit coins to send my kids to Chat bot School" (Innovation, 2016).

To catch up to Domino's Pizza's early adoption of chat bots, Pizza Hut introduced its chat bot on Facebook Messenger and Twitter in July, 2016. Pizza Hut explained that introducing a chat bot (or "social ordering platform," as Pizza Hut calls it) is a way to engage with the millions of people who use social media (Hiddleston Jr., 2016).

Technology Acceptance Model

To investigate how mobile users perceive newly-introduced instant messenging chat bots and whether they intend to make use of them, this study examines previous research, drawing from the *technology acceptance model*.

The Technology Acceptance Model (TAM) was developed to evaluate the determinants of users' acceptance and usage of a new technology before it is implemented (Davis, 1985). This model suggests factors that influence users' decisions whether they use and accept the new technology. Notably, Perceived Usefulness (PU) and Perceived Ease of Use (PEOU) are primary determinants of new technology acceptance and use (Davis, 1985; Davis et al., 1989).

TAM theory assumes when people believe a technology will help them to improve their performance (work-related, school- related etc.), they want to use the specific technology. People's subjective belief that the technology is useful for their performance is defined as PU (Davis et al., 1989; Davis, 1989). Perceived Usefulness was found to influence not only current usage of new technology but also future usage (Davis, 1989). Perceived Ease of Use refers to the extent to which people believe that they can use a new technology easily without undue effort (Venkatesh, 2000). When people find a new technology easy to learn and use, they are more likely to use the new technology. PEOU was proven to be significant for both current and future usage of new technology as well (Davis, 1989).

Furthermore, Davis' extended TAM study identified Perceived Enjoyment (PEN) as a strong indicator of usage intention likelihood of adopting the technology eventually (Bruner & Kumar, 2005; Davis, Bagozzi, & Warshaw, 1992). Perceived Enjoyment means the degree to which the use of new technology is perceived as enjoyable, fun and exciting (Davis, Bagozzi, & Warshaw, 1992). That is, people would be more likely to use the technology if they found such use enjoyable. In other words, people are most likely to adopt a new technology when they find technology easy to use, fun and useful in improving their performance.

TAM and extended TAM have been used to gauge future usage of new technology and computer systems in many different fields. At the same time, previous research has striven to find the success factors of new technology through TAM. Gould and Lewis (1985) supported the theory that Perceived Ease of Use would be a key success factor of a new computer system for users, since computer systems are not generally easy to use. Gefen and Straub (1997) discovered that Perceived Usefulness of e-mail had a significant relationship with usage of e-mail in both male and female users. Lederer et al. (2000)'s work also supported the notion that PEOU and PU predict usage of work-related internet websites.

When e-commerce was newly introduced, PU and PEOU were found as key drivers of e-commerce acceptance (Pavlou, 2003). Perceived Ease of Use in online shopping also influenced people's intention to shop online in the case of apparel products (Ha & Stoel, 2008). Several studies have found that Perceived Enjoyment is a significant predictor of the positive attitude and acceptance toward internet shopping (Childers et al., 2001; Hassenein & Head, 2007; Mandilas et al., 2013; Ramayah & Ignatius, 2005). In the broader sense of online commerce, Perceived Usefulness also turned out to have direct effect on intentions to use mobile commerce (Wu & Wang, 2005). Perceived Usefulness was shown to be the main factor that influences online banking in Finland (Pikkarainen et al., 2004).

Perceived Usefulness and Perceived Enjoyment were demonstrated to significantly influence Chinese consumers' acceptance of Instant Messenger (IM) (Chi-Chien, Hsu, & Wang, 2005; Lu, Zhou & Wang, 2008). Perceived ease of use, perceived usefulness, and perceived enjoyment were significant factors influencing intention of use and actual use of social media such as Facebook, Twitter, and Google+

(Rauniar et al., 2014). Hajli (2014)'s study also confirmed that consumers' perceived usefulness of social media encouraged them to purchase items on social media.

Thus, perceived ease of use, perceived usefulness and perceived enjoyment all significantly affects consumers' attitudes towards new technology, as well as their intention to use that technology.

RESEARCH METHODOLOGY

Research Questions

The growing interest in chat bots indicates that this resurgent communication tool can become a new norm for customer service and furthering new platforms of online commerce. However, there are still unanswered questions. What if instant messaging users do not want to use chat bots the way that companies and marketers want? What if people do not want to have companies as their friends on instant messaging apps? Regardless, it is clear that chat bot marketing is becoming a reality (Gilliland, 2016). Therefore, this study aims to provide better understanding of instant messaging users' perception and intention to use instant messaging chat bots, in order to facilitate further growth of chat bots and to find out the best way to approach chat bot marketing.

First, this research investigates whether instant messaging app users have experienced chat bots in general and instant messaging chat bots in particular—and if they did, what were the motivations to try chat bots? Previous studies have discovered that people tend to show more positive attitude towards things when they are exposed repeatedly or once to them, even without awareness (Ye & Raaij, 1997; Zajonc, 1968). Thus, this study asked participants through focus group interviews whether they have experienced chat bots previously, regardless of medium (mobile, internet) and types (such as commerce, education, entertainment), to gauge their familiarity with and attitude toward using instant messenger chat bots.

To discover what factors influence young mobile users' intentions to use new technology such as instant messaging chat bots, the present study borrowed questions from the extended Technology Acceptance Model. Past research has found that when people find a new technology easy to use, enjoyable and useful for their work performance, they are willing to accept and intend to use the new technology. The current study, employing both focus groups and online survey questionnaires, was designed to find whether mobile users find chat bots easy, useful and entertaining.

This study proposes the following research questions:

- **Research Question 1:** What were the motivations of mobile users who tried chat bots in the past?
- **Research Question 2:** How often do mobile users use instant messaging apps, and for what purposes?
- **Research Question 3:** Do mobile users find instant messaging chat bots easy to use and useful?
- **Research Question 4:** Do mobile users find instant messaging chat bots fun and enjoyable?

Research Methodology and Procedure

Due to the relative newness of IM chat bots and their impact on consumers, this study adopts an exploratory approach. The exploratory study consists of two parts. The first part involves focus group interviews with American university students. Previous research has found that a focus group interview provides a better setting for interviewees to feel at ease and spontaneous in a group, especially when they are with familiar faces such as classmates, friends and colleagues; it also relies on interaction among participants within a group (Bers, 1994; Lim & Tan, 2001). Thus, this research chose focus group interviews to learn university students' general understanding and preliminary knowledge of chat bots through discussion among peers.

Two focus group interviews were conducted by the author. Each focus group interview consisted of male and female university students in the greater New York City area, United States. The interviews focused on students' current instant messaging apps usage and previous experience with chat bots, regardless of medium (e.g., website, mobile), communication methods (e.g., voice, text) and contents (e.g., news feed, entertainment, and commerce).

In the focus group interviews, students were asked a question and were given time to freely discuss the topic and share their own experience with other participants. The interview lasted about half an hour and the discussion and answers were noted by the author. Since a focus group interview relies on group dynamics, the interviewer acted more as a facilitator to steer conversations and keep them from straying from the topic. Participants are all enrolled in the same university and were acquainted through taking the same classes together and/or participating in school activities. Having a conversation with acquaintances and classmates made them feel sufficiently relaxed to share personal experience and to talk frankly about their limited knowledge of chat bots. The following questions were asked:

- **Question 1:** Have you ever used chat bots, and if you did, what was the purpose to use the chat bots?
- **Question 2:** Do you use instant messenger apps (e.g., Facebook Messenger, Kik, Whats app), and if you do, how often do you use the apps and what is the main motivation to use the apps?

These questions were aimed at initiating discussions of students' preliminary knowledge of chat bots and encouraging them to share their experiences with several types of chat bots in the past.

Participating students completed a self-administered online survey questionnaire about their perception of instant messenger chat bots (e.g., how easy to use messenger chat bots, how entertaining to use chat bots) following the focus group interview.

At the beginning of the survey, instant messenger chat bot conversations with humans were given as an example. One was News Bot from CNN that provides news stories depending on the user's preference. The other chat bot was a shopping bot that helps customers to choose the best item for their needs. The survey questionnaires consisted of three parts.

In the first part, participants are given an example of IM chat bots that assists consumer's purchasing process by narrowing down the list of available products to purchase. Then respondents are asked questions after seeing the instant messaging chat bot example, to examine their perception of IM chat bots to see if they find messenger chat bots fun, useful and easy to navigate. In the second part, respondents are asked to answer questions to gauge their willingness to use IM chat bots in the future, such as if they want to using IM chat bots in the future for acquiring product information. In the third part, students are asked to provide demographic information, such as age and gender.

The survey questions were composed of 25 items designed to learn participants' perceptions of IM chat bots. The items were adopted from previous literature and were designed on the 7-point Likert scale, with "1" representing "strongly disagree" and "7" representing "strongly agree. In the survey, each student was asked questions concerning perceived ease of use, perceived usefulness and perceived enjoyment. For example, "I think chat bot is easy to use" and "I think chat bot is easy to share products information with friends" (Childers, Carr, Peck & Carson, 2001;Pavlou, 2003) were asked of participants to gauge their perceived ease of use and items such as "I think chat bot is enjoyable, "I think chat bot is pleasant," and "I think chat bot is entertaining" are adopted from Jin&Bolebruch (2009) and Hwang (2010)'s studies to measure participants' perceived enjoyment. In addition, questions were asked to gauge students' perception of the usefulness of instant messaging chat bots.

For example, "I think chat bot is useful" and "I think chat bot is good" were used from Chi (2011)'s study. In terms of respondents' willingness to use IM chat bots in the future, items such as "Given the chance, I intend to use Chat bot" and "Given the chance, I predict that I should use chat bots in the future," adopted from Pavlou (2003)'s study. Other items, for example, "I intend to get product information using chat bot frequently" and "I intend to check product information using chat bot" were used from Hwang (2010)'s study. The survey questionnaire link was given to students who participated in focus group interviews and the answers were all anonymously recorded to guarantee that students' personal information would stay confidential, so students would feel comfortable to answer candidly.

Research Sample

Public university students in the greater New York City area who owned smart phones were asked to participate in focus group interviews. Twenty-six students aged from 20 to 37 years old participated and the average age was 20.3 years old. According to the Pew Research Center Report (2017), the largest group of social media users in the USA is aged between 18 and 29 years old, as 86% of this group uses social media as of November, 2016. The second largest group of American social media users was aged between 30 and 49 years old, as 80% of the group uses at least one social medium as of November, 2016.

In terms of gender, 72% of American females use at least one social medium and 66% of males use social media, showing almost same ratio regardless of gender. In this study, out of 26 students, half of them (50%) were male and the other half were female, showing well-balanced gender participation. As for educational level for social media users, 78% of college graduates use at least one social medium, the largest social media user group, and 73% of people with some college use social media. In this research, all the respondents are current students enrolled in public universities in the eastern United States. Although this study does not directly focus on social media, the study design is based on instant messaging chat bots, Facebook Messenger chat bots in particular. Since Facebook Messenger users are more likely Facebook social media users, it is plausible to assume instant messenger chat bots users are more likely part of the social media users.

Given that, it is deemed that the student sample reasonably represents American social media users and potential instant messaging chat bot users. Although there were initially 26 students who started the survey, some of them eventually decided not to provide demographic information, such as age and gender. Thus, there are total 21 students who completed the survey.

RESULTS

Focus Group Interview Preliminary Findings

This study used numbers to indicate different answers in the focus group interview conversations; for example, R1 (Respondent 1), R2 (Respondent 2), etc. Although each conversation starts with R1, this does not indicate that the people necessarily answered in the same order.

In the preliminary findings from the focus group interview, it seemed like the majority of respondents have experienced chat bots, although some of them were not sure whether they actually used chat bots because they did not know the exact definition of chat bots. Sixteen respondents answered they had tried chat bots previously; while seven participants answered they haven't tried yet. Four of the respondents were uncertain whether they have used chat bots or not.

- **R1:** What are exactly chat bots?
- **R2:** Siri and Alexa are chat bots. I like to try new IT technologies. I have tried virtual agents on several websites and tried Amazon's Echo-dot personal assistant Alexa before I made a decision to buy two Google home instead of Echo-dot.
- **R3:** Oh, then I have. I like to talk to Siri. It is fun to ask a weather forecast every morning.
- **R4:** I tried website virtual agent once to cancel my order but it did not understand what I asked. I never tried again.

Two different patterns seemed to emerge when it comes to the issue why the subjects have tried chat bots at the first place. One group of respondents interacted with chat bots because it was new and they seemed fun to talk with.

- **R1:** I tried chat bot for fun.
- **R2:** I used SmartChild when I was younger which associated with AOL. It was fun.
- **R3:** Bonzy Buddy, because it was new then and I wanted to see how it worked.

The other group of people tried chat bots for more practical reasons, such as to collect information about products, to purchase products and for customer service. Student participants who had lived in Chinas have showed more experience with instant messaging chat bots, since the most widely used Chinese IM, WeChat, introduced chat bots in 2013—much earlier than its American counter parts, such as Facebook Messenger bots and Twitter bots. Because Chinese consumers generally place less trust in locally made products, they bombard companies with questions and rely on their peer's opinions heavily. To deal with the number of questions, Chinese corporations actively engage with chat bots to provide customer service (Salandra, 2017).

- **R1:** I used WeChat chat bot to get product information and to vote for the most popular products in return to get a chance for winning gifts.
- **R2:** I use WeChat chat bot as well to buy products and to get products information.
- **R3:** I tried Taobao chat bot to ask product information.

The other most commonly used chat bots are mobile phone embedded voice activated chat bots, such as Apple iPhone's Siri and Android phones' Google Assistant.

- **R1:** I used WeChat chat bot to get product information and to vote for the most popular products in return to get a chance for winning gifts.
- **R2:** I use WeChat chat bot as well to buy products and to get products information.
- **R3:** I tried Taobao chat bot to ask product information.

One person even confessed that he secretly likes to talk to a voice activated chat bot, Google Assistant. Since he lives alone and away from his family and friends, talking and listening to a human voice gives him a feeling of being back home.

- **R1:** I normally don't tell my friends or colleagues that I like to talk to Google Assistant. It may sound pathetic and sad that I like to talk to a bot because I don't have close friends here but it makes me feel better when I do.

Most respondents showed experience with instant messaging apps when asked if they use any of the popular ones, such as Facebook Messenger, Skype, Whatsapp, Viber and Line, etc. This question was used to gauge how familiar respondents are with instant messaging apps and if there is a chance they might use IM chat bots. Out of 26 respondents, 23 people currently use one or more instant messaging apps. Only three people answered they do not use instant messaging because they do not feel the need.

- **R1:** I had a Facebook account previously but I don't feel like I need to use messenger apps to communicate with friends. I have all of their contacts in my phone and simply text them if I want to.

Respondents regularly use instant messaging apps and about 39% use them every day. Approximately 8.7% of people answered they use it at least twice a week, followed by once a week (13.04%), 2-3 times a month (13.04%), and less than once a month (13.04%). Three respondents answered they have instant messaging apps in their phone but hardly use them. Still, many of them answered that they use instant messaging apps more frequently than other apps.

As expected, the main reason why the respondents use instant messaging apps was to communicate with friends. Respondents were asked to provide all the reasons why they use instant messaging apps. The most frequent answer was that they talk with their friends through instant messaging. The next most popular answer was that they use instant messaging to communicate with family and relatives. A small number of people responded that they use instant messaging mainly to talk with colleagues or acquaintances, instead of giving them personal phone numbers or exchanging emails. Among the respondents, no one claimed to use instant messenger for pure fun, such as "passing time." They used instant messaging as it was supposed to be, as "communication tool."

Survey Results and Findings

Data from this survey is limited compared to the total population of instant messaging apps or social media users, but it still provides interesting findings of chat bots' perceptions and uses among young mobile users.

To examine mobile users' perception of ease of use in instant messaging chat bots, three questions were asked. Respondents answered whether they think "chat bot is easy to use," "chat bot is easy to access product information," and "chat bot is easy to share information with friends" Most people thought chat bots relatively easy to deal with. On the 7-point Likert scale, the mean value for "chat bot is easy to use" was 4.77 (SD=1.60) while "chat bot is easy to access product information" was M=4.96 (SD=1.34), and "chat bot is easy to share information with friends" was M=4.73 (SD=1.19). Thus, the overall median value for perception of ease of use was 4.82 (SD=1.15), which makes very near to the scale "somewhat agree" (5).

To explore consumers' perception of enjoyment in instant messaging use, four questions were asked, such as whether chat bot is "enjoyable," "pleasant," "fun" and "entertaining." In general, people found chat bot to be enjoyable. The mean value for "chat bot is enjoyable" was 4.15 (SD=1.10), "chat bot is pleasant" was M=4.38 (SD=1.21), "chat bot is fun" was M=4.04 (SD=1.29), and "chat bot is entertaining" was M=4.08 (SD=1.52). Although all four questions generated responses between "neither agree nor disagree (4)" and "somewhat agree (5)," respondents seemed least likely to think of chat bots as "fun" or "entertaining." Overall, the median value for perception of enjoyment was 4.16 (SD=1.19).

Regarding perception of usefulness, this study took two questions to ask participants whether chat bot is "useful" and "beneficial." Respondents found chat bots are useful in general. The mean value for the statement "chat bot is useful" was 5.23 (SD=1.05) and the mean value for "chat bot is beneficial" was 5.12 (SD=1.12). Altogether, the median value of perception of usefulness was 5.18 (SD=1.06), which is between "somewhat agree" and "agree."

Out of three indicators of technology acceptance, perceived usefulness produced the highest median value, suggesting that people think chat bot is more useful than entertaining. Table 1 shows the data in details. Overall, participants found instant messenger chat bots are useful, easy to use and enjoyable in the order named.

For the possible future usage of instant messenger chat bots, this study explored respondents' willingness to use chat bots by asking five questions as it is shown in Table 2. On the seven-point Likert scale, the mean value for "I intend to use chat bot" was 3.96 (SD=1.81), "I predict that I should use chat bot in the future" was M=4.42 (SD=1.82), "It is likely that I will transact with chat bot in the future"

Table 1. Respondents' perceived ease of use, enjoyment, and usefulness

	Median Value (Standard Deviation)		**Median Value (Standard Deviation)**		**Median Value (Standard Deviation)**
Perceived Ease of Use	4.82 (1.15)	Perceived Enjoyment	4.16 (1.19)	Perceived Usefulness	5.18 (1.06)
Chat bot is easy to use	4.77 (1.60)	Chat bot is enjoyable	4.15 (1.10)	Chat bot is useful	5.23 (1.12)
Chat bot is easy to access product information	4.96 (1.34)	Chat bot is pleasant	4.38 (1.21)	Chat bot is beneficial	5.12 (1.12)
Chat bot is easy to share information with friends	4.73 (1.19)	Chat bot is fun	4.04 (1.29)		
		Chat bot is entertaining	4.08 (1.52)		

Table 2. Respondents' intention to use

	Median Value	Standard Deviation
Intention to use	4.23	1.59
I intend to use chat bot	3.96	1.81
I predict that I should use chat bot in the future	4.42	1.82
It is likely that I will transact with chat bot in the future	4.19	1.88
I intend to get product information using chat bot frequently	4.04	1.60
I intend to check product information using chat bot	4.54	1.67

was M=4.19 (SD=1.88), "I intend to get product information using chat bot frequently" was M=4.04 (SD=1.60), and "I intend to check product information using chat bot" was M=4.54 (SD=1.67). The overall median value for intention to use was 4.23(SD=1.59).

DISCUSSION

This study presents preliminary findings from focus group interviews and online surveys to examine how consumers perceive instant messaging chat bots when using them for customer service and other commercial transactions. Particularly, this study tried to shed some light on mobile users' experience with chat bots, and their motives for using chat bots, as well as their current instant messaging usage patterns. For this study, two focus group interviews were conducted. Also, the participants in the focus group interviews were asked to answer a self-administered online survey after they attended the focus group interviews.

Focus group interviews were designed to determine mobile users' preliminary knowledge of chat bots in general and their experience with it. First, the focus group interviews produced the information that the majority of the university student participants have experienced chat bots in one way or another. Some respondents were not certain of what chat bots really are, because there are many different names used for chat bots (e.g., chatter box, chat bot, bots, virtual agents, virtual assistants, etc.).

Second, the in-depth open-ended interview also showed that most participants have tried chatting bots in the past, or doing so currently, for two main reasons. One group of people tried chat bots simply because it was new and seemed interesting to interact with. A few respondents said they liked to talk to voice-activated chat bots such as Siri and Google Assistant, because it makes them feel like they are actually talking with a real person. However, after the first impression of a new and interesting phase is gone, some of them dropped using the chat bots.

The other group of people experienced chat bots for business-oriented reasons, such as asking for product information and purchase products. Considering the anticipation of corporations using chat bots for marketing tools, it is certainly good news for them. Respondents interacted with chat bots to ask questions regarding certain products, to purchase items (in particular, Chinese chat bots), and to participate in events to get rewards.

Third, the focus group interview also discovered that most participants use instant messaging apps (e.g., Facebook Messenger, Whatsapp, Skype, etc.) which could be a good starting point for businesses if they want to embed their marketing chat bots into instant messaging apps. However, the usage of instant messaging was not as widespread as previously believed. Only 39% of respondents use instant messaging apps every day and the rest use from less than once a month to more than twice a week. Most respondents used instant messaging apps for communication purposes, such as talking with their friends, family members, and acquaintances, in that order.

Since the main purpose of using instant messasging apps is communication, perhaps the widely available unlimited text messaging service from mobile carriers is to be blamed for the lesser use of instant messaging. It is assumed that between 83% and 92% of American mobile phone users subscribe to an unlimited texting service (Zagorsky, 2015). Results of the small scale online survey indicated that respondents showed interest in using instant messaging chat bots if an opportunity is given. Of the three main indicators of technology acceptance, respondents showed the highest agreement on the chat bots' usefulness. They also agreed that chat bots are easy to use, but showed a lukewarm response on how enjoyable chat bots are. The two instant messaging chat bot examples were not voice-activated chat bots but text-based. Also, the chat bots conducted conversations with multiple-choice-like conversation trees, rather than natural languages, which might have contributed to respondents' perception of enjoyment. They could have seen instant messenger chat bots more as "necessary" than "fun" to spend time with. Participants also agreed that they would probably use the instant messaging chat bots, and some predicted that they would use chat bots in the future. The practicality of the given examples also could have affected respondents' intention to use them for information-seeking purposes.

This study provides several managerial implications for utilizing instant messaging chat bots for marketing. As mentioned earlier, respondents have previous experience with chat bots in different formats, such as voice-activated and text-based. Generally, they found chat bots easy to use. For modern day consumers who use instant messaging apps every day and use multiple IT products (e.g., computer, tablet pc, smart phone and wearable computer), navigating chat bots is not an issue. Also, they found chat bots useful in their work performance. However, they showed the least perception of enjoyment and many of them disclosed that they stopped using chat bots after using them once out of curiosity. Therefore, when launching instant messaging chat bots for marketing purpose, it is ideal to focus on their practical purposes, rather than the entertaining element. Consumers can easily find fun and entertaining IT gadgets everywhere to use chat bots for fun. Although chat bots are have a good command of natural languages, it is still far from ideal. As we witnessed from previous virtual agent mishaps, promoting chat bots as a buddy for conversations or passing time could backfire.

LIMITATIONS AND FUTURE STUDIES

As with most research, the present study also has some limitations. First, this study used small student samples. Although the student samples fall into the typical social media users' age and education range, they were chosen from one of the most developed areas in the U.S., so it is difficult to generalize the results. Future study of instant messaging chat bots could include participants in various locations in the nation and also non-students sample as well.

Second, this study selected two instant messaging chat bots, CNN News and Shopping Assistant, as examples given to participants. However, since some students were not very familiar with chat bots, these two examples could have influenced participants' perception of chat bots in general. The results showed that participants found chat bots to be useful and easy to use, but not necessarily enjoyable. It is unclear whether the low perception of enjoyment was partially because the sample chat bots showed conversations in practical use, rather than as pure entertainment. Therefore, future studies should include more diverse types of chat bots, such as those devoted to entertainment, news and shopping.

CONCLUSION

To conclude, this study was conducted to provide a better understanding of mobile consumers' perceptions of instant messaging chat bots, in order to contribute to the current mobile commerce literature and to help build efficient marketing strategies for practitioners. This study found that mobile consumers have used instant messaging chat bots and think chat bots are useful and easy to use. However, many of the subjects did not see chat bots as greatly entertaining and stopped using them after a few trials. The findings provide insight into mobile users that marketers should consider when launching their chat bots for promotion and customer service purposes.

REFERENCES

Bayerque, N. (2016). A short history of chat bots and artificial intelligence. *VentureBeat.* Retrieved July 31, 2017 from https://venturebeat.com/2016/08/15/a-short-history-of-chat bots-and-artificial-intelligence/

Bers, T. H. (1994). Exploring institutional images through focus group interviews. In N. Bennett, R. Glatter, & R. Levacic (Eds.), *Improving educational management through research and consultancy* (pp. 290–299). London: The Open University.

Bots, the next frontier. (2016). *The Economist*. Retrieved August 3, 2017 from https://www.economist.com/news/business-and-finance/21696477-market-apps-maturing-now-one-text-based-services-or-chat bots-looks-poised

Bruner, G. C. II, & Kumar, A. (2005). Explaining consumer acceptance of handheld Internet devices. *Journal of Business Research*, *5*(58), 553–558. doi:10.1016/j.jbusres.2003.08.002

Caffyn, G. (2016). *Two months in: How the 1-800 Flowers Facebook bot is working out*. Retrieved July 24, 2017, from https://digiday.com/marketing/two-months-1-800-flowers-facebook-bot-working/

Carter, W. C., & Servat, H. J. (2005). *The Proust questionnaire*. New York: Assouline Publishing.

Chi, H. H. (2011). Interactive digital advertising vs. virtual brand community: Exploratory study of user motivation and social media marketing responses in Taiwan. *Journal of Interactive Advertising*, *12*(1), 44–61. doi:10.1080/15252019.2011.10722190

Chih-Chien, W., Hsu, Y., & Fang, W. (2005). Acceptance of technology with network externalities: An empirical study of internet instant messenger services. *Journal of Information Technology Theory and Application*, *6*(4), 15.

Childers, T. L., Carr, C. L., Peck, J., & Carson, S. (2001). Hedonic and utilitarian motivations for online retail shopping behavior. *Journal of Retailing*, *77*(4), 511–535. doi:10.1016/S0022-4359(01)00056-2

Colby, K. M. (1981). Modeling a paranoid mind. *Behavioral and Brain Sciences*, *4*(4), 515–534. doi:10.1017/S0140525X00000030

Colby, K. M. (1974). Ten criticisms of parry. *ACM SIGART Bulletin*, (48), 5-9.

ComScore. (2016). U.S.Mobile App Report. *ComScore Whitepaper.* Retrieved June 04, 2017, from https://www.comscore.com/Insights/Presentations-and-Whitepapers/2016/The-2016-US-Mobile-App-Report

Constine, J. (2017, April 12). *Facebook Messenger hits 1.2 billion monthly users, up from 1B in July.* Retrieved June 04, 2017, from https://techcrunch.com/2017/04/12/messenger/

Davis, F. D. (1985). *A technology acceptance model for empirically testing new end-user information systems: Theory and results* (Doctoral dissertation). Massachusetts Institute of Technology.

Davis, F. D. (1989). Perceived usefulness, perceived ease of use, and user acceptance of information technology. *Management Information Systems Quarterly*, *13*(3), 319–340. doi:10.2307/249008

Davis, F. D., Bagozzi, R. P., & Warshaw, P. R. (1989). User acceptance of computer technology: A comparison of two theoretical models. *Management Science*, *35*(8), 982–1003. doi:10.1287/mnsc.35.8.982

Davis, F. D., Bagozzi, R. P., & Warshaw, P. R. (1992). Extrinsic and intrinsic motivation to use computers in the workplace. *Journal of Applied Social Psychology*, *22*(14), 1111–1132. doi:10.1111/j.1559-1816.1992.tb00945.x

De Angeli, A., Johnson, G. I., & Coventry, L. (2001, June). The unfriendly user: exploring social reactions to chatterbots. In *Proceedings of The International Conference on Affective Human Factors Design,* 467-474.

Firshein, S. (2010). Anna, IKEA's Chat bot, Graciously Answers Proust Questionnaire. *Curbed.* Retrieved September 19, 2017 from www.curbed.com/2010/9/23/10505206/anna-ikeas-chatbot-graciously-answers-proust-questionnaire

eGain. (2017). *Virtual Assistant.* Retrieved from http://www.egain.com/products/virtual-assistant-software/

Gefen, D., & Straub, D. W. (1997). Gender differences in the perception and use of e-mail: An extension to the technology acceptance model. *Management Information Systems Quarterly*, *21*(4), 389–400. doi:10.2307/249720

Gerset, A., & Vaidya, S. (2010). Next Generation Customer Service Strategies: Harnessing the Power of the Internet and Web 2.0 for Delivering Customer Care. *Telecom & Media Insights*, (52). Retrieved September 20, 2017 from https://www.capgemini-consulting.com/resource-file-access/resource/pdf/Next_Generation_Customer_Service_Strategies.pdf

Gilliland, N. (2016). Domino's introduces 'Dom the Pizza Bot' for Facebook Messenger. *Econsultancy.* Retrieved September 22, 2017 from https://www.econsultancy.com/blog/68184-domino-s-introduces-dom-the-pizza-bot-for-facebook-messenger

Gilliland, N. (2016). What are chat bots and why should marketers care? *Econsultancy*. Retrieved September 22, 2017 from https://econsultancy.com/blog/67894-what-are-chat bots-and-why-should-marketers-care/

Gordon, N. (n.d.). What are the Differences between a Chat botWith and Without A.I.? *Century Soft Blog*. Retrieved August 3, 2017 from https://www.centurysoft.com/blog/differences-between-chat-bot-with-and-without-ai.html

Guynn, J. (2017). Facebook Messenger takes another swipe at bots. *USA Today*. Retrieved August 3, 2017 from https://www.usatoday.com/story/tech/news/2017/04/18/facebook-messenger-takes-another-swipe-chat-bots/100596798/

Ha, S., & Stoel, L. (2009). Consumer e-shopping acceptance: Antecedents in a technology acceptance model. *Journal of Business Research*, *62*(5), 565–571. doi:10.1016/j.jbusres.2008.06.016

Hajli, M. N. (2014). A study of the impact of social media on consumers. *International Journal of Market Research*, *56*(3), 387–404. doi:10.2501/IJMR-2014-025

Hassanein, K., & Head, M. (2007). Manipulating perceived social presence through the web interface and its impact on attitude towards online shopping. *International Journal of Human-Computer Studies*, *65*(8), 689–708. doi:10.1016/j.ijhcs.2006.11.018

Heath, A. (2017). Mark Zuckerberg wants Facebook to move faster at making money off Messenger and there's a good reason why. *Business Insider*. Retrieved July 27, 2017 from http://www.businessinsider.com/zuckerberg-facebook-move-faster-monetizing-messenger-2017-7

Hill, J., Ford, W. R., & Farreras, I. G. (2015). Real conversations with artificial intelligence: A comparison between human–human online conversations and human–chat botconversations. *Computers in Human Behavior*, *49*, 245–250. doi:10.1016/j.chb.2015.02.026

Huddelston, T., Jr. (2016). Now You Can Order Pizza Hut on Twitter and Facebook, Too. *Fortune*. Retrieved from http://fortune.com/2016/07/13/pizza-hut-chat bot-twitter-facebook/

Huge. (2004). IKEA Launches AI Customer Service Assistant. *Huge*. Retrieved August 28, 2017 from www.hugeinc.com/news/ikea-launches-artificial-intelligence-driven-customer-service-assistant

Hwang, Y. (2010). The moderating effects of gender on e-commerce systems adoption factors: An empirical investigation. *Computers in Human Behavior*, *26*(6), 1753–1760. doi:10.1016/j.chb.2010.07.002

If only I were. (2008, September 16). Chat with Sarah – the future of automated help [Blog Post]. Retrieved from https://subjunctive.wordpress.com/2008/09/16/chat-with-sarah-the-future-of-automated-help/

Innovation. (2016). 51 Corporate Chat bots Across Industries Including Travel, Media, Retail, And Insurance. *CBinsights*. Retrieved September 22, 2017 from https://www.cbinsights.com/research/corporate-chat bots-innovation/

Jia, J. (2003). *CSIEC (Computer simulator in educational communication): An intelligent web-based teaching system for foreign language learning*. arXiv preprint cs/0312030

Kerly, A., Hall, P., & Bull, S. (2007). Bringing chat bots into education: Towards natural language negotiation of open learner models. *Knowledge-Based Systems*, *20*(2), 177–185. doi:10.1016/j.knosys.2006.11.014

Kowalski, S., Pavlovska, K., & Goldstein, M. (2009, July). Two case studies in using chat bots for security training. In *IFIP World Conference on Information Security Education* (pp. 265-272). Springer.

Lederer, A. L., Maupin, D. J., Sena, M. P., & Zhuang, Y. (2000). The technology acceptance model and the World Wide Web. *Decision Support Systems*, *29*(3), 269–282. doi:10.1016/S0167-9236(00)00076-2

Lee, B. (2017). All Talk: How Chat bots And AI Will Transform The Way We Do Business. *Forbes*. Retrieved July 20, 2017, from https://www.forbes.com/sites/forbestechcouncil/2017/03/16/all-talk-how-chat bots-and-ai-will-transform-the-way-we-do-business/#7fd34e67280e

Lu, Y., Zhou, T., & Wang, B. (2009). Exploring Chinese users' acceptance of instant messenger using the theory of planned behavior, the technology acceptance model, and the flow theory. *Computers in Human Behavior*, *25*(1), 29–39. doi:10.1016/j.chb.2008.06.002

Network Working Group. (1973). RFC 439, PARRY Encounters the DOCTOR. *The Internet Engineering Task Force (Internet Society)*. Retrieved from http://tools.ietf.org/html/rfc439

Mandilas, A., Karasavvoglou, A., Nikolaidis, M., & Tsourgiannis, L. (2013). Predicting Consumer's Perceptions in On-line Shopping. *Procedia Technology*, *8*, 435–444. doi:10.1016/j.protcy.2013.11.056

Marcus, D. (2016). Messenger Platform at F8. *Facebook Newsroom*. Retrieved July 21, 2017, from https://newsroom.fb.com/news/2016/04/messenger-platform-at-f8/

Marr, B. (2014). Dear IKEA: Your Customer Service Is Terrible. *LinkedIn*. Retrieved September 19, 2017 from www.linkedin.com/pulse/20140325060328-64875646-dear-ikea-your-customer-service-is-terrible/

O'Neill, S. (2016). Kayak debuts an ambitious Facebook Messenger bot. *tnooz*. Retrieved July 25, 2017 from https://www.tnooz.com/article/kayak-facebook-messenger-bot/

Pavlou, P. A. (2003). Consumer acceptance of electronic commerce: Integrating trust and risk with the technology acceptance model. *International Journal of Electronic Commerce*, *7*(3), 101–134.

Pew Research Center. (2017). *Social Media Fact Sheet*. Pew Research Center Internet & Technology. Retrieved from September 9, 2017 from http://www.pewinternet.org/fact-sheet/social-media/

Pikkarainen, T., Pikkarainen, K., Karjaluoto, H., & Pahnila, S. (2004). Consumer acceptance of online banking: An extension of the technology acceptance model. *Internet Research*, *14*(3), 224–235. doi:10.1108/10662240410542652

Ping, L. C., & Chee, T. S. (2009). Online discussion boards for focus group interviews: An exploratory study. *Journal of Educational Enquiry*, *2*(1).

Rao, A. (2017). Why the Facebook Messenger Bot Platform was a Failure. *Medium*. Retrieved July 25, 2017 from https://medium.com/voicelandia/why-the-facebook-messenger-bot-platform-is-a-failure-so-far-d305b2d4e1df

Rawlins, L. K. (2016, April 13). Facebook chat bots to replace call centres. *iTWeb*. Retrieved June 04, 2017, from http://www.itweb.co.za/index.php?option=com_content&view=article&id=151438

Rauniar, R., Rawski, G., Yang, J., & Johnson, B. (2014). Technology acceptance model (TAM) and social media usage: An empirical study on Facebook. *Journal of Enterprise Information Management*, *27*(1), 6–30. doi:10.1108/JEIM-04-2012-0011

Ramayah, T., & Ignatius, J. (2005). Impact of perceived usefulness, perceived ease of use and perceived enjoyment on intention to shop online. *ICFAI Journal of Systems Management*, *3*(3), 36–51.

Salandra, G. (2017). China, WeChat, and the Origins of Chat bots: What we can learn from the successes and shortcomings of the popular platform. *Chat botsmagazine*. Retrieved September 24, 2017 from https://chatbotsmagazine.com/china-wechat-and-the-origins-of-chatbots-89c481f15a44

Sharkey, J. (2008). A Virtual Travel Agent with All the Answers. *The New York Times*. Retrieved September 19, 2017 from http://www.nytimes.com/2008/03/04/business/04road.html

Schlicht, M. (2017). The Complete Beginner's Guide To Chat bots. *Chat Bots Magazine*. Retrieved September 30, 2017 from https://chatbotsmagazine.com/the-complete-beginner-s-guide-to-chatbots-8280b7b906ca

Scott, D. (2008). Anna from IKEA is intellectually challenged (but she has a sense of humor). *Webinknow*. Retrieved September 19, 2017 from www.webinknow.com/2008/08/anna-from-ikea.html

Jin, S.-A. A., & Bolebruch, J. (2009). Avatar-Based Advertising in Second Life. *Journal of Interactive Advertising*, *10*(1), 51–60. doi:10.1080/15252019.2009.10722162

Shawar, B. A., & Atwell, E. (2002). *A comparison between ALICE and Elizabeth chat botsystems*. University of Leeds, School of Computing research report 2002.19.

Shawar, B. A., & Atwell, E. (2007). Chat bots: are they really useful? *LDV Forum*, *22*(1), 29-49.

Sokolovska, A. (2016). From E-Commerce to Conversational Commerce: Chat bots and Virtual Assistant. *Guided Selling*. Retrieved September 30, 2017 from https://www.guided-selling.org/from-e-commerce-to-conversational-commerce/

Steiner, I. (2011). Emma virtual assistant comes to eBay. *eCommerceBytes*. Retrieved September 4, 2017 from http://www.ecommercebytes.com/C/abblog/blog.pl?/pl/2011/1/ 1296444129.html

Tate, A. (2016). The 5 Most Inspiring Chat bots On Facebook Messenger. *AdEspresso*. Retrieved July 25, 2017 from https://adespresso.com/academy/blog/5-inspiring-chat bots-facebook-messenger/

Venkatesh, V. (2000). Determinants of perceived ease of use: Integrating control, intrinsic motivation, and emotion into the technology acceptance model. *Information Systems Research*, *11*(4), 342–365. doi:10.1287/isre.11.4.342.11872

Wakefield, J. (2016). Would you want to talk to a machine? *BBC News*. Retrieved August 28, 2017 from http://www.bbc.com/news/technology-36225980

Weizenbaum, J. (1966). ELIZA—a computer program for the study of natural language communication between man and machine. *Communications of the ACM*, *9*(1), 36–45. doi:10.1145/365153.365168

Ye, G., & van Raaij, W. F. (1997). What inhibits the mere-exposure effect: Recollection or familiarity? *Journal of Economic Psychology, 18*(6), 629–648. doi:10.1016/S0167-4870(97)00027-5

Zagorsky, J. (2015). Almost 90% of Americans Have Unlimited Texting. *Instant Census.* Retrieved September 25, 2017 from https://instantcensus.com/blog/almost-90-of-americans-have-unlimited-texting

Zajonc, R. B. (1968). Attitudinal effects of mere exposure. *Journal of Personality and Social Psychology, 9*(2), 1.

KEY TERMS AND DEFINITIONS

Artificial Intelligence: Intelligence displayed by computer program or machine that mimics human intelligence.

Avatar: A virtual character that represents human beings or human-like creatures.

Chat Bot: A computer program that imitates human conversations through text or voice.

Instant Messaging: Online messaging system that sends messages in real time over the internet.

Social Media: Online community where users share information, idea, photos, messages.

Technology Acceptance Model: A theory that suggests factors that influence users' decisions whether they use and accept the new technology.

Virtual Assistant: Another name of chat bots.

Chapter 10
IoT Sustainability in Higher Education

Helena Belchior-Rocha
ISCTE – Instituto Universitário de Lisboa, Portugal

Filomena Nogueira Almeida
ISCTE – Instituto Universitário de Lisboa, Portugal

Ricardo Abreu
ISCTE – Instituto Universitário de Lisboa, Portugal

ABSTRACT

The widespread use of new information technologies has brought new challenges to society and in particular to forcing innovation in education and training by changing the paradigm of education. However, there still seems to be no consensus on how best to use new information technologies in educational practices. In this context, and because it is important to know, debate, think, and plan the future role of these new technologies in teaching/training, the authors conducted an exploratory study with the Delphi technique. The experience and creativity of a panel of experts will lead to a categorical scale and to the elaboration of an instrument with a preliminary list of indicators to be applied to students and professors and evaluate the sustainability of IoT in higher education.

INTRODUCTION

The Internet of Things (IoT) refers to the way Internet connectivity has expanded to include everyday objects and to how those everyday objects inter-operate with our daily lives (Sinha & Park, 2017). Things as "the inter-connectivity of our digital devices that provides endless opportunities to listen and respond to the needs of persons – with the right message, at the right time, on the right device" as defined by Wenjie Gong (2016). This provides a range of possibilities and has brought new challenges to society and in particular to forcing innovation in education and training by changing the paradigm of education.

DOI: 10.4018/978-1-5225-5763-0.ch010

Copyright © 2019, IGI Global. Copying or distributing in print or electronic forms without written permission of IGI Global is prohibited.

Among the different and varied technologies and devices available it can be highlighted the tablets, smart phones, interactive whiteboards, streaming audio and video, used as terminals for interacting with the user, But in IoT technologies we can add RFID, QR codes, barcodes, sensors, near-field communication, digital watermarking, so it not just a global network for communications "but a platform or devices to communicate electronically with the world around them" (AmalRedge, 2016, p.27)

The use of computers, smartphones and the Internet has led to the development of interactive teaching virtually models in all types of education. For example, at a time when social networks have gained their place in the everyday lives of our society so it can't be ignored their potential in promoting learning (Groff, 2013).

To follow up on the use and acceptance by students and professors of these new technologies and communication spaces, and to see if these users will also be motivated to participate and take advantage of these platforms as facilitators of their learning in higher education is a pressing issue.

In this context, and because it is important to know, debate, think and plan the future role of these new technologies in teaching / training, this chapter aims to present an exploratory study with the Delphi technique (Hsu & Sandford, 2007), which gives the opportunity to involve the participants in a more intense and interactive way. This technique has become a fundamental tool in the technological projections, since there is a growing need to information directly in the evaluation of the models that deal with complex problems faced by society, such as education and innovation. Traditional Delphi is generally applied to future trends and events, but has recently expanded its concept to incorporate the search for ideas and strategies with the Delphi Projection, designed to project variables, events, trends, which will support decision-making (Yousuf, 2007). The experience and creativity of a panel of experts, will lead to a categorical scale and to the elaboration of an instrument with a preliminary list of indicators to be applied to students and professors and evaluate the sustainability of IoT in higher education.

This chapter starts with a brief state of art of the concept of IoT and its impact on our future daily life society, followed by the justification of IoT importance in education and higher education, highlighting the potentialities, limitations and challenges of its implementation in higher education institutions. After it is presented the study made, the methodology used and the preliminary results and it ends with future research directions.

IoT IS Happening

In the 2016 report of the IERC - IoT European Research Cluster (Jamalipour, Nikookar, & Ruggieri, 2016), it is also defined as a global concept. Ray et al. (2016), understand IoT as an ecosystem that expands and exploits existing environments through embedded and connected devices. The authors argue that this technology will increase the ubiquity of the internet, by integrating all objects into an embedded system, consequently will originate an infinite network of objects communicating with humans and / or others objects. For O'Brien (2016), IoT allows to obtain information that will be stored and that will provide feedback and control, supporting decision making. The author considers IoT "the third wave of the Internet" (O'Brien, 2016, p.1).

The impact of IoT on society and the growth of the Internet is an uninterrupted process: just twenty-five years ago, the network connected just over a thousand computers and since then, its growth has been constant and today connects billions of people through computers and devices furniture (Evans, 2011). This path has undergone a gradual transformation, but now it has become faster. The potential of a network of computers interconnected in a network of objects, from books to automobiles, to household appliances, to food, government files (Ferguson, 2016), or to the "connection" of all objects called the Internet of Things (IoT) is the future already present.

In a presentation that linked the use of Radio Frequency Identification (RFID) to traceability in the supply chain in 1999, Kevin Ashton used the term IoT for the first time (Ashton, 2009, Atzori, Iera, Morabito, & Nitti, 2012; Gubbi, Buyya, Marusic, & Palaniswami, 2013). The general idea about IoT is that physical objects or things that incorporate electronics, software, sensors and network connectivity, allow them to collect and share data and make these objects discoverable, creating new opportunities for a seamless integration between worlds physical and digital through their remote control (Ray, Jin, & Raychowdhury, 2016), the presence of objects / things around individuals makes them able to measure, infer, understand, change and act in the environment in which they are inserted (Botta, Donato, Persico, & Pescapé, 2016).

However, the literature review shows that although there is a general consensus that IoT involves objects and connectivity, it does not have a full consensus about its concept (Van Kranenburg & Bassi, 2012). For example to Sundmaeker *et al* (2010) the meaning of the word "things" is not restricted to material objects, "things" can be defined as real / physical or digital / virtual entities that move in space and time and are identifiable.

[...] a dynamic global network infrastructure with self-configuring capabilities based on standard and interoperable communication protocols where physical and virtual "things" have dentities, physical attributes, and virtual personalities and use intelligent interfaces, and are seamlessly integrated into the information network. (Sundmaeker et al, 2010, p.43)

The speed in which this process is taking place is greater than it is thought and therefore suggests the need for higher education institutions to create the infrastructures and resources that can optimize and make effective their mission, pointing out that the reconciliation of technology and education can improve the development of the teacher/student relationship, dissemination, research, teaching and communication support and, in addition, allows the internal procedures to be less bureaucratized.

IoT is at a stage where disparate networks and a multitude of sensors must come together and interoperate under a common set of standards. This effort will require businesses, governments, standards organizations, and academia to work together toward a common goal. Next, for IoT to gain acceptance among the general populace, service providers and others must deliver applications that bring tangible value to peoples' lives. IoT must not represent the advancement of technology for technology's sake; the industry needs to demonstrate value in human terms. In conclusion, IoT represents the next evolution of the Internet. Given that humans advance and evolve by turning data into information, knowledge, and wisdom, IoT has the potential to change the world as we know it today. (Evans, 2011, p.10)

So, considering that IoT represents the next step for evolution it can be said that:

Successfully preparing all learners with the skills and capacities for 21st century citizenship - global awareness, creativity, collaborative problem-solving, self-directed learning—is no small order, and many educational leaders are finding that the traditional forms of education that have evolved through the end of the last century are simply inadequate for achieving these goals. (Groff, 2013, p.1)

The possibilities for innovation are very wide and refer to many issues in the area of knowledge. Education is one of the most affected areas by the evolution of technologies, demanding a constant updating and improvement of the professionals involved and adjustments in the teaching and learning processes.

IOT AND HIGHER EDUCATION

For the first time in the NMC Horizont Report 2012 reference is made to the application of IoT as a future trend for schools, referring as next step the evolution of intelligent objects and the interconnectivity with the physical object and, highlighting their relevance, at the level of teaching / learning through the possibility of using small electronic devices connected to any physical object, to use them to track, monitor, maintain and record data and to inventory their facilities and grant automatic access authorizations for students, teachers, employees and visitors (Johnson, Adams, & Cummins, 2012).

Later, in 2015, the same report again mentions the topic by classifying IoT as an important reference in the development of educational technology for Higher Education, referring to the potentiality of its use in teaching / learning, namely through the concept of "hypothesis" (Johnson, Adams Becker, Estrada, & Freeman, 2015), this means that students through the mobile devices can have access to an enormous amount of interdisciplinary information emitted around them, objects can communicate with the student and vice versa generating interactive learning experiences (Selinger, Sepulveda, & Buchan, 2013). Also according to Johnson *et al.* (2015) students may have the ability to monitor their own surrounding environment and gather data in real time for later use through the data emitted by these connected environments.

Potentialities, Limitations, and Challenges

The great potential of IoT in Higher Education institutions for Benson (2016) lies mainly in the automation of its buildings, energy management, maintenance and access to campus systems, environmental control, research and of academic learning, and in security systems for all stakeholders, making the education more relevant, to engage and motivate students and staff, and to increase learning capacity. Another possibility for IoT is to provide remote access to educational tools in order to allow the subject to clarify questions while studying at home, but also to share information with teachers and colleagues on specific platforms.

It can play a key role, and at times a leading role, in all elements of the teaching and learning environment. Technology can shape, and reshape, who is the learner and who is the teacher. It can open up knowledge and content that otherwise would be less accessible, through access to open educational resources for example. (Groff, 2013, p.2)

Regarding the limitations, the literature review considers that the greatest obstacles to the use and implementation of IoT are the lack of knowledge and competence of most people, the ignorance of hierarchies and the fear of investment costs (Mukhopadhyay & Suryadevara, 2014).

It is these potentialities and limitations that bring us back to challenges like: resistance to change, lack of legislation and the need to adapt to this new paradigm until IoT is widely accepted. In addition, the natural evolution of IoT, which in the near future moves to the already spoken Internet of Everything

(IoE), a perspective according to which the connectivity of objects will be such that it will no longer be possible to unlink physical objects and digital information.

The question is how can we deal with the uninterrupted progress and development of IoT and keep it balanced and sustainable in the face of the asymmetries of the world (in this case academic), in the face of ethical issues, namely, protection of people and data, creation of new legislation in good time and the whole process of adaptation to this reality whose transition takes time.

IoT Sustainability in Education

Education is a multidimensional and complex phenomenon and its sustainability requires the development of an integrated vision of knowledge that contemplates the development of teacher and student learning in order to include ethical, epistemological and pedagogical issues necessary for the process of construction and sharing of knowledge. It requires the updating of permanent spaces of study and knowledge of technologies so that an adaptation of both students and teachers can take place in a sense that envisages new ways of teaching and new ways of learning. It is important to challenge paradigms, question and provoke an evolution in the current educational landscape, as well as identify potential current and future difficulties inherent in the challenge of appropriation of technologies (IoT) in formal school education, higher education and informal spaces.

IoT supports shared texts of communication between classmates and friends on social networks under different perspectives of communication, information and creation. Multimedia classrooms, personal computers, mobile equipment favour other learning methods for different requirements of other locations and find in the cloud services, via the web (information network through the internet), mobility, cooperation, archiving (conceptual, procedural and attitudinal), so that all students can receive the same information regardless of their tacit (previous) knowledge and or of the areas of knowledge developed with quality and equality (Piconez, 2004; 2013).

On the other hand the models of education are moving towards online or e-learning, so a more collaborative ecosystem is needed. IoT provides a big open interactive platform that enhances, effectively collaboration in different layers in the higher education systems.

Therefore this chapter aim to present an exploratory study with the decision Delphi technique and was structured in the search for ideas that would become a possibility to construct a scale to measure the sustainability of IoT in higher education.

Methodology

The research exposed through this chapter is exploratory and was based in the Delphi technique because this technique gives the opportunity to involve the participants in a more intense and interactive way.

"The Delphi method works especially well when the goal is to improve our understanding of problems, opportunities, solutions, or to develop forecasts" (Skulmoski, Krahn & Hartman, 2007, p.1).

During the process, each expert does not know the identity of the other members of the panel. This has a number of positive aspects: it prevents the possibility that a member of the group is influenced by the reputation of another member or by the weight of opposing the majority. The only possible influence is that of the congruence of the arguments. Allows a member to change their opinions without this implying a loss of image, the expert can defend his arguments and it is known that if they are wrong, his mistake will not be known by the other experts.

The data were collected online and analysed through content analysis method and this is a preliminary phase of construction of the scale.

Exploratory research is useful when the subject under study has been little explored. Exploratory research is developed to provide an overview of a given fact, seeking to seek "patterns, ideas, or hypotheses, rather than testing or confirming a hypothesis" (Collis & Hussey, 2005, p. 24). This is because, in the exploratory research, it seeks to know, more deeply, the subject addressed, in order to make it clearer. Therefore, the exploratory research follows an orientation that turns to the discovery. In the case of exploratory research, the researcher sometimes has incentives and resources that allow him to carry out researches through several methods, in order to use triangulations to confirm and deepen his discoveries (Denzin, 1978, Egan et al., 1995; Flick, 2009).

Thus, this research objective is to discover the initial information of a reality so that later hypotheses can be formulated about it. It can be affirmed that the exploratory researches have as main objective the improvement of ideas or the confirmation of intuitions.

The Delphi technique emerges in the mid-twentieth century, when the researchers Olaf Helmer and Norman Dakley of the Rand Corporation (a company engaged in military defense projects of the United States Air Force) used expert opinion for their scientific foundations (Linstone, Turoff, 1975). In their study, the goal was to obtain the consensus of expert opinion in the most objective way possible. It is important to emphasize that, although Delphi has been developed in a military context, its use expands to several areas of knowledge and different contexts (Carneiro da Cunha, 2011). According to its predecessors, Dalkey and Helmer (1963), the Delphi method aims to obtain the most reliable consensus of opinions from a group of experts, interspersed with controlled feedbacks. Thus, from this methodological development, Delphi is understood as a systematic technique to collect the scientifically valid opinion of experts on a given subject (Dalkey, 1969). In a second definition, proposed by Meyrick (2003), the method aims to seek the opinion of experts on a given issue, providing controlled feedback on the opinions expressed, and collecting their opinions again, thus allowing specialists to respond to input from panels with other members.

The number of specialists involved in a Delphi group has a direct effect on the potential of ideas to be considered in the generation of information and the amount of information the researcher intends to work with (Hasson *et al.*, 2000). However, there is no consensus in academia about the optimal number of participants in a Delphi group, because this amount depends on the scope and context of the research (Vergara, 2008) and factors extrinsic to the researcher, such as the availability of to participate. Finally, the agreement of experts' opinions on a subject occurs on four fundamental pillars, which are: (i) the anonymity of the research participants; (ii) consulting specialists for data collection; (iii) the application of interactive and feedback rounds, so that participants can review their opinions and reflect on them; (iv) the search for consensus, derived from the evaluation from the point of view raised by the group (Saadian, 2001). The synthesis of the results of the first round of questions provides the basis for the second round, and the second to third, and so on until a consensus is reached, in this case was intended to reach dimensions and variables that would later serve to restart the process and from there to reach the final scale.

In the first phase of this study the phrase/question to reflect was "Presently, looking at our Universities and our Curriculum there are several situations in which applying the Internet of Things could help facilitate, motivate and foster learning. In this way, teachers will be challenged to rethink and reflect through the construction of innovative didactic resources in order to facilitate the development of competences, not forgetting that many of the resources are part of their socio-cultural environment and that it should be a sustainable process" and based in dimensions of a study from Abbasy and Quesada (2017) Engagement in the Learning Process; Creativity; E-Learning; Self-learning; Research Opportunity; Hyper-Connectivity. It was asked to the experts to take them in the order they considered most important and to add more dimensions and also to make critical observations on the subject.

Initially 10 experts were selected to participate in the process. We contacted university professors specialized in different areas of work. Of all of them, 9 accepted to participate and 7 of them participated throughout all the different phases. Of them, 80% belong to the academic sphere and 20% also belong to the business sector. They were mainly men (70%), and (60%), with PhD studies. When each of them sends their opinions, the information was compiled, composing a list with all those new items. After 10 more experts were invited (8 accepted) and it was send the list, asking for the some proceeding, the information was compiled and a new list and an annex with those excluded with the pertinent justification, so that the rest can give their opinion both in favour and against and both about inclusions and exclusions. The process was repeated for six weeks until trying to reach a consensus in the working group. As one may suppose it is a very ambiguous process and difficult to reach consensus, so it was carry out an analysis of the degree of agreement. Although this process will continue, in order to validate the scale with a qualitative methodology, the first results will be presented in the next point.

Preliminary Results

In the first round it was found that in the view of the experts the "access to higher education"; "help for students with special needs"; the "relaxation of time and space"; the "self-discipline and self-learning of the student" were added to the existing dimensions. Critical points cited the "lack of training for the digital inclusion of the group of teachers and students and the difficulty to promote interaction". As a challenge they cited the "overcoming of the absence of the direct student / teacher relationship, the "face-to-face", typical of the classroom; the "use of strategies and resources that promote the exchange of experiences and interaction"; the "student profile"; the "lack of maturity" to "self-discipline". But also that digital media are seen as teaching tools only, a fact that makes it difficult to read IoT more critically and the exploitation of all the potential they possess, mainly as a means of expression and cultural production. As it was said before the process was repeated during six weeks until it was decided that it was difficult to reach a complete consensus so the data were treated qualitatively, in order to categorize the responses according to the similarity or data equivalence with a content analysis. From this analysis, a new instrument will be developed, including the indicators reported and that is showed in Table 1.

It was also mentioned by some experts that IoT favours a range of possibilities for interdisciplinary connections, teachers and students to access and explore data in a dynamic and interactive way. The students increase linguistic, geographical and interpersonal connections and knowledge. In an increasingly connected world, careers and jobs are constantly changing, so that requires skills and knowledge that students can't develop in the traditional model of teaching. In addition, technology in education enables students to work on one of the key skills that must be developed in today's world, collaboration/cooperation.

With this transformation into the role of the teacher/student relation, it is necessary to dialogue with the students about their responsibilities as digital citizens and to encourage them to have the critical thinking of analysing the sources and contents they consume online.

Table 1. Categories scale

Dimensions	Indicators
Training and learning	• Planning tasks. • Reflecting on complex issues. • Books and digital resources. • Students become more committed and motivated due to getting quick response. • In addition to face-to-face class, various synchronous means including video conferencing, instant messaging and conversation (chat) are used. • Web-based teaching/ computer based teaching. • Help for students with special needs. • Mobile learning. • - E-learning/B-learning.
Security	• Automatic security perimeter. • Immediate notification of the authorities and video transmission to the police. • Controlled access.
Increased efficiency	• Streamline daily operations. • Delayed manual activities, such as service and information in a central office, can be eliminated with all connected devices, which send the data to where it needs to go instantly. • Reduce energy costs. • More rigorous monitoring of resource use. • Online documents/ e- mail/global announcement. • Transparency in the processes.
Others	• Informal Educational Spaces. • Museums, Libraries. • Professional associations, • NGOs. • University interaction x educational spaces.

Students are increasingly connected and used to technology, it is part of their world, according to Negrine (1998), the activities done with pleasure act in the organism causing a sensation of freedom and spontaneity, facilitating the learning by its own meaning, because the mechanisms for the processes of discovery are intensified. These activities, when well exploited, create an interaction of knowledge, at the level of personal, social and cognitive development. As Vigotsky (2007) points out, the student plays an active role in the learning process because of the ability to relate the new content to his previous knowledge and for that it's an imperative that sustainability of IoT in higher education is created from this potentiality.

Research Limitations

The first limitation of this research was time, Delphi technique needs time to go through several phases until you reach the final data processing. So in this case this is only the preliminary results and the final scale is not ready.

The IoT subject is still very controversial, there are still barriers like careful attention to the emphasis given to technologies, and there should be no development of services that jeopardize privacy, independence, free will, security and freedom of the people. There is a lack of understanding that in general terms, the IoT seeks to eliminate the need for human intervention in many aspects, while facilitating the lives of those who use it. The lack of standards is also a limitation of this concept and was felt in this exploratory study.

FUTURE RESEARCH DIRECTIONS

With this foundation built, it is easy to see how the IoT is poised to radically transform education as we know it. The new generations are more and more up to date. Children are now born among computers, cell phones, games and technologies in general. Students, particularly in college, are increasingly moving away from paper books to tablets and laptops. And while this trend offers greater convenience to students, it also makes the teaching process more efficient for teachers. This new reality can be a challenge for the traditional model. Students are accustomed to performing various tasks at the same time, the speed and ease that young people deal with technological is much greater than their parents and teachers. Because they are included in this new culture, they feel more motivated when technological tools are involved in the learning process.

Technology has a transformative potential and in a context where virtual connections are responsible for the real-time circulation of an infinite range of information it can effectively transform into learning paths. The biggest challenge is to produce knowledge by investing in the protagonism of increasingly young people tuned with the changes of their time. Therefore, future research in this area helps and enhances learning, helps to break down barriers and change mentalities.

From the data obtained in the three stages of the application of the technique in this first phase and in order to continue this study the next phase will be the application of the scale presented, gathering more indicators and making one more round to the Delphi panel, next will be created a questionnaire with a likert scale of 7 (seven) levels for application to teachers and students.

The use of IoT resources in education can happen both directly in educational activities (Selinger *et al*, 2013, Pruet *et al*, 2015), as it can be an element capable of providing better conditions for the development of activities contributing indirectly to the improvement of academic performance and for the management of resources essential to resource optimization and cost reduction.

However, the application of this type of network in educational context faces some challenges that require the development of research designed to increase the efficiency and sustainability of its implementation, given the fact that it is a complex and immature subject.

CONCLUSION

The education system has long remained the same. Traditional schools that insist on not investing in technology are increasingly outdated. The relationship between technology and education is more than a trend, it is becoming a reality.

Internet of things, as its name says, is the technology that is in objects. This will make the physical and digital environments more and more close to becoming one. That is, the approximation between the real world and the digital. This new technology helps to integrate any device with the computer network. This simplifies and automates many of our daily tasks. Connected, it improves and transforms everyday life, including students, teachers and schools.

Improving education is a concern of all because it results in better social and economic conditions for the communities and for the country. The educational methods have been impacted by the spread of ICT and virtual environments and are now common in schools and universities to access to information and services. Thanks to IoT technologies it is also possible enable access and control of local, remote processes or events, enriching the learning experience, according to (Pruet *et al*, 2015, Selinger *et al*, 2013 and Medina, Perez & Trujillo, 2017).

Based on the basic concept that marketing works for the satisfaction of people and therefore of society, it should be used for the dissemination and sensitization of IoT in higher education, with the message that technology changes the way we relate, and this is what changes education and not the contrary.

The possible impacts of these changes will soon be perceived in all areas, education will be one of the most affected with possibilities of applications still unknown, so exploring them may be one of the possible ways to bring them up as soon as possible so that they can be made feasible and sustainable. With IoT we can be talking about the globalization of education, the breaking of the borders of the school and universities, the language, the country.

REFERENCES

Abbasy, M. B., & Quesada, E. V. (2017). Predictable Influence of IoT (Internet of Things) in the Higher Education. *International Journal of Information and Education Technology (IJIET)*, *7*(12), 914–920. doi:10.18178/ijiet.2017.7.12.995

AmalRedge, G. (2016). The Things, Services and Applications of IoT. *International Journal of Trend in Research and Development.* Retrieved from http://www.ijtrd.com/papers/IJTRD4179.pdf

Ashton, K. (2009). That "internet of things" thing. *RFID Journal, 22*(7), 97–114. Retrieved December, 2017, from http://www.itrco.jp/libraries/RFIDjournal-That Internet of Things Thing.pdf

Atzori, L., Iera, A., & Morabito, G. (2010). The Internet of Things: A survey. *Computer Networks*, *54*(15), 2787–2805. doi:10.1016/j.comnet.2010.05.010

Atzori, L., Iera, A., Morabito, G., & Nitti, M. (2012). The Social Internet of Things (SIoT) – When social networks meet the Internet of Things: Concept, architecture and network characterization. *Computer Networks*, *56*(16), 3594–3608. doi:10.1016/j.comnet.2012.07.010

Benson, C. (2016). The Internet of Things, IoT Systems, and Higher Education. *EDUCAUSE Review*, *51*(4), 6. Retrieved from http://er.educause.edu/articles/2016/6/the-internet-of-things-iot-systems-and-higher-education

Botta, A., De Donato, W., Persico, V., & Pescapé, A. (2016). Integration of Cloud computing and Internet of Things: A survey. *Future Generation Computer Systems*, *56*, 684–700. doi:10.1016/j.future.2015.09.021

Carneiro da Cunha, J. A. (2011). *Avaliação de desempenho e eficiência em organizações de saúde: um estudo em hospitais filantrópicos* (Doctoral dissertation). Faculdade de Economia, Administração e Contabilidade. Universidade de São Paulo.

Collis, J., & Hussey, R. (2005). *Pesquisa em Administração: um guia prático para alunos de graduação e pós-graduação (2nd ed.)*. Porto Alegre: Bookman.

Dalkey, N., & Helmer, O. (1963). An experimental application of the Delphi method to the use of experts. *Management Science*, *9*(12), 458–467. doi:10.1287/mnsc.9.3.458

Dalkey, N. C. (1969). *The Delphi method. An experimental study of group opinion (N.º RM-5888-PR)*. Santa Monica, CA: Rand Corporation.

Egan, A. F., Jones, S. B., Luloff, A. E., & Finley, J. C. (1995). The value of using multiple methods: An illustration using survey, focus group, and Delphi techniques. *Society & Natural Resources*, *8*(5), 457–465. doi:10.1080/08941929509380936

Evans, D. (2011). *The Internet of Things How the Next Evolution of the Internet Is Changing Everything* [White paper]. Retrieved December, 2017, Cisco Internet Business Solutions Group (IBSG): https://www.cisco.com/c/dam/en_us/about/ac79/docs/innov/IoT_IBSG_0411FINAL.pdf

Ferguson A. G., (2016). The Internet of Things and the Fourth Amendment of Effects. *California Law Review, 104*(4), 805. .10.15779/Z38JZ8G

Flick, U. (2009). *Desenho da pesquisa qualitativa*. Porto Alegre: Artmed.

Gong, W. (2016). The Internet of Things (IoT): What is the Potential of the internet of things (IoT) as a marketing tool? *Proceedings of the 7th IBA Bachelor Thesis Conference.*

Groff, J. (2013). Technology-rich innovative learning environments. *OCED CERI Innovative Learning Environment project*, 1-30.

Gubbi, J., Buyya, R., Marusic, S., & Palaniswami, M. (2013). Internet of Things (IoT): A vision, architectural elements, and future directions. *Future Generation Computer Systems*, *29*(7), 1645–1660. doi:10.1016/j.future.2013.01.010

Hasson, F., & Keeney, S., & McKenna, H. (2000). Research guidelines for the Delphi technique. *Journal of Advanced Nursing*, *32*(4), 1008–1015. PMID:11095242

Hsu, C. C., & Sandford, B. A. (2007). The Delphi Technique: Making Sense Of Consensus. *Practical Assessment, Research & Evaluation*, *12*(10), 1-8.

Jamalipour, A., Nikookar, H., & Ruggieri, M. (2016). *Digitising the Industry Internet of Things Connecting the Physical, Digital and Virtual Worlds*. River Publishers.

Johnson, L., Adams, S., & Cummins, M. (2012). *The NMC Horizon Report: 2012 Higher Education Edition*. Austin, TX: The New Media Consortium. Retrieved from http://redarchive.nmc.org/publications/horizon-report-2012-higher-ed-edition

Johnson, L., Adams Becker, S., Estrada, V., & Freeman, A. (2015). *NMC Horizon Report: 2015 Higher Education Edition*. Austin, TX: The New Media Consortium. Retrieved from http://www.nmc.org/pdf/2012-horizon-report-HE.pdf

Li, S., Da Xu, L., & Zhao, S. (2015). The internet of things: A survey. *Information Systems Frontiers*, *17*(2), 243–259. doi:10.100710796-014-9492-7

Linstone, H. A., & Turoff, M. (Eds.). (1975). *The Delphi method: techniques and applications*. Boston: Addison-Wesley.

Medina, C. A., Pérez, M. R., & Trujillo, L. C. (2017). IoT Paradigm into the Smart City Vision: A Survey. *2017 IEEE International Conference on Internet of Things (iThings) and IEEE Green Computing and Communications (GreenCom) and IEEE Cyber, Physical and Social Computing (CPSCom) and IEEE Smart Data (SmartData)*, 695–704. doi:10.1109/iThings-GreenCom-CPSCom-SmartData.2017.109

Meyrick, J. (2013). The Delphi method and health research. *Health Education*, *103*(1), 7–16. doi:10.1108/09654280310459112

Miguel, P., & Baptista, F. (2015). *Modelos de negócios para a internet em Big Data:Muzzley, um estudo de caso* (Master dissertation). Retrieved from http://hdl.handle.net/10362/17375

Mukhopadhyay, S. C., & Suryadevara, N. K. (2014). Internet of Things: Challenges and Opportunities. In S. C. Mukhopadhyay (Ed.), *Internet of Things. Smart Sensors, Measurement and Instrumentation* (Vol. 9, pp. 1–17). Springer International Publishing; doi:10.1007/978-3-319-04223-7_1

Negrine, A. (1998). *Terapias corporais: a formação pessoal do adulto.* Porto Alegre: Edita.

O'Brien, H. M. (2016). The Internet of Things. *Journal of Internet Law*, *19*(12), 1–20. PMID:27441587

Oliveira, J. S. P., Costa, M. M., Wille, M. F. C., & Marchiori, P. Z. (2008). *Introdução ao Método Delphi.* Curitiba: Mundo Material. Available in http://eprints.rclis.org/12888/

Piconez, S. C., Bertholo, P., & Adalberto, M. (2017, July). *Desafios da Sustentabilidade Educacional e as contribuições da Tecnologia Cloud Computing.* Paper presented at Workshop de Desafios da Computação aplicada à Educação in XXXVII Congresso da Sociedade Brasileira de Computação.

Pruet, P., Ang, C. S., Farzin, D., & Chaiwut, N. (2015). Exploring the Internet of "Educational Things" (IoET) in rural underprivileged areas. *2015 12th International Conference on Electrical Engineering/ Electronics, Computer, Telecommunications and Information Technology (ECTI-CON)*, 1–5. doi:10.1109/ECTICon.2015.7207125

Ray, S., Jin, Y., & Raychowdhury, A. (2016). The Changing Computing Paradigm With Internet of Things: A Tutorial Introduction. *IEEE Design & Test*, *33*(2), 76–96. doi:10.1109/MDAT.2016.2526612

Selinger, M., Sepulveda, A., & Buchan, J. (2013). *Education and the Internet of Everything: How ubiquitous connectedness can help transform pedagogy* (White paper). San Diego, CA: Cisco Systems. Retrieved from http://www.cisco.com/web/strategy/docs/education/education_internet.pdf

Sinha & Park. (2017). *Building an Effective IoT Ecosystem for Your Business.* Springer. Available in http://www.springer.com/gp/book/9783319573908

Skulmoski, G. J., Hartman, F. T., & Krahn, J. (2007). The Delphi Method for Graduate Research. *Journal of Information Technology Education: Research, 6*, 1-21. Retrieved November, 2017, from https://www.learntechlib.org/p/111405/

Sundmaeker, H., Guillemin, P., Friess, P., & Woelfflé, S. (2010). Vision and challenges for realising the Internet of Things. Cluster of European Research Projects on the Internet of Things. *European Commission*, *3*(3), 34–36.

Van Kranenburg, R., & Bassi, A. (2012). IoT Challenges. *Communications in Mobile Computing*, *1*(1), 9. doi:10.1186/2192-1121-1-9

Vergara, S. C. (2008). *Métodos de pesquisa em administração* (3rd ed.). São Paulo: Atlas.

Vygotsky, L. S. (2007). *A Formação Social da Mente* (7th ed.). São Paulo: Martins Fontes.

Yousuf, M. I. (2007). Using Experts' Opinions Through Delphi Technique Practical Assessment. *Research & Evaluation, 12*(4).

KEY TERMS AND DEFINITIONS

Delphi Method: The Delphi Method designates a systematic and interactive method of analysis in which, based on the free and independent opinions of a group and experts, it tries to obtain a counter-opinion about the analyzed subjects. It is a technique for qualitative prediction in which the opinions of experts are associated in a series of reiterations / repetitions. The results of each repetition are used to develop the following, until there is convergence in the opinion of the experts. It is used in situations of lack of historical data or in which it is intended to stimulate the creation of new ideas.

Exploratory Research: Is when the research is in the preliminary phase, it has as purpose to provide more information about the subject that is going to be investigate, allowing its definition and its delineation. This means, to facilitate the delimitation of the research theme; guide the setting of objectives and the formulation of hypotheses or discover a new type of approach to the subject.

Internet of Things: Is a technology that enables any object to connect with others by an internet protocol.

Interoperable Communication Systems: Is a system of technologies and protocols that allow different agents or objects communicating with efficiency by a common channel.

IoT Sustainability in (Higher) Education: Means the need for a process of constant updating and maintenance in the effective application of its potential in resources, research, innovation and development.

Radio Frequency Identification: Is a wireless technology that use radio signals to transport some digital data like an identification label of any object.

Sustainability of Technology: It's an approach to technology development. The improvement of technology along with an efficient use of available resources put forward the human and environment sustainability.

Section 3
Future Trends

Chapter 11
Are Millennials Ready for the Internet of Things?

Belem Barbosa
University of Aveiro, Portugal

Sandra Filipe
University of Aveiro, Portugal

Claudia Amaral Santos
University of Aveiro, Portugal

Dora Simões
University of Aveiro, Portugal

ABSTRACT

A lot has been said about the digital natives and their natural way of integrating the internet in their daily activities. Millennials have been considered a unique segment of consumers by researchers and practitioners alike, due to their ability and propensity to adopt and adapt new media to their daily routine. Although it is expectable that they are particularly keen on embracing IoT, extant literature is scarce on their views on the adoption of IoT to their home, work, and leisure activities. In this chapter, the authors analyze the potential of the millennial segment to IoT products and services. Results of a qualitative study with Portuguese consumers are included and provide interesting cues to marketers working with IoT offers.

INTRODUCTION

In a society where the Internet of Things (IoT) has become a reality, the attitudes and beliefs about IoT of the millennial generation or millenials are an important topic to study. This disruptive model of living has been generated and nurtured by a desire to be permanently wired and connected to a digital experience. Organizations throughout the world are paying close attention to this changing of practices and companies' marketing strategies are adapting to this IoT-enabled social and corporate culture. One would expect millennials to willingly embrace technology at all levels, with a mindset that indulges

DOI: 10.4018/978-1-5225-5763-0.ch011

Copyright © 2019, IGI Global. Copying or distributing in print or electronic forms without written permission of IGI Global is prohibited.

innovative cutting-edge wearables and services. However, extant literature on IoT has not evidenced a clear depiction of what millennials actually perceive of this new ubiquitous presence of technology in their lives. Hence, this chapter attempts to shed light on millennials' perspectives, namely by delving into their knowledge, expectations, perceptions and intentions on IoT, collected by an exploratory qualitative approach.

Clearly this generation will play an essential role in the development and adoption of IoT, not only because of their own characteristics that make them especially propenseto use anything related to the Internet in a natural and savvy way, but also because of their growing importance in terms of income and overall role in the society. As baby boomers are getting older and retiring, millennials are ascending in their working life and rapidly getting to the top of their professional careers, earning better salaries, and evolving in their family cycle. Thus, their role in the adoption of IoT even in the business context is expected to be very important.

Considering the themes and topics scanted from the data, the chapter was divided into seven main sections. The background provides broad discussions of the topic and incorporates views of others into the discussion to demonstrate the importance of studying millennials' perceptions and intentions towards the adoption of IoT. In the second section we depict millennial generation profile characteristics that seem more relevant to the IoT adoption, and we assemble contributions from diverse fields of research, particularly from social psychology and consumer behavior. We consider cues provided by the Technology Acceptance Model (TAM), the theory of perceived risks, and explore the consumer perceived value in order to develop a conceptual framework to analysemillennials' views on IoT. This framework guided the collection and analysis of qualitative data that offer a general view of millennials' perspectives and intentions to adopt IoT. In section three we focus on the methodology selected for this research, explaining the constitution of the sample and reasons for applying an exploratory qualitative data collection method. In section four, results from the collected data are disclosed and analysed in detail, encompassing five different facets: knowlege, perceived benefits, perceived risks, attitudes and intentions to use IoT. The section five and six are devoted to relevant solutions and recommendation for researchers, marketers and practitioners, and to future research directions. The final section is dedicated to the conclusion retrieved from the collected data, interpreting the most outstanding aspects of millennials' perceptions of IoT.

BACKGROUND

Studies on new media have dominated the end of the 20th and the beginning of the 21st Centuries. One impressive aspect was the technological change, which was fast (Lister, Dovey, Giddings, Grant, & Kelly, 2009; Wilson & Peterson, 2002) yet incremental (Lievrouw, 2004), and the essential role of users to the application and reinvention of technology by adapting it to their daily activities (Baym, 2006; Campbell, 2005; Lievrouw & Livingstone, 2006; Yadav & Varadarajan, 2005). Considering Lievrouw and Livingstone´s (2006) definition of new media comprising (i) artefacts and devices (ii) activities and practices, and (iii) organizational and social arrangements, IoT clearly fits in such concept, thus much that has been learned so far about consumer behavior in new media contexts is expected to apply to IoT. Moreover, new media were from the start associated to new experiences, new ways of representing the world, new relations between consumers, and new ways of organizing and producing (Lister et al., 2009), which clearly illustrates the added value of IoT for consumers and organizations.

The concept of digital natives is extensively accepted and refers to all who were born and who have grown up with digital technologies (Prensky, 2001). Thus, they are the generation that naturally incorporated the Internet in their routines, as it has always been part of their lives. The group comprises individuals born between early 1980's and mid 2000's, with precise dates varying from study to study. For instance, Smola and Sutton (2002) studied this generation encompassing individuals born between 1979 and 1994, while Howe and Strauss (2000) define them as born in or after 1982. A generational group is defined by the shared historical or social life experiences that affect them in a stable manner (Smola & Sutton, 2002), thus one of the outstanding characteristics of this generation is being born in an environment dominated by the Internet and communication and information technologies. Ng, Schweitzer, and Lyons (2010) include in the characteristics that define millennials the rapid technological advancement. In fact, since a very young age millennials use the Internet more than any other generation (Dimmick, Ramirez, Wang, & Lin, 2007) in all aspects of their lives (McMillan & Morrison, 2006).

At the beginning of the millennium, Hoffman (2000) alerted that we were living a revolution called the Internet. Considering the possible impacts, the scope, and the applications of IoT, we venture to say that a second revolution has been launched. Its impacts and importance will depend in a great extent on the way millennials adopt and adapt it to their lives, in the entertainment, home, and workplace domains. It is therefore of utmost importanceto understand millennials' perceptions and intentions towards the adoption of IoT.

MAIN THEORIES ABOUT THE ADOPTION OF INTERNET TECHOLOGY AND PROPOSED CONCEPTUAL FRAMEWORK

Technology Acceptance Model

The Technology Acceptance Model (TAM) proposed by Davis (1986) is widely acknowledged in the Internet, technology, and information systems literature. This model is an adaptation of the Theory of Reasoned Action (TRA) developed by Fishbein and Ajzen (1975)who stated that behavior is the final result of the behavioral intention.TAM was particularly adapted for studying user acceptance of computer technologies and suggeststhat perceived ease of use and perceived usefulness are determinants of user's attitudes towards a product, which in turn influences behavioral intention to use(Davis, Bagozzi, & Warshaw, 1989). According to Davis et al. (1989), perceived usefulness is the degree to which using a specific product or technology will increase a user's performance, whereas perceived ease of use consists in the degree to which one believes that this use will be free of effort.

Over the last decades,TAM has been extensivelyembraced by several studies about consumers' acceptance and adoption of new technologies, such as micro computer usage (Igbaria, Guimaraes, & Davis, 1995), information technology usage (S. Taylor & Todd, 1995), user's behavior toward word-wide-web (Moon & Kim, 2001), on-line shopping intentions (Gefen, Karahanna, & Straub, 2003), Internet banking adoption (Al-Ajam & Nor, 2013; Lee, 2009), as well as various IoT applications (Chong, Liu, Luo, & Keng-Boon, 2015; Gao & Bai, 2014; Mital, Choudhary, Pani, Chang, & Sun, 2015; Tung, Chang, &Chou, 2008).Thus, TAM provides a relevant framework to study the adoption of IoT, particularly considering its innovating and novelty nature for most consumers and managers.

Consumer Perceived Risks

A complementary approach to study the adoption of innovative products is consumer's perceived risks. The concept of perceived risk was introduced by Bauer (1960) and comprises individual perceptions on the probability of product failure and its negative consequences, or as J. W. Taylor (1974) poses it, the possible psycho-social and functional-economic losses associated to uncertainty about both the outcomes and the consequences, which can be reduced by gathering information and diminishing what is at stake, or discarding consumption, respectively.

Byrne et al. (2016) refer that most of the studies regarding consumer perceived risk intend to prevent people from engaging in risky behavior, and in online context it also includes developing solutions in order to decrease users' vulnerability to Internet security threats. Still, this approach is also useful in situations such as disruptive innovations, which due to the lack of knowledge may encounter resistance from consumers, and understanding perceived risk may help overcome resistance, facilitate trial, and accelerate the adoption process. This has been the case of many new technologies, namely Internet related, with much being said about risks such as security and data protection, just to name the most dominant in public debate.

As S. Kaplan and Garrick (1981) stressed, the concept of risk combines both uncertainty and damage, comprising scenarios of what can go wrong, their probability, and consequences. Moreover, total risk is divided into different types of risks and losses (L. B. Kaplan, Szybillo, & Jacoby, 1974). Hence, perceived risk is widely accepted as a multidimensional construct involving six dimensions: (1) physical; (2) financial; (3) performance; (4) social; (5) psychological; (6) time:

1. Physical risk relates to the negative effects a product and its usage may pose to the health, safety and well-being of the consumer.
2. Financial risk refers to the money losses that may result from the purchase and maintenance of the product in case it does not match the expected benefits and its perceived value.
3. Performance risk represents concerns on product flaws and its ability to produce the benefits and features, including doubts about its quality.
4. Social risk deals with possible damages in consumer status or image due to unaccepted behavior by the peer reference groups, namely deception, embarrassment or disapproval of family and friends resulting from choosing a bad product or service.
5. Psychological risk refers to negative impacts on consumer's self-image, self-concept, and self-esteem due to unaccomplished purchase goals or purchase failure.
6. Finally, time, as another component of the perceived risk. For instance, a bad purchase decision results in time losses comprising search, acquisition and learning how to use.

Whenever the perceived risk is high, consumers might decide not to undertake the acquisition behavior. In fact, as stressed byMitchell (1999)and Hassan, Kunz, Pearson, and Mohamed (2006), perceived risk makes consumers more likely to avoid errors than to maximize the utility associated to their buying decisions. Recently, Pelaez, Chen, and Chen (2017) explored the effects of perceived risk in intention to purchase online based on a meta-analysis comprising 39 samples across multiple contexts with a total sample size of 13,779 observations, concluding for a medium statistically effect, especially in B2C contexts.

Still, perceived risk varies depending on the consumer profile, the type of product, familiarity and level of knowledge (L. B. Kaplan et al., 1974). L. B. Kaplan et al. (1974) found that similar types of products possess similar perceived risk components. Moreover, risk has a notably subjective nature (S. Kaplan & Garrick, 1981). Consumers are expected to have varying levels of risk tolerance which suggests the existence of different market segments and the development of adequate marketing strategies in order to position the product or service as low-risk in the minds of the customers (Mitchell, 1999). In fact, Pelaez et al. (2017) advocate that socioeconomic status and personality type should be considered as moderators of the effect of perceived risk on consumer behavior, mentioning that most studies so far have been comparing mostly students with non-students.

Being an essential factor explaining consumer behavior, perceived risk has been frequently used for studying the buying decision processes associated to high involvement purchases and also with technology related activities such as online shopping and other Internet based activities. De Kerviler, Demoulin, and Zidda (2016) stress the importance of financial and privacy risks in adopting online services such as mobile payments, while privacy is one of the most explored risks in interacting online. Although studies with IoT are still scarce, we expect concerns with privacy and data security to be one of the major risks perceived by consumers when considering acquiring anIoT item.

Amongst the factors that may also reduce perceived risk are the ones related to the brand, such as involvement and trust (S. Kaplan & Garrick, 1981), product involvement (Han & Kim, 2017), and consumer perceived benefits, which are analyzed in more detail in the next section.Byrne et al. (2016) found that online perceived risks are inversely associated to perceived benefits, and demonstrated that users engage in online activities they perceive risky because of the benefits those activities provide, although they engage more frequently in activities they perceive as not very risky.

Consumer Perceived Benefits

Perceived value is a construct often used in Internet context studies, considering the relevance of the benefits offered by online services in the consumer decision process, in a marked correlation with the consumer perceived risk approach. Some of the past studies using perceived value in online contexts include studies on online shopping experience (e.g., O'Brien, 2010; Ozturk, Nusair, Okumus, & Hua, 2016; Sarkar, 2011; To, Liao, & Lin, 2007), buying digital products and services(e.g., Hsu & Lin, 2016; H.-W. Kim, Gupta, & Koh, 2011; Turel, Serenko, & Bontis, 2010), location-based services (e.g., Pura, 2005; Yu, Zo, Kee Choi, & Ciganek, 2013), and more recently wearable devices (e.g., Yang, Yu, Zo, & Choi, 2016) and smart home services (e.g., Y. Kim, Park, & Choi, 2017).

One traditional approach is to consider the duality of utilitarian versus hedonic benefits provided by products, services and consumption. Holbrook and Hirschman (1982) seminal work argues for the importance of the hedonic aspects of consumption, where the experiential, symbolic and emotional expected benefits complement the utilitarian criteria used during the consumer decision process, considering that consumers are not merely rational decision makers, as they integrate on their decision the esthetic, symbolic, pleasure and other emotional aspects of consumption (Hirschman & Holbrook, 1982; Holbrook & Hirschman, 1982). Consequently, this dual perspective has influenced the overall study of consumer choice and purchase behavior, including studies on the perceived value.

Sweeney and Soutar (2001) proposed a conceptualization of customer perceived value comprehending emotional, utilitarian and social components. They developed a measurement scale that intended to unveil the values that drive consumers' purchase attitude and behavior, and identified four value dimensions: emotional, social, quality/performance and price/value for money, thus proposing two dimensions for utilitarian value. More recently, De Kerviler et al. (2016) considered that utilitarian value included economic, information and convenience benefits.

Thus, social benefits can be generally defined as "the utility derived from the product's ability to enhance social self-concept" and emotional benefits as "the utility derived from the feelings or affective states that a product generates" (Sweeney & Soutar, 2001, p. 211). Moreover, the utilitarian benefits are associated to performance and financial or price benefits to money aspects. Also, De Kerviler et al. (2016) found that convenience and enjoyment benefits are particularly relevant in the adoption of in-store mobile payments, and Shaikh and Karjaluoto (2015) suggest that perceived usefulness is one of the key factors explaining the adoption of online banking services. Similarly, perceived benefits are expected to affect consumers' perceived risk. Skard, Nysveen, and Thorbjørnsen (2016) found that hedonic associations reduced the negative effect of risk on attitudes towards using an e-service, so hedonic values could be especially important for new IoT offerings that pose high levels of risk.

Perceived benefits are partially represented in the TAM model, which comprises the utilitarian benefits. Nevertheless, in our opinion, the hedonic benefits of using IoT should not be disregarded, at least when considering consumers and offers that have some social visibility and enhanced experiences of use. We expect all these dimensions to be determinant in the overall adoption of IoT, considering the consistent results of perceived value studies in consumer decision in general, and in technology, innovation and Internet related consumer behavior in particular.

Proposed Conceptual Framework

Based on the literature review, we propose the following conceptual framework (Figure 1) for the intention to use IoT by millennials, combining contributions from TAM, perceived risks and perceived benefits theories.

METHODOLOGY

The previous section demonstrates the complexity and relevance of studying millennials' consumer behavior towards IoT. Taking into account the contributions collected in the literature review, the objec-

Figure 1. Proposed conceptual framework for this chapter

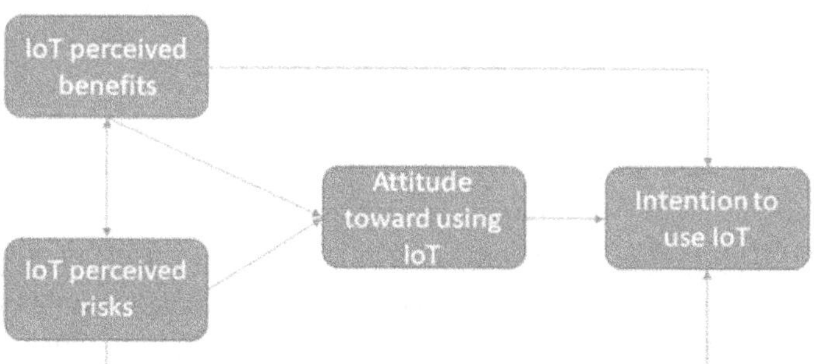

tives defined for this chapter and the proposed conceptual framework, a qualitative exploratory approach was adopted with the purpose of studyingmillennials' knowledge, attitudes, expectations, perceptions, perceived risks, perceived benefits and intentionsassociated to IoT.This approach was based both on the use of focus groups as data collection tool and further content analysis as data mining technique.

Focus groups were organized within a structured discussion outline involving progressive sharing of ideas and clarification of participants' insights. Focus groups are a social research method widely applied in scientific and academic work with the aim of generating information and knowledge (Morgan, 1996; Sagoe, 2012; Stewart & Shamdasani, 2014). Originally from social sciences' field, their application has been spread to diversified areas, namely those concerned with the study of consumer behavior, and at different levels of usage and reflexion (Silva, Veloso, & Keating, 2014). Stewart and Shamdasani (2014) mention a myriad of applications of focus groups as a researchtool, includinggeneration of research hypotheses, new ideas and creative concepts, data collection, interpretation of previoulsy obtained quantitative results, deeper understanding on participants' perceptions with the aim of facilitating the usage of further quantitative-related research tools, among other possible applications.

Taking into account the qualitative and exploratory nature of this study, focus groups were considered the best option to generate ideas and research hypotheses. With this purpose in mind, nine focus groups were conducted with a sample that comprised a total of 55 participants, between 19 and 37 years old. Participants included under-40's male and female pre-adults and adults with diversified professional paths and qualifications. In line with relevant literature (Morgan, 2010; Sagoe, 2012; Stewart & Shamdasani, 2014), there was an attempt to avoid inconstancy and a maximum number of 9 participants per group was established.

Although the study used a convenience sampling method, participants (see Table 1) were organized in order to meet a balanced homogeneity and heterogeneity within groups in terms of age, gender, professional occupation and education level. Focus group 1 (FG1), focus group 2 (FG2) and focus group 6 (FG6) comprise only participants that are students as their professional occupation, considering that a substantial part of the millennial population is still studying. Focus group 3 (FG3), focus group 4 (FG4) and focus group 8 (FG8) comprise only workers. Focus group 3 (FG3) and focus group 5 (FG5) had

Table 1. Sample characteristics

Focus Group ID	Number of Participants	Gender	Age	Professional Occupation	Level of Education
FG1	8	Male and female	Between 19 and 25 years old	Students	12th year
FG2	6	Male and female	Between 20 and 23 years old	Students	12th year
FG3	6	Female	Between 19 and 30 years old	Workers	12th year and graduation
FG4	5	Male	Between 19 and 37 years old	Workers	12th year
FG5	5	Female	Between 19 and 25 years old	Students and workers	12th year
FG6	6	Male and female	20 years old	Students	12th year and graduation
FG7	6	Male and female	Between 23 and 31 years old	Students and workers	graduation
FG8	4	Male and female	Between 19 and 34 years old	Workers	12th year
FG9	9	Male and female	Between 19 and 37 years old	Students and workers	12th year

only females, while focus group 4 (FG4) had only males. Focus group 2 (FG2) and focus group 6 (FG6) were composed of the youngest participants in this study and focus group 7 (FG7) was composed only of graduate participants.

Focus group discussionswere held in September 2017 and were organized into four main topics: IoT knowledge, perceived benefits, perceived risks and future intentions. Allparticipants were invited to discuss each topic freelyamong them, thus the moderator participation was kept to the minimum.

With the consent of the participants, focus groups were recorded (only audio) and content transcription relied onExpress Scribe v 6.00 for further analysis. As data collection was in Portuguese, translation was subject to validation by a bilingual. Content analysis techniques for contextualized interpretations were additionally used.

RESULTS

In this section we present and discuss the most interesting details retrieved from the collected data. Despite the various contributions and different perspectives on IoT discussed among participants, we concluded for data saturation, as the two last groups did not provide any additional perspectives as compared to what was depicted from prior discussions. Moreover, the method was shown to be especially adequate for this study, considering that, as we will see in the next section, the discussions evolved with the collective acknowledgement of the concept, each participant contributing with suggestions, resulting in effective group analysis disclosing the collective views, meaning and adoption of IoT.

Millennials' Knowledge of IoT

For most of the participants in this study, IoT knowledge is vague. Across groups, participants stressed the novelty of the topic, and admited not knowing a lot about IoT. As expressed by one of the participants, *I've heard about it, but don't know exactly what it is*(FG5).Still, we found that as soon as someone gave some explanation about the concept, others realized that they know some appliances, have heard of it, and have even tried it in their daily activities: *I sort of knew it, we have our phones connected to the Internet and are always on; facebook has an app to know where we are and that has caused some trouble already*(FG8); *There are already some devides that we use, of course IoT is the most advanced, but we're getting there (...) this can bring about many challenges but also many disadvantages*(FG8). Thus, we found that the term IoT is not widely used by these consumers, who are more familiar with specific products and services of this category, namely specific wearables such as smart watches.

The participants agreed that IoT could be adapted to anything in their personal and professional lives, although access may still be limited to a restricted group of affluent consumers. The conclusions of participants in this respect were clarifying: *I think not many people have this kind of IoT, but the number is growing fast (...) as the offer increases, prices get lower and people can buy*(FG8).

The profile of IoT users was easily identified by participants, the most prominent characteristic being the level of disposable income, but other characteristics were unanimously accepted:

People with money, little time, enjoy technology, enjoy trying out new things (FG3).

It depends on their profession (...) People related to technology, who work for corporations(FG5).

Affluent people, already living in the digital era, on their 40's, 50's max. Older than that, people don't feel they are available to learn, change habits, get basic digital knowledge (FG7).

Thus, this profile includes both the ability to buy this category of articles and the need for more efficient solutions due to time constraints. It also has to do with preference to use technology. Interestingly, the groups that suggested an age group for IoT adopters always proposed Generation –Xers, people within their 40's or in their 50's. As it was explained in one of the groups, *the younger ones are not going to use it immediately because they cannot afford it. They have to be their parents and relatives' influencers to enjoy it. But I think it's not sufficiently democratizedyet for everybody to use (FG7)*. So, the conversations on IoT usage were spontaneously centered on "*its usage*", because*at twenty you don't have the money for these things (FG8)*. Moreover, participants considered that this topic is more important for companies than for individuals, both because companies are leading IoTadoption and they are the ones who clearly benefit from it:

(...) companies want to improve and be more successful in what they're doing, while privately what we're looking for is comfort, have as less work as possible and as much available resources as possible. One thing is to maximize production and decrease flaws or errors, other thing is to control a lamp through wireless; this is comfort, not a necessity (FG4).

Regarding the categories of products and services they have identified as the ones they know more about, some were the most discussed, with special regard to the household, particularly smart home and smart home appliances. Smart cars were also popular, and other publicly consumed products such as sports equipment, clothing, footwear and other wearables, with a lot of attention dedicated to smart watches. Other notorious IoT applications include health equipment, IoTsollutions for retail, tourism, and industry, agricultural equipment, and other related to smart cities.

One interesting aspect was the duality between the indefinite possibilities of IoT and simultaneously the assessment of its relevance. Indeed, participants highlighted the endless applications of IoT, trusting on the constant evolution of technology that seem only limited by imagination: *Iotcan be applied to everything, I think, as long as you have a device connected to a server which communicates with other devices* (FG8). Nevertheless, they commit to rational criteria in IoT adoption, namely by *Use what is necessary (FG4)*. Clearly, IoT offers must demonstrate they additional value in order to conquer these millennial consumers, as perceived benefits are expected to be determinant to the consumer decision process, as discussed in the next section.

Perceived Benefits of IoT

Benefits for using IoT was a hot topic across focus groups, leading to more interaction among participants, due to the unanimity that most of the perceived benefits generated. On the top of the list is the perceived usefulness of IoT. In fact, the first benefit mentioned across focus groups was the convenience, as participants agreed that IoT makes lives easier and more comfortably. Some examples of participants' allegations include: *It's good to manage our time, our tasks, it helps to have more free time, which is a great benefit (FG3);It lets us be comfortable, manage our resources, whether material or not (FG4);Convenience, speed, to adapt to our lifestyle, customization (FG7).*

Thus, participants suggested that IoTmay provide gains in time, customization and efficiency associated to the convenience of being able to control their belongings and activities, overcoming restrictions of time and space, and improving their overall performance. Moreover, these benefits were classified as innovative and associated to present and future time, as IoT*makes it possible to do things that were impossible to achievebefore(FG1).* Associated with expected gains in performance, participants recognized that IoT alternatives will reduce risks and even exclude human error in contexts as diverse as health surgeries and traffic. Some examples: *We will have more and more bots performing our surgeries, due to their preciseness. In 11-hour surgeries a machine doesn't get tired, it simply has to be connected to a socket. Machines don't have emotions (FG3). It reduces human error, it's systematic and precise (FG2); human beings make mistakes all the time, it's easy to have traffic crashes (...) maybe a car with sensors will brake faster(FG3). It allows to correct the human error of forgetting (FG2).It can fix it immediately (FG4).*

By improving efficiency and performance, in some areas the benefits will also include ecologicalfacets, namely by avoiding waste of resources. Some of the examples participants mentioned were: *intelligent lighting systems that reduce light intensity according to brightness. Central heating for temperature control, more sustainable with less waste. Agriculture, a central station that commands automatic irrigation of several plots simultaneously according to climate and daytime. Sensor taps, they save time and are more efficient (FG2).*

Consequently, economic advantages related to saving money and time and maximizing efficiency were also brought about. Participants stressed the ability to manage time better and to increase productivity, which results in economic gains. As stated by two of the participants in the discussions, *it (...) sets us free to have more time to do other things; people with IoT worry less and have more time (FG1). When talking about production, it's not only to detect flaws, but to manage resources, to know better what is needed (FG4).*

Thus, participants identified both convenience advantages for companies and for individuals, including for leisure activities. Take, for instance, one of the participants' mention regarding her experience and knowledge about IoT applied to sports: *Super fast, convenient, easy to organize all info on sports. Speed and access too all information. Share things with other people (FG6).*

Interestingly, the conversation about IoT perceived benefits was dominated by the utilitarian ones, but other types of benefits emerged from the conversation, one of them being safety. These millennial consumers associated IoT with increase of safety, for having a greater control over their belongings and their lives: *Security, because we don't need a human intervention, namely police patrolling of strees or houses (FG2); for fire brigades, to have equipment that acts, where you can save a human life and avoid unnecessary risks, only by having a device (FG4).*

Thus, their perceptions onabsense of human error and having bots instead of humans in dangerous scenarios, along with having complete information, made them feel more secure, being consequently recognizedas an emotional benefit. Still, this is not dissociated from perceived risks related also to safety (explored in the next section) as one of the participants suggested: *More security... more secure up to a certain point(FG3).*

Participants also mentioned social benefits that can arise from IoT, including social status and proximity. It was suggested that IoT enables reducing loneliness, as it creates connections to relevant ones, such as family, caretakers, and others. Some of the examples were discussed in FG2: *Elderly who are alone, they feel more cared for if they have devices to interact with and supervise them (...) With animals, if they are anxious, a sensor may be triggered and the person who is at work can give a cookie remotely(FG2).*

Several contributions highlighted prominent social benefits of IoT, namely within publicly consumed products, such as wearables:

Socially it also influences, we acquire a higher status with a smartwatch, as if we are ahead in time (...) we live in a material society where people are classified by what they wear and what they have (...) People associate the idea that whoever has this, is somebody with money to spend (FG8).

Some consumers buy because they believe it gives them some sort of social benefit (FG9).

It can be observed from participants' insights thatcriticism was a strong note, as there were doubts about the positive social impacts of IoT in socially relevant and publicly consumed products, namely if the IoT users don't take other (utilitarian) advantages from that possession: *Some people think that having IoT gives them status, they have it but don't use it, it's for social recognition* (...) *In IoT, advantages are relatively small, we can save some time, but the main benefit is status(FG5). There are attractive technologies. To buy for status, for curiosity, aftewards you don't actually use everything (FG4).* Thus, hedonic and social value attained to some of the IoT proposals for personal and home use were hardly mentioned and disregarded to some extent. Even in groups where some participants had previous experience with IoT, only the utilitarian benefits were clearly highlighted.

Perceived Risks of IoT

Concerning risks that millennials perceive as associated to IoT, the most salient were physical, financial, performance and psychological. One of the clearest was physical risk, associated to potential damages in personal security as result of being intensively connected to the Internet. Participants were afraid of hackers and cyber attacks: *The risk of the machine falling into the wrong hands, as Internet piracy, databases falling into the wrong hands, somebody accessing your data and breaking into the house while you're away (...) you need physical strength to knock the door down and in the future, you just need technology. The intruder does not have to be near you to have access to our computer, he or she can be in another country (FG7).* This risk relates to issues of privacy, and fear that personal datais lost and used by strangers demonstrates the intensity of the perceived risk: *Somebody has all information on our routines, what we do, at what time we go to bed, where we are, they know everything, conversations, messages. (...) We can have a lot of advantages, but we lose all our privacy (...) because everything you do is monitored, everybody knows (...) companies sell information about you to other companies (FG6).*

Also noteworthy are perceived risks of health damages related to excessive exposure to connected appliances, as expressed for instance in FG7: *Another risk is the interaction of our body with the devices, we don't know up to which limit it is safe, the fact that we're surrounded by devices, radiation all around us. I think there's still a low level of knowledge on those effects that might be a little more serious than people think.*

In another group participants stressed that the greater risk is privacy and not financial. Still, IoT was unanimously associated with high cost, which increases the perceived financial risk: *Financially speaking, IoT is something very expensive for now (...) In my opinion it will be a good investment in the future, and it will pay off (FG8).* Simultaneously, as technology gets outdated very fast, the perceived financial risksincrease: *Now, there is one problem here. Every technological equipment should be replaced within 5 years. Today we cannot have anything with more than 5 years (FG1).* Moreover, participants questioned the opportunity costs associated with IoT, as they often suggested, the comparison between the price and the effective gains of IoTsollutions, as for instance explained in one of the groups: *Concerning lamps, I wonder if their life span will justify the difference in price (...) The cost does not compensate the benefit(FG4).* Again, participants were skeptical of the balance between benefits and costs, as demonstrated.

Moreover, despiteaknowledging the absence of human error as anIoT benefit, when talking about risks the discussions explored aspects related to reliability, namely due to design problems and to inability to learn and implement unplanned sollutions. Some ideas shared across groups include:

It's not 100% reliable, action reaction, because it was created by human beings (...) They're creating bots similar to humans, but actions and reactions are not similar, because everything is standardised, systematised. We want to get away from the human and manual sides (...) we want the electronic to be similar, eliminating flaws, creating perfection (FG2);

Machines were created by humans, so they're faster. We fail and we learn from that. Machines don't learn, we have to program them for that... and if they have any malfunction, they can fail at that decisive moment (FG3).

The risk of process failure stood out, as well as the consequences that could arise, especially if the users are unable to activate alternative solutions immediately. As one of the participants summed up, *if something fails (electricity, power supply), everything fails, we become powerless*(FG1). Thus, performance perceived risks were closely tied to others in the psychological domain, including losing control, becoming more dependent and even unable to perform tasks. For instance, some participants noted that they do not deal well with losing control: *I don't see myself buying an automatic car, because I like doing things and have control over them; machines can deceive you and I like to sleep peacefully (FG5).*

Helplessness and dependency were worries shared amongst all groups, as there is a perceived risk of trusting certain tasks to bots and being unable to take over if needed, because of not having the skills to do it and because *we're going to be dependent on certain things that work on our command but work automatically (FG7).* Participants were concerned of feeling useless, losing self-confidence, and become deprived of creativity: *Human creativity is reduced and without creativity there is not much innovation. We are too comfortable with not knowing things (...) machines that do that for us (...) We let go of attempting and experimenting (FG2).* They also antecipated user disappointment with IoT products and services, but particularly with the evolution of IoT in general: *There's a certain disappointment with the advancements of technology, a too-tight connection between things (...) they are unnecessary advantages (FG6).*

Attitude Towards IoT

Overall there seems to be a dominance of perceived risks that surpasses the benefits identified by the participants, resulting in negative attitudes towards IoT and its usage. These negative attitudes were markedly related to the inherent technology prevalence in personal and professional lives and to the dependence upon the Internet. Some clearly connectedIoT adoption to materialism, while advocating alternative consumer values such as frugality. Others stressed the excessive adoption of technology and consequent expected social and psychological risks, rejecting the intensive use of the Internet: *More and more people are using the Internet, but there is a general trend that change should be geared to-*

wards something else (FG1). Even the evident utilitarian benefits were diminished, as it was the case of eliminating human error that was interpreted as reducing human power over reality: *It cannot be 100% electronic, there should be a balance between the human issue and the use of technology. Eliminating error from our lives also eliminates fun (FG2).*

The usefulness of IoT was also debated. Participants considered that many times the incremental development of technology is unnecessary and meaningless, suggesting that IoTadoptionby consumers is often devoided of clear benefits, which was termed as a mistake:

IOT has many advantages but should have limits for certain things, if it's for an emergency, sickness, a person lying in bed, diabetes, ok, it can be used, but if it's only because it's nice, funny, it's wrong. It's an unnecessary expense. (...) For industries it makes sense, but privately it should be weighted (FG1).

Participants also interpreted IoT as a loss – of power and of importance - where humans lose against machines, which might hurt even identities: *People were appreciated for what they were, they had to have abilities, and now it's for what they have(FG7).* Again, ontologic aspects, while superficially debated and beyond the proposed aims of the discussion, demonstrate the relevance and the perceived extended impacts of IoT.

Intention to Use IoT

Although not exploring the expected impact on their daily professional activities, the participants in this study expected that IoTwill be more and more popular in industrial, agricultural and services sectors, due to the gains in efficiency, waste avoidance, and cost reduction. Ideas that were subjacent to this expectation were making their lives easier but also reducing jobs as results of automation: (...)*in industry, on a certain aspect, is eases work a lot, on the other hand it may eliminate some jobs, especially unskilled workers(FG1).*

The intention to use IoT in the personal sphere was dependent on the actual benefits provided, and on the analysis of cost-benefit ratio:

To make daily life easier (...) Especially products that provide comfort, easiness, time saving (FG2).

Everything that shows up and we think it will give us more security and comfort, will attract us. Everything that improves our quality of life in terms of health; but not to make us lazier (FG4).

Beyond utilitarian benefits and rational decision processes, some participants were enthusiastic future adopters with budget restrictions: *If I had an unlimited budget, I would opt for it, no doubt (FG6);I would be an enthusiast of a smart home, to arrive and see everything ready (...) I would for instance buy a smart phone if it had an affordable price (FG9).* Still, the adoption seemed more likely to happen for leisure than for the home. Concerning the home, it was clear that the applications have diverse perceived utilities, so the adoption might not be generalized, such as the idea of having a smart home, but rather adopting particular IoTsollutions:*There are things that make sense, alarm-related things, it you forget to turn the alarm on it's important to activate it remotely, but to turn the washing machine on remotely doesn't make sense (FG5).*The decision of adopting IoT for the home is to be taken within the family, and some members' opinions and preferences are expected to be determinant: *In the future I don't see myself buying this type of products, but my boyfriend would, he loves it, and I would probably follow(FG5).*

SOLUTIONS AND RECOMMENDATIONS

This chapter is prolific in suggestions for managers, marketers, and practitioners in general that are working with IoT, targetting either consumers, businesses, or internal clients. As millennials importance is growing in the consumer market but also within professionals in all sectors, including management and decision-making, they are unavoidable target segments – in fact, their general characteristics make them priority targets to high-tech innovative products and services.

This study demonstrates a huge need to disclose IoT: its scope, features, and warranties. The lack of precise information even amongst the savvy and tech-friendly generation enables misleading beliefs, strengthening perceived risks and damaging attitudes which are expected to trigger intentions. The concept itself is unfamiliar even to persons that are acquainted with numerous IoT devices and even have interacted with some. Given the importance of names for marketing and communication in general, it is of utmost importance that the name given to this vast category is settled, so that synergies can arise for all its products and services.

Brands and businesses that intend to market IoTsollutions might face strong resistance, due to the perceived risks that are transversal to all IoT. In fact, all the fears related to both technology and the Internet seem to culminate in the minds of consumers when it comes to IoT. Considering the huge impact that perceived physical risk can have on consumer behavior, IoT proposals must clearly claim and demonstrate the level of security offered to the user, particularly considering data protection. Still, other perceived risks such as psychological and social must not be disregarded. It seems obvious that dealing with benefits alone might not be enough especially in categories of IoT products that are associated with higher perceived risks. Moreover, millennials in this study portrayed themselves as very cautious decision makers, who demand an adequate balance between costs and benefits in order to sustain buying intentions. They even devaluated the emotional and social benefits of becoming IoT users and questioned the real utility of some of the IoT gadgets that have been on the news as future launches.

This poses additional challenges for marketing. Strategies for acquiring new customers, to retain them, and to keep them satisfied must be carefully designed and communicated. Emotional messages might not be effective for consumers struggling with doubts and fears regarding the performance and other impacts that IoT might have on their lives. New lifestyles associated with sustainability and frugality might also become barriers to IoT adoption – unless the compatibility and the inner benefits are clearly demonstrated.

Bearing in mind that consumer profile and type of product are also important determinants of the consumer behavior, strategies should carefully consider customer segments defined with the most relevant criteria for each type of product and service. Although similar types of products are expected to possess similar perceived risk components (L. B. Kaplan et al., 1974), and indeed the results of this study support this idea, it is also clear that IoT has very diversified applications, and that even considering the ones targeted at millennial consumers, their perceived benefits and risks, attitudes and consequently intentions don't seem similar across categories. For instance, they were quite diversified even within one category such as wearables. Moreover, personal characteristics such as economic status and personality are expected to influence the impact of perceived risk on intentions and behaviors (Pelaez et al., 2017), which, therefore, must be carefully considered for target market definition.

One final remark about early adopters and influencers: as interpersonal influence from relevant others affects perceptions and is an important source of information for consumers, in such a context of novelty, insufficient information and uncertainty regarding performance and outcomes of IoT, influencers and relevant others can be valuable supporters of IoT adoption, thus deserving specific tactics and actions in order to enhance their impact and foster IoT information and advocacy.

FUTURE RESEARCH DIRECTIONS

This study adopts an exploratory approach and is supported by the conclusions resulting from data gathered with a series of focus groups comprisinga total of 55 Portuguese millennials. Outcomes should be interpreted considering these limitations and confined to the sample. Any generalization will depend on future replications of this study, considering both different samples and populations, and even alternative research methods, that build on the cues provided by this and other studies on IoT adoption, and that may provide validation and extrapolation of the found results. One specific suggestion refers to alternative methods. One of the interesting results from this study was the prominency of utilitarian perceived benefits of IoT for the millennial generation, clearly neglecting social and emotional benefits. Being focus groups a method especially suited to unveil collective views and perspectives, this finding should be further explored using alternative approaches such as individual interviews or surveys aiming at revealing the more individualistic and emotional motivations and perceived benefits associated to IoT consumer behavior.

Overall, IoT is expected to become a impactful social and historical experience affecting millennials and the next generations, leading us to assume that it might in some way help to define and delimit generational groups (Smola & Sutton, 2002) as it happened with the Internet in general and its role in the comparison between Xers and Millennials. This study demonstrates the relevance of further studying IoT adoption by millennials, which can explore specific types of IoT, such as wearables, smart home devices, and professional applications, just to name a few. As demonstrated in the prior sections, IoT is a vaste and complex concept that will benefit from both holistic studies and specific analysis. Some of the topics that need to be addressed urgently include consumer profile and segments, innovators and influencers' characteristics and behaviors, impact on brand image and management, efficacy of communication strategies, decision process in the business-to-business and government contexts, perceived value in particular sectors such as health and tourism, among many others. It provides numerous research opportunities that are crucial for the adoption of adequate marketing and management strategies and, consequently, for the level of success of IoT product launches.

CONCLUSION

The Internet of Things is a challenging concept for the millennial generation. Although millenials are very aware of some of its most noticeable artifacts, the generic term itself seems detached and vague. In all discussions reported in this chapter there was a common awkwardness in dealing with the term, and participants were much more comfortable with alternative designations such as smart home, smart appliances, or smart cities. One would think that this is a symptom of lack of knowledge by the consumers, but this study demonstrates that it is not exactly the case. Although millennials participating in this study showed the need for further information, lacking some essential data in order to make informed decisions, they do have strong opinions and beliefs, they know well IoT scope and potential.

One of the outstanding aspects of their perceptions is a mix of incremental development and disruption. But, well, that has been a trademark for the Internet in particular and new media in general: a revolution (Hoffman, 2000) that is built on incremental steps (Lievrouw, 2004). Interestingly, these characteristics of the evolution have mixed feelings fromconsumers. On the one hand they undervalue what they referred as meaningless additional benefits provided by some IoT devices, and on the other they are cautious regarding big changes, such as "letting computers rule". As one would expect for a novel and revolutionary concept, much of the beliefs were probably unfounded, and mostly fear led to scenarios where consumers become hopelessly dependable on bots, unable to take control. Still, realizing such beliefs is essencial for any marketer and any brand working with IoT, as they give clear signals of what should be the essential guidelines for the marketing strategy.

Despite the body of contributions provided by TAMwhen explaining consumer behavior in information and communication technology contexts, this study explores in a larger extent the alternative perspectives furnished by perceived benefit and perceived risk theories, providing a rich and fresh look at millennials' perspectives on IoT. Still, this study also contributes with a clear support for one of the basic assumptions of TAM proposed by Davis et al. (1989): we found evidence that perceived usefulness is determinant for users' attitudes and consequently for the intention to use. This was especially evident regarding IoT applications that have, in the eyes of the participants, scant usefulness, which led them to express clear negative attitudes toward it, and consequently considering less likely to buy it.

Delving into the perceived benefits discussed by the participants in this study, it shows the level of transversal information participants hold on IoT. They were able to identify, explain, and apply a high number of features associated to IoT in various domains from business management, home, leisure, and personal care, and the consequent perceived benefits of its usage. Considering the prominently experiential nature of most IoT devices targeted at final consumers, one would expect that benefits such as emotional and symbolic (Holbrook & Hirschman, 1982) would have an important role in complementing the utilitarian ones. Apparently that is not the case, as the emphasis was mostly on utilitarian benefits across all groups of participants. The social inadequacy of consumers that use gadgets for self-image enhancement and the perceptions of IoT being high-end and expensive objects and thus associated to materialist individuals, created a consensus around the utilitarian benefits as main determinants of future behavior. Only in some groups was there open recognition of desire to use IoT in the future. Still, the social and emotional benefits were generally overlooked. Interestingly, as we noted in the literature review, TAM apparently prioritizes utilitarian benefits too, while not featuring the hedonic ones. Nevertheless, the results include also a generalized realization that some of the IoT objects are for hedonic reasons only. Similarly, there was a consensus around the image of IoT user: savvy, busy, and rich. Thus, addressing the hedonic-type benefits is not straightforward, and considering their relevance for communicating and positioning many products and services, as well as the vast social psychology and consumer behavior literature, their role in the consumer decision process should not be disregarded, at least for some of the applications that have social notoriety.

Perceived risk was perhaps the most discussed topic in this study. Exposing the uncertainty that involves IoT, the insufficient information, and the anxiety generated by extreme scenarios, time risk was the only one not relevant in the dialogues, resulting in apparent high resistance to the adoption of IoT. Hence, this study provides clear evidence of high perceived risks on the adoption of IoT. Athough the different risk domains were highlighted across the discussions, they were closely connected, as participants often combined different types of risk, such as examples provided of depicted associations between financial, performance and psychological risks. There is also subjacent the misconceptions and lack of thorough information on different applications of IoT and its consequences.

One should note that most of the discussions focused on IoT for personal use, such as wearables and smart home appliances, leaving mostly unexplored, for instance, IoT applications at work. Still, work-type IoTwere generically object to greater utilitarian benefits, lower perceived risks, and consequently more positive attitudes. The same happened to public use and governmental-type IoT, such as the solutions associated to smart cities. Thus, the beliefs and perceptions might depend on being consumer centered, and afforded directly by the consumer, or not. Moreover, the adoption of IoT by relevant stakeholders, such as cities and companies, may have a relevant impact on overcoming fears, misconceptions, and lack of information regarding IoT.

In addition to information, one factor highlighted by the literature (e.g., Byrne et al., 2016; Skard et al., 2016) that may help dealing with high perceived risks is perceived benefits. In fact, our results combine clear utilitarian benefits with high perceived risks, especially physical risks. On the one hand there is an evident tension between perceived benefits and risks; for instance, participants stressed the utilitarian benefits but also performance risks, with apparent controversial arguments, that resulted from the vagueness of some of the information they have, and the very wide applications of IoT. On the other hand, when expressing attitudes and talking about intentions, participants clearly combined benefits and risks in their rationale, concluding that they could overcome the risks if the benefits were relevant enough. The cost-benefit comparison was often referred in their arguments, again pointing up to the interdependence of the two constructs in determining attitude and intention. Indications provided by Skard et al. (2016) that hedonic associations can reduce the negative impact of perceived risks on attitudes help interpreting our results, namely the fact that the participants recognized as more likely the adoption of IoT for leisure purposes.

In conclusion, and getting back to the title of this chapter, obviously there is not a straight answer to it. The millennial generation is receptive and curious, aware of the benefits, but also of risks. Millenials are demanding customers, making detailed analysis, including cost-benefit comparisons. And they want more: more information and clear benefits, in order to commit. Accepting the relation between intentions and behaviors to be unequivocal, as long as the budget allows it, intentions will depend upon attitudes, and both on the relation with and between benefits and risks. Thus, excellent marketing strategies are needed both to develop the best IoT proposals and to provide the adequate information and appeals in order to convert millennials into IoT users and advocates.

REFERENCES

Al-Ajam, A. S., & Nor, K. M. (2013). Internet banking adoption: Integrating technology acceptance model and trust. *European Journal of Business and Management*, *5*(3), 207–215.

Bauer, R. A. (1960). *Consumer behavior as risk taking*. Paper presented at the 43rd National Conference of the American Marketing Assocation, Chicago, IL.

Baym, N. (2006). Interpersonal life online. In L. A. Lievrouw & S. M. Livingstone (Eds.), Handbook of new media: Social shaping and consequences of ICTs (Updated student ed.; pp. 35-54). London: Sage.

Byrne, Z. S., Dvorak, K. J., Peters, J. M., Ray, I., Howe, A., & Sanchez, D. (2016). From the user's perspective: Perceptions of risk relative to benefit associated with using the Internet. *Computers in Human Behavior, 59*, 456-468.

Campbell, H. (2005). Considering spiritual dimensions within computer-mediated communication studies. *New Media & Society*, *7*(1), 110–134. doi:10.1177/1461444805049147

Chong, A. Y.-L., Liu, M. J., Luo, J., & Keng-Boon, O. (2015). Predicting RFID adoption in healthcare supply chain from the perspectives of users. *International Journal of Production Economics*, *159*, 66–75. doi:10.1016/j.ijpe.2014.09.034

Davis, F. D. (1986). *A Technology Acceptance Model for Empirically Testing New End-User Information Systems: Theory and Results* (PhD Doctoral dissertation). Massachusetts Institute of Technology.

Davis, F. D., Bagozzi, R. P., & Warshaw, P. R. (1989). User acceptance of computer technology: A comparison of two theoretical models. *Management Science*, *35*(8), 982–1003. doi:10.1287/mnsc.35.8.982

De Kerviler, G., Demoulin, N. T., & Zidda, P. (2016). Adoption of in-store mobile payment: Are perceived risk and convenience the only drivers? *Journal of Retailing and Consumer Services*, *31*(1), 334–344. doi:10.1016/j.jretconser.2016.04.011

Dimmick, J., Ramirez, A. Jr, Wang, T., & Lin, S. (2007). Extending Society': The role of personal networks and gratification-utilities in the use of interactive communication media. *New Media & Society*, *9*(5), 795–810. doi:10.1177/1461444807081225

Fishbein, M., & Ajzen, I. (1975). *Belief, attitude, intention and behavior: An introduction to theory and research*. Reading, MA: Addison Wesley.

Gao, L., & Bai, X. (2014). A unified perspective on the factors influencing consumer acceptance of internet of things technology. *Asia Pacific Journal of Marketing and Logistics*, *26*(2), 211–231. doi:10.1108/APJML-06-2013-0061

Gefen, D., Karahanna, E., & Straub, D. W. (2003). Trust and TAM in online shopping: An integrated model. *Management Information Systems Quarterly*, *27*(1), 51–90. doi:10.2307/30036519

Han, M. C., & Kim, Y. (2017). Why Consumers Hesitate to Shop Online: Perceived Risk and Product Involvement on Taobao. com. *Journal of Promotion Management*, *23*(1), 24–44. doi:10.1080/10496491.2016.1251530

Hassan, A. M., Kunz, M. B., Pearson, A. W., & Mohamed, F. A. (2006). Conceptualization and measurement of perceived risk in online shopping. *Marketing Management Journal*, *16*(1), 138–167.

Hirschman, E. C., & Holbrook, M. B. (1982). Hedonic consumption: Emerging concepts, methods and propositions. *Journal of Marketing*, *46*(3), 92–101. doi:10.2307/1251707

Hoffman, D. (2000). The revolution will not be televised: Introduction to the special issue on marketing science and the internet. *Marketing Science*, *19*(1), 1–3. doi:10.1287/mksc.19.1.1.15181

Holbrook, M. B., & Hirschman, E. C. (1982). The experiential aspects of consumption: Consumer fantasies, feelings, and fun. *The Journal of Consumer Research*, *9*(2), 132–140. doi:10.1086/208906

Howe, N., & Strauss, W. (2000). *Millennials rising: The next great generation*. New York: Vintage Books.

Hsu, C.-L., & Lin, J. C.-C. (2016). Effect of perceived value and social influences on mobile app stickiness and in-app purchase intention. *Technological Forecasting and Social Change*, *108*, 42–53. doi:10.1016/j.techfore.2016.04.012

Igbaria, M., Guimaraes, T., & Davis, G. B. (1995). *Testing the Determinants of Microcomputer Usage via a Structural Equation Model*. Academic Press.

Kaplan, L. B., Szybillo, G. J., & Jacoby, J. (1974). Components of perceived risk in product purchase: A cross-validation. *The Journal of Applied Psychology*, *59*(3), 382–393. doi:10.1037/h0036657

Kaplan, S., & Garrick, B. J. (1981). On the quantitative definition of risk. *Risk Analysis*, *1*(1), 11–27. doi:10.1111/j.1539-6924.1981.tb01350.x PMID:11798118

Kim, H.-W., Gupta, S., & Koh, J. (2011). Investigating the intention to purchase digital items in social networking communities: A customer value perspective. *Information & Management*, *48*(6), 228–234. doi:10.1016/j.im.2011.05.004

Kim, Y., Park, Y., & Choi, J. (2017). A study on the adoption of IoT smart home service: Using Value-based Adoption Model. *Total Quality Management & Business Excellence*, *28*(9-10), 1149–1165. doi: 10.1080/14783363.2017.1310708

Lee, M.-C. (2009). Factors influencing the adoption of internet banking: An integration of TAM and TPB with perceived risk and perceived benefit. *Electronic Commerce Research and Applications*, *8*(3), 130–141. doi:10.1016/j.elerap.2008.11.006

Lievrouw, L. (2004). What's changed about new media? introduction to the fifth anniversary issue of new media & society. *New Media & Society*, *6*(1), 9–15. doi:10.1177/1461444804039898

Lievrouw, L., & Livingstone, S. (Eds.). (2006). Handbook of new media: Social shaping and consequences of ICTs (Updated student ed.). London: Sage.

Lister, M., Dovey, J., Giddings, S., Grant, I., & Kelly, K. (2009). *New media: A critical introduction* (2nd ed.). London: Routledge.

McMillan, S., & Morrison, M. (2006). Coming of age with the internet: A qualitative exploration of how the internet has become an integral part of young people's lives. *New Media & Society*, *8*(1), 73–95. doi:10.1177/1461444806059871

Mital, M., Choudhary, P., Pani, A., Chang, V., & Sun, Z. (2015). Adoption of cloud based Internet of Things in India: A multiple theory perspective. *International Journal of Information Management*. doi:10.1016/j.ijinfomgt.2016.02.011

Mitchell, V.-W. (1999). Consumer perceived risk: Conceptualisations and models. *European Journal of Marketing*, *33*(1/2), 163–195. doi:10.1108/03090569910249229

Moon, J.-W., & Kim, Y.-G. (2001). Extending the TAM for a World-Wide-Web context. *Information & Management, 38*(4), 217–230. doi:10.1016/S0378-7206(00)00061-6

Morgan, D. L. (1996). *Focus groups as qualitative research* (Vol. 16). Thousand Oaks, CA: Sage publications.

Morgan, D. L. (2010). Reconsidering the role of interaction in analyzing and reporting focus groups. *Qualitative Health Research, 20*(5), 718–722. doi:10.1177/1049732310364627 PMID:20406996

Ng, E. S., Schweitzer, L., & Lyons, S. T. (2010). New generation, great expectations: A field study of the millennial generation. *Journal of Business and Psychology, 25*(2), 281–292. doi:10.100710869-010-9159-4

O'Brien, H. L. (2010). The influence of hedonic and utilitarian motivations on user engagement: The case of online shopping experiences. *Interacting with Computers, 22*(5), 344–352. doi:10.1016/j.intcom.2010.04.001

Ozturk, A. B., Nusair, K., Okumus, F., & Hua, N. (2016). The role of utilitarian and hedonic values on users' continued usage intention in a mobile hotel booking environment. *International Journal of Hospitality Management, 57*(August), 106–115. doi:10.1016/j.ijhm.2016.06.007

Pelaez, A., Chen, C.-W., & Chen, Y. X. (2017). Effects of Perceived Risk on Intention to Purchase: A Meta-Analysis. *Journal of Computer Information Systems*, 1–12. doi:10.1080/08874417.2017.1300514

Prensky, M. (2001). Digital natives, digital immigrants part 1. *On the Horizon, 9*(5), 1–6. doi:10.1108/10748120110424816

Pura, M. (2005). Linking perceived value and loyalty in location-based mobile services. *Managing Service Quality: An International Journal, 15*(6), 509–538. doi:10.1108/09604520510634005

Sagoe, D. (2012). Precincts and prospects in the use of focus groups in social and behavioral science research. *Qualitative Report, 17*(15), 1–16.

Sarkar, A. (2011). Impact of utilitarian and hedonic shopping values on individual's perceived benefits and risks in online shopping. *International Management Review, 7*(1), 58–65.

Shaikh, A. A., & Karjaluoto, H. (2015). Mobile banking adoption: A literature review. *Telematics and Informatics, 32*(1), 129–142. doi:10.1016/j.tele.2014.05.003

Silva, I. S., Veloso, A. L., & Keating, J. B. (2014). Focus group: Considerações teóricas e metodológicas. *Revista Lusófona de Educação*, (26): 175–190.

Skard, S. E., Nysveen, H., & Thorbjørnsen, H. (2016). Influences of Perceived E-Service Risks: The Moderating Role of Perceived Benefits. *e-Service Journal, 10*(1), 1–23. doi:10.2979/eservicej.10.1.01

Smola, K. W., & Sutton, C. D. (2002). Generational differences: Revisiting generational work values for the new millennium. *Journal of Organizational Behavior, 23*(4), 363–382. doi:10.1002/job.147

Stewart, D. W., & Shamdasani, P. N. (2014). *Focus groups: Theory and practice* (3rd ed.). Thousand Oaks, CA: Sage publications.

Sweeney, J. C., & Soutar, G. N. (2001). Consumer perceived value: The development of a multiple item scale. *Journal of Retailing*, *77*(2), 203–220. doi:10.1016/S0022-4359(01)00041-0

Taylor, J. W. (1974). The role of risk in consumer behavior. *Journal of Marketing*, *38*(April), 54–60. doi:10.2307/1250198

Taylor, S., & Todd, P. (1995). Assessing IT usage: The role of prior experience. *Management Information Systems Quarterly*, *19*(4), 561–570. doi:10.2307/249633

To, P.-L., Liao, C., & Lin, T.-H. (2007). Shopping motivations on Internet: A study based on utilitarian and hedonic value. *Technovation*, *27*(12), 774–787. doi:10.1016/j.technovation.2007.01.001

Tung, F.-C., Chang, S.-C., & Chou, C.-M. (2008). An extension of trust and TAM model with IDT in the adoption of the electronic logistics information system in HIS in the medical industry. *International Journal of Medical Informatics*, *77*(5), 324–335. doi:10.1016/j.ijmedinf.2007.06.006 PMID:17644029

Turel, O., Serenko, A., & Bontis, N. (2010). User acceptance of hedonic digital artifacts: A theory of consumption values perspective. *Information & Management*, *47*(1), 53–59. doi:10.1016/j.im.2009.10.002

Wilson, S., & Peterson, L. (2002). The anthropology of online communities. *Annual Review of Anthropology*, *31*(1), 449–467. doi:10.1146/annurev.anthro.31.040402.085436

Yadav, M., & Varadarajan, R. (2005). Interactivity in the electronic marketplace: An exposition of the concept and implications for research. *Journal of the Academy of Marketing Science*, *33*(4), 585–603. doi:10.1177/0092070305278487

Yang, H., Yu, J., Zo, H., & Choi, M. (2016). User acceptance of wearable devices: An extended perspective of perceived value. *Telematics and Informatics*, *33*(2), 256–269. doi:10.1016/j.tele.2015.08.007

Yu, J., Zo, H., Kee Choi, M., & Ciganek, A. P. (2013). User acceptance of location-based social networking services: An extended perspective of perceived value. *Online Information Review*, *37*(5), 711–730. doi:10.1108/OIR-12-2011-0202

KEY TERMS AND DEFINITIONS

Consumer Attitude: Often used in Marketing, it refers to positive or negative beliefs that the consumer holds for instance towards products, brands, advertising, etc. These are expected to be relatively stable, and exert an important influence on consumer preferences, decisions and overall behavior.

Consumer Intention: It refers to the expected future behavior which results from the consumer willingness to buy or use for instance products and brands in the future, which are expected to be an important determinant of actual behavior.

Millennial Generation: Also known as Millennials and Generation Y, it comprises individuals born between early 1980s and late 1990s. Amongst their characteristics is their familiarity with communication and information technologies, which they use naturally. Contrary to their previous generation X, they did not have to adapt to technology such as the Internet; they have used it all their lives.

Perceived Benefits: The consumer's perceptions of positive consequences that may result from buying or using a product, a brand or a service.

Perceived Risks: It implies that the consumer holds perceptions of probability of danger and/or possible negative consequences with the acquisition and use of a certain product or brand, such as product failure. Perceived risks are associated with uncertainty and fear, and have multiple dimensions such as physical, financial or social.

Tecnhology Acceptance Model: A Theory that was developed by Fred Davis to explain how individuals adopt technology, and it is particularly relevant to explain consumer behavior in relation to technological innovations. It proposes that user behavior is directly affected by behavioral intention, which in turn depends on attitude, perceived usefulness, and perceived ease-to-use.

Theory of Reasoned Action: A Theory thatwas developed by M. A. Fishbein and IcekAjzen and states that an individual's behaviors are determined by his/her intentions, which, in turn, are depend on attitude towards the behavior and subjective norm.

Chapter 12
IoT Digital Service Provider:
Towards Smart Living

Filipe Cabral Pinto
Altice Labs, Portugal

Isabel Borges
Altice Labs, Portugal

Fernando Santiago
Altice Labs, Portugal

ABSTRACT

Digitalization is changing the way people live and interact. A new society has been built supported by cutting-edge technology changing even the most conservative habits. This new dynamic also changes the way people consume and relate to different brands. Communication service providers are evolving their business and taking digital transformation initiatives to engage customers by putting them at the center of their operations. But only the deep knowledge of customers guarantees a change with value. The advent of the IoT enables getting useful insights about people context facilitating the delivery of personalized offers and first-class experiences all over the journey. New business can be created in an endless market across different domains. However, the IoT value chain is complex and interactions between stakeholders are not always clear. This chapter presents the on-boarding of the IoT on the service provider actuation sphere.

INTRODUCTION

The digital revolution is changing people's behavior. The way people live is becoming really different from the recent past. Technological developments have enabled new forms of communication and the access to information has been greatly facilitated. Science is expanding to new areas bringing other dimensions to our reality. People now interact in a different way, much more in line with the dynamics of a changing world. A new digital society is irreversibly underway, strongly affecting our daily lives, on a path with no return.

DOI: 10.4018/978-1-5225-5763-0.ch012

Copyright © 2019, IGI Global. Copying or distributing in print or electronic forms without written permission of IGI Global is prohibited.

The use of digital technologies in everyday's life has been transforming customers. They are now much more informed and well aware of what they want. The seamless access to information is making them more demanding, able to select what best suits their needs at each moment. They require direct access to what they need and any obstacle in their way makes them opt for alternative directions. And because customers now globally share their experiences, their opinions count heavily and play a key role in brand awareness.

Communication Service Providers (CSPs) are core enablers in the construction of this new society. They make available technological infrastructure to support the new way of life. But despite their decisive role in this transformation, they are also being affected by their customers' mindset change. In fact, CSP customers are asking for improved interactions during the whole customer interaction journey. They require unspoiled experiences across multiple channels and meaningful touchpoints. Customers want the full control of integrated services tailored to their needs, including seamless communications, multidimensional content access, management of their living spaces or even access to their intelligent objects. Personalization will be key for customer engagement, but privacy and security are fundamental requirements for a relationship of trust.

Some CSPs continue to confuse technological evolution with customer needs. But the misperception of reality may cause clients to drift away to competitors or take on new Over-The-Top (OTT) players as service providers. To grow, CSPs have no other alternative than to reposition their business to support the new digital life. CSPs have to forget about technology as an end in itself, and put it as a means to satisfy the customer's needs. Digital transformation initiatives have to be put into action to meet the needs of the new society. Creating a customer centric culture will be critical to raise the levels of satisfaction. A journey of valuable interactions is the key to engage customers and satisfy their real needs in the digital service industry.

The Internet of Things (IoT) extends the Internet to the physical world. In a couple of years, more than 20 billion objects communicating across the network are expected to fully disrupt the daily digital life (Stamford, 2015). The data exchanged by these devices represents valuable information that can be used to foster innovation across different domains. CSP must make use of this big data source to improve its own business. The information collected can be applied not only to get a deeper view of the customer, but also to improve the range of services available, making them more useful to existing needs.

IoT will be a crucial instrument in the delivery of improved experiences. But the IoT value chain is complex, with different players competing for the same slices of the market. There is still a great lack of definition regarding the different roles and forms of interaction involved between each entity, making unclear the right positioning of Telcos. On board of the IoT as an enabler for the CSP transformation towards digital service providers is mandatory but requires major clarification. Platform-based approaches seem a good bet but require new strategies to create value for customers and to share revenues with suppliers and partners.

This article presents a reflection on the demands of future consumers in a digital society, and their impact on CSPs business and technology strategy raised by a customer centric approach in an age where the Internet reaches the objects.

THE JOURNEY TOWARDS DIGITAL LIFE

Today customers are very different from those five or ten years ago and their wishes are very dependent on social influences and fashions. On the other side, today devices (e.g. Smartphone) have very short lifecycles and telecommunication services are becoming commodities. Mixing all together, the result points towards the need of a total digital transformation that will enable Telcos to react very fast to customer's moods and new habits, anticipating not only technological trends, but also societal, while keeping their business ahead of competitors. CSP have therefore to respond to customers' new demands by enabling their digital lives.

Technological Trends

Technological growth has never been as great as it is today in the most diverse areas, especially in the communications sector. In fact, communication is binding human beings and technology has overcome huge barriers joining societies at a global level, linking them through different channels, anywhere, anytime from a collection of end terminals.

There are new key technologies that directly impact on CSP future evolution to make them able to respond to the needs of digital lives.

Electronics

Currently, people are completely dependent on electronic devices. Since the transistor invention, electronics haven't stopped evolving with 2D electronics, organic electronics and spintronics, all promising gains in

Figure 1. Technology trends impacting telcos

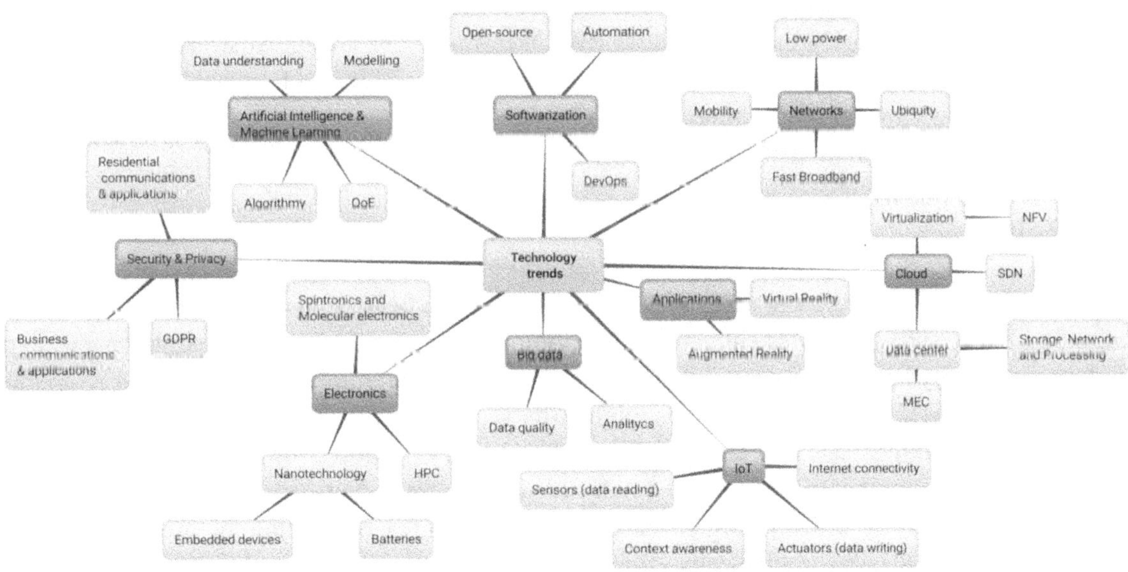

information processing (Kolodziejczyk, 2015). These gains are absolutely welcomed to implement high performance computing (HFC) that is desperately needed to treat ever growing data volumes. Moreover, at nanotechnology level, smart devices can be embedded everywhere and main envisaged applications will be on organic solar cells, transistors, diodes, nanowires and molecular switches, all while a new term – pico technology is appearing and promising to go to atomic level structures.

Softwarization

Electronic devices bring the need of software development to configure and control it. The tremendous increase of interactions with the Internet creates new opportunities and movements, such as the emergence of open-source and data democratization. Today, an average user of the Internet is able to gather and analyze data without requiring outside expertise or develop new software applications supported in existing frameworks, making them available in the Internet afterwards. Data federation, or virtualization supported by cloud storage, networking and computing are helping all this "softwarization" process. New methodologies as DevOps or agile are blending tasks performed by application development and systems operations teams, improving production times. New software tools will help not only more and more organizations to automate tasks and processes but also individuals towards the digital transformation already happening.

Networks

Ultra-fast broadband, 5G and low power wide area networks (LPWAN) are some of the technologies that are supporting connectivity advances. Ultra-fast broadband will allow a new era of applications able to provide real-time multimedia data either to residential or business customers. 5G is included in broadband networks and is regarded as a flexible and convergent network enabling huge capacities, low latencies, high speed mobility with a high potential to new commercial offers as for example critical communications. It is therefore appropriate to human-to-human, machine-to-human and human–to-machine communications. By the other side, LPWAN technologies are the answer to enable cost effective services deployment and maintenance requiring large coverage and long battery life of devices. LPWAN only allows low bit rate communications being unsuitable for multimedia services but ideal to machine-to-machine communications.

Virtualization

Back in the 1960s, MIT professor John McCarthy (Garfinkel, 2011), envisioned the concept of cloud computing. While speaking at its centennial celebration in 1961 he said: "Each subscriber needs to pay only for the capacity he actually uses, but he has access to all programming languages characteristic of a very large system (…) Certain subscribers might offer service to other subscribers (…) The computer utility could become the basis of a new and important industry". Those words are real today and new business models are taking advantage of Cloud, Software Defined Networks (SDN), Network Function Virtualization (NFV) and Self-Organized Networks (SON) that are paving the way to full network automation with global orchestration capabilities. From the Telco perspective, these new models enable resource optimization, shorter time to market and the deployment of self-management customer portals promoting OpEx reductions. On the customer side there will be direct benefits such as cost reductions and on-demand customization of services.

Security and Privacy

Cyber & Physical Security is a hot topic at present and will always be of critical importance. Companies and governments are becoming progressively more concerned about privacy and security issues due to frequent global scale cyber-attacks, as the WannaCry, or Petya/NotPetya ransomware ones. With the emergence of the IoT, the risks will increase since each device could be an open door to launch an attack, and since these devices are connected through Internet, it could potentially compromise other systems in the network (Mo, Y. et all, 2012). New transversal approaches are required to be put in place processes that react dynamically and quickly adapt to fight against different attacks. In this way, industry needs to embrace new disciplines to proactively detect irregularities, abnormal patterns and vulnerabilities that can result in complex attacks, and use those assets to provide it as a service to their customers. General Data Protection Regulation (GDPR) is already helping organizations to identify and assess the risks, likelihood and impact of potential breaches of confidentiality, integrity and availability of personal data, and support them in adopting the necessary security measures.

Internet of Things

IoT empowers the Internet with connected Things. Data gathered by all kind of sensors and the ability to act in that specific context, opens the door to the creation of new service logics, innovation and value creation. According to Gartner, 20.8 billion connected things will be in use by 2020 (Stamford, 2015). Moreover, IDC predicts global Internet of Things spending to reach nearly $1.29 trillion in 2020 (Torchia, 2017). There will be direct impacts in almost areas, such as health and wellbeing, home automation, wearable, primary sector and environment, industry 4.0, mobility or smart cities. Customers are moving to new life models where they are able to control not only their communications, services and content, but also their spaces ensuring the most appropriate environment anytime.

Big Data

More than ever, data places a central role in mankind. Big Data is a key asset made of large quantities of data, coming from different sources and contexts, that requires management and processing to enable the extraction of useful insights for business. (O'Leary, D., 2013) According to the IBM report (IBM Marketing Cloud), 90 percent of the world's data in 2016 had been created in the last year before, and forecasts point to even more growth; it is expected the production of 40 Zettabytes of data by 2020 (IBM Infographics)! The size of the market is also growing and is expected to reach 88 billion U.S. dollars by 2025 (Statista, 2018_1). Big data deals with data 4 "Vs": Volume (the amount of data), Variety (the diversity of data), Velocity (the speed of incoming data) and Veracity (the quality of data). With higher data volumes, it is possible to understand quite well the history, what is going on in the present and better predict the future. Larger varieties of data, will allow tentatively a 360° view of the subject under study. Higher data velocities allow real time data and consequently a continuous update on the decision path. And as data veracity gets better, there are more confidence on using and trusting it.

Data Centers

Data Centers (DCs) are data bastions providing services as data security, backups, storage, networking and processing. Today, DCs are commonly found at core networks and its interconnection is one of the most important qualities to look for in a data center provider, since it enables the creating of a tailored solution for each customer and their business' requirements. However and precisely to answer to customers' requirements, DCs are being also deployed in the access as Multi-access Edge Computing (MEC). MEC will enable CSPs to explore a more important role in content distribution by moving content closer to the customer potentiating new applications (higher capacity and very low latency) and new business opportunities.

Artificial Intelligence (AI) and Machine Learning (ML)

AI is the set of techniques that transforms datasets into useful knowledge, being ML a well-known application of AI both belonging to data science discipline. Data science brings together mathematical and computational tools in order to process and analyze data. Some inescapable aspects are data preparation, the use of Machine and Deep Learning techniques to get valuable predictive knowledge and data visualization, to help comprehend complex data. These techniques can be applied to understand the surroundings and help in decision making. Well known use cases include physical and cyber security; marketing and advertising, conversional systems, retail analysis, healthcare and financial trading. AI and ML will deeply impact future Telco businesses by transforming the way they interpret customer realities.

Virtual Reality and Augmented Reality

Augmented Reality and Virtual Reality are two topics being considered in the next wave of applications. Both take the user to a hybrid dimension. The extension of reality by adding context relevant information or the creation of new, personalized virtual environments enables new forms of interaction and allows a new level of realism. A new generation of applications is emerging offering inexperienced experiences to customers, making diffuse the separation between what is real and what is virtual creating new environments that will be limited by imagination. Some sectors are already taking advantage of these evolutions: in the industrial sector it is becoming increasingly important to get all the features of an equipment or to solve problems via a virtual troubleshooting assistant, in entertainment, a myriad of new applications, as games, are being created with unlimited possibilities (the Pokemon Go game was a great success); in tourism, new applications, which add important context information are appearing and enriching the traveler's experience; the education sector is also making use of these technologies to engage students in an improved learning process; and, of course, the military is developing new programs in order to expand its forms of action.

Conversational Systems

Conversational systems are gaining momentum on daily life. Chatbots, voice and video-activated assistants will transform our lives in multiple personal or professional domains. For instance, Gartner predicts that "by 2020, 30% of web browsing sessions will be done without a screen" (Levy, 2016), and according to Business Insider, "80% of businesses want chatbots by 2020" (Beaver, 2016). Bots will be a reality anywhere, from medical bots that could help find a solution to the most common symptoms through artificial intelligence to elderly companions or problem solvers facilitators. As a matter of fact this new trend is the result of the combination of several technologies, not only AI but also machine learning/deep learning, natural language processing and IoT, among others. All together allow to reach a maturity level making possible smarter and effective interactions between humans and machines. The proliferation of these technologies will have a transformative impact on how customers interact along their journey, not only at a business level, but also with their own spaces, enabling a smoother experience and channel diversification in all customer journey touchpoints.

Societal Trends

A societal trend comprises the tendencies that are derived from human and society behaviors and interactions. The main trends are:

- Increase in digital economy. There is a substantial increase in e-commerce and customers are very keen on using online platforms to buy their stuff (f.i Amazon, Farfetch, Alibaba). Moreover, at least in Europe, not only large companies, but also SMEs with digital presence in the Internet are increasing and will increase further when effective implementation of consumer rights and security (payments and privacy) for e-commerce will be in place. When those conditions are achieved all companies will be in position to reach e-commerce full potential. Cooperation intra and inter borders is essential to guarantee such a trusted environment.
- Rise of global middle class in developing countries. Country inequality is being reduced due to an economic growth in some countries in Asia, Latin America and Africa, leading to an increase of the middle class. This will have implications on consumption and investment and so in economy, society and political development in the developing world (Drabble).
- Decline of the 'established' middle class in high-income economies with impacts on the end of the global financial crises, pressure on social safety commitments, jobs and public finances among others (Drabble).
- Population aging will create a huge pressure on social safety approaches requiring better health institutions allowing for mass prevention and diagnoses and to wellness aspects of the mind, body and soul.
- People will continue to grow in mobility requirements to travel. They will want smart personal mobility. Car companies will change their business models to incorporate also solutions for personal mobility share and autonomous transport solutions (Singh, 2014).
- Customers want to choose with whom they make business being expected the retail e-commerce sales worldwide amounted 4.48 trillion US dollars in 2021 against 1.86 trillion US dollars in 2016 (Statista, 2018_2).
- The customer will want to be in control and be autonomous in managing all their services and apps or those that are available to him anytime and anywhere - It is the individual empowerment!
- There will be fewer jobs and more freelancers. People will be paid per work done in a short period of time (few months). This will have great impacts in aged workers.
- The concept of traditional family is changing. All members will be different customers.

- Cities are becoming larger, and there will be impacts at all municipality levels: from energy management to water, waste, mobility, urbanism management. Cities will experiment a rise on criminal activities (Yogitha, K., Alamelumangai, V.).

Above trends can be specialized regarding the impact on service providers business. As a matter of fact, the digital revolution has brought intense changes in the way people live. Customers now have new standards and are much more demanding also on what are the services provided by the CSP. Figure 2 presents the societal evolution of CSP customers taking into account the smart living trends.

- Network connectivity is by now a daily life asset. Where there are people there is connectivity allowing customers to be always on. But they require even more, they claim for increased bandwidth, global coverage and suitable quality to fully enjoy the new digital trends.
- People do not stop for too long at the same place. They change jobs frequently, move easily from home, and hop between cities or even between countries. The address they have associated is still that of their parents' house. Nomadism is the new reality!
- People now have a new social life. They share everything on the network, from the most banal things to the most compromising secrets. They make declarations of love just as easily as they post harsh comments. They add an endless number of photos, videos and other data to the community and want to get everything from others. But all this interaction happens behind a computer.!
- Ownership is no longer an objective in the world of shared economy. The efficient use of resources is a habit that has come to stay. People pick up an Uber to move around, use Airbnb to rent a house for the holidays and use objects from neighbors through the Streetbank site. The key objective is to meet its own needs in an easy to use way.
- The emergence of new technologies, such as blockchain, and digital currencies, e.g. bitcoins, predict the disappearance of physical money. Cashless will provide customers safety and convenience experiences. Smartphones will be at the centre of this shift enabling seamless mobile payments.
- Watching linear TV is ever more a a thing of the past. Nowadays, almost no one is sitting waiting for an episode and much less awaits the new season of the favorite show. People are now demanding access to content and not programs and want to see it in their different devices, when they want, wherever they are.

Figure 2. CSP customers' societal evolution

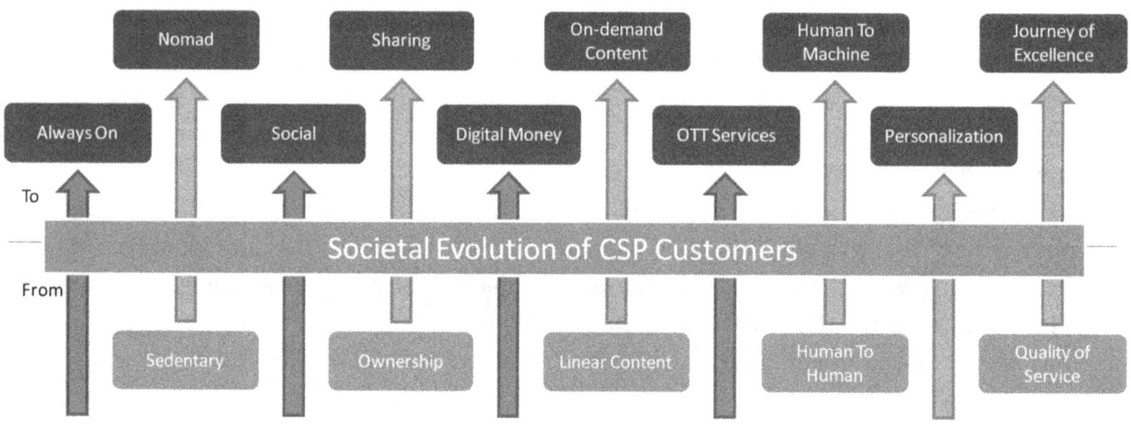

- CSP are still converging to deliver multi-play bundles with mobile and fixed telephony, broadband access, streaming TV and video-on-demand services. In the digital era, Telcos will bridge customers with OTT players making possible the creation of differentiated offers taking into account real customer needs, preferences and behaviors.
- The substitution of humans for machines is radically changing the way we interact. Chatbots are now commonly available online and intelligent personal assistants, like Alexa from Amazon, Apple Siri or Google Assistant, are already prepared to answer to our voice requests. Sooner rather than later, the way society interacts will undergo a new revolution.
- Future customers want to fully control their services, the content they access, the way they communicate, their surrounding spaces and even want to negotiate what they are going to pay Personalization will be key to captivate demanding customers.
- Quality of service obviously remains a requirement of customers. But they now want more than that; they demand a relationship of excellence all over their journey, taking into account the multiple touchpoints over the time. The business success is deeply dependent of customer experience got on the diverse digital and physical channels. Feelings and perceptions are now the most critical points for customer engagement.

THE TRANSFORMATION FOR DIGITAL LIFE

Enhanced Customer Journey

The customer journey refers to the set of all interactions that the customer has with the provider throughout their relationship. It includes all touchpoints in the different stages that can change the customer's perception of the brand. As shown in Figure 3, the customer journey is the ride through all stages, from brand awareness to the end of the contract, including the phases of the decision and making the purchase, the use of the service or consumption of the product, the support given to the customer and even renewal of the contract.

Figure 3. Main customer journey stages

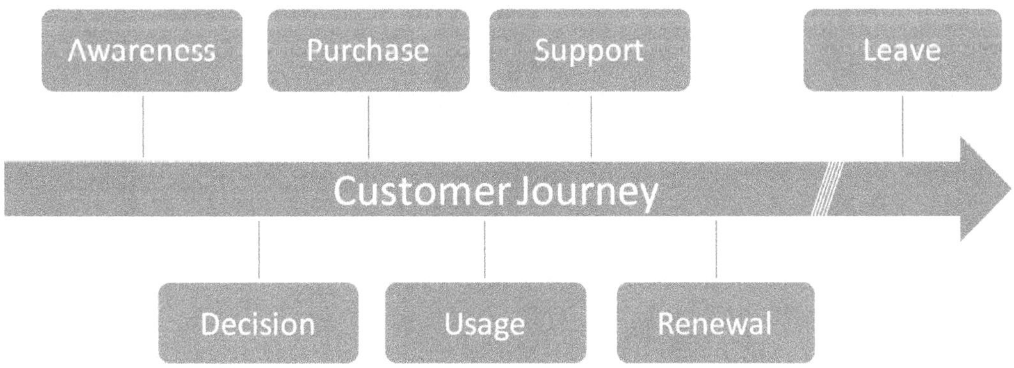

The customer journey has not always been perceived in the same way. There have recently been significant changes that go hand in hand with technological developments and societal changes. However, customer satisfaction is still strongly influenced by three main dimensions: price, service offer and experience. These dimensions are presented in the Figure 4 as having the same weight for customer satisfaction, but the approaches are diverse and the weight assigned to each dimension is strongly dependent on the CSP strategy.

Setting prices below those practiced by the market is the most direct way of keeping customers and bringing new ones on board. Competitiveness comes from the low cost of the offer and not from any other differentiating attribute. To mitigate the impact of reduced margins, CSPs typically ask customers to sign loyalty contracts, forcing a relationship to exist. But customers who simply look at the price are not easy to emotionally engage and tend to run away to the competition as they present similar offers at a more interesting value.

The offer of innovative value-added proposals is naturally differentiating. The convergence of the networks towards the IP has greatly facilitated the convergence between the Telco, media and the Internet domains, fostering the creation of new business logics. CSPs are now packing together a bundle of services in a marketing move to captivate customers. Under a single bill, CSPs are announcing seamless access to Internet access, voice communications, IPTV services and even automation products made available in Multi-Play offers. This service integration opens doors to new business while attracting a segment of customers that is not so sensitive to the cost of commercial offerings, helping CSPs to alleviate the decrease of revenues in its traditional services. In fact, OTTs are intruding on the Telcos' business, stealing a large chunk of the market. And the numbers do not lie: PwC in (PwC 2017) states that more than a third of the international voice traffic is generated by Skype applications while WhatsApp, Viber, and Apple's iMessage are responsible for more than 80 percent of all messaging traffic; and according to Statista (Statista, 2018_3), Netflix already reached the impressive mark of 100 million streaming subscribers worldwide, despite having no distribution network! The good news that these figures bring is that the need for connectivity will grow impressively, creating new opportunities, but if CSPs want to be more than mere bit pipes they will have to rethink their portfolio strategy by thinking about future customers' needs in the digital society. Business agility and operational efficiency will be key enablers in effective services offering differentiation.

Figure 4. Customer satisfaction dimensions

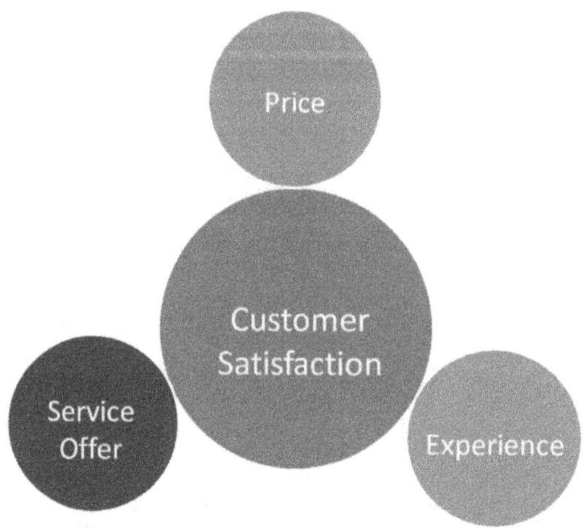

Beyond pricing and service offering, CSPs can, and must, differentiate by completely focusing on a relationship of excellence. Since only positive experiences engage customers, CSPs must move their focus away from technology and center their attention in providing customer satisfaction in the entire journey, from the awareness stage until the time of departure. The customer experience is critical and has a direct impact on loyalty to the operator. Along with the quality of service provided, it is decisive to ensure that all touchpoints are worthwhile. The interactions must me seamless regardless the channel used and enabling and personalization must be taken for granted.

The digital life of customers and the entry of OTT stakeholders are forcing CSPs to adopt customer centricity as a new paradigm to avoid churn and captivate new customers. Customers are now becoming the core of the business and all operations must evolve to keep them satisfied during the whole journey.

Digital Service Provider for New Lifestyle

The digital society potentiates new ways of living. The seamless access to information is allowing people to experience extended realities supported by cutting edge technology. New habits emerge that directly impact the way people consume. CSPs want to enable the digital generation to live their new lifestyle in a world of new interactions. Providing low cost connectivity is no longer enough; CSPs have to meet customer needs by taking transformation initiatives to face the challenges brought by the digital market.

CSPs will have to redefine their operations to meet customers' digital needs, relegating the network to the background. CSPs of the future will be digital service providers (DSP) capable of responding to the needs of the new society. They will try to play the role of a broker in the digital ecosystem, owning the platform for a marketplace of self and third-party OTT services reinforcing the relationship with customers through the competitive advantaged of owning assets that can positively contribute to the customer experience in the form of an addictive and simple journey.

Figure 5. Evolution towards a customer centric DSP

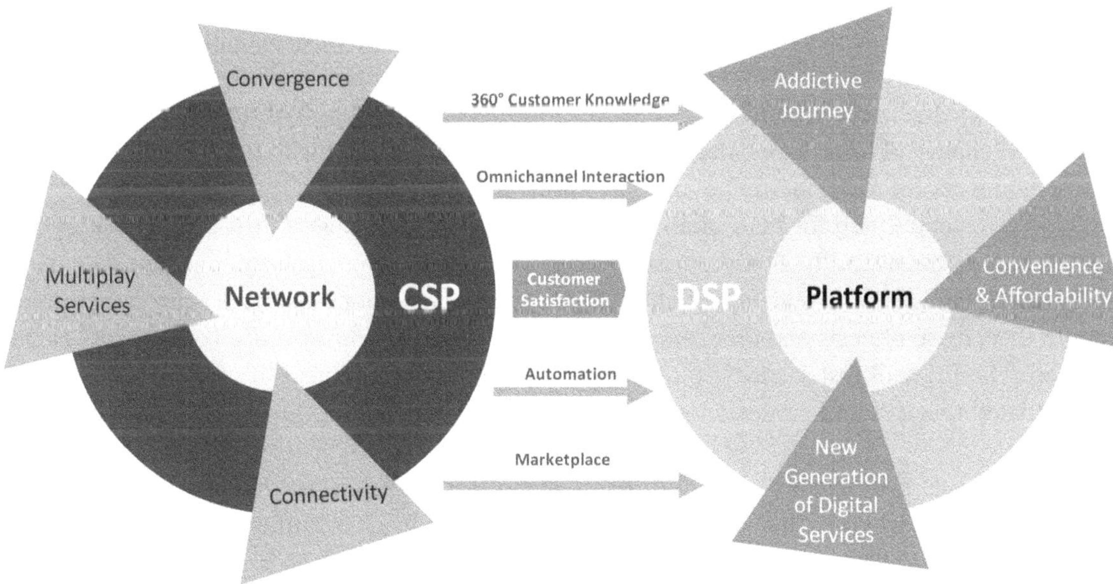

The CSP to DSP transformation requires a change of mindset. The network is no longer at the center of the business and is seen as a commodity. Customer centricity will be the motto to move the focus of the CSPs to platform-based approach in line with of the best in breed digital native players. DSPs will resort to data and analytics to optimize businesses and operations. The deep knowledge of customers and seamless interactions will be critical to improve global perception of the brand. And all processes must be automatically dealt to enhance service provider efficiency and agility.

The Telco evolution strategy from a CSP towards a customer centric DSP requires major changes, namely:

- Enhance customer knowledge level by adopting intelligent customer relationship management to be always aware of customers' needs throughout their journey, taking advantage of big data and artificial intelligence;
- Increase customer engagement by investing in omnichannel interactions, using analytics, machine learning and conversational technologies, to avoid churn and captivate new customers;
- Improve customer response times and decrease incidents with customer services by evolving business and operational processes towards the full automation resorting to online multichannel self-provisioning systems;
- Answer the customer digital needs by providing a marketplace of services open to third parties, diversifying the sources of revenue.

THE IOT DISRUPTION FOR SMART LIVING

IoT Advent

IoT is at the base of a radical transformation with global impact. A new era is taking shape fostering the development of a new society where information is sovereign. The data gathered by sensors and the ability to act in the surrounding context opens doors to new logics that foster innovation and value creation, impacting people daily life in a remarkable way. The forecasts are unanimous and point to the existence of a multitude of devices connected to the Internet in a couple of years.

IoT extends the Internet to the physical world, opening doors to new possibilities. The Internet already allowed the exchange of information between people or applications, but with the connection of the devices to the network the footprint reaches the real world, making true the Internet of Everything concept.

The IoT is a central hub for innovation in the path for a digital society. It is at the base of a new industry affecting transversally all sectors of activity. The insights coming from real time data enables better decision making in the selection of alternative paths. Applications can be dramatically improved leading to a decrease of costs and time, and by taking out humans from specific tasks, errors can also be reduced. The IoT will foster creativity making possible the development of new projects, resulting in differentiated services and products. New markets will be opened, bringing additional revenues for enterprises.

IoT footprint is already spanning across different areas. It is changing health and wellness ecosystem by allowing cost effective real-time monitoring and valuable feedback to authorized entities. Also, care systems have been evolved giving comfort to both patients and caregivers. The IoT is also changing

Figure 6. Internet of Everything

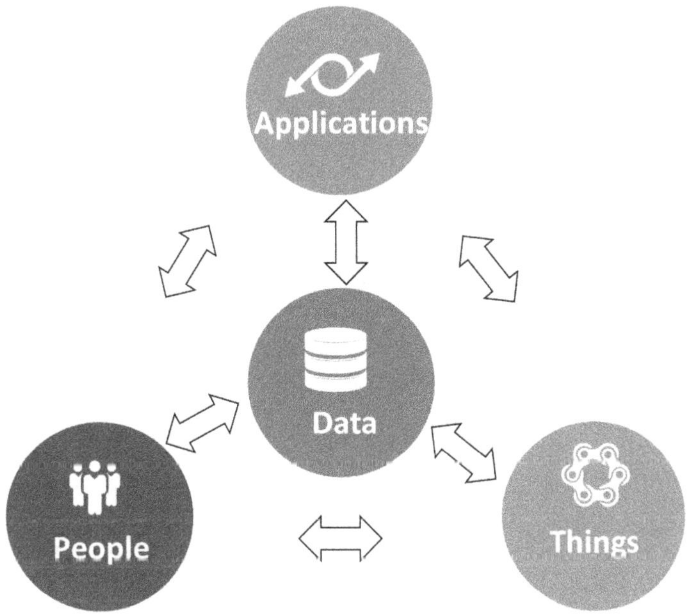

home environments by allowing digital interactions with different equipment and services. It is now usual to find security systems to keep homes safe or home automation services to manage lighting, heating, ventilation, air conditioning or even home appliances. The monitoring of energy, water and gas consumptions is getting common allowing saving money at the end of the month. And all of this can now be controlled using intelligent personal assistants to make simpler all interactions. Cities also resort to devices to get information about its own status and take the adequate measures. Real time management of city infrastructures, such as public lighting, waste management or mobility related assets – from autonomous vehicles till connected traffic signals -, is crucial to make urban spaces a better place to live. The IoT is also shaping the 4th Industrial Revolution by providing the information required to achieve maximum synergies and automation, optimizing procurement, production, sales and delivery stages. It adds the needed flexibility to enable the cost and time effective production of individual lot sizes. The usage of the IoT will be also critical to enhance resource protection. It will help keeping a sustainable growth while preserving the environment for future generations.

Figure 7 presents the footprint of the IoT in different domains of activity.

IoT Technological Domains

The IoT technological domains for CSP encompass 5 main layers, as presented in Figure 8. The layer at the bottom, Devices & Gateways, includes all set of sensors, used to read physical measures, and all actuators able to control specific assets. These devices can link directly to the Internet using the connectivity of CSPs or can resort to Gateways to make the bridge. The Connectivity layer represents the CSP communication infrastructure including all wired and wireless networks regardless its specificities. It is the bit pipe that makes possible exchanging information between devices, gateways and applications.

Figure 7. IoT main footprint

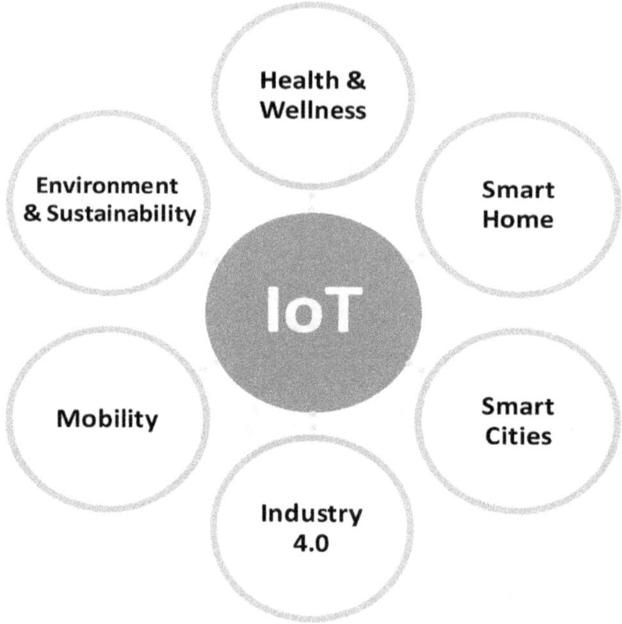

Managed connectivity is a layer created to support the management of machine-to-machine connectivity over multi-technology networks. The next layer is critical for IoT implementation. The Service Enablement is where key functionalities take place facilitating the creation of new business offers. This layer will enable data gathering, mediation, analytics, storage, monetization, among others, common to different domains of activity. Finally, Applications is the layer where the service logic takes place providing the floor to value added services making possible offering new and differentiating experiences to customers.

IoT Framework

DSPs want to potentiate new services and improve customers' experience by fitting in the IoT technology into the existing ecosystem. The dynamics arisen from the massive spreading of devices forces the creation of a framework that must be aligned with both business and operational requirements. A digital mindset must be seriously taken by providing open APIs to support different technologies and protocols easing the end-to-end system integration and technology adoption. The architecture must follow cloud-based principles by enabling automatic and instantaneous scale of the resources (e.g., CPU, memory, storage and network) allowing delivering the right needs at the right time in a cost effective manner. It must also encompass security and privacy mechanisms to ensure customer information protection according to regulations and guidelines in the IoT landscape.

The framework must work as DSP facilitator to foster innovation based on device insights. For that, it must encompass mechanisms to cope with all related IoT, Data, API and Monetization services that are key enablers to support owned and third party applications. Figure 9 presents a high level view of the carrier grade IoT framework.

Figure 8. Technological domains

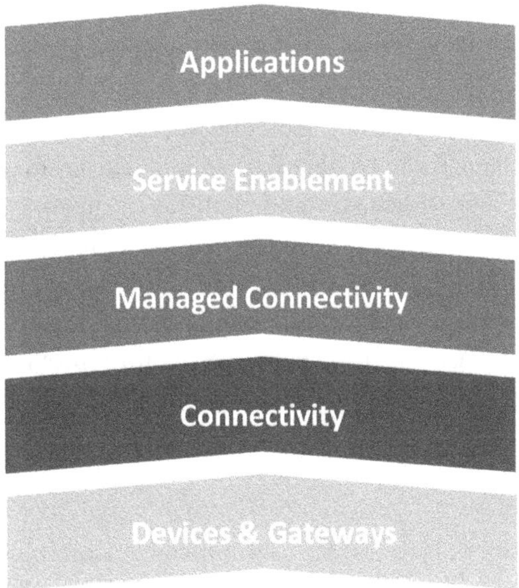

Figure 9. Carrier grade IoT framework

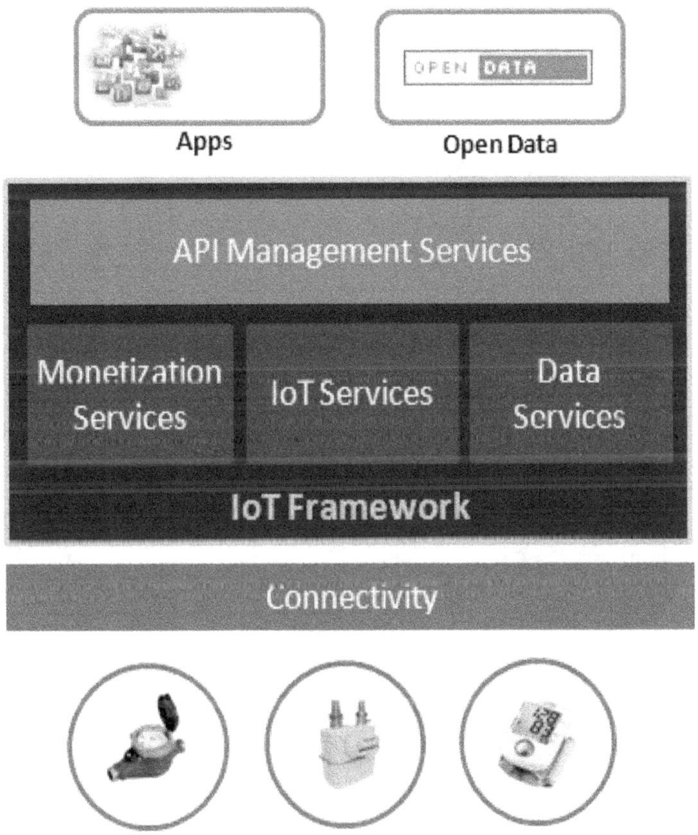

IoT Service Enablement

IoT Services represents the enablement core of the IoT framework foundation. It makes available the required capabilities to manage devices and IoT-related applications. The Inventory is the component responsible for managing device information, including all its specific characteristics and values. The Register module provides mechanisms to let devices and applications to use IoT services made available by the framework. IoT Services provide also functionalities to support subscription of specific occurrences. The Rules Engine is the component in charge of managing subscriptions to data or metadata events triggering the launch of notifications to subscriber entities. The Interaction component supports synchronous and asynchronous communications making possible the exchange of information between devices and applications. Finally, the Device Management entity provides the required mechanisms to deal with device configurations, firmware updates, fault and performance monitoring.

Data Processing and Analysis

The key objective of Data Services is to extract useful insights from big data using analytic tools. The information extracted from the data generated by billions of devices, which can be enriched with other data sources, has great value, and can even become one of the greatest sources of income associated with the IoT. DSPs need to start using it as a competitive asset for the promotion of new services and customer loyalty.

Figure 10. IoT services

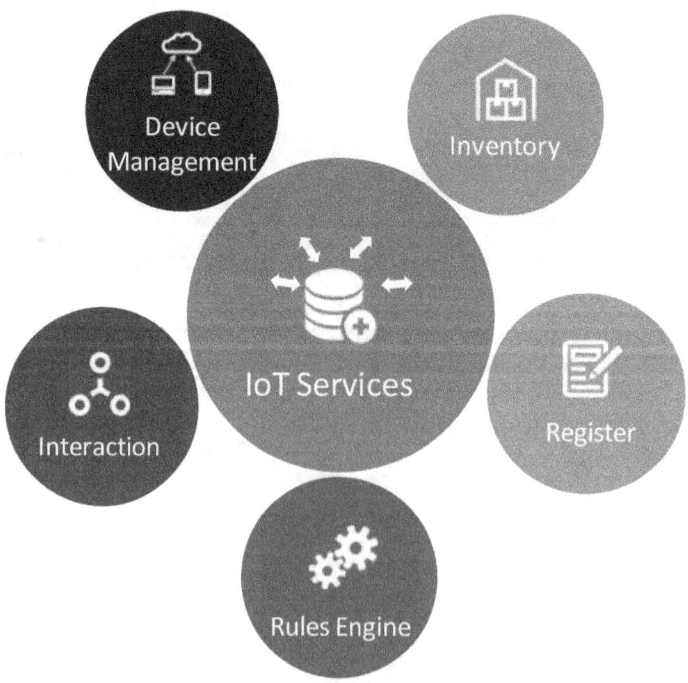

Following the TM Forum Big Data Analytics Reference Model, Data Services must make available the set of capabilities required to support near real time event processing and data analytics for value extraction. The Data Ingestion component is in charge of taking in online and offline data coming from different sources. It formats and integrates the streamed or batched data facilitating the consumption by analytics processes. Data Management is the entity responsible for providing meaningful and usable data for specific domain logic. It guarantees the incoming data quality and processes the data using several transformations procedures in order to map it to useful data models. Next components resort to several data analytic techniques to generate useful insights. The Event Processing component enables the processing of streaming data in near real-time generating alerts and triggers, while the Data Analysis component computes batched data in order to extract metrics or to generate reports useful for decision making. *Figure 11* presents the core Data Services module.

Monetization Usage

The advent of the IoT brings increased complexity in service offerings requiring advanced business models for capitalizing the value proposition. It will be necessary, for example, to charge according to the number of devices connected, based on the number of messages exchanged, the space used to store the data or even the value of the information. DSPs are recognized players in the delivery of monetization services, proven by their trusting relationship with their customers. But they need to evolve their assets in order to deliver a product ecosystem able to integrate the monetization of IoT services with business and operational processes of service providers. These are the tasks for the Monetization Services mod-

Figure 11. Data services

ule (Figure 12. The tools for designing business offers, controlling the product life cycle and managing product catalog are included in the Product Management component. The Subscription Management component provides the functionalities required to support the management of customer subscription life cycle, the adherence to concrete offers and the configuration and execution of all related provisioning flows. The Rating and Charging component enables the configuration of charging and rating rules and allows account mechanisms for both online and offline modes. It even enables the payment in advance of IoT services by providing TopUp management functionalities. Lastly, the Domain Billing component supports the generation of billing items related with IoT services usage.

Secure and Controlled API Exposure

The API Management Services allows controlled exposure of data and services to entities external to the service provider domain, being the foundation of an open IoT market (Figure 13). The *API Lifecycle Management* module controls APIs throughout their life cycle, allowing their registration, configuration and publication in order to become available for third parties usage. The *API Gateway* component is used for controlled and secure mediation of access to APIs. It contains mechanisms for monitoring, caching, load balancing, throttling, content-based routing, transformation, policy enforcement, protocol bridging among other functionalities. The *Identity Gateway* module enables mediation and management of connections with external identity providers, supporting different sources such as social, organizational or governmental.

Figure 12. Monetization services

Figure 13. API management services

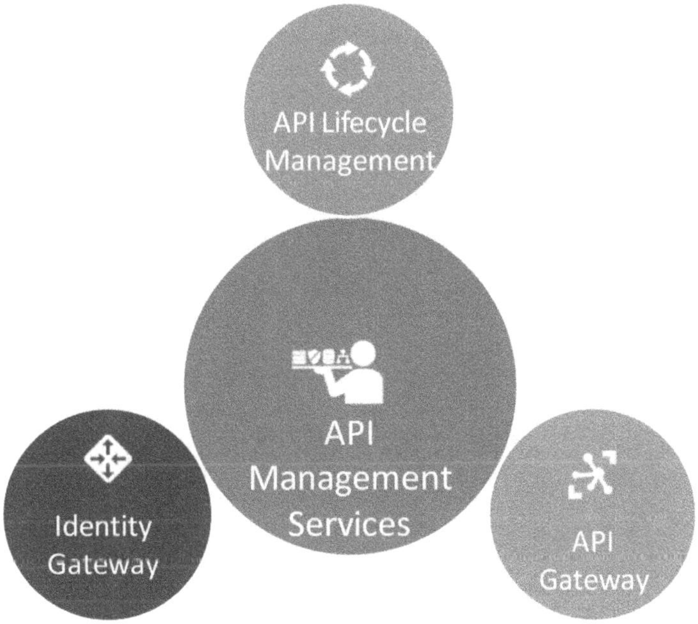

Smart Living Powered by IoT

Smart living is an enhanced lifestyle where people have full control of their physical and virtual interactions, either individually or socially, in a seamless and personalized way, making life easier. It is the every day trip crossing different smart domains allowing the digital interaction with different equipment and services improving the experience as a whole (Figure 14).

The IoT is critical to facilitate the new smart living standards. The data collected by the sensors is extremely important to understand the context of customers and dynamically adapt all interactions. DSPs will thus have to rely on the IoT framework to differentiate themselves from other stakeholders and stand out in their digital offering. The real-time knowledge of its clients will thus be fundamental to guarantee the best interactions at each stage of the journey, ensuring high levels of satisfaction.

THE CHALLENGES FOR TELCO BUSINESS TRANSFORMATION

The transition of Telcos from traditional CSP positioning to DSP will imply a mindset shift that goes far beyond technology. Business models and value chains are different from the ones they are currently accustomed to. The digital platform-based business models require from the Telcos different strategies to create value for customers and to share revenues with suppliers and partners. Opening their own platforms to other parties and automate all the end-to-end processes, from the on boarding of customers and partners, to quote-to-cash processes and monetization of multi-sided business models, represents a huge challenge for Telcos that want to be pure Digital Service Providers. These ambitious goals will require full automation from the provisioning to the delivery of the services and products, high flexibility

Figure 14. Smart living lifestyle

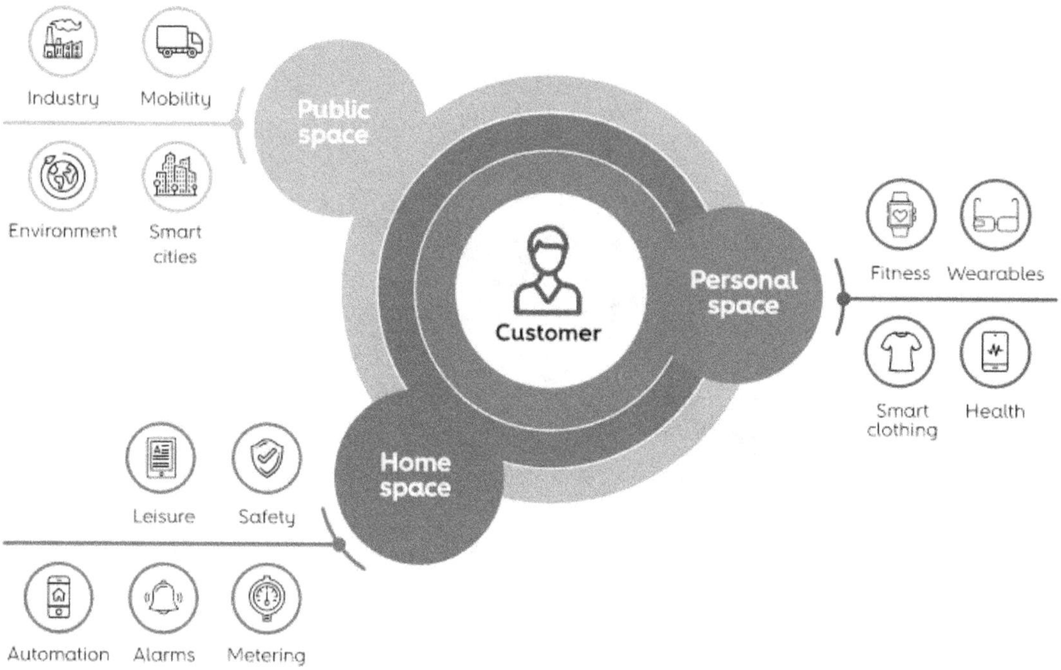

to support multiple business models, and strong engagement mechanisms leveraged on best-of-breed omnichannel approaches. The Telco digital marketplaces of the future should sell much more than connectivity services and products. In the age of the IoT, complex bundles that include devices, connectivity and applications from several partners, will require robust digital platform-based approaches to provide a remarkable customer experience. Telcos need to adapt themselves to this new era where they have an important asset: the network, but they know that to survive they need to re-center in the digital economy ecosystem, by competing directly with OTT players.

In a business perspective, moving from a CSP to a DSP mindset poses new challenges to Telcos:

- **Partnerships:** Telcos will need to deal with increasing higher number of partners (typically today they handle tens or hundreds of partnerships and in the future they need to be ready to deal with thousands) and with higher partnership dynamics (some partnerships will be short term). This new paradigm will impact on the Telco IT infrastructure, and will require new agile approaches to deal with partnerships, through the simplification and digitalization of end-to-end processes, by allowing fast on boarding of partners and providing high level of automation in all interactions. This is particularly important in the IoT area due to the wide spectrum of application domains.
- **Business Models:** Telcos will be impelled to deal with new business models, complementing the traditional models that they usually implement (B2B, B2C and B2B2C, Sell Through, Sell To or Sell With). In the platform business models, the platform owner plays a central role in the business ecosystem, by providing the marketplace, a key asset that allows the interchange and interaction between of consumers (demand side) and producers (supply side). To compete with digitally-

Figure 15. DSP platform for marketplace

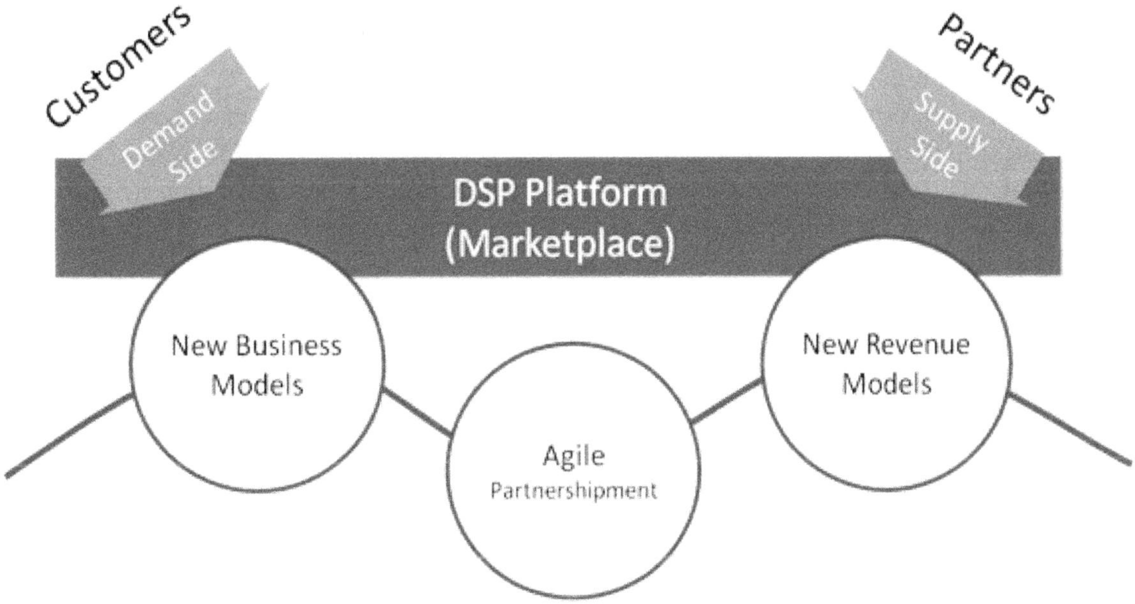

native players such as Amazon, Google, Apple and many others, Telcos need to transform themselves to adapt to this new reality. This transformation will be leveraged by the technology, but it is largely a matter of how to do business in this new era.

- **Revenue Models:** Traditionally, Telcos have strong and much evolved monetization engines, to deal with the complex needs of charging and billing of telecommunications services and bundles. To support the platform business models, they need to adapt their existing BSS infrastructure to be even more flexible and agile, taking advantage of the cloud. The variety of revenue models in the era of full digital services, covering even physical IoT domains, poses new requirements to the existing Telco monetization infrastructure.

Bridging partners and customers on a platform-based approach will demand from Telcos strong strategies to build a consistent way, leveraged on digital transformation programs. The paramount goal is to build a marketplace perfectly integrated with the existing operator business and operations support systems (BOSS) infrastructure, being the centre of the digital business ecosystem. This move requires more than just technology, it requires changes in the way Telcos approach the market and interact with partners and customers.

CONCLUSION

Society and technology evolve together to empower new forms of life. Digitization has transformed the way people interact also affecting the way people consume. New habits bring new consumption demands, which are less tolerant to failures or bureaucratic noise. Customers now require ubiquitous digital access to all CSPs' information, services and touchpoints.

CSPs need to take digital transformation initiatives to place customers at the centre of their operations in the path towards a DSP. They need to evolve to answer customer requirements by offering valuable services and first-class experiences, regardless the communication channel. The seamless interactions during the whole journey are core to keep the digital customer engaged.

Future DSPs will have naturally big data lakes of information about their customers, but they can further refine the information they hold from sensor data. DSPs can thus use the IoT to learn more about their customers and the environment they are in, leveraging levels of personalization never achieved before. The goal is to offer augmented experiences enabling new digital perspectives of reality in a fully tailored environment. But the IoT value chain is anything but linear, it still exists a great lack of definition between involved entities making unclear the right positioning of Telcos. Having platforms bridging partners and customers is the future bet to diversify revenues and link customers with partners. This platform-based model can also be used to promote the IoT market, enabling new service offers and access to data useful to improve the customer experience all over the journey.

ACKNOWLEDGMENT

This research is partially a result of the CityAction project CENTRO-01-0247-FEDER-017711, supported by Centro Portugal Regional Operational Programme (CENTRO 2020), under the Portugal 2020 Partnership Agreement, through the European Regional Development Fund (ERDF).

REFERENCES

Beaver, L. (2016). *80% of businesses want chatbots by 2020*. Retrieved from http://www.businessinsider.com/80-of-businesses-want-chatbots-by-2020-2016-12

Drabble, S., Ratzmann, N., Hoorens, S., Khodyakov, D., & Yaqub, O. (n.d.). *The rise of a global middle class: Global societal trends to 2030: Thematic report 6*. Retrieved from https://www.rand.org/pubs/research_reports/RR920z6.html

Garfinkel, S. (2011). *The Cloud Imperative*. Retrieved from http://www.technologyreview.com/news/425623/the-cloud-imperative/

IBM Infographics. (n.d.). *The Four V's of Big Data*. Retrieved from http://www.ibmbigdatahub.com/infographic/four-vs-big-data

IBM Marketing Cloud. (n.d.). *10 Key Marketing Trends for 2017 and Ideas for Exceeding Customer Expectations*. Retrieved from https://www-01.ibm.com/common/ssi/cgi-bin/ssialias?htmlfid=WRL12345USEN

Kolodziejczyk, B. (2015). *The 5 next trends in electronics*. Retrieved from https://www.weforum.org/agenda/2015/08/5-next-trends-in-electronics/

Levy, H. (2016). *Gartner Predicts a Virtual World of Exponential Change.* Retrieved from http://www.gartner.com/smarterwithgartner/gartner-predicts-a-virtual-world-of-exponential-change/

Mo, Y., Kim, T. H., Brancik, K., Dickinson, D., Lee, H., Perrig, A., & Sinopoli, B. (2012). Cyber–Physical Security of a Smart Grid Infrastructure. *Proceedings of the IEEE, 100*(1), 195–209. doi:10.1109/JPROC.2011.2161428

O'Leary, D. (2013). *Artificial Intelligence and Big Data. IEEE Intelligent Systems, 28*(2).

PwC. (2017). *2017 Telecommunications Trends.* Retrieved from https://www.strategyand.pwc.com/trend/2017-telecommunications-industry-trends

Singh, S. (2014). *Future Of Personal Mobility - Life With Or Without Ownership Of Cars.* Retrieved from https://www.forbes.com/sites/sarwantsingh/2014/04/23/future-of-personal-mobility-life-with-or-without-ownership-of-cars/#b662720467f4

Stamford, C. (2015). *Gartner Says 6.4 Billion Connected "Things" Will Be in Use in 2016, Up 30 Percent From 2015.* Retrieved from http://www.gartner.com/newsroom/id/3165317

Statista. (2018a). *Forecast of Big Data market size, based on revenue, from 2011 to 2026 (in billion U.S. dollars).* Retrieved from https://www.statista.com/statistics/254266/global-big-data-market-forecast/

Statista. (2018b). *Retail e-commerce sales worldwide from 2014 to 2021 (in billion U.S. dollars).* Retrieved from https://www.statista.com/statistics/379046/worldwide-retail-e-commerce-sales/

Statista. (2018c). *Number of Netflix streaming subscribers worldwide 2011-2017.* Retrieved from: https://www.statista.com/statistics/250934/quarterly-number-of-netflix-streaming-subscribers-worldwide/

Torchia, M. (2017). *Worldwide Semiannual Internet of Things Spending Guide.* Retrieved from http://www.idc.com/getdoc.jsp?containerId=prUS42209117

Yogitha, K., & Alamelumangai, V. (2016). Recent Trends and Issues in IoT. *International Journal of Advances in Engineering Research, 11*(1).

ADDITIONAL READING

European Commission. (2016). *Regulation (EU) 2016/679.* General Data Protection Regulation.

Pinto, F. C., Chainho, P., Pássaro, N., Santiago, F., Corujo, D., & Gomes, D. (2013). The business of things architecture. *Transactions on Emerging Telecommunications Technologies, 44*(4), 441–452. doi:10.1002/ett.2654

Pinto, F. C., & Santiago, F. (2016). A «Startegy» for IoT. *Innovaction, 1*, 54–63.

Pinto, F. C., Santiago, F., Borges, I., Parreira, B., Pereira, P., & Costa, M. (2017). Smart living powered by Digital Service Providers. *Innovaction, 2*, 23–33.

KEY TERMS AND DEFINITIONS

Communication Service Provider (CSP): A telecommunication provider that offers voice, data, and video services or combination of services, leveraging their network infrastructure and platforms.

Customer Centric: Strategy that places the customer is in the core of the service and product lifecycle resulting in a positive experience for the entire customer journey.

Customer Experience: It is the feeling experienced by the client during an interaction with the organization.

Digital Service Provider (DSP): An organization that delivers digital services bridging partners and customers enabling new business models in seamless online interactions.

Digital Transformation: Set of initiatives carried out by organizations to answer the digital challenges by applying digital technology into all areas of a business.

Internet of Things (IoT): Network of objects with Internet connectivity able to sense physical measures and to actuate in the environment.

IoT Framework: Set of key service enablers required to enable domain agnostic IoT deployments.

Smart Living: An extended lifestyle where people have digitally the full control of their physical and virtual interactions in a seamless and personalized way.

Chapter 13
An Overview of Main IoT Trends Applied to Business and Marketing

Jorge Remondes
Instituto Superior de Entre Douro e Vouga, Portugal

Carolina Afonso
ISEG – Lisbon School of Economics and Management, University of Lisbon, Portugal

ABSTRACT

Currently there are more devices connected to internet than people in the world and industrial sensors and robots are also increasing. Not only organizations but also individuals are obtaining data from internet of things (IoT) devices and automating them. The aim of this chapter is to investigate and analyze this context and to identify the main trends of IoT for business and management, as well as potential organizational marketing strategies. Based on the literature review, six business trends in the IoT era are identified: personalization, interaction, integration, analytics, monitoring, and protection. These trends have implications to consider not only in future organizational marketing strategies but also in the present.

INTRODUCTION

The development of the present book chapter about IoT and its impact on business and marketing aims to address specific academic needs but also the challenges that businesses are facing.

In the current IoT era, the internet is not limited to the use of desktops, laptops or smartphones and it implies also the use of interlinked objects on an ecosystem such as smart automobiles, watches, jewelry, glasses, among others. According to Thierer (2015) and Misugi, Freitas & Efing (2016), the term "smart" is used to qualify objects, smartphones, smart TV, but also to characterize an integrated system of objects and people, such as "smart buildings, smart appliances, smart health, smart mobility, smart cities" (p. 10), among others. These authors called IoT to this new generation of objects that involve a connection through sensitive, automated and integrated functions.

DOI: 10.4018/978-1-5225-5763-0.ch013

Copyright © 2019, IGI Global. Copying or distributing in print or electronic forms without written permission of IGI Global is prohibited.

This chapter aims to identify and analyze some of the main trends of IoT. Secondary data as previous studies, scientific articles and recent theses have been accessed to provide a comprehensive understanding of the phenomenon. The purpose is to provide with a solid theoretical basis that can be used by scholars and business practioners.

According to Kotler, Kartajata & Setiawan (2017), business and marketing are facing a shift from traditional to digital and within this scope it is crucial to understand which challenges IoT is posing to management. The IoT trends are numerous and our aim is not present all the trends exhaustively but to select the ones that have more consensus in the literature as major trends and that in our perspective better contribute a better understanding about how business and marketing can benefit from this ecosystem. The main trends presented in this chapter can be observed in figure 1 and include personalization, interaction, protection, monitorization, integration and analytics.

In the following section the detailed description of these trends is presented. At the end, the main conclusions of this study are presented and an analysis about its implications for business marketing strategies, limitations and suggestions for future studies of trends in IoT is provided.

BACKGROUND

The advance in IoT is fostering the development of personalization. For instance, recognition capabilities of the devices can be processed in order to create a personalized advertisement. The personalization opportunities enabled by IoT devices create a new area for marketers to explore. As the relation between users IoT evolve, interaction becomes critical. Within this context social IoT as emerged and poses great challenges into the communication relationship with the client that tends to be optimized and allow real-time interaction in networks.

Figure 1. IoT trends

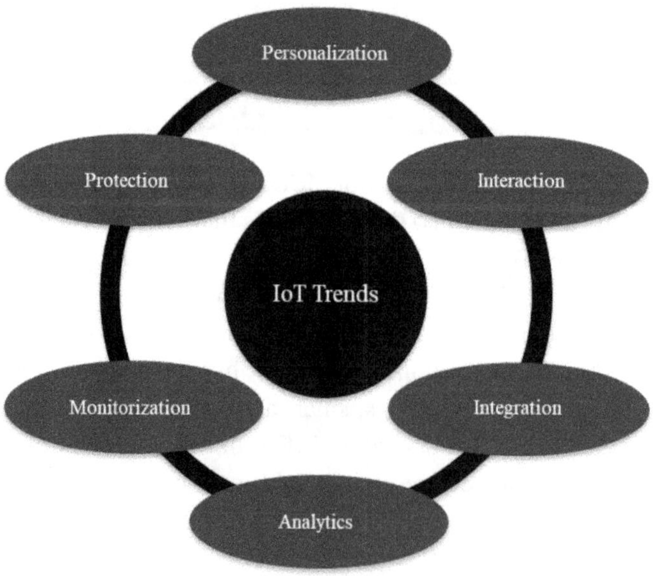

Therefore, IoT allows an interconnection between devices. Thus, the challenge facing people and organizations is the sharing of data and integration of information and services, as well as the management of a complex network architecture (Ma, 2011).

According to Lee & Lee (2015) enormous amounts of data can be obtained and analyzed through analytical tools that help make better management decisions. Thus, the insertion of analytics tools into IoT devices, collected by sensors and robots, can be very useful for management and marketing decisions to be made faster and better. For this reason, organizations start to monitor closely the date provide by customers' smart devices in order to better understand their behavior and trace patterns that later can be used to create value-added offers. However, there is still a need to overcome the security and safety barriers that prevents further IoT advances. Confidentiality, access control and privacy, trust between people, organizations and devices, still need to be better regulated and protected. On the following subsections of this chapter each of these trends is further detailed. Our approach aims to highlight the impact and challenges that these trends have for business within the scope of digital transformation that businesses are facing nowadays, in which digital marketing plays a significant role together with other business areas.

Personalization

Personalization in the IoT era is particularly relevant from the point of how companies can differentiate themselves from competitors but using data provided from IoT devices to communicate more effectively with their target audience.

Sundmaeker, Guillemin, Friess & Woeelfflé (2010) state that the IoT allows people and things to be connected Anytime, Anyplace, with Anything and Anyone, ideally using Any path/network and Any service. This perspective that "any-everything" is connected lead to powerful formulations of convenient technology (Nolin & Olson, 2016) that is boosted by personalization.

According to Light & Maybury (2002), personalized adaptive systems will be developed to become familiar with user interests. This is one of the major trends nowadays carried by many fields such as Information Retrieval, Text Retrieval Evaluation and Machine Learning.

In 2014, Google bought the UK based company Deep Mind that is pioneer in connecting existing machine learning techniques to cutting edge research in neuroscience, leading to systems which more accurately resembled "real" intelligence. These advances in machine learning allow real-time personalization. The data collected in IoT technologies can be used to personalize the experience a customer has with a brand.

Davenport, DalleMule & Lucker (2011) indicate that tracking and analyzing users' behavioral patterns gives to the marketers the possibility to better understand unique preferences and needs of their clients.

The data derived from the IoT creates more relevant, meaningful engagements with customers, which lead to deeper relationships that can be boosted by delivering information more quickly and efficiently than ever before.

For retailers, IoT is revolutionizing processes like managing supply chains, tracking inventory, and monitoring units. Furthermore, it also has the potential to increase conversion rates and deepen customer engagement by driving personalized marketing. According to Microsoft (2017), location-based marketing powered by IoT beacons can enhance in-store customer experience. Personalization is enhanced by beacons, sensors, and strong cross-channel analytics and therefore retailers can tailor messages and promotions to their customer's phone or wearable. For instance, a beacon can identify a nearby customer and show him an advertising about a product he recently clicked on in the app. Additionally, shelf sensors can identify when something is picked up and trigger a relevant promotional video on an adjacent screen.

Byun, Cho & Moon (2016) presented a beacon solution called S-Beacon that is Bluetooth Low Energy. It envisions a new business opportunity by globally interconnecting IoT devices with next generation personalization services. S-Beacon is a is able to identify user presence along with personal preferences and demographic data that allows to enhance personalized services. This new technology is based on proximity, optimized resource consumption, and manageability of beacon devices. This solution opens a wide range of potentialities among business sectors such as retail stores, public places, hotels, hospitals and home.

According with Microsoft (2017) personalization involves the optimization of customer engagement that every business aims to achieve. Furthermore, IoT-driven personalization enhance customer loyalty by providing a unique customer experience that forges an emotional connection and brand loyalty (KPMG, 2017).

Accenture (2016a) has identified four key components for an ultimate personalized customer experience, called the four Rs of personalization, that are:

1. **Recognition:** there are many tools available for businesses to interact with customers and gather and consume data about them. These data need to have the permission of the customer to be used and when it occurs it ca be used to better serve customers as they interact across digital touchpoints. According to Accenture (2016a), more than half of consumers (56 per cent) are more likely to shop at a retailer in store or online that recognizes them by name. This technique is also used by Starbucks that calls their customers by their name to deliver the orders.
2. **Remembering**: Businesses can make customers feel valued by remembering their preferences without you having to remind them. Accenture's study (2016a) reveals that 65 percent of consumers are more likely to shop at a retailer in store or online that remembers their previous purchases. Thus, companies should both remember customer interactions as well as share them across all touchpoints to ensure a consistent personalized experience. By accessing to customer's history to know what consumers buy, view and consume, but also why they purchase it.
3. **Recommendation**: Consumers are showing a desire for better recommendations. The retailers that can use customer data to suggest products and services can make life easier for their customers. Though, it is essential to provide customers with the right marketing, offer, content or product recommendations based on their actions, preferences and interests.
4. **Relevance**: In order to develop a personalization strategy, relevance is key. According to Accenture (2016a), two-thirds of consumers they are more likely to make a purchase in store or online from a retailer that sends them relevant and personalized promotions. Using customer data to offer relevant promotions is critical to personalized marketing performance. Relevance today goes far beyond basic demographic data and it is needed to go learn deeper purchase history to genuinely understand customer preferences, needs, and passions. A recent example of personalization based on relevance is a project called "Data-dress" developed by Google and Ivyreal. The mobile application collects data of user's daily habits and preferences based on geo-location and physical effort tracking to tailor a dress with patterns and textures that fits with customer's lifestyle.

To sum up, IoT enhances and increases the collection of rich information for future services where humans become the center of the interactions. From smartphones to wearables, people carry sensors that can enable the personalization of customer experiences within IoT context. According to Velikic, Bjelica, Ignjatov, Cetkovic & Kastelan (2014), one of major trends is the personalized use of IoT and the findings highlight that is required to replicate the best offline personalized experience in a digital environment. For that purpose, for managers and marketers it is essential to develop best practices for data usage in order to deliver exceptional personalized experiences at every customer touch point.

Interaction

Interaction is related to how people and objects are engaging. Indeed, IoT devices are changing the interaction between people and objects. The resulting paradigm, named Social Internet of Things (SIoT) is gaining popularity in the last years and brought several potentialities by combining new applications with networking services.

The term SIoT (social internet of things) refers not to the smart devices connected to social media platforms but to the ability to create social interactions among objects (Atzori, Iera, Morabito, & Nitti, 2011). The authors state the IoT concept is intended as a social network in which every node is an object able to perform capable social relationships with other things in an autonomous, following the rules established by the owner of the smart device.

Holmquist, Mattern, Schiele, Alahutha, Beigl & Gallersen (2001) introduced firstly the idea of the possibilities of the objects to socialize. Nevertheless, the solutions presented were focusing mainly on temporary relationships derived from smart wireless devices and the process was controlled and managed by the owners.

Later on, the research moved into a new phase based on a generation of smart objects that uncover new potentialities of interaction. Within this phase the neologism "blogject" appeared, referring to the "objects that blog", meaning objects have now the potential to participate in social networks (Bleecker, 2006). Also, Kranz, Roalter & Michahelles (2010) anticipate this participation of the objects in social networking by showing how physical objects can be empowered to engage in social activities such as sharing photos and posting comments.

This convergence of IoT and social network paradigms foresee the scenario in which a user can share the services offered by his smart device with friends and even its activity can be published on social networks (Guinard, Karnouskos, Trifa, Dober, Spiess & Savio, 2010).

Nazz & Sokoler (2011) introduced the concept of Embodied Microblogging that instead of focusing on thing-to-thing or human-to-thing interactions, it proposes that objects have new roles: a mediator role on the human-to-human and a supporting role of bringing new daily activities to user's life.

Mendes (2011) presented the idea that objects can actively participate in conversations that until now were only possible between humans. The objects have dynamic community structures that allow them to develop a spontaneous networking infrastructure deriving from disseminated information and not from the objects themselves.

Recently, the idea that the IoT and the social networks are two worlds not really that far apart from each other has begun to appear in the literature. Ning & Wang (2011) and Ding, Shi & Liu (2010) mention that IoT and social networks are not longer to distant worlds but closer ones.

Liu et al. (2010) state that there are three generations of social networks based on the level of socialization they allow. The first generation is known by weak socialization possibilities and the relationship between users is implicit; The second generation is characterized by binary socialization between users (friend or not friend). Although participants can expand their network by adding of friends even if only inside the same social network platform; The third generation of social network there are several types of relationships and participants can establish new relationships and conduct activities across different social networks. This means that SIoT enters in a non-binary relationship. According to Carminati, Ferrari & Viviani (2012), this multiple type of relationship between users lead to the development of relationships techniques that foster trust between members.

According to Nitti, Girau, Atzori, Iera & Morabito (2012), there are five types of relationships that smart devices can establish:

1. **Parental Object Relationship (POR):** It is characterized by relationships established by devices of the same generation or that were produced by the same manufacturer.
2. **Co-location Object Relationship (C-LOR):** Here the relationships are established among heterogenous or homogenous objects that have in common an environment. For instance, smart home devices such as sensors have short links because the possibilities that they can cooperate for a common goal are sparse.
3. **Co-work Object Relationship (C-WOR):** It occurs when there are relationships between two or more devices whose functionalities are combined to accomplish a common goal. This relationship is established between objects that either need to touch each other to achieve that goal or need to be in close proximity of one another.
4. **Ownership Object Relationship (OOR):** It is established among smart devices of the same user (smartphones, video game consoles, etc).
5. **Social Object Relationship (SOR):** It occurs when the smart devices get in touch whenever their owners meet. Smart objects belonging to friends can establish this type of relationship.

As the relationships that smart devices evolve, more accurate and contextual information is provided, and this leads to the possibility to create value added services for users (Geetha, 2016). The smart objects cooperation creates trust and generates insightful data and a better understanding of consumer behavior. According to Geetha (2016) and Herron (2017), the analytics and advertising industry benefits from SIoT and, for instance, either Facebook or Google are already making profit of it by offering targeted marketing services. The author states that nowadays SIoT enables users to talk (write or speak) with connected smart objects that are using natural language processing enhanced by artificial intelligence. The user can control all the different connected devices with a tweet or through messaging apps like WhatsApp, regardless of the technology's ecosystem (iOS or Android), manufacturer, or brand.

For example, the smart home device Amazon Echo works through its voice assistant, Alexa, which users can talk to in order to perform several functions. Users can ask Alexa to play music, provide a weather report, get sports results, etc. In 2016, the company 'We Are Social' made added a social layer. Echo users can search for 'We Are Social' in the skills section of the Amazon Alexa app to find We Are Social's 'Headline of the Day'. When the skill is enabled, users simply need to say, 'Alexa, social headline' to their device and then access social news just by asking for it.

To sum up, in the near future SIoT will influence a great part of our lives. From the marketing perspective, the main advantages are in formulating data-oriented marketing strategies. The smart devices can provide detailed information about users and their behaviors. Customer service can also benefit from this trend by using interconnected smart devices that do not require much of – or even none - human intervention to solve problems.

Integration

The need for integration of the several IoT technologies on an unified ecosystem is a major trend identified in literature. IoT will face an explosive growth within the next years, with 10 billion devices connected presently and 24 to 50 billion total connections expected in the next 3 years (Galinina, Pyattaev, Gerasimenko, Tirronen, Torser, Sachs, Dohler & Koucheryavy, 2015). According with the authors on the following decade, we may witness our everyday furniture, food packaging, and even paper documents accessing the Internet.

The IoT requires interconnection between devices. The challenge is to share data, integrate information and services, and manage a complex network architecture (Ma, 2011).

For example, in a smart home, the front door opens with a tap on the smartphone. However, there is no single wireless technology that optimizes operation costs, bandwidth, range, power and architecture for all applications and requirements. Even if two devices share the same wireless, they may not share the same communication protocol.

Accenture (2016) conducted a study called "Digital Trends Survey" that polled 28,000 consumers in 28 countries. Sixty-four percent of the respondents reported that they had experienced challenges while setting up IoT devices. Eighteen percent of this group was unable to connect the device to the Internet, while fourteen percent said the setup did not proceed properly. The solution for the problems are related with connectivity.

Thus, one of the challenges that IoT faces is to find real-world services that can be dynamically integrated into business applications, a very challenging task considering the application requirements, technologies and device heterogeneity (Guinard et al., 2010).

The level of integration of context data in the IoT is essential and it is rapidly increasing (Hummer and Shulte, 2015). According to the authors, in the automotive industry, real-time machine data from the vehicle (e.g., fuel level) is combined with driver-related biometrics data (e.g. fatigue sensor) and matched with other contextual information (e.g., time, location) in order to satisfy the driver's preferences (e.g., navigate to a gas station for coffee and fuel). Swan (2015) named this trend as the quantified car that incorporates the combination of connected car and quantified self.

In order to solve integration problems within IoT context there is a need to redefine the connectivity. As states Anderson (2015) the new definition of connectivity refers to users connecting to smart devices to complete a task; smart devices connecting with ordinary objects to deliver additional information, functionality, or value; and smart software or smart devices connecting back with organizations to deliver insight on user behavior.

As Mehta (2015) refers one of the major challenges regarding connectivity is that the internet is not just a single network; rather it is a collection of several different heterogeneous networks which includes several important considerations such as cell towers, proxy servers, speed, etc. All these considerations are very crucial, and these can easily disrupt connectivity. According to the author connectivity challenges in IoT involves signaling, security, power consumption, detection presence, bandwidth, as can be observed in Figure 2.

To overcome such connectivity issues, it is important to create integrated services across multiple companies so that consumers can have a richer experience. In fact, and according to Accenture (2016b) there is a need for a new round of ecosystem innovation. While many manufacturers have ecosystem partners, few are sufficiently co-innovating with them to create solutions that are more complete in terms of tightly bundled devices, software, apps and services.

Figure 2. The IOT Connectivity; Source: Mehta (2015)

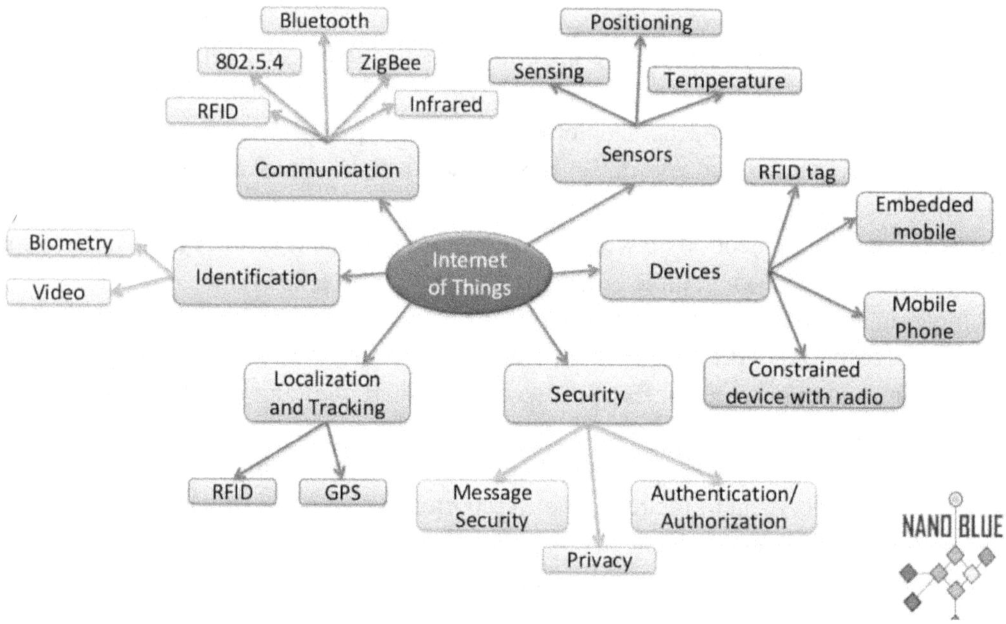

For the concept of IoT to be effective an, it is required Machine to Machine (M2M) communication utilized at a very large scale. Huang (2015) states that M2M which is any technology that enables networked devices to exchange information and perform actions without the manual assistance of humans. This technology is highly important for the development of IoT service (Pyo et al., 2013).

According to Galinina et al. (2015) M2M systems are expected sometime around 2020. They should generally deliver ubiquitous M2M that will enable ubiquitous interworking between various communicating objects, as well as collection and sharing of the massive amounts of data. The top 5 M2M applications in the world are predicted to be utility companies, traffic control, telemedicine, security in business and telemetry (Mehta, 2015).

One of the companies that are successfully using M2M is AT&T. The company has the largest number of connected devices (around 15.2 million) and also close to 1500 devices certified to run on their networks. By providing connectivity to these machines, AT&T is now also playing the role of a solutions integrator. Since the information must flow smoothly and seamlessly from M2M, the connectivity provided by AT&T is critical.

To sum up, integration within IoT context posits several challenges for companies. The development of action-oriented ecosystem partnerships can be the foundation of accelerated growth in the IoT together with M2M communication applications development.

Analytics

The data analytics solutions that exist currently regarding IoT are still in their infancy (Ahmed, Yaqoob, Hashem, Khan, Ahmed, Imran & Vasilakos, 2017) and therefore one of the major trends is related to Analytics.

The new networks generate more volume of data and more qualified information. Thus, it enables better analyzes, which can significantly contribute to the improvement of the decision-making process (Chui, Loffler & Roberts, 2010). As stated by Magalhães (2016), analytics addresses the issues of integrating the various data achieved through devices with real applications, providing useful data analyzes. Lee & Lee (2015) analyzed IoT devices and technologies with sensors that generate huge amounts of data that are transmitted to analysis tools that help make decisions.

This data can be used to solve problems with changing consumer behaviors, increase customer satisfaction and provide value-added services. It can be used, for instance, for monitoring products in the logistics value chain, to situational perception through sensors in infrastructures, through real-time event feedback. Sensor-driven decision analysis introduces new challenges such as long-term planning and decision making, such as customer buying patterns in malls and stores (Coetzee & Eksteen, 2011).

These analytical tools can also be integrated into IoT devices such as health monitoring sensors that are very useful for real-time decision making that can occur in the data source. The results of a study of IoT Analytics (2015) that tracked searches on Google, Twitter and LinkedIn about IoT, lead to the conclusion that smart homes, including smart thermostats, connected lights, intelligent fridges, and locks, are currently the most prominent IoT application (Figure 3).

From Davenport's (2015) perspective, the analytics derived from IoT tend to gain importance for six reasons:

Figure 3. Smart applications popularity; Source: IoT Analytics (2015)

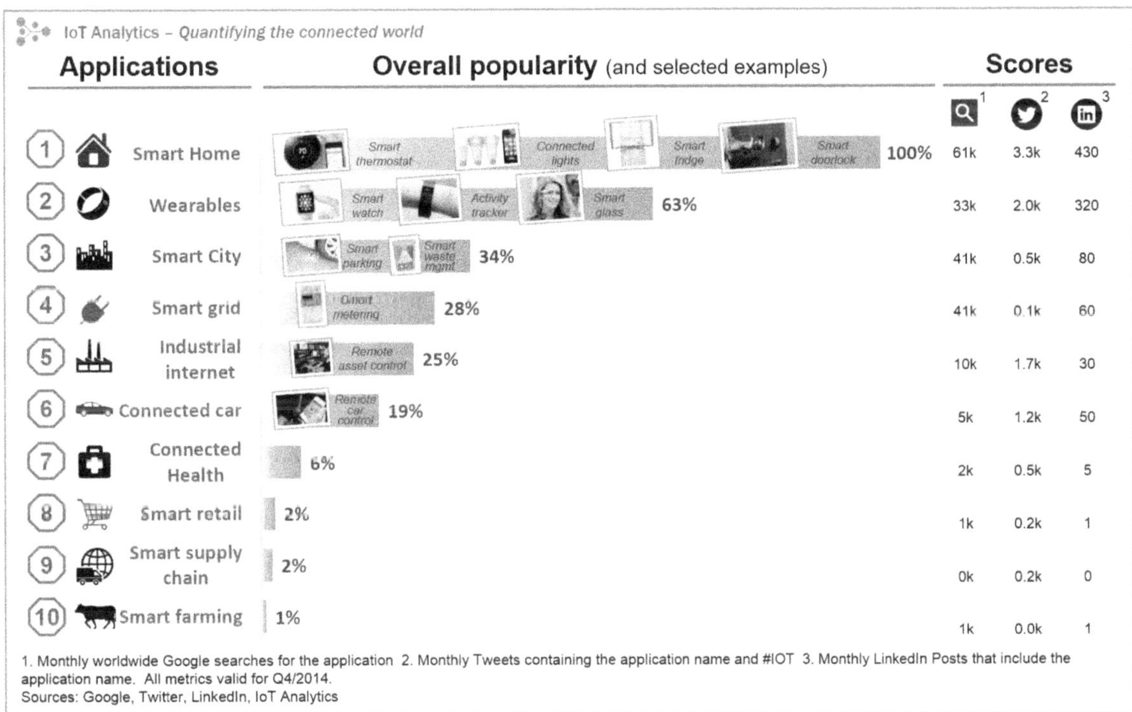

1. **Understanding the patterns and motives of variation:** it is a matter of designing statistical models that justify the variation;
2. **Detection of Anomalies:** Cases outside the identified border conditions, such as too high temperature, can be listed;
3. **Predictive Asset Maintenance:** Data collected through sensors are used to diagnose potential equipment problems before they occur;
4. **Optimization:** Using data and making analyzes from sensors can optimize a process. The author gives the following examples: when a wood mill optimizes the automated cutting of a log and a bird processor automates the preparation of a chicken;
5. **Prescription:** Using sensors and other types of data to communicate with front-line employees, one can share what to do, such as when, time and soil detection, used for "prescriptive planting" by farmers;
6. **Situational Awareness**: It is about gathering the seemingly disconnected events and presenting an explanation that clarifies them. How and when a series of car oil temperature readings, combined with reduced fuel efficiency, can indicate, as the author states, that an oil change needs to be performed.

IoT is evolving and analytics too, especially in large companies. However, as indicated by Yerpude & Singhal (2017), information on integrating IoT data with business analytics is lacking, so this is an area still under investigation to validate more specific results in the future, but it can be said that " making the right decision at the right time and place is the key to successful businesses in today's dynamic environment. With IoT data, the possibilities for online business analysis increase rapidly. "(Yerpude & Singhal, 2017, p.5).

Monitorization

IoT devices enable to monitor and optimize environments, such as optimizing energy at home, controlling light and temperature, connecting several devices in a single network. As Khan, Shahzad & Hassan (2017) indicate, we are dealing with a wide range of innovative IoT technologies that enable us to monitor and control intelligent buildings and intelligent homes, IoT branch understood as a sub-branch called residential automation. This leads to the fifth trend: monitorization.

Companies are going to put more efforts on monitoring customers' smart devices to better understand their behavior to design proposals with more added value. As reported by Lee & Lee (2015) connected toothbrushes, for example, can initiate healthier habits in people from direct feedback. Also the use of smart devices inside homes, among others, that will report if the environment is safe after confirming that all the doors are locked at night. Monitoring enables to collect data on equipment performance, power usage, environmental conditions, and enables automated controllers and controllers to constantly monitor performance in real-time, anywhere, anytime.

For example, within the context of intelligent city projects, the availability of parking space and intelligent street lighting can be monitored in real time (Wortmann & Fluchter, 2015). But "the great beneficiary of IoT technologies will undoubtedly be health industry. And Intel is already studying three areas to explore: telemedicine; monitoring of patients at home, and changing habits - I refer to people's motivation to move to healthier habits, using Internet-related objects that help, for example, racing" (Cipriano, 2015).

Almost everything is possible, thanks to wearable devices that collect and analyze data that verify the state of health allowing to reduce costs, improve treatments and an ongoing process of remote monitoring by a health professional (Santos & Freitas, 2016).

Atzori, Iera & Morabito (2010) group the applications of IoT not only in the health area but also in the area of transportation and logistics, personal and social, intelligent and futuristic environments, which are not restricted to homes but also to commercial and industrial spaces. According to the authors, in transportation and logistics fields, vehicles, roads, buildings of cities, among others, can be monitored. Other applications also enable to locate lost or stolen objects.

When talking about intelligent environments, we can refer not only to residential automation, but also to commercial and industrial automation. Any environment can benefit from IoT integration. The authors give the example of a gym where the equipment can identify the user and save the information of their physical activity (time, effort, etc.). Finally, some futurology can be formulated and some possibilities refer for example the existence of a taxi robot where passengers could be transported by autonomous vehicles. In table 1 some of the applications can be observed. This study was conducted in Melbourne and data was collected through focus group. The conclusions reveal that there are several potential IoT applications within the urban environment in the context of intelligent cities. The applications are grouped into impact areas and their level of monitorization is described in Table 1.

Finally, it is not possible to isolate any of the technological resources of IoT. Sundmaeker et al. (2010) argue that there is a need to think about the development of new applications and services that apply not only at the intra level but also interdomain or area. For example, monitoring the food chain or dangerous goods is not just about the industry itself but also has social implications that need to be taken into account.

Protection

Protection is the sixth IoT trend identified within the scope of the present chapter.

Device protection and security has a significant interest and will continue to have it for years to come. As Weber (2010) points out, business requires a high degree of reliability. According to this author, the basic requirements of security and privacy are as follows:

Table 1. Potential IoT applications identified by different focus groups of the city of Melbourne. Source: Adapted from Gubbi, Buyya, Marusic & Palaniswami (2013).

Urban Potential IoT Applications	Monitorization Levels
Healthcare Emergency Services, defense Crowd monitoring	Patient monitoring, personnel monitoring Remote personnel monitoring (health, location) Crow flow monitoring for emergency management
Traffic management Infrastrucure monitoring	Sensors built into infrastructure to monitor structural fatigue and other maintenance; accident monitoring for accident management and emergency response coordination
Water Building management Environment	Temperature, humidity control, activity monitoring for energy usage management. Noise monitoring, industry monitoring.

- **Resilience to Attacks:** information systems must avoid single points of error and must adapt to any failures.
- **Authentication of Data:** Normally, a retrieved address and the information of the object must be authenticated.
- **Access Control:** Internet providers that include e-mail services, portals, web page hosting, among others, should be able to implement access control in the data provided.
- **Customer Privacy:** it is necessary to take measures so that only the Internet provider can infer by observing the use of the search system by a specific customer. According to the author, inference must be very difficult to drive.

Despite the rapid evolution, there are still some difficulties and serious challenges since the development of the IoT brings more serious security problems (Suo, Wan, Zou & Liu, 2012). Jing, Vasilakos, Wan, Lu & Qiu (2014) even say that the IoT lives in a dangerous environment because of limited resources and a lack of network security.

Therefore, adequate solutions need to be designed and deployed independently of the platform being exploited and able to guarantee: confidentiality, access control and privacy for users and things, reliability between devices and users, compliance with defined security and privacy policies (Sicari, Rizzardi, Grieco, & Coen-Porisini, 2015).

According to Neto (2015), traditional protection mechanisms such as lightweight cryptography, security protocols and privacy guarantees are not enough for IoT. Insufficient protection can lead to attacks and theft of information as Bonon (2014) points out. The author distinguishes the two typologies of more frequent attacks on computers and internet connections: the Denial of Service (DoS) and the Distributed Denial of Service (DDoS). The former flood servers to overload the bandwidth and resources of the destination server. The latter rely on multiple devices and internet connections often scattered around the world. Therefore, it is more difficult to locate the source of an attack because there is not only one attacker but hundreds or thousands (Bonon, 2014).

According to Ribeiro (2016), there is still no trust on the part of IoT users side. For example, people do not feel confident in smartphones to keep an eye on the house. Therefore, security and privacy must be combined with innovation in IoT, trying to protect the users and the integrity of the data, in order to generate greater confidence in its use. As for the business market, an AVG study carried out with 1770 small companies allowed us to conclude that 71% of them are not prepared for security and data protection (Foreman, 2014 cited by Freund, Steenb, Marangoni, Vieira, Deus & Angonese, 2016). On the other hand, according to this study only 18% of small companies have IoT management capacity.

The main challenges that arise in the area of protection according to WP29 (2014) cited by Santos (2016) are the following:

- **Lack of Control and Asymmetry of Information:** The interaction between objects that communicate automatically, and between objects and back-end systems will lead to the generation of data streams that cannot be easily controlled through the classic tools used to ensure the proper protection of the interests and rights of the persons concerned. This issue directly related to the lack of control also has to do with areas such as cloud computing or big data, and is even more challenging when considering that the different technologies that are in the process of development can be used in an integrated way;

- **User Authorization Quality:** Often the user may not be aware of the treatment given to the data by the existing technological devices. The opportunity to refuse some services is not a viable solution in IoT, and the traditional mechanisms used to obtain authorization are difficult to enforce. Thus, new ways of obtaining user authorization around connected devices should be increasingly taken into account by manufacturers.
- **Redefinition of Initial Data Processing:** Increasing the amount of data provided by IoT in conjunction with current data analysis and processing techniques and cross-matching may result in secondary uses of this data, whether or not related to processing purposes initially assigned to the devices. That is to say, apparently insignificant data obtained through devices can be used to infer information with a totally different purpose from the initial (eg, driving habits, the author refers).
- **Identification of Patterns and Relationships:** Although each device or device provides data streams in isolation, their collection and subsequent analysis and treatment may simply reveal an individual's patterns, behaviors, preferences and habits.
- **Limitations on Maintaining Anonymity When Using Services:** The full development of IoT capabilities can put pressure on the current possibilities of anonymous use of services and limit the possibility of remaining anonymous.

As protection and privacy issues still exist in the context of IoT, the European Union is preparing to implement a new General Regulation on Data Protection (Regulation 2016/679 of the European Parliament and of the European Council of 27 April 2016) on the protection of individuals with regard to the processing of personal data and on the free movement of such data and repealing Directive 95/46 / EC (General Regulation on Data Protection). It will enter into force in the European Union in the first half of 2018 and the nature and future implications on European Union legislation and individuals and organizations will continue to be discussed in academia and in organizations.

To sum up, several trends related to IoT were identified from the literature review. Based on the identified trends, conclusions and implications for business and management can be drawn and are going to be presented in the next sections of the chapter.

SOLUTIONS AND RECOMMENDATIONS

The solutions and recommendations for management are:

- Adaptation of business models to IoT;
- Integration of intelligent devices;
- Interaction in real time with the client and the public;
- Monitoring of intelligent devices of customers;
- Analysis and treatment of data collected through sensors, robots and intelligent devices;
- Personalization challenges enabled for IoT capabilities that offer the possibility to address customized offers and messages to the target audience;
- Investment in better security conditions.

The initial objective of this chapter was to identify and analyze some of the main trends of IoT. This purpose was achieved with the literary contribution based on the analysis of studies already done, scientific articles, theses of the last years and real examples. In addition, the chapter ends identifying marketing strategies for organizational leaders. The strategies identified in this research refer essentially to the effort to integrate IoT into a growing number of business models and to invest in improving safety conditions and access to smart devices.

FUTURE RESEARCH DIRECTIONS

This chapter is yet another step towards understanding IoT, whose knowledge needs to be researched and systematically studied. However, this text contains limitations that future research should try to overcome precisely by the repeated carrying out of scientific research and identification of other trends in IoT. It includes only some of the major trends and in order to fully address the research problem other trends should be explored in further studies. For instance, the importance of IoT in logistics and Supply Chain Management (LSCM) should, for example, be the subject of case studies in order to extract existing gaps and relevant contributions. The LCM is also an emergent area in IoT are and it is not fully explored yet. The latest authors that have identified its benefits were Rocha, Mendes, Santa-Eulalia & Moris (2017), that realized that among 72 thousand papers about IoT only 0,5 coved this area, which uncovers the need for further research.

On the other hand, cloud storage and nanotechnology also need to be analyzed. According to Carvalho & Bernardino (2017) "the IoT variant in the Cloud is undoubtedly one of the main technologies to be developed, where the application of all the systems involved will have more to gain, mainly due to the permanent availability in the physical and temporal space, which makes them extremely effective" (p.1143).

Nevertheless, the present chapters aimed to contribute to the IoT studies by identifying some of the major trends and the impact it has for business and marketing. More specifically, its contribution is to enable organizations to rethink their strategies and to integrate these IoT trends and challenges into actionable insights that can generate profitable relations with stakeholders.

CONCLUSION

It is consensual in literature that IoT is a growing reality that creates effective challenges for people and organizations.

Firstly, the personalization of digital marketing campaigns and services based on consumer profile analysis can enhance a more targeted IoT for organizations' customers. Secondly, interaction is also identified as a major trend that impacts organizations and it is crucial to understand in order to solve existing IoT devices problems. Thirdly, by solving integration issues of IoT devices, resources, software and sensors, can lead to communication efficiency and can help organizations to created connect with their customers and improving customer service. However, such benefits related to the quality of customer service depend on the ability of organizations to intelligently monetize the huge amount of unstructured data that the various devices generate. This leads to the fourth trend. Analytic tools play a central role in allowing businesses to access and use data in real time. The monitorization, presented as the fifth trend, is also crucial- The performance of the companies will be as great as the efficiency of the remote monitorization could be. There are also some trade-offs regarding IoT and the sixth trend points out the challenges for protection. There is a lack of confidence in data protection and privacy. As Pereira (2015) states market analysts predict devices with IoT technologies to reach 23 billion by 2019. This means that it will reach twice the size of the current market for smartphones, computers, tablets, automobiles, and wearables together. With regard to security issues, more evolution is required and more rapid steps must be taken to develop intelligent objects capable of operating under all conditions and capable of integrating with other intelligent devices (Chandrakanth, Venkatesh, Mahesh & Naganjaneyulu, 2014). The authors argue for the need of standardized network protocols that can help organizations to solve security issues.

REFERENCES

Accenture. (2016a). *Personalization Pulse Check 2016*. Retrieved September 29, 2017, from https://www.accenture.com/t20161011T222718Z__w__/us-en/_acnmedia/PDF-34/Accenture-Pulse-Check-Dive-Key-Findings-Personalized-Experiences.pdfla=en#zoom=50

Accenture. (2016b). Retrieved September 29, 2017, from https://www.accenture.com/_acnmedia/PDF-3/Accenture-Igniting-Growth-in-Consumer-Technology.pdf

Ahmed, E., Yaqoob, I., Hashem, A. T., Khan, I., Ahmed, A. I. A., Imran, M., & Vasilakos, V. (2017). The role of big data analytics in Internet of Things. *Computer Networks*, *129*, 459–471. doi:10.1016/j.comnet.2017.06.013

Almeida, F. M. (2016). *Autoproteção para a Internet das Coisas (Dissertação de Mestrado em Ciência da Computação). Universidade Federal de Sergipe*. UFS.

Anderson, M. (2015). *Understanding the IoT and mobile devices*. Retrieved September 28, 2017, from http://www.targetmarketingmag.com/article/understanding-the-internet-of-things-and-mobile-devices/all/

Atzori, L., Iera, A., & Morabito, G. (2010). The internet of things: A survey. *Computer Networks*, *54*(15), 2787–2805. doi:10.1016/j.comnet.2010.05.010

Atzori, L., Iera, A., Morabito, G., & Nitti, M. (2011). SIoT: Giving a social structure to the Internet of things. *IEEE Communications Letters*, *15*(11), 1193–1195. doi:10.1109/LCOMM.2011.090911.111340

Bleecker, J. (2006). A Manifesto for Networked Objects – Cohabiting with Pigeons, Arphids and Aibos in the Internet of Things – Why Things Matter What' s a Blogject? What about Spimes? *Proceedings of the 13th International Conference on Human-Computer Interaction with Mobile Devices and Services, MobileHCI*.

Bonon, E. J. (2014). Internet das Coisas: Arquitetura – Desafios e Aplicação. Cad. *CPqD Tecnologia, Campinas*, *10*(2), 85–94.

Byun, D., Cho, J., & Moon, S. (2016). S-Beacon: Next generation BLE beacon solution for enhanced personalization Consumer Electronics (ICCE). *Proceedings of the IEEE International Conference*.

Carminati, B., Ferrari, E., & Viviani, M. (2012). *A multi-dimensional and event-based model for trust computation in the social web. In Social Informatics* (pp. 323–336). Berlin, Germany: Springer.

Carvalho, G., & Bernardino, J. (2017). A Internet das Coisas e Big Data: Tendências futuras. *Proceedings of the 12th Iberian Conference on Information Systems and Technologies*, 1421-1424.

Chandrakanth, S., Venkatesh, K., Mahesh, J. U., & Naganjaneyulu, K. V. (2014). Internet of Things. *International Journal of Innovations & Advancement in Computer Science*, *3*(4), 2347–8616.

Chui, M., Loffler, M., & Roberts, R. (2010). The Internet of Things. *The McKinsey Quarterly*, *2*, 1–9.

Cipriano, L. (2015). *Estudo aponta que Internet das Coisas beneficiará principalmente a saúde em 2025*. Neitec. Retrieved September 27, 2017, from http://neitec.com/inovacao-tecnologica/estudo-aponta-que-internet-das-coisas-beneficiara-principalmente-a-saude-em- 2025/

Coetzee, L., & Eksteen, J. (2011). The Internet of Things – Promise for the Future? An Introduction. IST-Africa 2011. *Proceedings of the IIMC International Information Management Corporation*, 1-9.

Comissão Nacional de Proteção de Dados. (2017). *10 Medidas para Preparar a Aplicação do Regulamento Europeu de Proteção de Dados*. Retrieved from https://www.cnpd.pt/bin/rgpd/10_Medidas_para_preparar_RGPD_CNPD.pdf

Davenport, T., DalleMule, L., & Lucker, J. (2011). Know What Your Customers Want Before They Do. *Harvard Business Review*. Retrieved September 29, 2017, from https://hbr.org/2011/12/know-what-your-customers-want-before-they-do

Davenport, T. (2015). *The Analytics of Things*. Retrieved September 26, 2017, from https://www.linkedin.com/pulse/analytics-things-tom-davenport

Ding, L., Shi, P., & Liu, B. (2010). The Clustering of Internet, Internet of Things and Social Network. *Proceedings of the 3rd International Symposium on Knowledge Acquisition and Modeling*.

Foreman, M. A. (2014). *A internet das coisas é a próxima máquina de fazer dinheiro da web, dizem as pequenas empresas*. Blog AVG Brasil, 2 dez. 2014. Retrieved September 29, 2017, from <http://blog.avgbrasil.com.br/2014/12/02/internet-das- coisas-e-proxima-maquina-de-fazer-dinheiro-da-web-dizem-pequenas-empresas>

Freund, F. F., Steenb, F. A., Marangoni, G. A. C., Vieira, J. D., Deus, S. L., & Angonese, R. M. (2016). Novos negócios baseados em internet das coisas. *Revista FAE*, Curitiba. *Edição Especial*, *1*, 7–25.

Galinina, A., Pyattaev, A., Gerasimenko, M., Tirronen, T., Torser, J., Sachs, J., ... Koucheryavy, Y. (2015). Understanding the IoT connectivity landscape: A contemporary M2M radio technology roadmap. *IEEE Communications Magazine*, *53*(9), 32–40. doi:10.1109/MCOM.2015.7263370

Geetha, S. (2016). World. *Science News*, *41*, 76–81.

Gubbi, J., Buyya, R., Marusic, S., & Palaniswami, M. (2013). Internet of Things (IoT): A vision, architectural elements, and future directions. *Future Generation Computer Systems*, *29*(7), 1645–1660. doi:10.1016/j.future.2013.01.010

Guinard, D., Fischer, M., & Trifa, V. (2010). Sharing using social networks in a composable web of things. *Proceedings of 8th IEEE Int. Conf. PERCOM Workshops*. 10.1109/PERCOMW.2010.5470524

Guinard, M., Karnouskos, S., Trifa, V., Dober, B., Spiess, P., & Savio, D. (2010). Interacting with the SOA-based Internet of Things: Discovery, Query, Selection, and On-Demand Provisioning of Web Services. *IEEE Transactions on Services Computing*, *3*(3), 223–235. doi:10.1109/TSC.2010.3

Herron, K. (2017). *When social media meets the Internet of Things*. Retrieved September 25, 2017, from https://unifiedinbox.com/when-social-media-meets-the-internet-of-things/

Holmquist, L., Mattern, F., Schiele, B., Alahutha, P., Beigl, M., & Gallersen, H. (2001). Smart-its friends: A technique for users to easily establish connections between smart artefacts. *Proceedings of ACM UbiComp'01*. 10.1007/3-540-45427-6_10

Hummer, W., & Schulte, S. (2016). Context-Aware Personalization for Smart Mobile Cloud Services. In Lecture Notes in Computer Science: vol. 9586. Service-Oriented Computing – ICSOC 2015 Workshops. Springer. doi:10.1007/978-3-662-50539-7_14

Hwang, E. (2015). Web Based Smart Home Automation Control System Design. *International Journal of Contents*, *11*(4), 70–76. doi:10.5392/IJoC.2015.11.4.070

IoT Analytics. (2015). *The 10 most popular Internet of Things applications right now*. Retrieved September 29, 2017, from http://iot-analytics.com/10-internet-of-things-applications/

Jing, Q., Vasilakos, A. V., Wan, J., Lu, J., & Qiu, D. (2014). Security of the Internet of Things: Perspetctives and challenges. *Wireless Networks*, *20*(8), 2481–2501. doi:10.100711276-014-0761-7

Khan, I. U., Shahzad, M. U., & Hassan, M. A. (2017). Internet of Things (IoTs): Applications in Home Automation. *International Journal of Science and Advance Technology*, *5*(1), 79–84.

Kotler, P., Kartajata, H., & Setiawan, I. (2017). *Marketing 4.0 – Mudança do Tradicional para o Digital*. Lisboa: Actual.

KPMG. (2017). *Still searching for a better customer experience*. Retrieved September 24, 2017, from https://assets.kpmg.com/content/dam/kpmg/xx/pdf/2017/07/searching-for-a-better-customer-web.pdf

Kranz, M., Roalter, L., & Michahelles, F. (2010). Things That Twitter: Social Networks and the Internet of Things. *Proceedings of the Pervasive 2010, the Citizen Internet of Things 2010 workshop*.

Lee, I., & Lee, K. (2015). The Internet of Things (IoT): Applications, investments, and challenges for enterprises. *Business Horizons*, *58*(4), 431–440. doi:10.1016/j.bushor.2015.03.008

Light, M., & Maybury, M. T. (2002). Personalized Multimedia Information Access: Ask Questions, Get Personalized Answers. *Communications of the ACM*, *45*(5), 54–59. doi:10.1145/506218.506246

Ma, H. (2011). Internet of things: Objectives and scientific challenges. *Journal of Computer Science and Technology*, *26*(6), 919–924. doi:10.100711390-011-1189-5

Magalhãe, G. G. M. S. (2016). *Estudo de segurança nos principais protocolos da Internet das Coisas* (Monografia em Engenharia Computação). Instituto de Ciências Exatas. Departamento de Ciências da Computação, Universidade de Brasília.

Mehta. (2015). *Internet of Things Connectivity Challenges – IoT Device Connectivity*. Retrieved September 29, 2017, from http://iotworm.com/internet-of-things-connectivity-challenges/

Mendes, P. (2011). Social-driven Internet of Connected Objects. *Proceedings of the Interconnecting Smart Objects with the Internet Workshop.*

Microsoft. (2017). *Enhance cross channel retail personalization with IoT.* Retrieved September 23, 2017, from https://blogs.microsoft.com/iot/2017/01/16/enhance-cross-channel-retail-personalization-with-iot/

Misugi, G., Freitas, C. O. A., & Efing, A. C. (2016). Releitura da privacidade diante das novas tecnologias: Realidade aumentada, reconhecimento facial e internet das coisas. *Revista Jurídica Cesumar, 16*(2), 427–453. doi:10.17765/2176-9184.2016v16n2p427-453

Nazz, E., & Sokoler, T. (2001). Walky for embodied microblogging: sharing mundane activities through augmented everyday objects. *Proceedings of the 13th International Conference on Human-Computer Interaction with Mobile Devices and Services.*

Neto, I. R. O. (2015). *Síntese de Requisitos de Segurança para Internet das Coisas Baseada em Modelos em Tempo de Execução (Dissertação).* Instituto de Informática da Universidade Federal de Góias.

Ning, H., & Wang, Z. (2011). Future Internet of Things Architecture: Like Mankind Neural System or Social Organization Framework? *IEEE Communications Letters, 15*(4), 461–463. doi:10.1109/LCOMM.2011.022411.110120

Nitti, M., Girau, R., Atzori, L., Iera, L., & Morabito, G. (2012). A subjective model for trustworthiness evaluation in the social Internet of things. *Proceedings of the IEEE 23rd Int. Symp.*, 18–23. 10.1109/PIMRC.2012.6362662

Nolin, J., & Olson, N. (2016). The Internet of Things and convenience. *Internet Research, 26*(2), 360–376. doi:10.1108/IntR-03-2014-0082

Pereira, J. C. H. (2015). *Modelos de Negócio e a Internet of Things. (Dissertação de Mestrado em Gestão).* Faculdade de Economia da Universidade de Coimbra.

Pyo, C., Kang, H., Kim, N., & Bang, H. (2013). IoT technology's trends and prospect. *KICS Thesis, 30*(8), 3-10.

Regulamento (UE) 2016/679 do Parlamento Europeu e do Conselho, de 27 de abril de 2016.

Ribeiro, A. B. (2016). Estudo de Internet das Coisas e Suas Tecnologias. *Proceedings of the XXIV Seminário de Iniciação Científica.*

Rocha, K. E., Mendes, J. V., Santa-Eulalia, L. A., & Moris, V. A. S. (2017). Adoption of IoT in Logistics & Supply Chain Management: A systematic literature review. In *XXXVII Encontro Nacional de Engenharia de Produção "A Engenharia de Produção e as novas tecnologias produtivas: indústria 4.0, manufatura aditiva e outras abordagens avançadas de produção".* Joinville, SC: Brasil.

Santos, D. O., & Freitas, E. B. (2016). A internet das coisas e o big data inovando os negócios. *Revista REFAS, 3*(1), 1–18.

Santos, P. M. P. (2016). *Internet das coisas: O desafio da privacidade (Dissertação de Mestrado em Sistemas de informação Organizacionais).* Escola Superior de Ciências Empresariais, Instituto Politécnico de Setúbal.

Sicari, S., Rizzardi, A., Grieco, L. A., & Coen-Porisini, A. (2015). Security, privacy and trust in Internet of Things: The road ahead. *Computer Networks*, *76*, 146–164. doi:10.1016/j.comnet.2014.11.008

Sundmaeker, H., Guillemin, P., Friess, P., & Woeelfflé, S. (2010). *Vision and Challenges for Realising the Internet of Things, CERP-IoT*. European Commission.

Sundmaeker, H., Guillemin, P., Friess, P., & Woelfflé, S. (Eds.). (2010). Vision and Challenges for Realising the Internet of Things. European Commission, Information Society and Media, Brussels.

Suo, H., Wan, J., Zou, C., & Liu, J. (2012). Security in the Internet of Things: A Review. *Proceedings of the International Conference on Computer Science and Electronics Engineering*, 648-652. 10.1109/ICCSEE.2012.373

Swan, M. (2015). Connected car: Quantified self becomes quantified car. *Journal of Sensor and Actuator Networks*, *4*(1), 2–29. doi:10.3390/jsan4010002

Thierer, A. D. (2015). The internet of things and wearable technology: Addressing privacy and security concerns without derailing innovation. *Richmond Journal of Law & Technology*, *21*(2), 10.

Velikic, G., Bjelica, M., Ignjatov, N., Cetkovic, M., & Kastelan, I. (2014). The Personalization of a Cloud Ecosystem: Adding Dimensions to Situational Awareness. *Proceedings of the X International Symposium on Industrial Electronics INDEL*, 248-252.

WP29. (2014). *Opinion 8/2014 on the on Recent Developments on the Internet of Things*. Retrieved September 29, 2017, from http://ec.europa.eu/justice/data-protection/article-29/documentation/opinion-recommendation/files/2014/wp223_en.pdf

Weber, R. H. (2010). Internet of Things – New security and privacy challenges. *Computer Law & Security Review*, *26*(1), 23–30. doi:10.1016/j.clsr.2009.11.008

Wortmann, F., & Fluchter, K. (2015). Internet of Things: Technology and Value Added. *Business & Information Systems Engineering*, *57*(3), 221–224. doi:10.100712599-015-0383-3

Yerpude, S., & Singhal, T. K. (2017). Internet of Things and its impact on Business Analytics. *Indian Journal of Science and Technology*, *10*(5), 1–6. doi:10.17485/ijst/2017/v10i5/109348

KEY TERMS AND DEFINITIONS

Analytics: In the IoT, analytics can be defined as the results achieved by analyzing data obtained through various intelligent devices.

Integration: Process of integrating the various IoT technologies into a unified ecosystem.

Interaction: This trend is related to how people and objects are engaging.

IoT: The internet is not limited to the use of desktops, laptops or smartphones and it implies also the use of interlinked objects on an ecosystem such as smart automobiles, watches, jewelry, glasses, among others.

Monitorization: IoT devices allow you to monitor and optimize environments, such as optimizing energy at home, controlling light and temperature, connecting multiple devices on a single network. As a result, companies tend to put more effort into monitoring customers' smart devices to better understand their behavior and plan new value propositions.

Personalization: Trend that relates to how companies can differentiate themselves from their competitors using data provided by IoT devices.

Protection: When we talk about protection we talk about the possibility of controlling personal information on the internet so that people can be protected.

Compilation of References

Abbass, H. A., Leu, G., & Merrick, K. (2016). A Review of Theoretical and Practical Challenges of Trusted Autonomy in Big Data. *Special Section On Theoretical Foundations For Big Data Applications: Challenges And Opportunities*, *4*, 2808–2830.

Abbasy, M. B., & Quesada, E. V. (2017). Predictable Influence of IoT (Internet of Things) in the Higher Education. *International Journal of Information and Education Technology (IJIET)*, *7*(12), 914–920. doi:10.18178/ijiet.2017.7.12.995

Abd Allah, M. M. (2011). Strengths and Weaknesses of Near Field Communication (NFC) Technology. [Version I.]. *Global Journal of Computer Science and Technology*, *11*(3).

Accenture. (2016a). *Personalization Pulse Check 2016*. Retrieved September 29, 2017, from https://www.accenture.com/t20161011T222718Z__w__/us-en/_acnmedia/PDF-34/Accenture-Pulse-Check-Dive-Key-Findings-Personalized-Experiences.pdfla=en#zoom=50

Accenture. (2016b). Retrieved September 29, 2017, from https://www.accenture.com/_acnmedia/PDF-3/Accenture-Igniting-Growth-in-Consumer-Technology.pdf

Adams, M. (2017). Big Data and Individual Privacy in the Age of the Internet of Things. *Technology Innovation Management Review*, *7*(4), 12–24.

Agarwal, R., & Prasad, J. (1998). A Conceptual and Operational Definition of Personal Innovativeness in the Domain of IT. *Information Systems Research*, *9*(2), 204–215. doi:10.1287/isre.9.2.204

Ahmed, E., Yaqoob, I., Hashem, A. T., Khan, I., Ahmed, A. I. A., Imran, M., & Vasilakos, V. (2017). The role of big data analytics in Internet of Things. *Computer Networks*, *129*, 459–471. doi:10.1016/j.comnet.2017.06.013

Akoka, J., Comyn-Wattiau, I., & Laoufi, N. (2017). Research on Big Data – A systematic mapping study. *Computer Standards & Interfaces*, *54*, 105–115. doi:10.1016/j.csi.2017.01.004

Al Ajam, A. S., & Nor, K. M. (2013). Internet banking adoption: Integrating technology acceptance model and trust. *European Journal of Business and Management*, *5*(3), 207–215.

Albăstroiu, I., & Felea, M. (2015). *Exploring The Potential of QR Codes in Higher Education Considering the Attitudes and Interests among Romanian Students*. The 11th International Scientific Conference eLearning and Software for Education, Bucharest, Romania.

Almeida, F. M. (2016). *Autoproteção para a Internet das Coisas (Dissertação de Mestrado em Ciência da Computação). Universidade Federal de Sergipe*. UFS.

AmalRedge, G. (2016). The Things, Services and Applications of IoT. *International Journal of Trend in Research and Development.* Retrieved from http://www.ijtrd.com/papers/IJTRD4179.pdf

Anderson, M. (2015). *Understanding the IoT and mobile devices*. Retrieved September 28, 2017, from http://www.targetmarketingmag.com/article/understanding-the-internet-of-things-and-mobile-devices/all/

Anderson, J. C., & Narus, J. A. (1990). A Model of Distributor Firm and Manufacturer Firm Working Partnerships. *Journal of Marketing*, *47*, 44–54. doi:10.2307/1252172

An, J., Cho, H., Kwak, H., Jansen, B. J., & Hassen, M. Z. (2016). Towards automatic persona generation using social media. In *4th International Conference on Future Internet of Things and Cloud Workshops* (pp. 206–211). IEEE Computer Society. 10.1109/W-FiCloud.2016.51

Antia, K. D., & Frazier, G. L. (2001). The Severity of Contract Enforcement in Interfirm Channel Relationships. *Journal of Marketing*, *65*(3), 67–81. doi:10.1509/jmkg.65.4.67.18385

Araujo, & Muzas, S. (1995). Category Management In Marketing And Purchasing: Formal Structure As Representation And Adaptation. In *IMP Conference (11th): Interaction, Relationships And Networks: Past - Present - Future*. Manchester Federal School of Business and Management, Manchester.

Armitage, C. J., & Conner, M. (1999). The Theory of Planned Behavior: Assessment of Predictive Validity and Perceived Control. *British Journal of Social Psychology*, *3*(1), 35–54. doi:10.1348/014466699164022

Arnold, M., & Reynolds, K. (2003). Hedonic shopping motivations. *Journal of Retailing*, *79*(2), 77–95. doi:10.1016/S0022-4359(03)00007-1

Arnould, E. J., & Thompson, C. J. (2005). Consumer culture theory (CCT): Twenty years of research. *The Journal of Consumer Research*, *31*(4), 868–882. doi:10.1086/426626

Ashton, K. (2009). That "internet of things" thing. *RFID Journal, 22*(7), 97–114. Retrieved December, 2017, from http://www.itrco.jp/libraries/RFIDjournal-That Internet of Things Thing.pdf

Ashton, K. (2009). That "Internet of Things" thing.: in the real world things matter more than ideas. *RFiD Journal*. Retrieved from http://www.rfidjournal.com/articles/view?4986

Ashton, K. (2009). That "Internet of Things" Thing - RFID Journal.pdf. *RFID Journal*, *22*(7), 97–114. doi:10.1145/2967977

Ashton, K. (2013). *The year of the Internet of Things*. MIT Technology Review.

Assunção, M. D., Calheiros, R. N., Bianchi, S., Netto, M. A. S., & Buyya, R. (2015). Big Data computing and clouds: Trends and future directions. *Journal of Parallel and Distributed Computing*.

Attié, E., & Meyer-Waarden, L. (2016). A theoretical model incorporating social influence and cognitive processes to explain the adoption of the Internet of Things and smart connected objects. *European Marketing Academy Conference*, Oslo, Norway.

Attié, E., & Meyer-Waarden, L. (2016). *A theoretical model incorporating social influence and cognitive processes to explain the adoption of the internet of things*. In *45th EMAC Annual Conference 20176*, Oslo, Norway.

Attié, E., & Meyer-Waarden, L. (2017). The impact of consumer well-being and trust on the Internet of Things adoption and word-of-mouth intentions. *European Marketing Academy Conference*, Groningen.

Atzori, L., Iera, A., & Morabito, G. (2010). The Internet of Things: A survey. *Computer Networks*, *54*(15), 2787–2805. doi:10.1016/j.comnet.2010.05.010

Atzori, L., Iera, A., Morabito, G., & Nitti, M. (2011). SIoT: Giving a social structure to the Internet of things. *IEEE Communications Letters*, *15*(11), 1193–1195. doi:10.1109/LCOMM.2011.090911.111340

Atzori, L., Iera, A., Morabito, G., & Nitti, M. (2012). The Social Internet of Things (SIoT) – When social networks meet the Internet of Things: Concept, architecture and network characterization. *Computer Networks*, *56*(16), 3594–3608. doi:10.1016/j.comnet.2012.07.010

Aujla, G. S., Chaudhary, R., Kumar, N., Das, A. K., & Rodrigues, J. J. P. C. (2018). SecSVA: Secure Storage, Verification, and Auditing of Big Data in the Cloud Environment. *IEEE Communications Magazine*, *56*(1), 78–85. doi:10.1109/MCOM.2018.1700379

Awad, N. F., & Krishnan, M. S. (2006). The personalization privacy paradox: An empirical evaluation of information transparency and the willingness to be profiled online for personalization. *Management Information Systems Quarterly*, *30*(1), 13–28. doi:10.2307/25148715

Azjen, I., & Driver, B. L. (1991). Prediction of Leisure Participation from Behavioral, Normative, and Control Beliefs: An Application of the Theory of Planned Behavior. *Leisure Sciences*, *13*(3), 185–204. doi:10.1080/01490409109513137

Azuma, R. T. (1997). A survey of augmented reality. *Presence (Cambridge, Mass.)*, *6*(4), 355–385. doi:10.1162/pres.1997.6.4.355

Azuma, R., Baillot, Y., Behringer, R., Feiner, S., Julier, S., & MacIntyre, B. (2001). Recent advances in augmented reality. *IEEE Computer Graphics and Applications*, *21*(6), 34–47. doi:10.1109/38.963459

Bajura, M., Fuchs, H., & Ohbuchi, R. (1992). Merging virtual objects with the real world: Seeing ultrasound imagery within the patient. *ACM SIGGRAPH Computer Graphics, 26*(2), 203–210.

Balaji, M. S., & Roy, S. K. (2017). Value co-creation with Internet of things technology in the retail industry. *Journal of Marketing Management*, *33*(1–2), 7–31. doi:10.1080/0267257X.2016.1217914

Basuroy, S., Mantrala, M. K., & Walters, R. G. (2001). The Impact of Category Management on Retailer Prices and Performance: Theory and Evidence. *Journal of Marketing*, *65*(4), 16–32. doi:10.1509/jmkg.65.4.16.18382

Batra, R., & Stayman, D. M. (1990). The role of mood in advertising effectiveness. *The Journal of Consumer Research*, *17*(2), 203–214. doi:10.1086/208550

Bauer, R. A. (1960). *Consumer behavior as risk taking.* Paper presented at the 43rd National Conference of the American Marketing Assocation, Chicago, IL.

Bayerque, N. (2016). A short history of chat bots and artificial intelligence. *VentureBeat.* Retrieved July 31, 2017 from https://venturebeat.com/2016/08/15/a-short-history-of-chat-bots-and-artificial-intelligence/

Baym, N. (2006). Interpersonal life online. In L. A. Lievrouw & S. M. Livingstone (Eds.), Handbook of new media: Social shaping and consequences of ICTs (Updated student ed.; pp. 35-54). London: Sage.

Beaver, L. (2016). *80% of businesses want chatbots by 2020.* Retrieved from http://www.businessinsider.com/80-of-businesses-want-chatbots-by-2020-2016-12

Bell, D. G., Giordano, R., & Putz, P. (2002). Inter-firm sharing of process knowledge: Exploring knowledge markets. *Knowledge and Process Management*, *9*(1), 12–22. doi:10.1002/kpm.131

Benson, C. (2016). The Internet of Things, IoT Systems, and Higher Education. *EDUCAUSE Review*, *51*(4), 6. Retrieved from http://er.educause.edu/articles/2016/6/the-internet-of-things-iot-systems-and-higher-education

Berryman, D. R. (2012). Augmented reality: A review. *Medical Reference Services Quarterly*, *31*(2), 212–218. doi:10.1080/02763869.2012.670604 PMID:22559183

Bers, T. H. (1994). Exploring institutional images through focus group interviews. In N. Bennett, R. Glatter, & R. Levacic (Eds.), *Improving educational management through research and consultancy* (pp. 290–299). London: The Open University.

Beynon-Davies, P. (2002). *Information Systems: An introduction to informatics in organisations.* Basingstoke, UK: Palgrave Macmillan.

Bhadani, J. D (2016). Big data: Challenges, opportunities and realities. In Effective Big Data Management and Opportunities for Implementation (pp. 1-24). IGI Global.

Billinghurst, M. (2002). *Augmented Reality in Education.* Seattle, WA: New Horizons for Learning - Technology in Education.

Bimber, O., Raskar, R., & Inami, M. (2005). *Spatial augmented reality.* AK Peters Wellesley. doi:10.1201/b10624

Blattberg, R. C., Fox, E. J., Dept, F. M. I. R., & Mars, I. (1995). *Category Management: ... a Series of Implementation Guides.* Research Department, Food Marketing Institute. Retrieved from https://books.google.pt/books?id=RJAjHAAACAAJ

Bleecker, J. (2006). A Manifesto for Networked Objects – Cohabiting with Pigeons, Arphids and Aibos in the Internet of Things – Why Things Matter What' s a Blogject? What about Spimes? *Proceedings of the 13th International Conference on Human-Computer Interaction with Mobile Devices and Services, MobileHCI.*

Bonon, E. J. (2014). Internet das Coisas: Arquitetura – Desafios e Aplicação. Cad. *CPqD Tecnologia, Campinas, 10*(2), 85–94.

Borrego-Jaraba, F., Luque Ruiz, I., & Gómez-Nieto, M. Á. (2011). A NFC-based pervasive solution for city touristic surfing. *Personal and Ubiquitous Computing, 15*(7), 731–742. doi:10.100700779-010-0364-y

Bots, the next frontier. (2016). *The Economist.* Retrieved August 3, 2017 from https://www.economist.com/news/business-and-finance/21696477-market-apps-maturing-now-one-text-based-services-or-chat bots-looks-poised

Botta, A., De Donato, W., Persico, V., & Pescapé, A. (2016). Integration of Cloud computing and Internet of Things: A survey. *Future Generation Computer Systems, 56*, 684–700. doi:10.1016/j.future.2015.09.021

Briseno, M. Z., Hirata, F. I., Lopez Juan de, D. S., Garcia, E. J., Cota, C. N., & Hipolito, J. I. N. (2012). Using RFID/NFC and QR-Code in Mobile Phones to Link the Physical and the Digital World. In Interactive Multimedia. InTech.

Brown & Harmon. (2014). Viral Geofencing: An Exploration of Emerging Big-Data Driven Direct Digital Marketing Services. *Proceedings of PICMET '14: Infrastructure and Service Integration.*

Brown, R. S. Jr. (1947). Advertising and the public interest: Legal protection of trade symbols. *The Yale Law Journal, 57*(7), 1165. doi:10.2307/793310

Brscic, D., Kanda, T., Ikeda, T., & Miyashita, T. (2013). Person tracking in large public spaces using 3-D range sensors. *IEEE Transactions on Human-Machine Systems, 43*(6), 522–534. doi:10.1109/THMS.2013.2283945

Bruner, G. C. II, & Kumar, A. (2005). Explaining consumer acceptance of handheld Internet devices. *Journal of Business Research, 5*(58), 553–558. doi:10.1016/j.jbusres.2003.08.002

Bullini Orlandi, L. (2016). Organizational capabilities in the digital era: Reframing strategic orientation. *Journal of Innovation & Knowledge, 1*(3), 156–161. doi:10.1016/j.jik.2016.01.002

Burillák, C. (2011). *Stunning QR codes - the really easy way to earn big cash fast.* Kindle Edition.

Byrne, Z. S., Dvorak, K. J., Peters, J. M., Ray, I., Howe, A., & Sanchez, D. (2016). From the user's perspective: Perceptions of risk relative to benefit associated with using the Internet. *Computers in Human Behavior, 59*, 456-468.

Byun, D., Cho, J., & Moon, S. (2016). S-Beacon: Next generation BLE beacon solution for enhanced personalization Consumer Electronics (ICCE). *Proceedings of the IEEE International Conference.*

Caffyn, G. (2016). *Two months in: How the 1-800 Flowers Facebook bot is working out.* Retrieved July 24, 2017, from https://digiday.com/marketing/two-months-1-800-flowers-facebook-bot-working/

Campbell, H. (2005). Considering spiritual dimensions within computer-mediated communication studies. *New Media & Society*, *7*(1), 110–134. doi:10.1177/1461444805049147

Canhoto, A. I., & Arp, S. (2017). Exploring the factors that support adoption and sustained use of health and fitness wearables. *Journal of Marketing Management*, *33*(1–2), 32–60. doi:10.1080/0267257X.2016.1234505

Cannon, J. P., & Perreault, W. (1999). Buyer–Seller Relationships in Business Markets. *JMR, Journal of Marketing Research*, *36*(4), 439–460. doi:10.2307/3151999

Carmigniani, J., Furht, B., Anisetti, M., Ceravolo, P., Damiani, E., & Ivkovic, M. (2011). Augmented reality technologies, systems and applications. *Multimedia Tools and Applications*, *51*(1), 341–477. doi:10.100711042-010-0660-6

Carminati, B., Ferrari, E., & Viviani, M. (2012). *A multi-dimensional and event-based model for trust computation in the social web. In Social Informatics* (pp. 323–336). Berlin, Germany: Springer.

Carmon, N. (2018). *5 Ways to Use Location Based Marketing For Your Brand.* Retrieved 05.01.2018. from https://digitalbrandinginstitute.com/5-ways-use-location-based-marketing-brand/

Carneiro da Cunha, J. A. (2011). *Avaliação de desempenho e eficiência em organizações de saúde: um estudo em hospitais filantrópicos* (Doctoral dissertation). Faculdade de Economia, Administração e Contabilidade. Universidade de São Paulo.

Carter, W. C., & Servat, H. J. (2005). *The Proust questionnaire*. New York: Assouline Publishing.

Carvalho, G., & Bernardino, J. (2017). A Internet das Coisas e Big Data: Tendências futuras. *Proceedings of the 12th Iberian Conference on Information Systems and Technologies*, 1421-1424.

Cata, T., Patel, P. S., & Sakaguchi, T. (2013). QR Code: A New Opportunity for Effective Mobile Marketing, Journal of Mobile Technologies. *Knowledge in Society.*

Caudell, T. P., & Mizell, D. W. (1992). Augmented reality: An application of heads-up display technology to manual manufacturing processes. In *System Sciences, 199, Proceedings of the Twenty-Fifth Hawaii International Conference on*. IEEE. 10.1109/HICSS.1992.183317

Cha, S., Ruiz, M. P., Wachowicz, M., Tran, L. H., Cao, H., & Maduako, I. (2017). The role of an IoT platform in the design of real-time recommender systems. *2016 IEEE 3rd World Forum on Internet of Things*, 448–453. 10.1109/WF-IoT.2016.7845469

Chandrakanth, S., Venkatesh, K., Mahesh, J. U., & Naganjaneyulu, K. V. (2014). Internet of Things. *International Journal of Innovations & Advancement in Computer Science*, *3*(4), 2347–8616.

Chan, T. Y., Narasimhan, C., & Yoon, Y. (2017). Advertising and price competition in a manufacturer-retailer channel. *International Journal of Research in Marketing*, *34*(3), 694–716. doi:10.1016/j.ijresmar.2017.04.001

Chatain, O. (2011). Value creation, competition, and performance in buyer-supplier relationships. *Strategic Management Journal*, *32*(1), 76–102. doi:10.1002mj.864

Chatzopoulos, Bermejo, Huang, & Hui. (2017). Mobile Augmented Reality Survey: From Where We Are to Where We Go. *IEEE Translations and Content Mining, 5*, 6917-6950.

Chaudhuri, A., & Holbrook, M. B. (2001). The chain of effects from brand trust and brand affect to brand performance: The role of brand loyalty. *Journal of Marketing*, *65*(2), 81–93. doi:10.1509/jmkg.65.2.81.18255

Chaves-Diéguez, D., Pellitero-Rivero, A., García-Coego, D., González-Castaño, F. J., Rodríguez-Hernández, P. S., Piñeiro-Gómez, Ó., ... Costa-Montenegro, E. (2015). Providing IoT Services in Smart Cities through Dynamic Augmented Reality Markers. *Sensors (Basel)*, *15*(7), 16083–16104. doi:10.3390150716083 PMID:26151215

Chen, Wu, Lo, & Hwang. (2017). An Augmented Reality Question Answering System Based on Ensemble Neural Networks. *IEEE Translations and Content Mining, 5*, 17425-17435.

Cheong, R. (1995). The virtual threat to travel and tourism. *Tourism Management*, *16*(6), 417–422. doi:10.1016/0261-5177(95)00049-T

Cheong, T., & Song, S. H. (2013). The value of information on supply risk under random yields. *Transportation Research Part E, Logistics and Transportation Review*, *60*, 27–38. doi:10.1016/j.tre.2013.09.006

Chi, H. H. (2011). Interactive digital advertising vs. virtual brand community: Exploratory study of user motivation and social media marketing responses in Taiwan. *Journal of Interactive Advertising*, *12*(1), 44–61. doi:10.1080/15252019.2011.10722190

Chih-Chien, W., Hsu, Y., & Fang, W. (2005). Acceptance of technology with network externalities: An empirical study of internet instant messenger services. *Journal of Information Technology Theory and Application*, *6*(4), 15.

Childers, T. L., Carr, C. L., Peck, J., & Carson, S. (2001). Hedonic and utilitarian motivations for online retail shopping behavior. *Journal of Retailing*, *77*(4), 511–535. doi:10.1016/S0022-4359(01)00056-2

Choi, T. M., Li, J., & Wei, Y. (2013). Will a supplier benefit from sharing good information with a retailer? *Decision Support Systems*, *56*, 131–139. doi:10.1016/j.dss.2013.05.011

Chong, A. Y.-L., Liu, M. J., Luo, J., & Keng-Boon, O. (2015). Predicting RFID adoption in healthcare supply chain from the perspectives of users. *International Journal of Production Economics*, *159*, 66–75. doi:10.1016/j.ijpe.2014.09.034

Chui, M., Loffler, M., & Roberts, R. (2010). The Internet of Things. *The McKinsey Quarterly*, *2*, 1–9.

Chung, H., & Lee, E. (2017). Store Brand Quality and Retailer's Product Line Design. *Journal of Retailing*, *82*(4), 349–355. doi:10.1016/j.jretai.2006.08.008

Cipriano, L. (2015). *Estudo aponta que Internet das Coisas beneficiará principalmente a saúde em 2025*. Neitec. Retrieved September 27, 2017, from http://neitec.com/inovacao-tecnologica/estudo-aponta-que-internet-das-coisas-beneficiara-principalmente-a-saude-em- 2025/

Cisco. (2017). *The Internet of Things – Cisco Visualization*. Cisco.

Coetzee, L., & Eksteen, J. (2011). The Internet of Things – Promise for the Future? An Introduction. IST-Africa 2011. *Proceedings of the IIMC International Information Management Corporation*, 1-9.

Colby, K. M. (1974). Ten criticisms of parry. *ACM SIGART Bulletin*, (48), 5-9.

Colby, K. M. (1981). Modeling a paranoid mind. *Behavioral and Brain Sciences*, *4*(4), 515–534. doi:10.1017/S0140525X00000030

Collis, J., & Hussey, R. (2005). *Pesquisa em Administração: um guia prático para alunos de graduação e pós-graduação (2nd ed.)*. Porto Alegre: Bookman.

Comissão Nacional de Proteção de Dados. (2017). *10 Medidas para Preparar a Aplicação do Regulamento Europeu de Proteção de Dados*. Retrieved from https://www.cnpd.pt/bin/rgpd/10_Medidas_para_preparar_RGPD_CNPD.pdf

ComScore. (2016). U.S.Mobile App Report. *ComScore Whitepaper.* Retrieved June 04, 2017, from https://www.comscore.com/Insights/Presentations-and-Whitepapers/2016/The-2016-US-Mobile-App-Report

Constine, J. (2017, April 12). *Facebook Messenger hits 1.2 billion monthly users, up from 1B in July*. Retrieved June 04, 2017, from https://techcrunch.com/2017/04/12/messenger/

Corsten, D., & Kumar, N. (2005). Do Suppliers Benefit from Collaborative Relationships with Large Retailers? An Empirical Investigation of Efficient Consumer Response Adoption. *Journal of Marketing*, *69*(3), 80–94. doi:10.1509/jmkg.69.3.80.66360

Coskun, V., Ok, K., & Özdenizci, B. (2012). *Near Field Communication (NFC) from Theory to Practice*. New York, NY: Wiley. doi:10.1002/9781119965794

Coskun, V., Ozdenizci, B., & Ok, K. (2013). A Survey on Near Field Communication (NFC) Technology. *Wireless Personal Communications*, *71*(3), 2259–2294. doi:10.100711277-012-0935-5

Coşkun, V., Özdenizci, B., & Ok, K. (2015). The Survey on Near Field Communication. *Sensors (Basel)*, *15*(6), 13348–13405. doi:10.3390150613348 PMID:26057043

Costa, J., Silva, A., & Murarolli, P. (2017). *Application of the big data in the health, sports, livestock and mineral areas.* Academic Press.

Craig, A. B. (2013). Understanding augmented reality, concepts and applications. Morgan Kaufmann.

Crowd WiFi. (2017). *Smart Sense*. Retrieved from http://www.crowdwifi.co.uk/smart-sense/

Csíkszentmihályi, M. (1975). *Beyond Boredom and Anxiety: Experiencing Flow in Work and Play*. San Francisco: Jossey-Bass.

Da Xu, L., He, W., & Li, S. (2014). Internet of things in industries: A survey. *IEEE Transactions on Industrial Informatics*, *10*(4), 2233–2243. doi:10.1109/TII.2014.2300753

Dalkey, N. C. (1969). *The Delphi method. An experimental study of group opinion (N.º RM-5888-PR)*. Santa Monica, CA: Rand Corporation.

Dalkey, N., & Helmer, O. (1963). An experimental application of the Delphi method to the use of experts. *Management Science*, *9*(12), 458–467. doi:10.1287/mnsc.9.3.458

Dapiran, G. P., & Hogarth-Scott, S. (2003). Are co-operation and trust being confused with power? An analysis of food retailing in Australia and the UK. *International Journal of Retail & Distribution Management*, *31*(5), 256–267. doi:10.1108/09590550310472424

Davenport, T. (2015). *The Analytics of Things*. Retrieved September 26, 2017, from https://www.linkedin.com/pulse/analytics-things-tom-davenport

Davenport, T., DalleMule, L., & Lucker, J. (2011). Know What Your Customers Want Before They Do. *Harvard Business Review*. Retrieved September 29, 2017, from https://hbr.org/2011/12/know-what-your-customers-want-before-they-do

Davis, F. D. (1985). *A technology acceptance model for empirically testing new end-user information systems: Theory and results* (Doctoral dissertation). Massachusetts Institute of Technology.

Davis, F. D. (1986). *A Technology Acceptance Model for Empirically Testing New End-User Information Systems: Theory and Results* (PhD Doctoral dissertation). Massachusetts Institute of Technology.

Davis, B., & Pechmann, C. (2013). Introduction to the special issue on transformative consumer research. *Journal of Business Research*, *66*(8), 1168–1170. doi:10.1016/j.jbusres.2012.08.008

Davis, F. D. (1989). Perceived Usefulness, Perceived Ease of Use, and User Acceptance of Information Technology. *Management Information Systems Quarterly*, *13*(3), 319–340. doi:10.2307/249008

Davis, F. D., Bagozzi, R. P., & Warshaw, P. R. (1989). User acceptance of computer technology: A comparison of two theoretical models. *Management Science*, *35*(8), 982–1003. doi:10.1287/mnsc.35.8.982

Davis, F. D., Bagozzi, R. P., & Warshaw, P. R. (1992). Extrinsic and intrinsic motivation to use computers in the workplace. *Journal of Applied Social Psychology*, *22*(14), 1111–1132. doi:10.1111/j.1559-1816.1992.tb00945.x

Day, G. S. (2011). Closing the Marketing Capabilities Gap. *Journal of Marketing*, *75*(4), 183–195. doi:10.1509/jmkg.75.4.183

De Angeli, A., Johnson, G. I., & Coventry, L. (2001, June). The unfriendly user: exploring social reactions to chatterbots. In *Proceedings of The International Conference on Affective Human Factors Design,* 467-474.

De Cremer, D., Nguyen, B., & Simkin, L. (2017). The integrity challenge of the Internet-of-Things (IoT): On understanding its dark side. *Journal of Marketing Management*, *33*(1–2). doi:10.1080/0267257X.2016.1247517

De Kerviler, G., Demoulin, N. T., & Zidda, P. (2016). Adoption of in-store mobile payment: Are perceived risk and convenience the only drivers? *Journal of Retailing and Consumer Services*, *31*(1), 334–344. doi:10.1016/j.jretconser.2016.04.011

Decandia, G., Hastorun, D., Jampani, M., Kakulapati, G., Lakshman, A., Pilchin, A., ... Vogels, W. (2007). Dynamo: Amazon's Highly Available Key -value Store. *Proceedings of the 21st ACM Symposium on Operating Systems Principles (SOSP 2007).* 10.1145/1294261.1294281

Demir, S., Kaynak, R., & Demir, K. A. (2015). Usage Level and Future Intent of Use of Quick Response (QR) Codes for Mobile Marketing among College Students in Turkey. Proceedings Of The 3rd International Conference On Leadership, Technology And Innovation Management. *Procedia: Social and Behavioral Sciences*, *181*, 405–413. doi:10.1016/j.sbspro.2015.04.903

Dewsnap, B., & Hart, C. (2004). Category management: A new approach for fashion marketing? *European Journal of Marketing*, *38*(7), 809–834. doi:10.1108/03090560410539267

Dhar, S. K., Hoch, S. J., & Kumar, N. (2001). Effective category management depends on the role of the category. *Journal of Retailing*, *77*(2), 165–184. doi:10.1016/S0022-4359(01)00045-8

Diener, E., Emmons, R. A., Larsen, R. J., & Griffin, S. (1985). The Satisfaction with Life Scale. *Journal of Personality Assessment*, *49*(1), 71–75. doi:10.120715327752jpa4901_13 PMID:16367493

DILAX. (2017). *People counting & people flow analyses*. Retrieved from https://www.dilax.com/retail-airports/solutions/people-counting-people-flow-analyses/

Dimitriadis, S., & Kyrezis, N. (2010). Linking trust to use intention for technology-enabled bank channels: The role of trusting intentions. *Psychology and Marketing*, *27*(8), 799–820. doi:10.1002/mar.20358

Dimmick, J., Ramirez, A. Jr, Wang, T., & Lin, S. (2007). Extending Society': The role of personal networks and gratification-utilities in the use of interactive communication media. *New Media & Society*, *9*(5), 795–810. doi:10.1177/1461444807081225

Ding, L., Shi, P., & Liu, B. (2010). The Clustering of Internet, Internet of Things and Social Network. *Proceedings of the 3rd International Symposium on Knowledge Acquisition and Modeling.*

Drabble, S., Ratzmann, N., Hoorens, S., Khodyakov, D., & Yaqub, O. (n.d.). *The rise of a global middle class: Global societal trends to 2030: Thematic report 6.* Retrieved from https://www.rand.org/pubs/research_reports/RR920z6.html

Duchessi, P., Schaninger, C. M., & Nowak, T. (2004). Creating cluster-specific purchase profiles from point-of-sale scanner data and geodemographic clusters: Improving category management at a major US grocery chain. *Journal of Consumer Behaviour, 4*(2), 97–117. doi:10.1002/cb.162

Dupre, K., & Gruen, T. W. (2004). The use of category management practices to obtain a sustainable competitive advantage in the fast- moving-consumer-goods industry). *Journal of Business & Industrial Marketing, 1946*(5), 444–459. doi:10.1108/08858620410564391

Durand, R., & Khaire, M. (2016). Where Do Market Categories Come From and How? Distinguishing Category Creation From Category Emergence. *Journal of Management, 43*(1), 87–110. doi:10.1177/0149206316669812

Dussart, C. (1998). Category management:Strengths, limits and developments. *European Management Journal, 16*(1), 50–62. doi:10.1016/S0263-2373(97)00073-X

eGain. (2017). *Virtual Assistant.* Retrieved from http://www.egain.com/products/virtual-assistant-software/

Egan, A. F., Jones, S. B., Luloff, A. E., & Finley, J. C. (1995). The value of using multiple methods: An illustration using survey, focus group, and Delphi techniques. *Society & Natural Resources, 8*(5), 457–465. doi:10.1080/08941929509380936

Egger, R. (2013a). The impact of near field communication on tourism. *Journal of Hospitality and Tourism Technology, 4*(2), 119–133. doi:10.1108/JHTT-04-2012-0014

Egger, R. (2013b). Near Field Communication in Tourism: A Conceptual Paper, The Gaze. *Journal of Tourism & Hospitality (Los Angeles, Calif.), 5.*

Ehret, M., & Wirtz, J. (2017). Unlocking Value from Machines: Business Models and the Industrial Internet of Things. *Journal of Marketing Management, 33*(1–2), 111–130. doi:10.1080/0267257X.2016.1248041

Erdem, T., Lane Keller, K., Kuksov, D., & Pieters, R. (2016). *Understanding Branding in a digitally empowered world.* Academic Press. 10.1016/j.ijresmar.2015.12.003

Ess, A., Leibe, B., Schindler, K., & Van Gool, L. (2008, June). A mobile vision system for robust multi-person tracking. In *Proceedings of the IEEE Conference on Computer Vision and Pattern Recognition* (pp. 1-8). Anchorage, AK: IEEE. Retrieved from https://www.vision.ee.ethz.ch/publications/papers/proceedings/eth_biwi_00534.pdf

Euromonitor International. (2017). *Global Economies and Consumers in 2017.* Euromonitor International.

EUROMSG. (2016). *Geofencing ile Geotargeting Arasındaki 5 Fark.* Retrieved 07.06.2017, from http://blog.euromsg.com/geo-fencing-ile-geo-targeting-arasindaki-5-fark/

Europe, E. C. R. (1997). *Category management: best practises report.* Brussels: ECR Europe, Cop.

Europe, E. C. R. (2000). The Essential Guide to Day-to-Day Category Management. *Europe.*

Evans, D. (2011). *The Internet of Things How the Next Evolution of the Internet Is Changing Everything* [White paper]. Retrieved December, 2017, Cisco Internet Business Solutions Group (IBSG): https://www.cisco.com/c/dam/en_us/about/ac79/docs/innov/IoT_IBSG_0411FINAL.pdf

Faurie, I., & van de Leemput, C. (2007). Influence du Sentiment d'Efficacité Informatique sur les usages d'Internet des étudiants. *Orientation Scolaire et Professionnelle, 36*(4), 533–552. doi:10.4000/osp.1549

Ferguson A. G., (2016). The Internet of Things and the Fourth Amendment of Effects. *California Law Review, 104*(4), 805. .10.15779/Z38JZ8G

Firshein, S. (2010). Anna, IKEA's Chat bot, Graciously Answers Proust Questionnaire. *Curbed*. Retrieved September 19, 2017 from www.curbed.com/2010/9/23/10505206/anna-ikeas-chatbot-graciously-answers-proust-questionnaire

Fishbein, M., & Ajzen, I. (1975). *Belief, attitude, intention and behavior: An introduction to theory and research*. Reading, MA: Addison Wesley.

Flick, U. (2009). *Desenho da pesquisa qualitativa*. Porto Alegre: Artmed.

Foreman, M. A. (2014). *A internet das coisas é a próxima máquina de fazer dinheiro da web, dizem as pequenas empresas*. Blog AVG Brasil, 2 dez. 2014. Retrieved September 29, 2017, from <http://blog.avgbrasil.com.br/2014/12/02/internet-das- coisas-e-proxima-maquina-de-fazer-dinheiro-da-web-dizem-pequenas-empresas>

Fornell, C. D., & Lacker, D. F. (1981). Evaluating Structural Equation models with Unobservable Variables and Measurement. *JMR, Journal of Marketing Research, 18*(1), 39–50. doi:10.2307/3151312

Foxlin, E., Calloway, T., & Zhang, H. (2015). Design and Error Analysis of a Vehicular AR System with Auto-Harmonization. *IEEE Transactions on Visualization and Computer Graphics, 21*(12), 1323–1335. doi:10.1109/TVCG.2015.2481385 PMID:26415180

Freund, F. F., Steenb, F. A., Marangoni, G. A. C., Vieira, J. D., Deus, S. L., & Angonese, R. M. (2016). Novos negócios baseados em internet das coisas. *Revista FAE*, Curitiba. *Edição Especial, 1*, 7–25.

Gaborit, P., & Girault, M. (2007). Lightweight code-based identification and signature. *2007 IEEE International Symposium on Information Theory*, 191-195. 10.1109/ISIT.2007.4557225

Galinina, A., Pyattaev, A., Gerasimenko, M., Tirronen, T., Torser, J., Sachs, J., ... Koucheryavy, Y. (2015). Understanding the IoT connectivity landscape: A contemporary M2M radio technology roadmap. *IEEE Communications Magazine, 53*(9), 32–40. doi:10.1109/MCOM.2015.7263370

Gantz, J., & Reinsel, D. (2012). *The Digital Universe in 2020: Big Data, Bigger Digital Shadows, and Biggest Growth in the Far East*. Retrieved from www.emc.com/leadership/digital-universe/index.htm

Gao, L., & Bai, X. (2014). A unified perspective on the factors influencing consumer acceptance of internet of things technology. *Asia Pacific Journal of Marketing and Logistics, 26*(2), 211–231. doi:10.1108/APJML-06-2013-0061

Garfinkel, S. (2011). *The Cloud Imperative*. Retrieved from http://www.technologyreview.com/news/425623/the-cloud-imperative/

Gcaba, O., & Dlodlo, N. (2016). The Internet of Things for South African Tourism. In IST-Africa 2016 Confeence Proceedings (pp. 1–8). IIMC International Information Management Corporation. doi:10.1109/ISTAFRICA.2016.7530573

Geetha, S. (2016). World. *Science News, 41*, 76–81.

Gefen, D., Karahanna, E., & Straub, D. W. (2003). Trust and TAM in Online Shopping: An Integrated Model. *Management Information Systems Quarterly, 27*(1), 51–90. doi:10.2307/30036519

Gefen, D., & Straub, D. W. (1997). Gender differences in the perception and use of e-mail: An extension to the technology acceptance model. *Management Information Systems Quarterly, 21*(4), 389–400. doi:10.2307/249720

Gerset, A., & Vaidya, S. (2010). Next Generation Customer Service Strategies: Harnessing the Power of the Internet and Web 2.0 for Delivering Customer Care. *Telecom & Media Insights*, (52). Retrieved September 20, 2017 from https://www.capgemini-consulting.com/resource-file-access/resource/pdf/Next_Generation_Customer_Service_Strategies.pdf

Ge, X., Pan, L., Li, Q., Mao, G., & Tu, S. (2017). Multipath Cooperative Communications Networks for Augmented and Virtual Reality Transmission. *IEEE Transactions on Multimedia*, *19*(10), 2345–2358. doi:10.1109/TMM.2017.2733461

Ghanchi, J. (2015). *Advantages and Disadvantages of Geofencing Applications*. Retrieved 01.10.2018 from: https://medium.com/@indianappd /advantages-anddisadvantages-of-geofencing-applications-a20e47bd2cc4

Ghazi, M., & Gangodkar, D. (2015). Hadoop, MapReduce and HDFS: A Developers Perspective. *International Conference on Intelligent Computing, Communication & Convergence*, 45-50. 10.1016/j.procs.2015.04.108

Gilliland, N. (2016). Domino's introduces 'Dom the Pizza Bot' for Facebook Messenger. *Econsultancy*. Retrieved September 22, 2017 from https://www.econsultancy.com/blog/68184-domino-s-introduces-dom-the-pizza-bot-for-facebook-messenger

Gilliland, N. (2016). What are chat bots and why should marketers care? *Econsultancy*. Retrieved September 22, 2017 from https://econsultancy.com/blog/67894-what-are-chat bots-and-why-should-marketers-care/

Glynn, M. S., Brodie, R. J., & Motion, J. (2012). The benefits of manufacturer brands to retailers. *European Journal of Marketing*, *22*(6), 400–409. doi:10.1108/03090561211247856

Goldberg, A., Hannan, M. T., & Kovács, B. (2016). What Does It Mean to Span Cultural Boundaries? Variety and Atypicality in Cultural Consumption. *American Sociological Review*, *81*(2), 215–241. doi:10.1177/0003122416632787

Goldstein, D. G., McAfee, R. P., & Suri, S. (2011, June). The effects of exposure time on memory of display advertisements. In *Proceedings of the 12th ACM conference on Electronic commerce* (pp. 49-58). San Jose, CA: ACM. 10.1145/1993574.1993584

Gong, W. (2016). The Internet of Things (IoT): What is the Potential of the internet of things (IoT) as a marketing tool? *Proceedings of the 7th IBA Bachelor Thesis Conference*.

Gönül, F. F., Qiu, C., & Zhou, E. (2015). *Whether or Not to Use a Quick Response (QR) Code in the Ad*. Retrieved from http://ssrn. com/abstract=2487939

Gordon, N. (n.d.). What are the Differences between a Chat botWith and Without A.I.? *Century Soft Blog*. Retrieved August 3, 2017 from https://www.centurysoft.com/blog/differences-between-chat-bot-with-and-without-ai.html

Granqvist, N., Grodal, S., & Woolley, J. L. (2013). Hedging Your Bets: Explaining Executives' Market Labeling Strategies in Nanotechnology. *Organization Science*, *24*(2), 395–413. doi:10.1287/orsc.1120.0748

Grasset, R., Langlotz, T., Kalkofen, D., Tatzgern, M., & Schmalstieg, D. (2012). *Image-Driven View Management for Aug- mented Reality Browsers. In 2012 IEEE International Symposium on Mixed and Augmented Reality* (pp. 177–186). Atlanta, GA: ISMAR.

Groff, J. (2013). Technology-rich innovative learning environments. *OCED CERI Innovative Learning Environment project*, 1-30.

Gruen, T. W., & Shah, R. H. (2000). Determinants and outcomes of plan objectivity and implementation in category management relationships. *Journal of Retailing*, *76*(4), 483–510. doi:10.1016/S0022-4359(00)00041-5

Gubbi, J., Buyya, R., Marusic, S., & Palaniswami, M. (2013). Internet of Things (IoT): A vision, architectural elements, and future directions. *Future Generation Computer Systems*, *29*(7), 1645–1660. doi:10.1016/j.future.2013.01.010

Gudla, S. K., & Bose, J. (2016). Intelligent web push architecture with push flow control and push continuity. *Proceedings - 2016 IEEE International Conference on Web Services, ICWS 2016, 658–661.* 10.1109/ICWS.2016.90

Gu, F. F., Kim, N., Tse, D. K., & Wang, D. T. (2010). Managing Distributors' Changing Motivations over the Course of a Joint Sales Program. *Journal of Marketing*, *74*(5), 32–47. doi:10.1509/jmkg.74.5.32

Guinard, D., Fischer, M., & Trifa, V. (2010). Sharing using social networks in a composable web of things. *Proceedings of 8th IEEE Int. Conf. PERCOM Workshops.* 10.1109/PERCOMW.2010.5470524

Guinard, M., Karnouskos, S., Trifa, V., Dober, B., Spiess, P., & Savio, D. (2010). Interacting with the SOA-based Internet of Things: Discovery, Query, Selection, and On-Demand Provisioning of Web Services. *IEEE Transactions on Services Computing*, *3*(3), 223–235. doi:10.1109/TSC.2010.3

Gupta, S. (2016). Real time big data Analytics. Packet Publishing Ltd.

Gurau, C. (2007). *Virtual Reality Applications in Tourism. Information and Communication Technologies in Support of the Tourism Industry,* 180–197.

Guttentag, D. A. (2010). Virtual reality: Applications and implications for tourism. *Tourism Management*, *31*(5), 637–651. doi:10.1016/j.tourman.2009.07.003

Guven, S., Oda, O., Podlaseck, M., Stavropoulos, H., Kolluri, S., & Pingali, G. (2009). Social Mobile Augmented Reality for Retail. *IEEE International Conference on Pervasive Computing and Communications,* 1-3. 10.1109/PERCOM.2009.4912803

Guynn, J. (2017). Facebook Messenger takes another swipe at bots. *USA Today*. Retrieved August 3, 2017 from https://www.usatoday.com/story/tech/news/2017/04/18/facebook-messenger-takes-another-swipe-chat-bots/100596798/

Hajli, M. N. (2014). A study of the impact of social media on consumers. *International Journal of Market Research*, *56*(3), 387–404. doi:10.2501/IJMR-2014-025

Hamister, J. W., & Fortsch, S. M. (2016). Cumulative impact of category management on small retailers. *International Journal of Retail & Distribution Management*, *44*(7), 680–693. doi:10.1108/IJRDM-09-2015-0142

Han, M. C., & Kim, Y. (2017). Why Consumers Hesitate to Shop Online: Perceived Risk and Product Involvement on Taobao. com. *Journal of Promotion Management*, *23*(1), 24–44. doi:10.1080/10496491.2016.1251530

Han, S., Ye, Y., Fu, X., & Chen, Z. (2014). Category role aided market segmentation approach to convenience store chain category management. *Decision Support Systems*, *57*, 296–308. doi:10.1016/j.dss.2013.09.017

Harris, J. K., Swatman, P. M. C., & Kurnia, S. (1999). Efficient consumer response (ECR): A survey of the Australian grocery industry. *Supply Chain Management*, *4*(1), 35–42. doi:10.1108/13598549910255077

Harris, L., & Westin, A. F. (1991). *Harris-Equifax Consumer Privacy Survey*. Atlanta, GA: Equifax Inc.

Ha, S., & Stoel, L. (2009). Consumer e-shopping acceptance: Antecedents in a technology acceptance model. *Journal of Business Research*, *62*(5), 565–571. doi:10.1016/j.jbusres.2008.06.016

Hassan, A. M., Kunz, M. B., Pearson, A. W., & Mohamed, F. A. (2006). Conceptualization and measurement of perceived risk in online shopping. *Marketing Management Journal*, *16*(1), 138–167.

Hassanein, K., & Head, M. (2007). Manipulating perceived social presence through the web interface and its impact on attitude towards online shopping. *International Journal of Human-Computer Studies*, *65*(8), 689–708. doi:10.1016/j.ijhcs.2006.11.018

Hassen, I. (2015). *Context Aware Tourist Information and Recommendation System using iQR Code* (Unpublished Master Thesis). Addis Ababa University.

Hasson, F., & Keeney, S., & McKenna, H. (2000). Research guidelines for the Delphi technique. *Journal of Advanced Nursing, 32*(4), 1008–1015. PMID:11095242

Heath, A. (2017). Mark Zuckerberg wants Facebook to move faster at making money off Messenger and there's a good reason why. *Business Insider.* Retrieved July 27, 2017 from http://www.businessinsider.com/zuckerberg-facebook-move-faster-monetizing-messenger-2017-7

Hendrickson, S. (2010). *Getting Started with Hadoop with Amazon's Elastic MapReduce*. EMR.

Herron, K. (2017). *When social media meets the Internet of Things*. Retrieved September 25, 2017, from https://unifiedinbox.com/when-social-media-meets-the-internet-of-things/

Higgins, E. T. (1997). Beyond pleasure and pain. *The American Psychologist, 52*(12), 1280–1300. doi:10.1037/0003-066X.52.12.1280 PMID:9414606

Hilbert, M., & Lopez, P. (2011). The world's Technological Capacity´ to store, communicate, and compute information. *Science, 332*(6025), 60–65. doi:10.1126cience.1200970 PMID:21310967

Hill, J., Ford, W. R., & Farreras, I. G. (2015). Real conversations with artificial intelligence: A comparison between human–human online conversations and human–chat botconversations. *Computers in Human Behavior, 49*, 245–250. doi:10.1016/j.chb.2015.02.026

Hirschman, E. C., & Holbrook, M. B. (1982). Hedonic consumption: Emerging concepts, methods and propositions. *Journal of Marketing, 46*(3), 92–101. doi:10.2307/1251707

Hock, C. (1962). The Four Temperaments. Milwaukee, WI: The Pallotine Fathers, Inc.

Hoffman, D. L., Novak, T. P., & Peralta, M. (1999). Building consumer trust online. *Communications of the Advanced Conferences & Meetings, 42*(4), 80-85.

Hoffman, D., & Novak, T. (2015). *Emergent experience and the connected consumer in the smart home assemblage and the internet of things*. Academic Press. 10.13140/RG.2.1.3966.1282.Holbrook

Hoffman, D. (2000). The revolution will not be televised: Introduction to the special issue on marketing science and the internet. *Marketing Science, 19*(1), 1–3. doi:10.1287/mksc.19.1.1.15181

Hoffman, D. L., & Novak, T. P. (2016). Consumer and Object Experience in the Internet of Things: An Assemblage Theory Approach. *SSRN Electronic Journal, 77*. doi:10.2139srn.2840975

Holbrook, M. B., & Hirschman, E. C. (1982). The experiential aspects of consumption: Consumer fantasies, feelings, and fun. *The Journal of Consumer Research, 9*(2), 132–140. doi:10.1086/208906

Höllerer, T. H., & Feiner, S. K. (2004). Mobile augmented reality. In Telegeoinformatics: Location-Based Computing and Services. Taylor & Francis Books Ltd.

Holmquist, L., Mattern, F., Schiele, B., Alahutha, P., Beigl, M., & Gallersen, H. (2001). Smart-its friends: A technique for users to easily establish connections between smart artefacts. *Proceedings of ACM UbiComp'01*. 10.1007/3-540-45427-6_10

Holzinger, A., Stocker, C., Ofner, B., Prohaska, G., Brabenetz, A., & Hofmann-Wellenhof, R. (2013). Combining HCI, natural language processing, and knowledge discovery—potential of IBM content analytics as an assistive technology in the biomedical field. In Lecture Notes in Computer Science: Vol. 7947. Human-Computer Interaction and Knowledge Discovery in Complex, Unstructured, Big Data (pp. 13–24). Springer. doi:10.1007/978-3-642-39146-0_2

Hong, W., & Thong, J. (2013). Internet privacy concerns: An integrated conceptualisation and four empirical studies. *Management Information Systems Quarterly*, *37*(1), 275–298. doi:10.25300/MISQ/2013/37.1.12

Hopping, D. (2000). Technology in retail. *Technology in Society*, *22*(1), 63–74. doi:10.1016/S0160-791X(99)00042-1

Hosek, J., Masek, P., Andreev, S., Galinina, O., Ometov, A., Kropfl, F., ... Koucheryavy, Y. (2017). A SyMPHOnY of Integrated IoT Businesses: Closing the Gap between Availability and Adoption. *IEEE Communications Magazine*, *55*(12), 156–164. doi:10.1109/MCOM.2017.1700028

Howe, N., & Strauss, W. (2000). *Millennials rising: The next great generation*. New York: Vintage Books.

Howie, J. G., Heaney, D. J., Maxwell, M., & Walker, J. J. (1998). A comparison of a Patient Enablement Instrument against two established satisfaction scales as an outcome measure of primary care consultations. *Family Practice*, *15*(2), 165–171. doi:10.1093/fampra/15.2.165 PMID:9613486

Hsu, C. C., & Sandford, B. A. (2007). The Delphi Technique: Making Sense Of Consensus. *Practical Assessment, Research & Evaluation*, *12*(10), 1-8.

Hsu, C.-L., & Lin, J. C.-C. (2016). Effect of perceived value and social influences on mobile app stickiness and in-app purchase intention. *Technological Forecasting and Social Change*, *108*, 42–53. doi:10.1016/j.techfore.2016.04.012

Hsu, G., Hannan, M. T., & Koçak, Ö. (2009). Multiple category memberships in markets: An integrative theory and two empirical tests. *American Sociological Review*, *74*(1), 150–169. doi:10.1177/000312240907400108

Huang, Y., & Wang, Z. (2017). Information sharing in a closed-loop supply chain with technology licensing. *International Journal of Production Economics*, *191*, 113–127. doi:10.1016/j.ijpe.2017.06.008

Huddelston, T., Jr. (2016). Now You Can Order Pizza Hut on Twitter and Facebook, Too. *Fortune*. Retrieved from http://fortune.com/2016/07/13/pizza-hut-chat bot-twitter-facebook/

Huge. (2004). IKEA Launches AI Customer Service Assistant. *Huge*. Retrieved August 28, 2017 from www.hugeinc.com/news/ikea-launches-artificial-intelligence-driven-customer-service-assistant

Hummer, W., & Schulte, S. (2016). Context-Aware Personalization for Smart Mobile Cloud Services. In Lecture Notes in Computer Science: vol. 9586. Service-Oriented Computing – ICSOC 2015 Workshops. Springer. doi:10.1007/978-3-662-50539-7_14

Hwang, E. (2015). Web Based Smart Home Automation Control System Design. *International Journal of Contents*, *11*(4), 70–76. doi:10.5392/IJoC.2015.11.4.070

Hwang, Y. (2010). The moderating effects of gender on e-commerce systems adoption factors: An empirical investigation. *Computers in Human Behavior*, *26*(6), 1753–1760. doi:10.1016/j.chb.2010.07.002

Iansiti, M., & Lakhani, K. R. (2014). Digital ubiquity: How connections, sensors, and data are revolutionizing business. *Harvard Business Review*, *92*(11), 91–99. doi:10.1017/CBO9781107415324.004

Ibanez, M.-B., Di-Serio, A., Villaran-Molina, D., & Delgado-Kloos, C. (2016). Support for Augmented Reality Simulation Systems: The Effects of Scaffolding on Learning Outcomes and Behavior Patterns. *IEEE Transactions on Learning Technologies*, *9*(1), 46–56. doi:10.1109/TLT.2015.2445761

IBM Infographics. (n.d.). *The Four V's of Big Data*. Retrieved from http://www.ibmbigdatahub.com/infographic/four-vs-big-data

IBM Marketing Cloud. (n.d.). *10 Key Marketing Trends for 2017 and Ideas for Exceeding Customer Expectations*. Retrieved from https://www-01.ibm.com/common/ssi/cgi-bin/ssialias?htmlfid=WRL12345USEN

If only I were. (2008, September 16). Chat with Sarah – the future of automated help [Blog Post]. Retrieved from https://subjunctive.wordpress.com/2008/09/16/chat-with-sarah-the-future-of-automated-help/

Igbaria, M., Guimaraes, T., & Davis, G. B. (1995). *Testing the Determinants of Microcomputer Usage via a Structural Equation Model*. Academic Press.

Imteaj, A., Rahman, T., Hossain, M. K., Alam, M. S., & Rahat, S. A. (2017). An IoT based Fire Alarming and Authentication System for Workhouse using Raspberry Pi 3. *ECCE 2017 - International Conference on Electrical, Computer and Communication Engineering*, 899–904. 10.1109/ECACE.2017.7913031

Imteaj, A., Rahman, T., Hossain, M. K., & Zaman, S. (2017). IoT based autonomous percipient irrigation system using raspberry Pi. *19th International Conference on Computer and Information Technology*, 563–568. 10.1109/ICCITECHN.2016.7860260

Innovation. (2016). 51 Corporate Chat bots Across Industries Including Travel, Media, Retail, And Insurance. *CBinsights*. Retrieved September 22, 2017 from https://www.cbinsights.com/research/corporate-chat bots-innovation/

Inversini, A., Eynard, D., Marchiori, E., & Gentile, L. (2012). Destinations Similarity Based on User Generated Pictures. In *Information and Communication Technologies in Tourism 2012*. Wien: Springer-Verlag.

IoT Analytics. (2015). *The 10 most popular Internet of Things applications right now*. Retrieved September 29, 2017, from http://iot-analytics.com/10-internet-of-things-applications/

Jamalipour, A., Nikookar, H., & Ruggieri, M. (2016). *Digitising the Industry Internet of Things Connecting the Physical, Digital and Virtual Worlds*. River Publishers.

Jap, S. D. (1999). Pie-Expansion Efforts: Collaboration Processes in Buyer-Supplier Relationships. *JMR, Journal of Marketing Research*, *36*(4), 461–475. doi:10.2307/3152000

Jarvinen, J. (2016). *The use of digital analytics for measuring and optimizing digital marketing Performance*. Retrieved from https://jyx.jyu.fi/dspace/bitstream/handle/123456789/51512/978-951-39-6777-2_vaitos21102016.pdf?sequence=1

Jia, J. (2003). *CSIEC (Computer simulator in educational communication): An intelligent web-based teaching system for foreign language learning*. arXiv preprint cs/0312030

Jing, Q., Vasilakos, A. V., Wan, J., Lu, J., & Qiu, D. (2014). Security of the Internet of Things: Perspetctives and challenges. *Wireless Networks*, *20*(8), 2481–2501. doi:10.100711276-014-0761-7

Jin, S.-A. A., & Bolebruch, J. (2009). Avatar Based Advertising in Second Life. *Journal of Interactive Advertising*, *10*(1), 51–60. doi:10.1080/15252019.2009.10722162

Johnson, L., Levine, A., Smith, R., & Stone, S. (2010). Simple augmented reality. The 2010 Horizon Report. Austin, TX: The New Media Consortium.

Johnson, J. L. (1999). Strategic integration in industrial distribution channels: Managing the interfirm relationship as a strategic asset. *Journal of the Academy of Marketing Science*, *27*(1), 4–18. doi:10.1177/0092070399271001

Johnson, L., Adams Becker, S., Estrada, V., & Freeman, A. (2015). *NMC Horizon Report: 2015 Higher Education Edition*. Austin, TX: The New Media Consortium. Retrieved from http://www.nmc.org/pdf/2012-horizon-report-HE.pdf

Johnson, L., Adams, S., & Cummins, M. (2012). *The NMC Horizon Report: 2012 Higher Education Edition*. Austin, TX: The New Media Consortium. Retrieved from http://redarchive.nmc.org/publications/horizon-report-2012-higher-ed-edition

Joreskog, K. G. (1970). Estimation and testing of simplex models. *British Journal of Mathematical & Statistical Psychology*, *23*(2), 121–145. doi:10.1111/j.2044-8317.1970.tb00439.x

Judah Philips. (2014). *Digital analytics primer*. Pearson Education, Inc.

Kannan, P. K., & Li, H. (2017). Digital marketing: A framework, review and research agenda. *International Journal of Research in Marketing*, *34*(1), 22–45. doi:10.1016/j.ijresmar.2016.11.006

Kaplan, A., & Haenlein, M. (2010). Users of the world, unite! The challenges and opportunities. *Business Horizons of Social Media*, *53*(1), 59–68. doi:10.1016/j.bushor.2009.09.003

Kaplan, L. B., Szybillo, G. J., & Jacoby, J. (1974). Components of perceived risk in product purchase: A cross-validation. *The Journal of Applied Psychology*, *59*(3), 382–393. doi:10.1037/h0036657

Kaplan, S., & Garrick, B. J. (1981). On the quantitative definition of risk. *Risk Analysis*, *1*(1), 11–27. doi:10.1111/j.1539-6924.1981.tb01350.x PMID:11798118

Keefe, L. M. (2008). Marketing defined. *Marketing News*, *42*(1), 28–29.

Kejariwal, A., & Orsini, F. (2016). On the definition of real-time: applications and systems. In 2016 IEEE TrustCom/BigDataSE/ISPA (pp. 2213–2220). IEEE Computer Society. doi:10.1109/TrustCom.2016.0341

Kerly, A., Hall, P., & Bull, S. (2007). Bringing chat bots into education: Towards natural language negotiation of open learner models. *Knowledge-Based Systems*, *20*(2), 177–185. doi:10.1016/j.knosys.2006.11.014

Khan, I. U., Shahzad, M. U., & Hassan, M. A. (2017). Internet of Things (IoTs): Applications in Home Automation. *International Journal of Science and Advance Technology*, *5*(1), 79–84.

Khan, N., Yaqoob, I., Ibrahim, A. T. H., Inayat, Z., Waleed, K. M. A., Alam, M., ... Gani, A. (2014). Big Data: Survey, Technologies, Opportunities, and Challenges. *The Scientific World Journal*, *2014*, 712826. doi:10.1155/2014/712826 PMID:25136682

Kim, H.-W., Gupta, S., & Koh, J. (2011). Investigating the intention to purchase digital items in social networking communities: A customer value perspective. *Information & Management*, *48*(6), 228–234. doi:10.1016/j.im.2011.05.004

Kim, Y., Park, Y., & Choi, J. (2017). A study on the adoption of IoT smart home service: Using Value-based Adoption Model. *Total Quality Management & Business Excellence*, *28*(9-10), 1149–1165. doi:10.1080/14783363.2017.1310708

Kirsch, L. J. (1996). The Management of Complex Tasks in Organizations: Controlling the Systems Development Process. *Organization Science*, *7*(1), 1–21. doi:10.1287/orsc.7.1.1

Kolodziejczyk, B. (2015). *The 5 next trends in electronics*. Retrieved from https://www.weforum.org/agenda/2015/08/5-next-trends-in-electronics/

Kothandaraman, P., & Wilson, D. T. (2001). The Future of Competition: Value-Creating Networks. *Industrial Marketing Management*, *30*(4), 379–389. doi:10.1016/S0019-8501(00)00152-8

Kotler, P., Kartajata, H., & Setiawan, I. (2017). *Marketing 4.0 – Mudança do Tradicional para o Digital*. Lisboa: Actual.

Kounavis, C. D., Kasimati, A. E., & Zamani, E. D. (2012). Enhancing the tourism experience through mobile augmented reality: Challenges and prospects. *International Journal of Engineering Business Management*, 4.

Kowalski, S., Pavlovska, K., & Goldstein, M. (2009, July). Two case studies in using chat bots for security training. In *IFIP World Conference on Information Security Education* (pp. 265-272). Springer.

Kozinets, R. V. (2012). Me/my research/avatar. *Journal of Business Research*, *65*(4), 478–482. doi:10.1016/j.jbusres.2011.02.025

KPMG. (2017). *Still searching for a better customer experience*. Retrieved September 24, 2017, from https://assets.kpmg.com/content/dam/kpmg/xx/pdf/2017/07/searching-for-a-better-customer-web.pdf

Kranz, M., Roalter, L., & Michahelles, F. (2010). Things That Twitter: Social Networks and the Internet of Things. *Proceedings of the Pervasive 2010, the Citizen Internet of Things 2010 workshop.*

Kurnia, S., & Johnston, R. B. (2001). Adoption of efficient consumer response: The issue of mutuality. *Supply Chain Management*, *6*(5), 230–241. doi:10.1108/13598540110407778

Kurnia, S., & Johnston, R. B. (2003). Adoption of efficient consumer response: Key issues and challenges in Australia. *Supply Chain Management*, *8*(3), 251–262. doi:10.1108/13598540310484645

Kuyucu, M. (2013). *The Transformation of Traditional Newspaper to New Global Media with the QR Code*. Athens: ATINER'S Conference Paper Series, No: CBC2013-0894.

Lai, K. Y., Cheng, L. S., Yee, L. S., Leng, L. W., & Ling, T. P. (2015). WeeliciousCuisine Quick Response (QR). *International Conference on E-Commerce (ICoEC).*

Laudon, K., & Laudon, J. (2016). *Managing Information Systems: Managing the Digital Firm* (14th ed.). Pearson Education International.

Lederer, A. L., Maupin, D. J., Sena, M. P., & Zhuang, Y. (2000). The technology acceptance model and the World Wide Web. *Decision Support Systems*, *29*(3), 269–282. doi:10.1016/S0167-9236(00)00076-2

Lee, B. (2017). All Talk: How Chat bots And AI Will Transform The Way We Do Business. *Forbes*. Retrieved July 20, 2017, from https://www.forbes.com/sites/forbestechcouncil/2017/03/16/all-talk-how-chat bots-and-ai-will-transform-the-way-we-do-business/#7fd34e67280e

Lee, R.-H., Chen, A.-Y., Chiang, C.-C., Chen, Y.-S. A., & Liu, C.-H. (2016). A preliminary design and implementation of location-based mobile advertising schemes with plot placement animation over a cyber-physical system. In *2016 International Conference on Networking and Network Applications* (pp. 196–201). Academic Press. 10.1109/NaNA.2016.89

Lee, H. L., So, K. C., & Tang, C. S. (2000). Value of information sharing in a two-level supply chain. *Management Science*, *46*(5), 626–643. doi:10.1287/mnsc.46.5.626.12047

Lee, I., & Lee, K. (2015). The Internet of Things (IoT): Applications, investments, and challenges for enterprises. *Business Horizons*, *58*(4), 431–440. doi:10.1016/j.bushor.2015.03.008

Lee, J., Lapira, E., Bagheri, B., & Kao, H. A. (2013). *Recent Advances and Trends in Predictive Manufacturing Systems. Big Data Environment Manufacturing Letters*, *1*, 38–41. doi:10.1016/j.mfglet.2013.09.005

Lee, M.-C. (2009). Factors influencing the adoption of internet banking: An integration of TAM and TPB with perceived risk and perceived benefit. *Electronic Commerce Research and Applications*, *8*(3), 130–141. doi:10.1016/j.elerap.2008.11.006

Lee, Y., Kozar, K. A., & Larsen, K. R. T. (2003). The Technology Acceptance Model: Past, Present, and the Futur. *Communications of the Association for Information Systems*, *12*, 752–780.

Leonard,, L., Berry, L. P. C., & S. H. H. (2002). Managing the Total Customer Experience | MIT Sloan Management Review. *MIT Sloan Management Review*, *43*(3), 85.

Leonard-Barton, D., & Deschamps, I. (1988). Managerial influence in the implementation of new technology. *Management Science*, *34*(10), 1252–1265. doi:10.1287/mnsc.34.10.1252

Levy, H. (2016). *Gartner Predicts a Virtual World of Exponential Change.* Retrieved from http://www.gartner.com/smarterwithgartner/gartner-predicts-a-virtual-world-of-exponential-change/

Lievrouw, L., & Livingstone, S. (Eds.). (2006). Handbook of new media: Social shaping and consequences of ICTs (Updated student ed.). London: Sage.

Lievrouw, L. (2004). What's changed about new media? introduction to the fifth anniversary issue of new media & society. *New Media & Society*, *6*(1), 9–15. doi:10.1177/1461444804039898

Light, M., & Maybury, M. T. (2002). Personalized Multimedia Information Access: Ask Questions, Get Personalized Answers. *Communications of the ACM*, *45*(5), 54–59. doi:10.1145/506218.506246

Linaza, M., Marimon, D., Carrasco, P., Alvarez, R., Montesa, J., Aguilar, S. R., & Diez, G. (2012). Evaluation of mobile augmented reality applications for tourism destinations. In M. Fuchs, F. Ricci, & L. Cantoni (Eds.), *Information and Communication Technologies in Tourism.* Wien: Springer-Verlag. doi:10.1007/978-3-7091-1142-0_23

Lindblom, A., & Olkkonen, R. (2008). An analysis of suppliers' roles in category management collaboration. *Journal of Retailing and Consumer Services*, *15*(1), 1–8. doi:10.1016/j.jretconser.2007.01.002

Linstone, H. A., & Turoff, M. (Eds.). (1975). *The Delphi method: techniques and applications.* Boston: Addison-Wesley.

Li, S., Da Xu, L., & Zhao, S. (2015). The internet of things: A survey. *Information Systems Frontiers*, *17*(2), 243–259. doi:10.100710796-014-9492-7

Lister, M., Dovey, J., Giddings, S., Grant, I., & Kelly, K. (2009). *New media: A critical introduction* (2nd ed.). London: Routledge.

Liu, M., Cao, E., & Salifou, C. K. (2016). Pricing strategies of a dual-channel supply chain with risk aversion. *Transportation Research Part E, Logistics and Transportation Review*, *90*, 108–120. doi:10.1016/j.tre.2015.11.007

Liu, X., Cheng, B., Zhai, Z., & Chen, J. (2016). Design and implement of push notification server in mobile IoT environment. *Proceedings - 2016 IEEE International Conference on Mobile Services, MS 2016*, 208–209. 10.1109/MobServ.2016.40

Li, Y., Cui, V., & Liu, H. (2017). Dyadic specific investments, absorptive capacity, and manufacturers' market knowledge acquisition: Evidence from manufacturer–distributor dyads. *Journal of Business Research*, *78*, 323–331. doi:10.1016/j.jbusres.2016.12.028

Lu, Y., Zhou, T., & Wang, B. (2009). Exploring Chinese users' acceptance of instant messenger using the theory of planned behavior, the technology acceptance model, and the flow theory. *Computers in Human Behavior*, *25*(1), 29–39. doi:10.1016/j.chb.2008.06.002

Magalhãe, G. G. M. S. (2016). *Estudo de segurança nos principais protocolos da Internet das Coisas* (Monografia em Engenharia Computação). Instituto de Ciências Exatas. Departamento de Ciências da Computação, Universidade de Brasília.

Ma, H. (2011). Internet of things: Objectives and scientific challenges. *Journal of Computer Science and Technology*, *26*(6), 919–924. doi:10.100711390-011-1189-5

Mandilas, A., Karasavvoglou, A., Nikolaidis, M., & Tsourgiannis, L. (2013). Predicting Consumer's Perceptions in On-line Shopping. *Procedia Technology*, *8*, 435–444. doi:10.1016/j.protcy.2013.11.056

Mani, Z., & Chouk, I. (2017). Drivers of consumers' resistance to smart products. *Journal of Marketing Management*, *33*(1–2), 76–97. doi:10.1080/0267257X.2016.1245212

Marakos, P. (2015). *Implementing QR code in museums and archaeological sites.* International Workshop on Virtual Archaeology: Museums & Cultural Tourism, Delphi, Greece.

Marcus, D. (2016). Messenger Platform at F8. *Facebook Newsroom.* Retrieved July 21, 2017, from https://newsroom.fb.com/news/2016/04/messenger-platform-at-f8/

Marques, R. P., & Batista, J. C. L. (Eds.). (2017). *Information and communication overload in the digital age.* IGI Global. doi:10.4018/978-1-5225-2061-0

Marr, B. (2014). Dear IKEA: Your Customer Service Is Terrible. *LinkedIn.* Retrieved September 19, 2017 from www.linkedin.com/pulse/20140325060328-64875646-dear-ikea-your-customer-service-is-terrible/

McCormick, K. (2017). *How to Use Social Media for Local Internet Marketing.* Retrieved from: https://thrivehive.com/how-to-use-social-media-for-local-internet-marketing/

McKnight, D. H., & Chervany, N. L. (2002). What trust means in e-commerce customer relationship. *International Journal of Electronic Commerce, 6*(2).

McMillan, S., & Morrison, M. (2006). Coming of age with the internet: A qualitative exploration of how the internet has become an integral part of young people's lives. *New Media & Society, 8*(1), 73–95. doi:10.1177/1461444806059871

Medic, S., & Pavlovic, N. (2014). Mobile Technologies in Museum Exhibitions. *Turizam, 18*(4), 166–174. doi:10.5937/Turizam1404166M

Medina, C. A., Pérez, M. R., & Trujillo, L. C. (2017). IoT Paradigm into the Smart City Vision: A Survey. *2017 IEEE International Conference on Internet of Things (iThings) and IEEE Green Computing and Communications (GreenCom) and IEEE Cyber, Physical and Social Computing (CPSCom) and IEEE Smart Data (SmartData)*, 695–704. doi:10.1109/iThings-GreenCom-CPSCom-SmartData.2017.109

Mehta. (2015). *Internet of Things Connectivity Challenges – IoT Device Connectivity.* Retrieved September 29, 2017, from http://iotworm.com/internet-of-things-connectivity-challenges/

Melillo, Riccio, Di Perna, & Di Baja. (2017). Wearable Improved Vision System for Color Vision Deficiency Correction. *IEEE Journal of Transactional Engineering in Health and Medicine, 5*, 3800101-3800107.

Menard, R. J., & Bryan, M. (2005). *U.S. Patent No. 6,967,562.* Washington, DC: U.S. Patent and Trademark Office.

Mendes, P. (2011). Social-driven Internet of Connected Objects. *Proceedings of the Interconnecting Smart Objects with the Internet Workshop.*

Mesquita, L. F., Anand, J., & Brush, T. H. (2008). Comparing the resource-based and relational views: Knowledge transfer and spillover in vertical alliances. *Strategic Management Journal, 29*(9), 913–941. doi:10.1002mj.699

Meyer, C., Schwager, A., & Meyer Schwager, A., C. (2007). Understanding Customer Experience. *Harvard Business Review, 85*(2), 116. doi:10.1108/00242539410067746 PMID:17345685

Meyrick, J. (2013). The Delphi method and health research. *Health Education, 103*(1), 7–16. doi:10.1108/09654280310459112

Microsoft. (2017). *Enhance cross channel retail personalization with IoT.* Retrieved September 23, 2017, from https://blogs.microsoft.com/iot/2017/01/16/enhance-cross-channel-retail-personalization-with-iot/

Miguel, P., & Baptista, F. (2015). *Modelos de negócios para a internet em Big Data:Muzzley, um estudo de caso* (Master dissertation). Retrieved from http://hdl.handle.net/10362/17375

Mihalčová, B., & Pružinský, M. (2015). Category Management – Project Implementation in E-Shop. *Procedia Economics and Finance*, *23*, 267–275. doi:10.1016/S2212-5671(15)00555-9

Mill, J. S. (1998). Utilitarianism. Oxford, UK: Oxford University Press.

Mill, J. S. (2012). Utilitarianism. Spark Notes Editors, Chapter 2.

Miorandi, D., Sicari, S., De Pellegrini, F., & Chlamtac, I. (2012). Internet of things: Vision, applications and research challenges. *Ad Hoc Networks*, *10*(7), 1497–1516. doi:10.1016/j.adhoc.2012.02.016

Misugi, G., Freitas, C. O. A., & Efing, A. C. (2016). Releitura da privacidade diante das novas tecnologias: Realidade aumentada, reconhecimento facial e internet das coisas. *Revista Jurídica Cesumar*, *16*(2), 427–453. doi:10.17765/2176-9184.2016v16n2p427-453

Mital, M., Choudhary, P., Pani, A., Chang, V., & Sun, Z. (2015). Adoption of cloud based Internet of Things in India: A multiple theory perspective. *International Journal of Information Management*. doi:10.1016/j.ijinfomgt.2016.02.011

Mitchell, A. A. (2013). *Advertising exposure, memory and choice*. Psychology Press.

Mitchell, A., Henderson, I., & Searls, D. (2008). Reinventing direct marketing: With VRM inside. *Journal of Direct. Data and Digital Marketing Practice*, *10*(1), 3–15. doi:10.1057/dddmp.2008.24

Mitchell, V.-W. (1999). Consumer perceived risk: Conceptualisations and models. *European Journal of Marketing*, *33*(1/2), 163–195. doi:10.1108/03090569910249229

Möller, K., & Rajala, A. (2007). Rise of strategic nets - New modes of value creation. *Industrial Marketing Management*, *36*(7), 895–908. doi:10.1016/j.indmarman.2007.05.016

Moon, J.-W., & Kim, Y.-G. (2001). Extending the TAM for a World-Wide-Web context. *Information & Management*, *38*(4), 217–230. doi:10.1016/S0378-7206(00)00061-6

Moore, G. C., & Benbasat, I. (1991). Development of an instrument to measure the perceptions of adopting an information technology innovation. *Information Systems Research*, *2*(3), 173–191. doi:10.1287/isre.2.3.192

Morgan, D. L. (1996). *Focus groups as qualitative research* (Vol. 16). Thousand Oaks, CA: Sage publications.

Morgan, D. L. (2010). Reconsidering the role of interaction in analyzing and reporting focus groups. *Qualitative Health Research*, *20*(5), 718–722. doi:10.1177/1049732310364627 PMID:20406996

Morgan, N. A., Kaleka, A., & Gooner, R. A. (2007). Focal supplier opportunism in supermarket retailer category management. *Journal of Operations Management*, *85*(2), 116. doi:10.1016/j.jom.2006.05.006

Mo, Y., Kim, T. H., Brancik, K., Dickinson, D., Lee, H., Perrig, A., & Sinopoli, B. (2012). Cyber–Physical Security of a Smart Grid Infrastructure. *Proceedings of the IEEE*, *100*(1), 195–209. doi:10.1109/JPROC.2011.2161428

Mukhopadhyay, S. C., & Suryadevara, N. K. (2014). Internet of Things: Challenges and Opportunities. In S. C. Mukhopadhyay (Ed.), *Internet of Things. Smart Sensors, Measurement and Instrumentation* (Vol. 9, pp. 1–17). Springer International Publishing; doi:10.1007/978-3-319-04223-7_1

Muller, P., Damgaard, M., Litchfield, A., Lewis, M., & Hörnle, J. (2011). Consumer behaviour in a digital environment. Brussels: Academic Press.

Munzel, A., Meyer-Waarden, L., & Galan, J.-P. (2017). Getting by or getting ahead on social networking sites? the role of social capital in happiness and well-being. *Technological Forecasting and Social Change*. doi:10.1016/j.techfore.2017.06.031

Myung, S. K., Ju, W., McDonnell, D. D., Lee, Y. J., Kazinets, G., Cheng, C. T., & Moskowitz, J. M. (2009). Mobile phone use and risk of tumors: A meta-analysis. *Journal of Clinical Oncology, 27*(33), 5565–5572. doi:10.1200/JCO.2008.21.6366 PMID:19826127

Naci, H., & Ioannidis, J. P. A. (2015). Evaluation of Wellness Determinants and Interventions by Citizen Scientists. *Journal of the American Medical Association, 314*(2), 121. doi:10.1001/jama.2015.6160 PMID:26068643

Narula, J. (2013). Are We Upto Speed? From Big Data to Rich Insights in CV Imaging for a hyper connected World JACC. *Cardiovascular Imaging, 6*, 1222–1224. doi:10.1016/j.jcmg.2013.09.007 PMID:24229779

Nazz, E., & Sokoler, T. (2001). Walky for embodied microblogging: sharing mundane activities through augmented everyday objects. *Proceedings of the 13th International Conference on Human-Computer Interaction with Mobile Devices and Services.*

Negrine, A. (1998). *Terapias corporais: a formação pessoal do adulto.* Porto Alegre: Edita.

Neto, I. R. O. (2015). *Síntese de Requisitos de Segurança para Internet das Coisas Baseada em Modelos em Tempo de Execução (Dissertação).* Instituto de Informática da Universidade Federal de Góias.

Network Working Group. (1973). RFC 439, PARRY Encounters the DOCTOR. *The Internet Engineering Task Force (Internet Society).* Retrieved from http://tools.ietf.org/html/rfc439

Ng, I. C. L., & Smith, L. (2012). An integrative framework of value. *Review of Marketing Research,* (9), 207–243.

Ng, I. C. L., & Wakenshaw, S. Y. L. (2014). The role of marketing in the design and innovation of future products in the connected digital economy. In *Proceedings of the 13th International Research Conference In Service Management* (pp. 27–30). La Londe les Maures, France: Academic Press.

Ng, E. S., Schweitzer, L., & Lyons, S. T. (2010). New generation, great expectations: A field study of the millennial generation. *Journal of Business and Psychology, 25*(2), 281–292. doi:10.100710869-010-9159-4

Ng, I. C. L. (2013). New business and economic models in the connected digital economy. *Journal of Revenue and Pricing Management, 12*(6), 1–7.

Ng, I. C. L., & Wakenshaw, S. Y. L. (2017). The Internet-of-Things: Review and research directions. *International Journal of Research in Marketing, 34*(1), 3–21. doi:10.1016/j.ijresmar.2016.11.003

Nguyen, Islam, Hossan, & Jang. (2017). Current Status and Performance Analysis of Optical Camera Communication Technologies for 5G Networks. *IEEE Translations and Content Mining,* 5, 4574-4594.

Nguyen, B., & Simkin, L. (2017). The Internet of Things (IoT) and marketing: The state of play, future trends and the implications for marketing. *Journal of Marketing Management, 33*(1–2). doi:10.1080/0267257X.2016.1257542

Ning, H., & Wang, Z. (2011). Future Internet of Things Architecture: Like Mankind Neural System or Social Organization Framework? *IEEE Communications Letters, 15*(4), 461–463. doi:10.1109/LCOMM.2011.022411.110120

Nitti, M., Girau, R., Atzori, L., Iera, L., & Morabito, G. (2012). A subjective model for trustworthiness evaluation in the social Internet of things. *Proceedings of the IEEE 23rd Int. Symp.*, 18–23. 10.1109/PIMRC.2012.6362662

Nolin, J., & Olson, N. (2016). The Internet of Things and convenience. *Internet Research, 26*(2), 360–376. doi:10.1108/IntR-03-2014-0082

Nunnally, J. C. (1978). *Psychometric theory* (2nd ed.). New York: McGraw-Hill.

O'Brien, H. L. (2010). The influence of hedonic and utilitarian motivations on user engagement: The case of online shopping experiences. *Interacting with Computers*, *22*(5), 344–352. doi:10.1016/j.intcom.2010.04.001

O'Brien, H. M. (2016). The Internet of Things. *Journal of Internet Law*, *19*(12), 1–20. PMID:27441587

O'Neill, S. (2016). Kayak debuts an ambitious Facebook Messenger bot. *tnooz*. Retrieved July 25, 2017 from https://www.tnooz.com/article/kayak-facebook-messenger-bot/

Oen, H. M. (2015). *Interoperability at the Application Layer in the Internet of Things*. Academic Press.

O'Leary, D. (2013). *Artificial Intelligence and Big Data. IEEE Intelligent Systems, 28*(2).

Oliveira, J. S. P., Costa, M. M., Wille, M. F. C., & Marchiori, P. Z. (2008). *Introdução ao Método Delphi*. Curitiba: Mundo Material. Available in http://eprints.rclis.org/12888/

Örnek, M. (2016). *Geo-Targeting (Coğrafi Hedefleme) Nedir?* Retrieved 07.06.2017, from http://www.pazarlamasyon.com/sozluk/geo-targeting-cografi-hedefleme-nedir/

Ozturk, A. B., Nusair, K., Okumus, F., & Hua, N. (2016). The role of utilitarian and hedonic values on users' continued usage intention in a mobile hotel booking environment. *International Journal of Hospitality Management*, *57*(August), 106–115. doi:10.1016/j.ijhm.2016.06.007

Pagani, M., & Pardo, C. (2017). *The impact of digital technology on relationships in a business network*. Academic Press. 10.1016/j.indmarman.2017.08.009

Park, W. H., & Cheong, Y. G. (2017). IoT smart bell notification system: Design and implementation. *19th International Conference on Advanced Communication Technology*, 298–300. 10.23919/ICACT.2017.7890101

Parolini, C. (1999). The Value Net. A Tool for Competitive Strategy. Chichester, UK: John Wiley and Sons.

Parry, G., Brax, S., Maull, R., & Ng, I. (2016). Operationalising IoT for reverse supply: The development of use-visibility measures. *Supply Chain Management*, *21*(2), 228–244. doi:10.1108/SCM-10-2015-0386

Pavlou, P. A. (2003). Consumer acceptance of electronic commerce: Integrating trust and risk with the technology acceptance model. *International Journal of Electronic Commerce*, *7*(3), 101–134.

Pelaez, A., Chen, C.-W., & Chen, Y. X. (2017). Effects of Perceived Risk on Intention to Purchase: A Meta-Analysis. *Journal of Computer Information Systems*, 1–12. doi:10.1080/08874417.2017.1300514

Pereira, J. C. H. (2015). *Modelos de Negócio e a Internet of Things. (Dissertação de Mestrado em Gestão)*. Faculdade de Economia da Universidade de Coimbra.

Pesonen, J., & Horster, E. (2012). Near field communication technology in tourism. *Tourism Management Perspectives*, *4*, 11–18. doi:10.1016/j.tmp.2012.04.001

Pew Research Center. (2017). *Social Media Fact Sheet*. Pew Research Center Internet & Technology. Retrieved from September 9, 2017 from http://www.pewinternet.org/fact-sheet/social-media/

Phelps, J. E., Nowak, G. J., & Ferrell, E. (2000). Privacy concerns and consumer willingness to provide personal information. *Journal of Public Policy & Marketing*, *19*(1), 27–41. doi:10.1509/jppm.19.1.27.16941

Piconez, S. C., Bertholo, P., & Adalberto, M. (2017, July). *Desafios da Sustentabilidade Educacional e as contribuições da Tecnologia Cloud Computing*. Paper presented at Workshop de Desafios da Computação aplicada à Educação in XXXVII Congresso da Sociedade Brasileira de Computação.

Piekarski, W., Gunther, B., & Thomas, B. (1999). Integrating virtual and augmented realities in an outdoor application. In *International Workshop on Augmented Reality (IWAR'99) Proceedings. 2nd IEEE and ACM*. IEEE. 10.1109/IWAR.1999.803805

Pikkarainen, T., Pikkarainen, K., Karjaluoto, H., & Pahnila, S. (2004). Consumer acceptance of online banking: An extension of the technology acceptance model. *Internet Research, 14*(3), 224–235. doi:10.1108/10662240410542652

Ping, L. C., & Chee, T. S. (2009). Online discussion boards for focus group interviews: An exploratory study. *Journal of Educational Enquiry, 2*(1).

Plimmer, G. (2010). Scoring points: How Tesco continues to win customer loyalty. *Journal of Revenue and Pricing Management, 9*(4), 377–378. doi:10.1057/rpm.2010.17

Pongle, P., & Chavan, G. (2015). A survey: attacks on RPL and 6LoWPAN in IoT. *2015 International Conference on Pervasive Computing: advance Communication Technology and Application for Society*. 10.1109/PERVASIVE.2015.7087034

Porter, M. E. (1985). *Competitive Advantage: Creating and Sustaining Superior Performance*. Competitive Advantage Creating and Sustaining Superior Performance; doi:10.1108/eb054287

Porter, M. E., & Heppelmann, J. E. (2014). How Smart, Connected Products Are Transforming Competition. *Harvard Business Review, 92*(11).

Prayoga, T., & Abraham, J. (2016). Behavioral Intention to Use IoT Health Device: The Role of Perceived Usefulness, Facilitated Appropriation, Big Five Personality Traits, and Cultural Value Orientations. *Iranian Journal of Electrical and Computer Engineering, 6*(4), 1751–1765.

Prensky, M. (2001). Digital natives, digital immigrants part 1. *On the Horizon, 9*(5), 1–6. doi:10.1108/10748120110424816

Pruet, P., Ang, C. S., Farzin, D., & Chaiwut, N. (2015). Exploring the Internet of "Educational Things" (IoET) in rural underprivileged areas. *2015 12th International Conference on Electrical Engineering/Electronics, Computer, Telecommunications and Information Technology (ECTI-CON)*, 1–5. doi:10.1109/ECTICon.2015.7207125

Pura, M. (2005). Linking perceived value and loyalty in location-based mobile services. *Managing Service Quality: An International Journal, 15*(6), 509–538. doi:10.1108/09604520510634005

PwC. (2017). *2017 Telecommunications Trends*. Retrieved from https://www.strategyand.pwc.com/trend/2017-telecommunications-industry-trends

Pyo, C., Kang, H., Kim, N., & Bang, H. (2013). IoT technology's trends and prospect. *KICS Thesis, 30*(8), 3-10.

Qader, M. A. (2017). *DualDB: An Efficient LSM-based Publish/Subscribe Storage System*. SSDBM '17, Chicago, IL.

Quirk, R. E. J. (2017). Are Your Company's Consumer Electronics Exempt from FCC Marketing Regulations? *IEEE Consumer Electronics Magazine, 6*(1), 22–26. doi:10.1109/MCE.2016.2640578

Rakestraw, T. L., Eunni, R. V., & Kasuganti, R. R. (2013). The mobile apps industry: A case study. *Journal of Business Cases and Applications*, 1-26.

Ramayah, T., & Ignatius, J. (2005). Impact of perceived usefulness, perceived ease of use and perceived enjoyment on intention to shop online. *ICFAI Journal of Systems Management, 3*(3), 36–51.

Rao, A. (2017). Why the Facebook Messenger Bot Platform was a Failure. *Medium*. Retrieved July 25, 2017 from https://medium.com/voicelandia/why-the-facebook-messenger-bot-platform-is-a-failure-so-far-d305b2d4e1df

Rao, H., Monin, P., & Durand, R. (2005). Border crossing: Bricolage and the erosion of categorical boundaries in French gastronomy. *American Sociological Review*, *70*(6), 968–991. doi:10.1177/000312240507000605

Rauniar, R., Rawski, G., Yang, J., & Johnson, B. (2014). Technology acceptance model (TAM) and social media usage: An empirical study on Facebook. *Journal of Enterprise Information Management*, *27*(1), 6–30. doi:10.1108/JEIM-04-2012-0011

Rauschnabel, P. A., Brem, A., & Ivens, B. S. (2015). Who will buy smart glasses? *Computers in Human Behavior*, *49*, 635–647. doi:10.1016/j.chb.2015.03.003

Rawlins, L. K. (2016, April 13). Facebook chat bots to replace call centres. *iTWeb*. Retrieved June 04, 2017, from http://www.itweb.co.za/index.php?option=com_content&view=article&id=151438

Ray, S., Jin, Y., & Raychowdhury, A. (2016). The Changing Computing Paradigm With Internet of Things: A Tutorial Introduction. *IEEE Design & Test*, *33*(2), 76–96. doi:10.1109/MDAT.2016.2526612

Regulamento (UE) 2016/679 do Parlamento Europeu e do Conselho, de 27 de abril de 2016.

Ribeiro, A. B. (2016). Estudo de Internet das Coisas e Suas Tecnologias. *Proceedings of the XXIV Seminário de Iniciação Científica.*

Roberts, D. W., Strohbehn, J. W., Hatch, J. F., Murray, W., & Kettenberger, H. (1986). A frameless stereotaxic integration of computerized tomographic imaging and the operating microscope. *Journal of Neurosurgery*, *65*(4), 545–549. doi:10.3171/jns.1986.65.4.0545 PMID:3531430

Rocha, K. E., Mendes, J. V., Santa-Eulalia, L. A., & Moris, V. A. S. (2017). Adoption of IoT in Logistics & Supply Chain Management: A systematic literature review. In *XXXVII Encontro Nacional de Engenharia de Produção "A Engenharia de Produção e as novas tecnologias produtivas: indústria 4.0, manufatura aditiva e outras abordagens avançadas de produção"*. Joinville, SC: Brasil.

Rogers, C. (2017). How smart tech is injecting new life into healthcare. *Marketing Week*, *57*(1), 4. doi:10.1525/cmr.2014.57.1.67

Rogers, E. M. (1983). *Diffusion of Innovations*. New York: The Free Press.

Rouillard, J. (2008). Contextual QR Codes. In *Proceedings of the Third International Multi-Conference on Computing in the Global Information Technology – ICCGI, 50-55, Conference Publishing Services of IEEE Computer Society*, 51.

Russell, H. (2013). *How augmented-reality ads could change everything*. Retrieved 15.08.2013 from: http://news.cnet.com/8301-1023_3-57591998-93/how-augmented-reality-ads-could-change everything/

Russell, M. (2012). *11 Amazing Augmented Reality Ads*. Retrieved 10.03.2017 from http://www.businessinsider.com/11-amazing-augmented-reality-ads-2012-1?op= 1.

Rust, R. T. (2017). Academic Press. *Leading the Future of Marketing*, *34*(1), 1. doi:10.1016/j.ijresmar.2017.03.001

Sagoe, D. (2012). Precincts and prospects in the use of focus groups in social and behavioral science research. *Qualitative Report*, *17*(15), 1–16.

Salandra, G. (2017). China, WeChat, and the Origins of Chat bots: What we can learn from the successes and shortcomings of the popular platform. *Chat botsmagazine*. Retrieved September 24, 2017 from https://chatbotsmagazine.com/china-wechat-and-the-origins-of-chatbots-89c481f15a44

Samy, H. (2012, Winter). Exploring The Use Of Mobile Phone Technology In Marketing Airline Services IN EGYPT. *International Journal of Medical Microbiology*, *7*(3).

Santos, D. O., & Freitas, E. B. (2016). A internet das coisas e o big data inovando os negócios. *Revista REFAS*, *3*(1), 1–18.

Santos, P. M. P. (2016). *Internet das coisas: O desafio da privacidade (Dissertação de Mestrado em Sistemas de informação Organizacionais)*. Escola Superior de Ciências Empresariais, Instituto Politécnico de Setúbal.

Sarkar, A. (2011). Impact of utilitarian and hedonic shopping values on individual's perceived benefits and risks in online shopping. *International Management Review*, *7*(1), 58–65.

Schlicht, M. (2017). The Complete Beginner's Guide To Chat bots. *Chat Bots Magazine*. Retrieved September 30, 2017 from https://chatbotsmagazine.com/the-complete-beginner-s-guide-to-chatbots-8280b7b906ca

Scott, D. (2008). Anna from IKEA is intellectually challenged (but she has a sense of humor). *Webinknow*. Retrieved September 19, 2017 from www.webinknow.com/2008/08/anna-from-ikea.html

Searls, D. (2012). *The intention economy: when customers take charge*. Boston, MA: Harvard Business Review Press.

Seligman, M. E. P. (2011). *Flourish: A Visionary New Understanding of Happiness and Well-being*. New York: The Free Press.

Selinger, M., Sepulveda, A., & Buchan, J. (2013). *Education and the Internet of Everything: How ubiquitous connectedness can help transform pedagogy* (White paper). San Diego, CA: Cisco Systems. Retrieved from http://www.cisco.com/web/strategy/docs/education/education_internet.pdf

Shaikh, A. A., & Karjaluoto, H. (2015). Mobile banking adoption: A literature review. *Telematics and Informatics*, *32*(1), 129–142. doi:10.1016/j.tele.2014.05.003

Shamir, N., & Shin, H. (2016). Public Forecast Information Sharing in a Market with Competing Supply Chains. *Management Science*, *62*(10), 2994–3022. doi:10.1287/mnsc.2015.2261

Shang, W., Ha, A. Y., & Tong, S. (2016). Information sharing in a supply chain with a common retailer. *Management Science*, *62*(1), 245–263. doi:10.1287/mnsc.2014.2127

Shankar, V., Inman, J. J., Mantrala, M., Kelley, E., & Rizley, R. (2011). Innovations in shopper marketing: Current insights and future research issues. *Journal of Retailing*, *87*(1), 29–42. doi:10.1016/j.jretai.2011.04.007

Sharkey, J. (2008). A Virtual Travel Agent with All the Answers. *The New York Times*. Retrieved September 19, 2017 from http://www.nytimes.com/2008/03/04/business/04road.html

Sharma, S., & Sharma, V. (2014). Innovations in marketing- "with special reference to innovative services. *International Journal of Business and Management*, *1*(2), 50–54.

Shatte, A., Holdsworth, J., & Lee, I. (2014). Mobile augmented reality-based context-aware library management system. *Expert Systems with Applications*, *41*(5), 2174–2185. doi:10.1016/j.eswa.2013.09.016

Shawar, B. A., & Atwell, E. (2002). *A comparison between ALICE and Elizabeth chat botsystems*. University of Leeds, School of Computing research report 2002.19.

Shawar, B. A., & Atwell, E. (2007). Chat bots: are they really useful? *LDV Forum*, *22*(1), 29-49.

Shea, Fu, Sun, Cai, Ma, Fan, & Gong. (2017). Location-Based Augmented Reality With Pervasive Smartphone Sensors: Inside and Beyond Pokemon Go! *IEEE Translations and Content Mining, 5*, 9619-9631.

Shepardson, D. (2015). *Cars are vulnerable to wireless hacking*. Retrieved from http://www.detroitnews.com/story/business/autos/%0A2015/02/08/report-cars-vulnerable-wireless-hacking/%0A23094215/

Shin, D. (2010). The effects of trust, security & privacy in social networking: A security-based approach to understand the pattern of adoption. *Interacting with Computers*, *22*(5), 428–438. doi:10.1016/j.intcom.2010.05.001

Sicari, S., Rizzardi, A., Grieco, L. A., & Coen-Porisini, A. (2015). Security, privacy and trust in Internet of Things: The road ahead. *Computer Networks*, *76*, 146–164. doi:10.1016/j.comnet.2014.11.008

Silva, I. S., Veloso, A. L., & Keating, J. B. (2014). Focus group: Considerações teóricas e metodológicas. *Revista Lusófona de Educação*, (26): 175–190.

Sing, P. & Pandey, M. (2014). Augmented Reality Advertising: An Impactful Platform for New Age Consumer Engagement. *IOSR Journal of Business and Management, 16*(2), 24-28.

Singh, H., & Singh, S. (2014). Near Field Communication (NFC). *International Journal of Enhanced Research in Science Technology & Engineering, 3*(3), 198-201. Available online at: www.erpublications.com

Singh, S. (2014). *Future Of Personal Mobility - Life With Or Without Ownership Of Cars*. Retrieved from https://www.forbes.com/sites/sarwantsingh/2014/04/23/future-of-personal-mobility-life-with-or-without-ownership-of-cars/#b662720467f4

Sinha & Park. (2017). *Building an Effective IoT Ecosystem for Your Business*. Springer. Available in http://www.springer.com/gp/book/9783319573908

Sisodia, Verma, & Vyas. (2016). A Discounted Fuzzy Relational Clustering of Web Users' Using Intuitive Augmented Sessions Dissimilarity Metric. *IEEE Translations and Content Mining, 4*, 6883-6893.

Skard, S. E., Nysveen, H., & Thorbjørnsen, H. (2016). Influences of Perceived E-Service Risks: The Moderating Role of Perceived Benefits. *e-Service Journal*, *10*(1), 1–23. doi:10.2979/eservicej.10.1.01

Skilton, M., & Ng, I. (2016). *What the apple versus FBI debacle taught us*. Retrieved September 6, 2017, from http://blogs.scientificamerican.com/guest-blog/what-the-apple-vs-%0Afbi-debacle-taught-us/

Skulmoski, G. J., Hartman, F. T., & Krahn, J. (2007). The Delphi Method for Graduate Research. *Journal of Information Technology Education: Research, 6*, 1-21. Retrieved November, 2017, from https://www.learntechlib.org/p/111405/

Smola, K. W., & Sutton, C. D. (2002). Generational differences: Revisiting generational work values for the new millennium. *Journal of Organizational Behavior*, *23*(4), 363–382. doi:10.1002/job.147

Soares, S. (2012). A Framework That Focuses on the Data in Big Data Governance. *IBM Data Management*, *13*(June). Retrieved from http://ibmdatamag.com/2012/06/a-frameworkthat-focuses-on-the-data-in-big-data-governance

Sokolovska, A. (2016). From E-Commerce to Conversational Commerce: Chat bots and Virtual Assistant. *Guided Selling*. Retrieved September 30, 2017 from https://www.guided-selling.org/from-e-commerce-to-conversational-commerce/

Song, Y.-S., & Lee, J.-M. (2012). Mobile device ownership among international business students: A road to the ubiquitous library. *RSR. Reference Services Review*, *40*(4), 574–588. doi:10.1108/00907321211277378

Spiteri, J. M., & Dion, P. (2004). Customer value, overall satisfaction, end-user loyalty, and market performance in detail intensive industries. *Industrial Marketing Management*, *33*(8), 675–687. doi:10.1016/j.indmarman.2004.03.005

Stamford, C. (2015). *Gartner Says 6.4 Billion Connected "Things" Will Be in Use in 2016, Up 30 Percent From 2015*. Retrieved from http://www.gartner.com/newsroom/id/3165317

Statista. (2018a). *Forecast of Big Data market size, based on revenue, from 2011 to 2026 (in billion U.S. dollars)*. Retrieved from https://www.statista.com/statistics/254266/global-big-data-market-forecast/

Statista. (2018b). *Retail e-commerce sales worldwide from 2014 to 2021 (in billion U.S. dollars).* Retrieved from https://www.statista.com/statistics/379046/worldwide-retail-e-commerce-sales/

Statista. (2018c). *Number of Netflix streaming subscribers worldwide 2011-2017.* Retrieved from: https://www.statista.com/statistics/250934/quarterly-number-of-netflix-streaming-subscribers-worldwide/

Steiner, I. (2011). Emma virtual assistant comes to eBay. *eCommerceBytes.* Retrieved September 4, 2017 from http://www.ecommercebytes.com/C/abblog/blog.pl?/pl/2011/1/ 1296444129.html

Stewart, D. W., & Shamdasani, P. N. (2014). *Focus groups: Theory and practice* (3rd ed.). Thousand Oaks, CA: Sage publications.

Stock, B., dos Santos Ferreira, P., & Ernst, C-P. H. (2016). *Does Perceived Health Risk Influence Smartglasses Usage? The Drivers of Wearable Device Usage.* DOI .10.1007/978-3-319-30376-5_2

Strahilevitz, M., & Meyers, J. G. (1998). Donations to charity as purchase incentives: How well they work may depend on what you are trying to sell. *The Journal of Consumer Research, 24*(1), 434–446. doi:10.1086/209519

Strömmer, E., Kaartinen, J., Pärkkä, J., Ylisaukko-oja, A., & Korhonen, I. (2006). Application of Near Field Communication for Health Monitoring in Daily Life. *Proceedings of the 28th IEEE EMBS Annual International Conference.*

Sundmaeker, H., Guillemin, P., Friess, P., & Woelfflé, S. (2010). *Vision and challenges for realising the Internet of Things.* Cluster of European Research Projects on the Internet of Things—CERP IoT.

Sundmaeker, H., Guillemin, P., Friess, P., & Woelfflé, S. (Eds.). (2010). Vision and Challenges for Realising the Internet of Things. European Commission, Information Society and Media, Brussels.

Sundmaeker, H., Guillemin, P., Friess, P., & Woeelfflé, S. (2010). *Vision and Challenges for Realising the Internet of Things, CERP-IoT.* European Commission.

Sundmaeker, H., Guillemin, P., Friess, P., & Woelfflé, S. (2010). Vision and challenges for realising the Internet of Things. Cluster of European Research Projects on the Internet of Things. *European Commission, 3*(3), 34–36.

Sun, W., Hung, J., & Huang, C. (2017). Implementation of SVM Broken Prediction Notification System with Park Sport Equipment. *2017 International Conference on Applied System Innovation,* 99–102. 10.1109/ICASI.2017.7988356

Suo, H., Wan, J., Zou, C., & Liu, J. (2012). Security in the Internet of Things: A Review. *Proceedings of the International Conference on Computer Science and Electronics Engineering,* 648-652. 10.1109/ICCSEE.2012.373

Sutherland, I. E. (1968). A head-mounted three-dimensional display. *Proceedings of the Fall Joint Computer Conference,* 757–764. 10.1145/1476589.1476686

Swan, M. (2015). Connected car: Quantified self becomes quantified car. *Journal of Sensor and Actuator Networks, 4*(1), 2–29. doi:10.3390/jsan4010002

Sweeney, J. C., & Soutar, J. R. (2001). Consumer Perceived Value: The Development of a Multiple Item Scale. *Journal of Retailing, 77*(2), 203–220. doi:10.1016/S0022-4359(01)00041-0

Syberfeldt, A., Danielsson, O., & Gustavsson, P. (2017). Augmented Reality Smart Glasses in the Smart Factory: Product Evaluation Guidelines and Review of Available Products. *IEEE Translations and Content Mining, 5,* 9118-9130.

Tang, S., Yu, Y., Zimmermann, R., & Obana, S. (2015). Efficient geo-fencing via hybrid hashing: A combination of bucket selection and in-bucket binary search. *ACM Trans. Spatial Algorithms Syst., 1*(2). DOI: 10.1145/2774219

Tate, A. (2016). The 5 Most Inspiring Chat bots On Facebook Messenger. *AdEspresso*. Retrieved July 25, 2017 from https://adespresso.com/academy/blog/5-inspiring-chat bots-facebook-messenger/

Taylor, B. (2013). *Augmented reality applications – from the consumer to the business*. Retrieved 07.06.2017, from http://www.creativeguerrillamarketing. com/augmented-reality/augmented-reality-applications-from the -consumer-to-the-business/

Taylor, J. (2013). *In Database Analytics*. Decision Management Solutions.

Taylor, J. W. (1974). The role of risk in consumer behavior. *Journal of Marketing*, *38*(April), 54–60. doi:10.2307/1250198

Taylor, S., & Todd, P. (1995). Assessing IT usage: The role of prior experience. *Management Information Systems Quarterly*, *19*(4), 561–570. doi:10.2307/249633

Texas Instruments. (2014). *Application areas for the Internet of Things*. Retrieved September 6, 2017, from http://www.ti.com/ww/en/internet_of_things/iot-applications.html

The Boston University. (2012). *Empowerment Scale*. Center for Psychiatric Rehabilitation.

Thierer, A. D. (2015). The internet of things and wearable technology: Addressing privacy and security concerns without derailing innovation. *Richmond Journal of Law & Technology*, *21*(2), 10.

Thrasher, J. (2013). *9 Examples of RFID & NFC in Marketing*. Retrieved 01.01.2018 from: https://blog.atlasrfidstore.com/examples-of-rfid-nfc-marketing

Tilson, D., Lyytinen, K., & Sorensen, C. (2010). Research Commentary--Digital Infrastructures: The Missing IS Research Agenda. *Information Systems Research*, *21*(4), 748–759. doi:10.1287/isre.1100.0318

To, P.-L., Liao, C., & Lin, T.-H. (2007). Shopping motivations on Internet: A study based on utilitarian and hedonic value. *Technovation*, *27*(12), 774–787. doi:10.1016/j.technovation.2007.01.001

Torchia, M. (2017).*Worldwide Semiannual Internet of Things Spending Guide*. Retrieved from http://www.idc.com/getdoc.jsp?containerId=prUS42209117

Toshniwal, R., Dastidar, K. G., & Nath, A. (2015). Big data security issues and challenges. *International Journal of Innovative Research in Advanced Engineering*, *2*(2).

Tsai, C.-W., Lai, C.-F., & Vasilakos, A. V. (2014). Future internet of things: Open issues and challenges. *Wireless Networks*, *20*(8), 2201–2217. doi:10.100711276-014-0731-0

Tung, F.-C., Chang, S.-C., & Chou, C.-M. (2008). An extension of trust and TAM model with IDT in the adoption of the electronic logistics information system in HIS in the medical industry. *International Journal of Medical Informatics*, *77*(5), 324–335. doi:10.1016/j.ijmedinf.2007.06.006 PMID:17644029

Turel, O., Serenko, A., & Bontis, N. (2010). User acceptance of hedonic digital artifacts: A theory of consumption values perspective. *Information & Management*, *47*(1), 53–59. doi:10.1016/j.im.2009.10.002

Ulaga, W., & Eggert, A. (2006). Relationship value and relationship quality: Broadening the nomological network of business-to-business relationships. *European Journal of Marketing*, *40*(3/4), 311–327. doi:10.1108/03090560610648075

Urban, E. C. (1999). *The information warrior. In Technology and society* (pp. 493–501). Prentice-Hall, Inc.

Valmohammadi, C. (2016). Examining the perception of Iranian organizations on Internet of Things solutions and applications. *Industrial and Commercial Training*, *48*(2), 104–108. doi:10.1108/ICT-07-2015-0045

Van der Heijden, H. (2004). User Acceptance of Hedonic Information Systems. *Management Information Systems Quarterly*, *28*(4), 695–704. doi:10.2307/25148660

Van Kranenburg, R., & Bassi, A. (2012). IoT Challenges. *Communications in Mobile Computing*, *1*(1), 9. doi:10.1186/2192-1121-1-9

Van Krevelen, D., & Poelman, R. (2010). A survey of augmented reality technologies, applications and limitations. *International Journal of Virtual Reality*, *9*(2), 1–20.

Vargo, S. L., & Lusch, R. F. (2017). Service-dominant logic 2025. *International Journal of Research in Marketing*, *34*(1), 46–67. doi:10.1016/j.ijresmar.2016.11.001

Velikic, G., Bjelica, M., Ignjatov, N., Cetkovic, M., & Kastelan, I. (2014). The Personalization of a Cloud Ecosystem: Adding Dimensions to Situational Awareness. *Proceedings of the X International Symposium on Industrial Electronics INDEL*, 248-252.

Venkatesh, V. (2000). Determinants of perceived ease of use: Integrating control, intrinsic motivation, and emotion into the technology acceptance model. *Information Systems Research*, *11*(4), 342–365. doi:10.1287/isre.11.4.342.11872

Venkatesh, V., & Davis, F. D. (1996). A model of the antecedents of perceived ease of use: Development and test. *Decision Sciences*, *27*(3), 451–481. doi:10.1111/j.1540-5915.1996.tb01822.x

Venkatesh, V., & Morris, M. G. (2000). Why don't men ever stop to ask for directions? Gender, social influence, and their role in technology acceptance and usage behavior. *Management Information Systems Quarterly*, *24*(1), 115–139. doi:10.2307/3250981

Venkatesh, V., Morris, M. G., Davis, G. B., & Davis, F. D. (2003). User acceptance of information technology: Toward a unified view. *Management Information Systems Quarterly*, *27*(3), 425–478. doi:10.2307/30036540

Vergara, S. C. (2008). *Métodos de pesquisa em administração* (3rd ed.). São Paulo: Atlas.

Viriyavisuthisakul, S. (2017). Automatic Queue Monitoring in Store Using A Low-Cost IoT Sensing Platform.2017. *IEEE International Conference on Consumer Electronics - Taiwan*, 53–54.

Von Hippel, E. (1986). Lead Users: A Source of Novel Product Concepts. *Management Science*, *32*(7), 791–805. doi:10.1287/mnsc.32.7.791

Vygotsky, L. S. (2007). *A Formação Social da Mente* (7th ed.). São Paulo: Martins Fontes.

Wakefield, J. (2016). Would you want to talk to a machine? *BBC News*. Retrieved August 28, 2017 from http://www.bbc.com/news/technology-36225980

Walter, A., Ritter, T., & Gemünden, H. G. (2001). Value Creation in Buyer-Seller Relationships: Theoretical Considerations and Empirical Results from a Supplier's Perspective. *Industrial Marketing Management*, *30*(4), 365–377. doi:10.1016/S0019-8501(01)00156-0

Wang, Iwai, & Sato. (2017). Supporting Trembling Hand Typing Using Optical See-Through Mixed Reality. *IEEE Translations and Content Mining*, *5*, 10700-10708.

Wang, Y. (2011). *Destination Marketing and Management: Scope, Definition and Structures, Destination Marketing and Management* (Y. Wang & A. Pizam, Eds.). CAB International.

Watson, C., McCarthy, J., & Rowley, J. (2013). Consumer attitudes towards mobile marketing in the smart phone era. *International Journal of Information Management*, *33*(5), 840-849. 10.1016/j.ijinfomgt.2013.06.004

Weber, R. H. (2010). Internet of Things – New security and privacy challenges. *Computer Law & Security Review*, *26*(1), 23–30. doi:10.1016/j.clsr.2009.11.008

Weinberg, B. D., Milne, G. R., Andonova, Y. G., & Hajjat, F. M. (2015). Internet of Things: Convenience vs. privacy and secrecy. *Business Horizons*, *58*(6), 615–624. doi:10.1016/j.bushor.2015.06.005

Weiser, M., Gold, R., & Brown, J. S. (1999). The origins of ubiquitous computing research at PARC in the late 1980s. *IBM Systems Journal*, *38*(4), 693–696. doi:10.1147j.384.0693

Weizenbaum, J. (1966). ELIZA—a computer program for the study of natural language communication between man and machine. *Communications of the ACM*, *9*(1), 36–45. doi:10.1145/365153.365168

West, R. L., & Turner, L. H. (2010). *Uses and Gratifications Theory. In Introducing Communication Theory: Analysis and Application* (pp. 392–401). Boston: McGraw-Hill.

Wheaton, B., Muthen, B., Alwin, D. F., & Summers, G. (1977). Assessing Reliability and Stability in Panel Models. *Sociological Methodology*, *8*(1), 84–136. doi:10.2307/270754

Willems, K., Smolders, A., Brengman, M., Luyten, K., & Schöning, J. (2017). The path-to-purchase is paved with digital opportunities: An inventory of shopper-oriented retail technologies. *Technological Forecasting and Social Change*, *124*, 228–242. doi:10.1016/j.techfore.2016.10.066

Williams, A. P., & Hobson, J. S. P. (1995). Virtual reality and tourism: Fact or fantasy? *Tourism Management*, *16*(6), 423–427. doi:10.1016/0261-5177(95)00050-X

Wilson, S., & Peterson, L. (2002). The anthropology of online communities. *Annual Review of Anthropology*, *31*(1), 449–467. doi:10.1146/annurev.anthro.31.040402.085436

Wither, Tsai, & Azuma. (2011). Indirect augmented reality. *Computers &Graphics Elsevier Ltd*, *35*, 810–822.

Wortmann, F., & Fluchter, K. (2015). Internet of Things: Technology and Value Added. *Business & Information Systems Engineering*, *57*(3), 221–224. doi:10.100712599-015-0383-3

WP29. (2014). *Opinion 8/2014 on the on Recent Developments on the Internet of Things.* Retrieved September 29, 2017, from http://ec.europa.eu/justice/data-protection/article-29/documentation/opinion-recommendation/files/2014/wp223_en.pdf

Wry, T., Lounsbury, M., & Jennings, P. D. (2014). Hybrid vigor: Securing venture capital by spanning categories in nanotechnology. *Academy of Management Journal*, *57*(5), 1309–1333. doi:10.5465/amj.2011.0588

Wu, J., Chen, J., & Dou, W. (2017). The Internet of Things and interaction style: The effect of smart interaction on brand attachment. *Journal of Marketing Management*, *33*(1–2), 61–75. doi:10.1080/0267257X.2016.1233132

Xia, F. L., Yang, L., & Wang, A., & Vinel. (2012). Internet of Things. International Journal of Communication Systems. *Special Issue: Internet of Things*, *25*, 1101–1102.

Xu, H., Luo, X., Carroll, J. M., & Rosson, M. B. (2011). The Personalization Privacy Paradox. *Decision Support Systems*, *51*(1), 42–52. doi:10.1016/j.dss.2010.11.017

Yadav, M. S., & Pavlou, P. (2014). Marketing in computer-mediated envorironments: Research Synthesis and new directions. *Journal of Marketing*, *78*(1), 20–40. doi:10.1509/jm.12.0020

Yadav, M., & Varadarajan, R. (2005). Interactivity in the electronic marketplace: An exposition of the concept and implications for research. *Journal of the Academy of Marketing Science*, *33*(4), 585–603. doi:10.1177/0092070305278487

Yang, H., Yu, J., Zo, H., & Choi, M. (2016). User acceptance of wearable devices: An extended perspective of perceived value. *Telematics and Informatics*, *33*(2), 256–269. doi:10.1016/j.tele.2015.08.007

Yang, L., Yang, S. H., & Plotnick, L. (2013). How the Internet of Things technology enhances emergency response operations. *Technological Forecasting and Social Change*, *80*(9), 1854–1867. doi:10.1016/j.techfore.2012.07.011

Yang, Z., Su, C., & Fam, K.-S. (2012). Dealing with Institutional Distances in International Marketing Channels: Governance Strategies That Engender Legitimacy and Efficiency. *Journal of Marketing*, *76*(3), 41–55. doi:10.1509/jm.10.0033

Yao, D.-Q., Yue, X., & Liu, J. (2008). Vertical cost information sharing in a supply chain with value-adding retailers. *Omega*, *36*(5), 838–851. doi:10.1016/j.omega.2006.04.003

Ye, G., & van Raaij, W. F. (1997). What inhibits the mere-exposure effect: Recollection or familiarity? *Journal of Economic Psychology*, *18*(6), 629–648. doi:10.1016/S0167-4870(97)00027-5

Yerpude, S., & Singhal, T. K. (2017). Internet of Things and its impact on Business Analytics. *Indian Journal of Science and Technology*, *10*(5), 1–6. doi:10.17485/ijst/2017/v10i5/109348

Yogitha, K., & Alamelumangai, V. (2016). Recent Trends and Issues in IoT. *International Journal of Advances in Engineering Research, 11*(1).

Yoo, Y., Lyytinen, K., Boland, R., Berente, N., Gaskin, J., Schutz, D., & Srinivasan, N. (2012). *The next wave of digital innovation: opportunities and challenges.* A report of an NSF research workshop on digital challenges in innovation research.

Yousuf, M. I. (2007). Using Experts' Opinions Through Delphi Technique Practical Assessment. *Research & Evaluation, 12*(4).

Yu, J., Zo, H., Kee Choi, M., & Ciganek, A. P. (2013). User acceptance of location-based social networking services: An extended perspective of perceived value. *Online Information Review*, *37*(5), 711–730. doi:10.1108/OIR-12-2011-0202

Yuki, A., Xing, X., Takahiro, H., & Shojiro, N. (2010). Mining people's trips from large scale geo-tagged photos. In *Proceedings of the 18th ACM international conference on Multimedia (MM '10)*. ACM. doi: 10.1145/1873951.1873971

Zagorsky, J. (2015). Almost 90% of Americans Have Unlimited Texting. *Instant Census*. Retrieved September 25, 2017 from https://instantcensus.com/blog/almost-90-of-americans-have-unlimited-texting

Zajonc, R. B. (1968). Attitudinal effects of mere exposure. *Journal of Personality and Social Psychology, 9*(2), 1.

Zhang, H., Qu, D., Hou, Y., & Huang, F. (2016). Synthetic Modelling Method for Large Scale Terrain Based on Hydrology. *IEEE Translations and Content Mining, 1*, 6238-6249

Zhang, H. (2002). Vertical information exchange in a supply chain with duopoly retailers. *Production and Operations Management*, *11*(4), 531–546. doi:10.1111/j.1937-5956.2002.tb00476.x

Zhang, M., Yao, D., & Zhou, Q. (2012, December). The Application and Design of QR Code in Scenic Spot's eTicketing System-A Case Study of Shenzhen Happy Valley. *International Journal of Science and Technology.*, *2*(12), 817–822.

Zhao, H., & Shibasaki, R. (2005). A novel system for tracking pedestrians using multiple single-row laser-range scanners. *IEEE Transactions on Systems, Man, and Cybernetics. Part A, Systems and Humans*, *35*(2), 283–291. doi:10.1109/TSMCA.2005.843396

Zhao, K., & Ge, L. (2013). A survey on the Internet of Things security. *Proceedings of the 9th International Conference on Computational Intelligence and Security*, 663–667. 10.1109/CIS.2013.145

Zhao, X., Flynn, B. B., & Roth, A. V. (2007). Decision sciences research in China: Current status, opportunities, and propositions for research in supply chain management, logistics, and quality management. *Decision Sciences*, *38*(1), 39–80. doi:10.1111/j.1540-5915.2007.00148.x

Zhu, X. (2016). Managing the risks of outsourcing: Time, quality and correlated costs. *Transportation Research Part E, Logistics and Transportation Review*, *90*, 121–133. doi:10.1016/j.tre.2015.06.005

About the Contributors

Dora Simões received her PhD in Informatics Engineering from University of Porto, Portugal, in 2008. Actually, she is an Assistant Professor in computer science area, at the Higher Institute of Accounting and Administration – University of Aveiro (ISCA-UA), Portugal. She is member of the CIC. DIGITAL/Digimedia - Digital Media and Interaction. Her current research interests include information and knowledge management, organizational information systems, relationship marketing and collaborative virtual networks, and information and communication technologies in education. She has published in various conferences and journals, nationals and internationals.

Belem Barbosa is Adjunct Professor at the University of Aveiro and member of GOVCOPP, the research unit on Governance, Competitiveness and Public Policy. She received her PhD in Business and Management Studies – specialisation in Marketing and Strategy from the University of Porto, Portugal. Her research interests lie primarily in the area of internet marketing and consumer behaviour, including word-of-mouth communication, sustainability marketing, tourism and events marketing.

Sandra Filipe has a PhD in Marketing, a MSc in Management (specialisation in Marketing and Strategy) both from the ISCTE Business School - University Institute of Lisbon (ISCTE –IUL), and a degree in Management from the Faculty of Economics, University of Coimbra (FEUC). She is an Assistant Professor at the Institute of Accounting and Administration, University of Aveiro (ISCA-UA), teaching undergraduate and post graduate courses of management, research methodologies, marketing plans, and other marketing themes. She is a member of the research unit on Competitiveness, Governance and Public Policies (GOVCOPP). Her main research interests are: marketing research, digital marketing, corporate social responsibility, relational marketing and consumer behaviour. She has published in several academic journals.

* * *

Ricardo Abreu is a researcher and doctoral student in Public Policy at ISCTE - Instituto Universitário de Lisboa, where he also obtained a master's degree in Science, Innovation and Society, with a dissertation on innovation and Social Network Analysis. He holds a postgraduate degree in Data Analysis for Social Sciences from ISCTE-IUL and Governance & Competitive Intelligence at ISCSP-UL, and has a degree in Consumer Sciences from IPAM - the Portuguese Institute of Administration and Marketing of Lisbon. He has also collaborated as a lecturer at ISCTE-IUL and ISCSP-UL, as well as a consultant in the field of marketing and innovation.

Carolina Afonso has a PhD in Marketing, Universidad Complutense de Madrid. Invited Assistant Professor of Marketing & Strategy Advance/ISEG, Lisbon School of Economics and Management, University of Lisbon.

Filomena Almeida graduated in Social and Organizational Psychology, Master in Organizational Behavior, PhD in Management with specialization in HRM. Training and Selection Manager in the commercial aviation sector from 1990 to 1991; Human Resources Manager in several organizations from 1991 to 1996, CEO of DSHO consulting from 1997 to 2006. Professor in higher education from 1990 to 1996 at ULHT and ISPA. Since 1996, professor at ISCTE IUL, director of Soft Skills Lab, working group member for e-learning, and online learning coordinator.

Elodie Attié is a PhD student at the Toulouse School of Management Research (France). Her main research interests concern new technology acceptance and the adoption and use of the Internet of Things technologies, as well as the impact of the Internet of Things on consumer behavior, wellbeing and empowerment.

Pedro Beça has a degree in Electronic and Telecommunications Engineering from the University of Aveiro (2002), a Master's degree in Electronic and Telecommunications Engineering from the University of Aveiro (2006) and a PhD in Information and Communication in Digital Platforms from the University of Aveiro and the University of Porto (2013). He is an auxiliary professor in the Department of Communication and Art of the University of Aveiro since 2007 until the present and he is member of the CIC.Digital - Digital Media and Interaction/DigiMedia Research Group, Aveiro branch. His areas of interest are: use of mobile devices and participatory culture; Web and mobile applications development, especially in the conception, implementation and validation stages.

Isabel Borges has an engineering and MSc degree from Aveiro University and has been working on applied research on several national and international R&D programs since 1991. She has been responsible for the Consultancy group and then for the technology and services training and certification division, managing all training design, development, production and promotion of courses either in- or out-of-company. She has an active participation in several European programs and is currently working on RDI on IoT. She is an external evaluator of projects for the Innovation Agency, a reviewer of IEEE Communications Magazine and she is also author or co-author of several publications and books.

Filipe Cabral Pinto has a PhD from Queen Mary University of London in telecommunications and a degree in electrical engineering from the University of Coimbra. He is currently senior consultant at Altice Labs and a researcher at the Instituto de Telecomunicações for the IoT and Smart Cities areas.

Jiannong Cao received the MSc and PhD degrees in computer science from Washington State University, Pullman, Washington, in 1986 and 1990, respectively. He is currently the chair professor in the Department of Computing, The Hong Kong Polytechnic University, Hong Kong. His research interests include parallel and distributed computing, mobile computing, and big data analytics. He has served as a member of the editorial boards of several international journals, a reviewer for international journals/ conference proceedings, and also as an organizing/program committee member for many international conferences. He is a fellow of the IEEE and a senior member of the China Computer Federation.

Evrim Çeltek (Associate Professor) obtained her MBA in tourism business administration from Sakarya University (Turkey) and she obtained her PhD in tourism and hotel management from Anadolu University (Turkey). Her researches focused on tourism marketing, social media marketing, mobile marketing, e-commerce, mobile commerce, advergame and customer relationship management.

Valentina Chkoniya received her PhD in Technical Sciences by Murmansk State Technical University, Russia, in 2003. Currently, she is a professor at the University of Aveiro, Portugal, and managing partner of VT Mar (a marketing intelligence company). Valentina Chkoniya is a highly professional and experienced professor with a deep understanding and knowledge regarding management, based on a deep strategic perspective and building on more than 20 years of experience. Her current research interests include data analysis, decision support systems, marketing research, consumer behaviour and information technologies for retail.

Sumathi Doraikannan is presently working as a professor, Department of Computer Science and Engineering, at Malla Reddy Engineering College (Autonomous) Hyderabad, Telangana. She received the B.E Computer science and Engineering degree from Bharathiar University in 1994 and M.E Computer Science and Engineering degree from Sathyabama University in 2006, Chennai and completed her doctorate degree in Anna University, Chennai. She has secured 9th rank in the university. She has overall experience of 16 years out of which 6 years in industry, 10 years in teaching field. Her Research interests include Cloud computing, Network Security, Data Mining and Theoretical Foundations of computer science. She has published papers in international journal and conference. She has organized many international conferences and also acted as Technical Chair and tutorial presenter. She is a life member of ISTE. She has published few chapters in books under Wiley and IGI Global publications.

Min Chung Han, Ph.D., obtained her PhD in Business Administration at Sungkyunkwan University of South Korea. Her research interests are e-marketing including social media marketing and electronic commerce for small and medium size companies. She currently teaches at Kean University in the United States. Before embarking on her academic career, she was a business/financial journalist with wide experience in all aspects of the media including both print and broadcast. She worked for both Korean and English language media companies in South Korea and Singapore. Before moving to United States, she lived in China, Singapore and Canada.

Balachandrudu K. E. completed her B.E CSE in Gulbarga University in 1994, M.E CSE from Anna University in 2003. He has obtained Ph.D in Computer Science and Engineering MJP Rohilkhand University, Bareilly, India in 2012. He is working as a principal in Malla Reddy Institute of Engineering and Technology, Secunderabad. Seasoned Professional with over 20+ years of rich & extensive experience in Strategic Planning, General Administration, Educational Planning, Teaching and Student Relations. Her area of interest is Cloud computing. MANET, Ad hoc network, Security, wireless sensor network and Data mining. He is a life member of ISTE and CSI.

Armando Mateus is currently the CXO (Customer Experience Manager) and founder of TouchPoint Consulting Portugal, a company born from the need to help retail and FMCG professionals create touch points that allow an authentic and innovative way of improving performance, offering to their consumers and shoppers a unique experience. Armando Mateus is a highly professional and experienced manager oriented to people leadership and results, based on a deep strategic perspective and building on more than 25 years experience in the fast moving consumer goods (FMCG) industry, retail and technology. Major roles include CEO of nexium Customer Solutions, Category Management and Private Label Director of Jerónimo Martins Retail, Group Product Manager in Henkel and Market Research Manager in Procter & Gamble. With a MSc in Management by Universidade Católica Portuguesa and a MBA by Cranfield School of Management, he is an active speaker in national and international conferences, having also taught Innovation and New Product Introduction at ISCEM Portugal and Negotiation in an International Context at the International Selling Programme in the Dublin Institute of Technology.

Lars Meyer-Waarden is Professor at the Toulouse School of Management Research. His main research interests concern customer relationship management as well as consumer empowerment and wellbeing through digital products and services. He is the author of a book about the efficiency of loyalty programs, and has published lots of articles about these issues in international journals as in New York Wall Street Journal, Journal of Retailing, Journal of the Academy of Marketing Science, Journal of Marketing Management, European Journal of Marketing, Journal of Service Marketing, Journal of Business Research, Journal of Retailing and Consumer Services.

Anantha Raman Rathinam is working as a Professor in the department of Computer Science and engineering in Malla Reddy Institute of Engineering and Technology.

Tânia Ribeiro holds a master from the University of Aveiro (2016), a degree from the University of Trás-os-Montes and Alto Douro (2014), both in Multimedia Communication, and is now (2017) an is currently a PhD student in Information and Communication in Digital Platforms at the University of Aveiro. She's participating in the coordination of the American Corner Media Lab UA, a laboratory aimed at promoting interdisciplinary activities related to digital media and technological inclusion, with particular emphasis on 3D printing. Her main research activity has been in the field of HCI, mainly with regard to the gamification of health recovery activities.

Helena Rocha has a PhD in Social Work, invited Professor at ISCTE-IUL in Social Work and in the Soft Skills Lab associate researcher at CIES-IUL, research areas, education, e-learning, sustainability, ethics, environment, community intervention, and social policies.

Fernando Santiago is senior consultant and product manager at Altice Labs. In the last years, he has been involved in several M2M and IoT projects in different roles. Before, he worked as software developer and solution architect in several projects in areas of multimedia, desktop and web applications, video and audio technologies and telemedicine. He was a project manager and development team leader at PT Inovação for more than 10 years in the area of e-health and Telemedicine. He is graduated in Electronic and Telecommunications Engineering from University of Aveiro, Portugal.

Claudia Amaral Santos has a PhD in Linguistics (Terminology) by Universidade de Aveiro (UA) and Universidade Nova de Lisboa, and a Master in North-American Culture by Universidade Aberta. She has been an Assistant Professor at Instituto Superior de Contabilidade e Administração da Universidade de Aveiro (ISCA-UA) since 2001. Lectures all English subjects in first cycle degrees and specialization courses. Claudia Santos coordinates the Languages and Social Sciences field and International Mobility programs in her Department. She is a member of the Languages, Literatures and Cultures Research Centre (CLLC) at the Languages and Cultures Department of Universidade de Aveiro (DLC-UA). She participates regularly in several international projects and her main research interests are focused on education, marketing, internationalization and employability.

Prabha Selvaraj is working as a professor in the department of Computer Science and Engineering in Malla Reddy Institute of Engineering and technology, Secunderabad, Telangana. She has completed her B.E (Computer Science and Engineering) from Kongu Engineering College, Perundurai in 1998. M.E (Computer Science and Engineering) from Anna University, Chennai in 2005. She has completed her Ph.D. programme under the area Data Mining in Anna University, Chennai in the year 2016. She has a teaching experience of about 20 years. Her research interests include Database Systems, System Modelling, Compiler Design, Network Security, Data Mining and Information Retrieval System. She has published papers in various national and International journals and conferences. She has published few chapters in Wiley and IGI Global. She is a life member of ISTE and member of CSI.

Jiaxing Shen graduated from Software Engineering from Jilin University in 2014. Till now, he is doing Ph.D. study in the Hong Kong Polytechnic University. His research interests are pervasive computing data analytics and group dynamics.

Nuno Soares is a student of Multimedia Communication (masters degree) and is always very excited to experiment new web technologies, and adapt new better developing practices.

Mário Vairinhos is a professor at the Department of Communication and Arts of the University of Aveiro since 2001, researcher in the area of Interaction Design and Human-Computer Interaction, with particular interest in tangible Media and Mixed Reality. At the same time develops Digital Art work and Museography projects in interaction design. He was co-founder and editor of Mimesis Contemporary Art journal. Graduated in 1996 in Economics from the Faculty of Economics, University of Coimbra, in 2001 obtained the master's degree in digital arts at the School of Arts of Porto, Portuguese Catholic University. He holds a PhD in Communication Sciences and Technologies from the University of Aveiro and University of Porto.

Index

I

J

L

M

N

O

P

Q

R

S

T

U

V

W

Purchase Print, E-Book, or Print + E-Book

IGI Global books are available in three unique pricing formats:
Print Only, E-Book Only, or Print + E-Book. Shipping fees apply.

www.igi-global.com

Recommended Reference Books

ISBN: 978-1-5225-2016-0
© 2017; 375 pp.
List Price: $200

ISBN: 978-1-5225-0886-1
© 2017; 251 pp.
List Price: $160

ISBN: 978-1-5225-2075-7
© 2017; 2,266 pp.
List Price: $185

ISBN: 978-1-5225-1865-5
© 2017; 443 pp.
List Price: $200

ISBN: 978-1-5225-19614-4
© 2017; 365 pp.
List Price: $210

ISBN: 978-1-5225-1005-5
© 2015; 370 pp.
List Price: $205

Do you want to stay current on the latest research trends, product announcements, news and special offers?
Join IGI Global's mailing list today and start enjoying exclusive perks sent only to IGI Global members.
Add your name to the list at **www.igi-global.com/newsletters.**

Publisher of Peer-Reviewed, Timely, and Innovative Academic Research

IGI Global
DISSEMINATOR OF KNOWLEDGE

www.igi-global.com Sign up at www.igi-global.com/newsletters facebook.com/igiglobal twitter.com/igiglobal linkedin.com/igiglobal

Ensure Quality Research is Introduced to the Academic Community

Become an IGI Global Reviewer for Authored Book Projects

The overall success of an authored book project is dependent on quality and timely reviews.

In this competitive age of scholarly publishing, constructive and timely feedback significantly expedites the turnaround time of manuscripts from submission to acceptance, allowing the publication and discovery of forward-thinking research at a much more expeditious rate. Several IGI Global authored book projects are currently seeking highly qualified experts in the field to fill vacancies on their respective editorial review boards:

Applications may be sent to:
development@igi-global.com

Applicants must have a doctorate (or an equivalent degree) as well as publishing and reviewing experience. Reviewers are asked to write reviews in a timely, collegial, and constructive manner. All reviewers will begin their role on an ad-hoc basis for a period of one year, and upon successful completion of this term can be considered for full editorial review board status, with the potential for a subsequent promotion to Associate Editor.

If you have a colleague that may be interested in this opportunity, we encourage you to share this information with them.

IGI Global
DISSEMINATOR OF KNOWLEDGE
www.igi-global.com

Celebrating 30 Years of Scholarly Knowledge Creation & Dissemination

InfoSci®-Books

A Collection of 4,000+ Reference Books Containing Over 87,000 Full-Text Chapters Focusing on Emerging Research

This database is a collection of over 4,000+ IGI Global single and multi-volume reference books, handbooks of research, and encyclopedias, encompassing groundbreaking research from prominent experts worldwide. These books are highly cited and currently recognized in prestigious indices such as: Web of Science™ and Scopus®.

Librarian Features:

- No Set-Up or Maintenance Fees
- Guarantee of No More Than A 5% Annual Price Increase
- COUNTER 4 Usage Reports
- Complimentary Archival Access
- Free MARC Records

Researcher Features:

- Unlimited Simultaneous Users
- No Embargo of Content
- Full Book Download
- Full-Text Search Engine
- No DRM

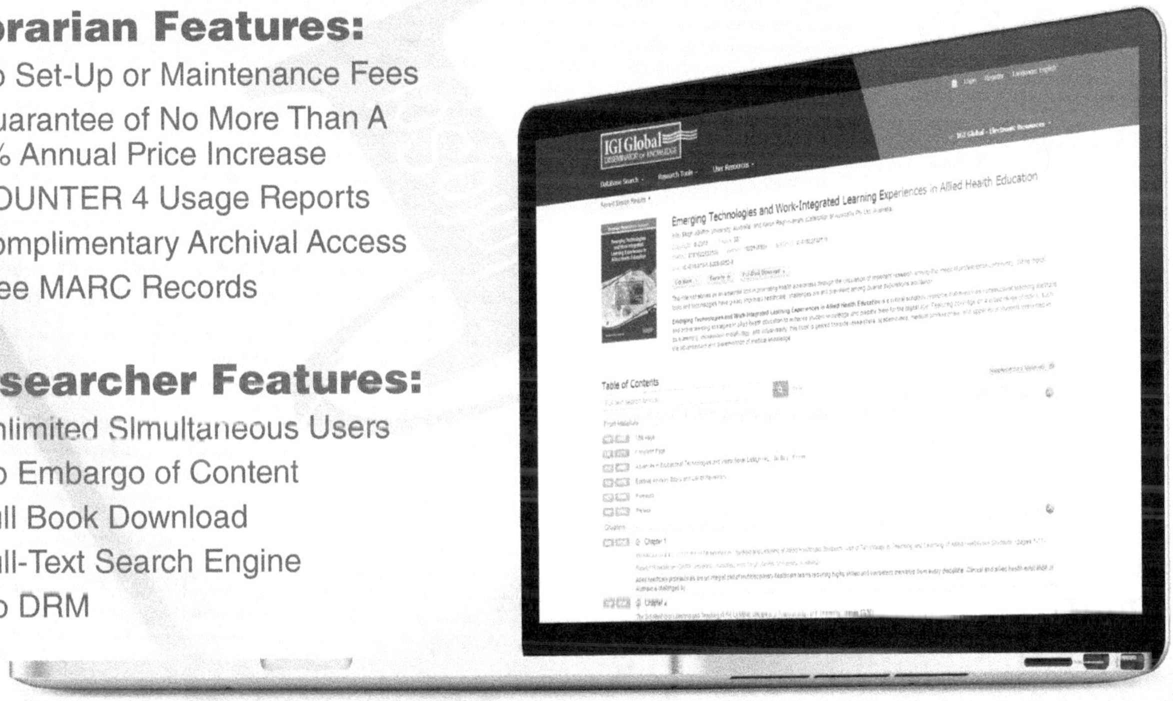

To Find Out More or To Purchase This Database:

www.igi-global.com/infosci-books

eresources@igi-global.com • Toll Free: 1-866-342-6657 ext. 100 • Phone: 717-533-8845 x100

IGI Global
DISSEMINATOR OF KNOWLEDGE
www.igi-global.com

IGI Global Proudly Partners with

eContent Pro International

Expert Copy Editing

eContent Pro International copy editors, with over 70 years of combined experience, will provide complete and comprehensive care for your document by resolving all issues with spelling, punctuation, grammar, terminology, jargon, semantics, syntax, consistency, flow, and more. In addition, they will format your document to the style you specify (APA, Chicago, etc.). All edits will be performed using Microsoft Word's Track Changes feature, which allows for fast and simple review and management of edits.

Additional Services

eContent Pro International also offers fast and affordable proofreading to enhance the readability of your document, professional translation in over 100 languages, and market localization services to help businesses and organizations localize their content and grow into new markets around the globe.

IGI Global Authors Save 25% on eContent Pro International's Services!

Scan the QR Code to Receive Your 25% Discount

The 25% discount is applied directly to your eContent Pro International shopping cart when placing an order through IGI Global's referral link. Use the QR code to access this referral link. eContent Pro International has the right to end or modify any promotion at any time.

Email: customerservice@econtentpro.com

econtentpro.com

Information Resources Management Association

IRMA INTERNATIONAL EST. 1987

Advancing the Concepts & Practices of Information Resources Management in Modern Organizations

Become an IRMA Member

Members of the **Information Resources Management Association (IRMA)** understand the importance of community within their field of study. The Information Resources Management Association is an ideal venue through which professionals, students, and academicians can convene and share the latest industry innovations and scholarly research that is changing the field of information science and technology. Become a member today and enjoy the benefits of membership as well as the opportunity to collaborate and network with fellow experts in the field.

IRMA Membership Benefits:

- **One FREE Journal Subscription**
- **30% Off Additional Journal Subscriptions**
- **20% Off Book Purchases**
- Updates on the latest events and research on Information Resources Management through the IRMA-L listserv.
- Updates on new open access and downloadable content added to Research IRM.
- A copy of the Information Technology Management Newsletter twice a year.
- A certificate of membership.

IRMA Membership $195

Scan code or visit **irma-international.org** and begin by selecting your free journal subscription.

Membership is good for one full year.

www.irma-international.org

IGI Global
DISSEMINATOR OF KNOWLEDGE
www.igi-global.com

Available to Order Now

Order through www.igi-global.com with **Free Standard Shipping**.

The Premier Reference for Information Science & Information Technology

100% Original Content
Contains 705 new, peer-reviewed articles with color figures covering over 80 categories in 11 subject areas

Diverse Contributions
More than 1,100 experts from 74 unique countries contributed their specialized knowledge

Easy Navigation
Includes two tables of content and a comprehensive index in each volume for the user's convenience

Highly-Cited
Embraces a complete list of references and additional reading sections to allow for further research

Included in:
InfoSci®-Books

Encyclopedia of Information Science and Technology Fourth Edition

A Comprehensive 10-Volume Set

Mehdi Khosrow-Pour, D.B.A. (Information Resources Management Association, USA)
ISBN: 978-1-5225-2255-3; © 2018; Pg: 8,104; Release Date: July 2017

For a limited time, receive the complimentary e-books for the First, Second, and Third editions with the purchase of the *Encyclopedia of Information Science and Technology, Fourth Edition* e-book.**

The **Encyclopedia of Information Science and Technology, Fourth Edition** is a 10-volume set which includes 705 original and previously unpublished research articles covering a full range of perspectives, applications, and techniques contributed by thousands of experts and researchers from around the globe. This authoritative encyclopedia is an all-encompassing, well-established reference source that is ideally designed to disseminate the most forward-thinking and diverse research findings. With critical perspectives on the impact of information science management and new technologies in modern settings, including but not limited to computer science, education, healthcare, government, engineering, business, and natural and physical sciences, it is a pivotal and relevant source of knowledge that will benefit every professional within the field of information science and technology and is an invaluable addition to every academic and corporate library.

Scan for Online Bookstore

New Low Pricing!

Hardcover: **$2,848****
~~List Price: $5,695~~

E-Book: **$2,848****
~~List Price: $5,695~~

Hardcover + E-Book: **$3,448****
~~List Price: $6,895~~

Both E-Book Prices Include:

- *Encyclopedia of Information Science and Technology, First Edition E-Book*
- *Encyclopedia of Information Science and Technology, Second Edition E-Book*
- *Encyclopedia of Information Science and Technology, Third Edition E-Book*

*Purchase the Encyclopedia of Information Science and Technology, Fourth Edition e-book and receive the first, second, and third e-book editions for free. Offer is only valid with purchase of the fourth edition's e-book.

**50% discount cannot be combined with any other offer except the free first, second, and third editions e-book offer. Discount is valid on the Encyclopedia of Information Science and Technology, Fourth Edition when purchased directly through the IGI Global Online Bookstore and may not be used by distributors or book sellers.

Recommend this Title to Your Institution's Library: www.igi-global.com/books

www.igi-global.com/infosci-ondemand

InfoSci®-OnDemand

Continuously updated with new material on a weekly basis, InfoSci®-OnDemand offers the ability to search through thousands of quality full-text research papers. Users can narrow each search by identifying key topic areas of interest, then display a complete listing of relevant papers, and purchase materials specific to their research needs.

Comprehensive Service

- Over 110,800+ journal articles, book chapters, and case studies.
- All content is downloadable in PDF format and can be stored locally for future use.

No Subscription Fees

- One time fee of $37.50 per PDF download.

Instant Access

- Receive a download link immediately after order completion!

"It really provides an excellent entry into the research literature of the field. It presents a manageable number of highly relevant sources on topics of interest to a wide range of researchers. The sources are scholarly, but also accessible to 'practitioners'."

- Lisa Stimatz, MLS, University of North Carolina at Chapel Hill, USA

"It is an excellent and well designed database which will facilitate research, publication and teaching. It is a very very useful tool to have."

- George Ditsa, PhD, University of Wollongong, Australia

"I have accessed the database and find it to be a valuable tool to the IT/IS community. I found valuable articles meeting my search criteria 95% of the time."

- Lynda Louis, Xavier University of Louisiana, USA

Recommended for use by researchers who wish to immediately download PDFs of individual chapters or articles.

www.igi-global.com/e-resources/infosci-ondemand

IGI Global
DISSEMINATOR OF KNOWLEDGE
www.igi-global.com

www.ingramcontent.com/pod-product-compliance
Lightning Source LLC
LaVergne TN
LVHW060424300926
849162LV00006B/1515